· WILLIAN

Bernard Nesfield-ᴄᴏᴏᴋson
was educated at a Rudolf Steiner school
in London and at the Universities of
Jena, London, and Bristol. He is
Principal of Hawkwood College, an
independent centre for adult education
in Gloucestershire, and the author of
Rudolf Steiner's Vision of Love (Aquarian
Press, 1983).

WILLIAM BLAKE

PROPHET OF
UNIVERSAL BROTHERHOOD

BERNARD NESFIELD-COOKSON

Foreword by Sir George Trevelyan

First published 1987
© **Bernard Nesfield-Cookson 1987**

British Library Cataloguing in Publication Data
Nesfield-Cookson, Bernard
William Blake: prophet of universal brotherhood.
1. Blake, William, *1757–1827*
Criticism and interpretation
I. Title
821'.7   PR4147

ISBN 0-85030-562-4

Crucible is an imprint of
The Aquarian Press,
part of the Thorsons Publishing Group

Printed and bound in Great Britain

CONTENTS

FOREWORD

William Blake has rightly been called the prophet of the New Age, but many of us have been somewhat bewildered by the complexity of his cosmology. We need help through interpretation in a manner which relates directly to the emergence of the spiritual world-view, the holistic vision which is awakening in our time.

Blake was the great precursor and visionary who could explore and chart the supersensible worlds. His map is composed of complex symbolism and we need a lesson in map-reading.

It is all there — all that is now being found out in spiritual research and the new transpersonal psychology. The emerging of holistic thinking brings recognition that the Life of God animates all creation, that the universe is essentially mind, not mechanism, that an ocean of life and thought is perpetually pouring forth from the creative source, re-animating the dying earth existence.

In our dark age of alarm and foreboding of doom a conviction is rising that spirit is the primary power of the universe. Advanced scientific thought now comes into line with the vision of the mystics and initiates. The two streams, separated for so long, begin to merge. The conception of the spiritual nature of man and the universe is filling many people with the hope that in very truth a cleansing of the planet is about to take place. Perhaps much of the darkness and gloom of our time is a secondary effect. It is not the real news!

The great truth is that energies of light and love are beginning to pour into this world of ours and human consciousness is beginning to rise into a wider perspective and dimension. We grasp in Imagination that the unified, collective consciousness of all humankind is our own true identity. We are conscious nerve-endings of God in matter. The earth is an integral, living creature and humanity is becoming the brain and nervous system of the planet.

An awakening, indeed a spiritual rebirth, is about to take place. To quote from Evelyn Nolt's poem, 'The Glory Which is Earth':

> O Earth, living, breathing, thinking Earth
> On the day we treasure you
> As you have treasured us
> Humanness is born.
>
> And throughout all Light
> A Radiance leaps from star to star
> Singing: A Son is born
> HUMANITY

Blake foresaw it all — the true coming of the New Age and the experience of Oneness. Indeed he wrote:

> Rouze up, O Young Men of the New Age!

And:

> Awake! awake O sleeper of the land of shadows, wake! expand!
> I am in you and you in me, mutual in love divine.

Each one of us is potentially the vast being of the Imagination. As apostle of Imagination, Blake shows how human consciousness can expand to apprehend the living spiritual whole. As droplets of Divinity, the human mind can rise and blend with the Ocean of Mind, which is God-thought poured out into the universe.

The most startling psychological phenomenon is the breakthrough into higher knowledge experienced by the initiates, the illuminati, the talented mystics who have lifted consciousness into immediate perception of the spiritual worlds. This reveals in truth that the human potential is virtually unlimited. The hope comes of a true science of the spirit.

It seems that this beautiful planet carries a precious cargo of self-consciousness, a point in creation which has become reflective and can itself become creative. Humanity stands at the threshold when it is becoming possible to step out of the imprisonment in matter and rigid form, and expand with Imaginative Vision into the living whole. Indeed, we are discovering that the key to our prison is on the inside of the door and we merely have to unlock it and walk out.

The universe is spirit and the world of matter and form is the expression of the living Idea of the Creator. The human mind can apprehend these living Ideas. Indeed, in Rudolf Steiner's words:

In taking possession of the Idea, thinking merges itself into the World-Mind. What was working without, now works within. Man has become one with the World Being at its highest potency.

Holding this world-view, Bernard Nesfield-Cookson has looked again at Blake, and with his width of scholarship is able to interpret the complex writings in the light of the spiritual vision. Thus this volume offers something of special value for our time, since it goes beyond a merely academic study and directly to those who have found their way into the spiritual world-view. It will help many to see the greatness and relevance of the work of that great artist, poet, and visionary, who, nearly two centuries ago, wrote directly for our time as we approach the threshold of expanding consciousness. A great service has been done to Blake — and therefore to us all.

Read it and be glad!

Sir George Trevelyan, Bt., M.A.

ACKNOWLEDGEMENTS

This book has been written with the interests of the general reader, not the scholar, in mind. This means that I have not thought it relevant to distinguish the original from the borrowed parts of my exposition and have therefore not acknowledged specific debts in the text itself. Those to whom I owe a special debt and whose scholarship forms the foundation of much that I have learnt about — and from — William Blake are: John Beer, Harold Bloom, Leopold Damrosch, Jr., Thomas R. Frosch, Northrop Frye, George Mills Harper, John Howard, Mary Lynn Johnson, Morton D. Paley, Kathleen Raine, Mark Schorer and Brian Wilkie.

I owe more immediate debts to Denise Wynne for her painstaking typing of the manuscript, and, as on earlier occasion, to my wife, Ruth, for her encouragement throughout the process of gestation and her patient reading and criticism of the first draft.

Hawkwood College, August 1985

PROLOGUE

On the occasion of the bicentenary of William Blake's birth,[1] Northrop Frye writes:

Blake's deep love of England is clearly not an unrequited love, nor is the sense that he is one of us confined to Englishmen. People get attracted to him through feeling that he is for them a personal discovery and something of a private possession. I constantly hear of doctors, housewives, clergymen, teachers, manual workers, shopkeepers, who are, in the most frequent phrase used, 'frightfully keen on Blake' . . . I have taught him to Communist organizers; I have taught him to deans of women and I have taught him to ferocious young poets of unpredictable rhythms and unprintable . . . diction. His admirers have nothing in common except the feeling that Blake says something to them that no one else can say: that whatever their standards and values may be, Blake has the charity to include them, not as part of a general principle of benevolence, which Blake himself would have despised, but uniquely as individuals . . .
. . . some poets travel better than others, and just as Byron and Pope in the nineteenth century proved to be more readily exportable than Wordsworth or Hawthorne, so in the twentieth century Blake seems the easiest of all our poets to export to India or Japan.[2]

Blake himself makes the fascinating statement:

I am happy to find a Great Majority of Fellow Mortals who can Elucidate My Visions, & Particularly they have been Elucidated by Children, who have taken a greater delight in contemplating my Pictures than I even hoped.[3]

These occur in a letter addressed to the Revd Dr Trusler, which begins by Blake expressing his regret that the learned man has 'fall'n out with the Spiritual World'.[4] He is surely being over-generous when, in the same letter, he claims that the majority of his fellowmen are 'on the side of

Imagination or Spiritual Sensation'.[5] Indeed, some nine years later, he writes: 'The Foundation of Empire is Art & Science. Remove them or Degrade them, & the Empire is No More. Empire follows Art & Not Vice Versa as Englishmen suppose.'[6]

But he is surely right when he states that those who are not ensnared by Baconian rationalism, and still possess 'Spiritual Sensation', have an immediate rapport with his work. Of Baconian man — that is, of those who claim that reason, not imagination, is the supreme mental faculty, Blake writes: '[He] calls Intellectual Arts Unmanly. Poetry, Painting, Music are in his opinion Useless.'[7]

William Blake is, of course, primarily a poet, but his poetry and his prose are concerned with philosophy. As a lad in his teens he had, according to his own statement, already read, criticized and rejected the conventional philosophers and their materialistic view of life.[8] Blake, the philosopher-poet, places Imagination 'above' Reason and thus rejects what is usually regarded as the foundation of the doctrines propounded by his countrymen, Bacon, Newton and Locke. Moreover, they placed God 'above' and separate from man, whereas Blake regards human imagination as the essential divine quality by which God manifests himself in man.

In the following pages the attempt is made to put complex issues into as simple a language as possible, so that the reader who may not have the time, the facility, or even the inclination, to delve into the rich background of thought and imagery which lies behind Blake (cabbalistic, hermetic, neoplatonic, biblical, Boehmian, Swedenborgian, Lockian, Baconian, Newtonian, etc.), may nevertheless gain a fair picture and, perhaps, a living experience, of Blake the poet, prophet and thinker.

A study of Blake is a lifelong affair and the more one lives with him, the more one realizes that he addresses himself in an exceptionally living and creative way to the perennial questions: What is man? What is the meaning of life? What is reality? What is illusion? and so on. And the more one realizes, too, that none of these questions, and many others, can be answered with a clear-cut, definitive answer. Flexibility of thought is what Blake asks of us, not rigidity. Selfless devotion, too, not arrogance. Constantly to start afresh; to see the widening circumference of life; to look 'within' to recognize the 'without', to look 'without' to recognize the 'within'; to overcome set patterns, habits and conventions, and yet to see the past as essential to the total growth of soul and spirit; to recognize the eternity of the moment, and, in imagination, to strive towards the future constantly coming towards us; to take responsibility, not only for our own destinies, but also for those of our fellowmen. All this, and more, Blake pleads we should do, if we are to be born anew and grow into our true selves.

Blake belongs to that relatively small group of men and women whose works have special relevance to every age: young, middle-aged or old, past, present or future. He seems to have everyone in mind. He is as vitally relevant in the last two decades of the present century as he was in his own and will be in the centuries to come.

The author makes no apology for stressing the 'idealistic' aspects of Blake's conception of the world and man, for Blake speaks directly and unequivocally to a deep longing in the breast of every man and every woman, the longing to find a finer purpose in life than the mere accumulation of material possessions and wealth, of demonstrable physical facts and computerized information. Discernible today, faint though it yet may be, is a new dawn, a new recognition of the reality of a creative spiritual world. Blake, for all the limitations one may find in his view of life, world and man, offers to mankind an everfresh spiritual soil, cultivated against the current of an age of profound materialism and intimately relevant to it. He offers us a vision of the world and of life through which we can grow spiritually.

We might be tempted to look upon Blake as an 'otherworldly' man, but to do so would be to do him an injustice; he is equally at home in the material and spiritual worlds. His writings can be read on different levels and approached from various angles. They speak of down-to-earth matters in the social, political and economic spheres of everyday life, and they are also profoundly concerned with philosophical, psychological, theological and cosmological questions. They show that his responses to the transitory and to the eternal are both concrete and specific. His 'Eye of Imagination',[9] though not without its shortcomings (which Blake himself admits), is nevertheless all-embracing, directed as much towards his next-door neighbour as towards Eternity. His reactions to social injustices — slavery and child labour, for instance — are never solely concerned with the 'outer' circumstances, but also with the 'inner', spiritual causes. He touches the 'heart' of things and so can establish a direct human contact with men and women no matter how remote they may be — in time and space — from the 'charter'd streets' of London[10] in which Blake himself spent most of his life.

With reference to such abuses of human beings as child labour and slavery (or their equivalents in our own time) Blake draws our attention not merely to the obvious inhumanity, cruelty, involved but, equally importantly to the complacency with which such evil is rationalized. Blake never fails to try to make us see that the rationalizing of inhumanity is in itself an essential part of the evil. Indeed, the rationalizing can be the very essence of evil. This is why he gives so much attention to what he considers to be intellectual errors · – to abstractions and deism and natural religion.

In all his relative poverty and simplicity William Blake clearly lived life to the full. Far from being an ascetic mystic, he constantly stresses the importance of experience in the world of generation and he shows us his evident delight in living. But, for Blake, life on earth devoid of Imagination is inhuman and 'dead'. It is the very power of Imagination which endows life with joy and nature with 'holiness'. The 'dark Satanic Mills',[11] divorced from Imagination are tantamount to the destruction of the human race; imbued with Imagination both the 'Mills', which do not merely represent industrialized society but also the materialistic philosophy under which humanity suffers, and the human race can be redeemed.

Imaginative Vision and awareness of the physical condition of man are both strong in Blake, but the stress lies always with the former. Blake constantly speaks of his desire to recall his fellow men to the Divine Vision, to awareness of Christ 'within', yet he is also the poet who can write:

> Dear Mother, dear Mother, the Church is cold.
> But the Ale-house is healthy & pleasant & warm.[12]

Blake believes in the essential humanness of God and in the spark of divinity at the core of human nature. He modifies the orthodox views of the transcendence of God Almighty and the unworthiness of Man. Blake is both a Christian and a humanist. Yet he is neither in the usually accepted sense. For instance, Blake's fashioning of God in the image of man cannot be accepted by orthodoxy.

> Thou art a man, God is no more
> Thy own humanity learn to adore.[13]

Similarly, the liberal humanist is not in accord with the stringency of Blake's standards of 'humanity'. True humanity, as Blake sees it, is not to be found by ascertaining the average of the mass of men and women as we find them, but is to be glimpsed whenever an individual lives by his or her own inward vision. From the fullness of such vision most, if not all, of us have fallen away.[14] (See Chapter 6.)

Blake's humanism is neither an attempt to resuscitate the sixteenth-century endeavour to provide a synthesis between reason and faith, nor the still-prevailing nineteenth-century attempt to elevate reason above faith. The rationalist agnostic is a humanist of the latter type. He believes in the ability of the technologist to provide a better material standard of living for all and regards human nature as being simply a part of 'Nature'. Neither of these tenets of agnostic rationalism is characteristic of Blake's humanism. In particular, Blake insists that behind the characteristics of each individual man and woman there exist the lineaments of the 'Eternal Man' which are most nearly apprehended when we see our fellow man radiant with his own creative imagination freely exercised, and acting from immediate inspiration, from the direct perception of truth.

The view of the individual which emerges from Blake's writing

is governed both by the power of Blake's own imagination and by his indignation at social injustices. The two qualities combine into a condition which might be described as that of 'visionary humanism'. In some of the prophetic books indeed, the power of his imagination is so overwhelming that it might be more accurate to call him a 'humanist visionary'. ... When Blake thought about social and political questions it was the eternal man that was most present to him, the eternal humanity which stood judgement on all acts of inhumanity and injustice and deplored society's failure to allow individual self-fulfilment.[15]

Blake shows himself to be always keenly aware of the ills of his time — ills which still obtain in ours. His awareness is always accompanied by a conviction that social 'ills' are most surely dealt with by curing the mental 'ills' which lie behind them, 'within' man himself. Dark 'Satanic Mills', horrendous highrise flats, arise in towns because men have 'dark Satanic Mills' and horrendous flats in their minds.

Most of us still find it a strange idea that we should form part of a spiritual reality which we can experience from two sides: from the soul within and the social reality without. The Western world still lives under the influence of 'the old man of Königsberg', Immanuel Kant (1724–1804), considered by many to be the foremost philosopher of the modern age, who stated that there are boundaries to human knowledge and that what lies on the other side of them can only be a matter of supposition. From Kant, in his *Critique of Pure Reason*,[16] we learn that knowledge of ultimate realities, the world of the spirit, cannot be reached by the human mind. Real knowledge, he maintains, is obtainable only by things pertaining to the world of space and time. Blake, as we shall become increasingly aware in these pages, is clearly opposed to such limitations imposed by rationalism on man's potential abilities to gain knowledge. He does not acknowledge the cleavage which Kant would have us accept.

It was Francis Bacon (1561–1626), the founder of experimental science, who, well before Kant, systematically established the division between the 'within' and the 'without'. He mistrusted human perception, stating that it is subjective and that, as far as possible, we have to substitute mechanical instruments, which can measure and weigh, for human perceptions. He also maintained that thinking could only be trusted when it can be set out in mathematical formulae.[17] In short, Bacon would exclude man, both as a perceiving and as a thinking being, from the process of knowledge. Such a procedure inevitably resulted in a science wherein man can no longer rediscover his true self. He is, in fact, left out of account as a perceiver and a knower. In a society which is based on such a science there is no room for man at all! Materialism has brought about a world in which man is left desolate. He is alienated, not only from his true, spiritual self, but also from his fellow men, and he finds no answers to his fundamental questions about nature and his own being. We live in a society based on a technology, psychology and sociology, which are all 'soulless' and without any vision of Eternity. The spiritual in man, Christ in man, has no place in such a society. Throughout his life, Blake battles in 'Mental Fight' against a rationalism which, rejecting man's true being, brings about a spectral society, a society without a human face.

Blake is of a select company who show us a human society, a civilization, which is no longer satisfied by appearances and the transistory, but which strives, with all the powers of creative imagination, 'Spiritual Sensation', to awaken from deathful sleep and bring into being the New Jerusalem, spiritual freedom. Empirical rationalism, reason, can only give us knowledge of the 'outside', the transitory; Intellect, that is, the Imagination which constitutes the only 'true Man',[18] is the guardian and 'brother' of the Eternal, the Divine vision.

In the following pages the endeavour is made to show how Blake's Vision can aid our 'visionary realism' so that we can rise out of the mire of death-bringing analysis and doubt, isolation and alienation, into the clarity of awareness of spiritual reality and realization of universal brotherhood.

Blake gives us:

> ... the end of a golden string,
> Only wind it into a ball,
> It will lead you in at Heaven's gate
> Built in Jerusalem's wall.[19]

As we approach the end of the twentieth century the signs are encouraging. An increasing number of people are responding to Blake's exhortation and are beginning to grasp the 'golden string'.

In the New Jerusalem all men and women, united by the bond of spiritual freedom, enjoy their own individualities without let or hindrance — and also 'adore' the humanity in each other.[20]

Blake is the courageous champion of spiritual freedom. Such freedom involves a more complete transformation of things as we find them today than any political programme can ever bring about.

In the following pages we shall find Blake consistently 'attacking' both natural religion – deism – and the orthodox Churches. Both natural religion and orthodoxy preach the doctrine of future reward and punishment for moral action (Urizenic moralistic judgement). Blake sees this doctrine as constituting a mechanism for gaining political power over men and women through control of their minds. Although, in the eighteenth century, natural religion had begun to erode the power of orthodoxy, it also showed signs of allying itself with the established seat of political power. As Blake states:

> Seeing the Churches at their Period in terror & despair
> Rahab created Voltaire, Tirzah created Rousseau.[21]

Natural religion was merely a substitute for orthodoxy. Both, therefore, could be forms of state religion. In his criticism of this tendency Blake attacks the suppressive weapon of both orthodoxy and natural religion: the inculcated belief that moral action earned eternal rewards and punishments for man. As John Howard points out, Blake's view of this tendency need not be seen as historically accurate, but it is possible to find examples that demonstrate his conception. We need not here go into any detail as to the justification of Blake's distrust of Rousseau and Voltaire, but it is certainly evident that both favoured an alliance between Church and State. Both 'taught the doctrine of morality and a system of rewards and punishments. It is for this reason that Blake focuses on them as manifestations of Rahab and Tirzah, the symbols of religious domination'.[22]

Deism, natural religion, we may note here, was the universal religion current among rationalists (and free-thinkers) in the eighteenth century. We may be tempted to think that deism is of no concern to us today and that Blake's vehement opposition to it is therefore irrelevant to the twentieth century. However, we would be gravely mistaken if we were to assume such an attitude, for basic to natural religion is rationalism, the exclusion of the spiritual from creation, and the assumption that knowledge of this transitory material world — and that derived from it — is the sum total of knowledge that man is capable of achieving, thus denying the eternal, spiritual world of Blake's 'Spiritual Perception'.[23] Such a limited, materialistic outlook on life is still very much with us today. The failure to 'see beyond one's nose', 'beyond' the limits of outer physical space, is part of a larger failure of human vision intimately interwoven with the mechanistic, analytical, scientific method which dominates contemporary life.

Blake consistently 'attacks' the dominance of reason. Now, as will be stressed on more than one occasion, Blake does not advocate the elimination of man's reasoning power — on the contrary, he stresses the necessity of Urizen's (Reason's) co-operation with man's other soul-faculties. What he calls for is a shift of emphasis: from one-sided domination to harmonious co-operation.

Moreoever, we need to bear in mind that Blake opposes the domination of rational-discursive thought, of reason in a restricted sense, 'fallen' Reason, functioning within set limits. Purely discursive thought is limited in its function to the phenomenal world. Blake goes straight to the heart of the matter when he writes: 'He who sees the Infinite in all things sees God. He who sees the Ratio only, sees himself only.'[24]

'Ratio' (measure), proportionality and comparison,[25] play an essential role in rational discursive thought, the very nature of which limits its scope to the finite:

> The Visions of Eternity, by reason of narrowed perceptions
> Are become weak Visions of Time & Space.[26]

It is in finiteness that our notions of time and space are rooted, and on this our conception of causality thus depends. Discursive thought operates by arranging things in a clock-time sequence, thus creating a

distinction between a beginning and an ending. For discursive (logical
–rational) thought Christ's declaration that He is both 'Alpha and
Omega, the beginning and the ending'[27] is clearly nonsensical.
Moreover, as limited as it is, discursive thought, which can only operate
in the phenomenal world, can only recognize that a physical effect has a
physical cause. For Visionary Man, for the 'Eye of Imagination',[28] on the
other hand, perceiving a spiritual order,

> ...every Natural Effect has a Spiritual Cause, and not
> A Natural; for a Natural Cause only seems; it is a Delusion
> Of Ulro & a ratio of the perishing Vegetable Memory.[29]

When we pass beyond discursive thought — and therefore also beyond
notions of finite time and space, beyond conceptions of natural causality,
we reach intuition, which, as we shall see Regenerate Man doing, sees all
simultaneously and is thus able to perceive the true Infinity and Eternity,
the Whole, God, Christ Himself, Who is both 'within' us and in
Heaven. Such an experience, writes Agnes Arber, leads 'beyond even
intuitive intellection, since the Ultimate One can be realized only in the
still higher phase — the *Unio mystica*'.[30]

Blake gives expression to the rational materialist who would persuade
us that we are no more than mortal worms 'of sixty winters'[31] or 'seventy
inches':

> ... that Human Form
> You call Divine is but a Worm seventy inches long
> That creeps forth in a night & is dried up in the morning sun.[32]

Those who think along such materialistic lines:

> ... know not why they love nor wherefore they sicken & die.[33]

Such a man has lost his 'inner' world. Only so-called facts — verifiable
by mechanistic science — are valid for him. Mechanistic science
inevitably has to lead us to deny our very humanity; one-sided discursive
thought, proceeding by a rigidly logical process, persuades us, in Kath-
leen Raine's words,

to confess ourselves to be mere parts in a lifeless mechanism, to define life itself in
mechanistic terms, our sensations as mere devices directed towards survival,
definable only in terms of function and usefulness within a system of physical
cause and effect, spare parts within a mindless mechanism, our consciousness a
function of the brain, which can be replaced, for all practical purposes, by the
computer.[34]

If he is honest enough and carries his ideology to its logical conclusion, life is meaningless for a materialist.

In his argument against mechanistic science and the philosophy of the five senses Blake writes: 'As the true method of knowledge is experiment, the true faculty of knowledge must be the faculty which experiences.'[35] It is this faculty with which Blake is concerned and he affirms that the Human Imagination, 'the Poetic Genius is the true Man'.[36]

The Imagination, 'God Himself, the Divine Body, Jesus'[37] is neither in clock-time nor in measurable space, but in living consciousness. Imagination 'existed' before time and space. In *A Vision of the Last Judgement* Blake writes:

Many suppose that before [Adam *del.*] the Creation All was Solitude & Chaos. This is the most pernicious Idea that can enter the Mind, as it takes away all sublimity from the Bible & Limits all Existence to Creation & to Chaos, To the Time & Space fixed by the Corporeal Vegetative Eye, & leaves the Man who entertains such an Idea the habitation of Unbelieving demons. Eternity Exists, and All things in Eternity, Independent of Creation.[38]

In eternity there is neither time nor space; nor is it subject to death and decay. Blake speaks of it as the spiritual world into which the spiritual body, 'true Man', is resurrected in a spiritual birth:

The world of Imagination is the world of Eternity; it is the divine bosom into which we shall all go after the death of the Vegetated body. This World of Imagination is Infinite & Eternal, whereas the world of Generation, or Vegetation, is Finite & [for a small moment *del.*] Temporal. There Exist in that Eternal World the Permanent Realities of Every Thing which we see reflected in this Vegetable Glass of Nature. All Things are comprehended in their Eternal Forms in the divine body of the Saviour, the True Vine of Eternity, The Human Imagination, who appear'd to Me as Coming to Judgement among his Saints & throwing off the Temporal that the eternal might be Establish'd.[39]

The Imagination — here called the Saviour, Christ, Who is the 'Divine Body', the Divine Being, in every man — rescues natural man from the temporal and spatial condition and enables him to enter the living experience of spiritual existence.

For Urizenic man, the mind of the ratio,

Who publishes doubt & calls it knowledge, whose Science is Despair,[40]

such an experience is mere subjective illusion and he can do not other than

Charge Visionaries with decieving
And call Men wise for not Believing[41]

Blake would have us understand that mechanistic science and the philosophy of materialism eliminate the concept of life itself. All they can do is to define life in terms of biochemistry, biophysics, vibrations, wavelengths, and so on; they reduce 'life' to conceivable measurement, but such a conception of life does not embrace the most evident element of all: that life can only be known by a living being, by 'inner' experience. No matter how exact measurement may be, it can never give us an experience of life, for life cannot be weighed and measured on a physical scale.

For Blake the universe is not a mechanism. It is a living organism; it is alive, an experience. Kathleen Raine expresses this very succinctly:

Blake reverses the positive view to affirm that the universe has its existence from, and within, a living mind whose organs we are; therefore the world lives with the life of the beholder. Not only in its whole but in its parts the world lives in and by the creative power of the Imagination.[42]

When Blake says that:

There exist in that Eternal World the Permanent Realities of Every Thing which we see reflected in this Vegetable Glass of Nature,[43]

he is asking us to see the life of the universal spirit mirrored in sense-perceptible nature. 'Thus', to quote Kathleen Raine again,

nature becomes not an object of analysis and classification but an experience. The visible world remains of course measurable, still the same inexhaustible treasury of marvels that science has observed, but by a reversal of premises not its aspect but its nature undergoes a metamorphosis: it becomes a living universe.[44]

Life itself is eternal, immeasurable. The 'inner' world, the world of experience, is inexhaustible,

... in your own Bosom you bear your Heaven
And Earth & all you behold; tho' it appears Without, it is Within,
In your Imagination, of which this world of Mortality is but a Shadow.[45]

The only reality for materialistic science, restricted to discursive thought, is objective, quantitative fact. Objectivity demands that every subjective response should be eliminated, for such subjectivity is irrelevant in a picture of man and universe in which experience, the human element, is non-essential. For Blake, for the man of imagination, experience, the inner, human response, *is* the reality. Life, devoid of inner experience, is spiritual death, is meaningless — in fact, it is 'lifeless'. A world of pure fact is a lifeless world.

Blake's consistent and basic objection to natural religion and materialistic philosophy — to 'objective' science — is that the universe 'invented' by the Urizenic mind is lifeless. It is a 'Void Outside of Existence',[46] outside of experience, living consciousness, or human Imagination, and, Blake insists, is illusory and therefore destructive to man's true humanity. A universe which is 'outside' Imagination is a 'building of eternal death'.[47] Such a world is inhuman, a spiritual desert:

The Cities & Villages of Albion become Rock & Sand Unhumanized.[48]

The consequence of rationalistic materialism (Urizenic discursive thought) is alienation between man and the universe, man and nature, and between man and man. Universe, nature and man become mere cold, lifeless abstractions; men and women become 'Spectres' who 'ravin/Without the food of life';[49]

The rational materialist 'invents' a world of matter, a lifeless and heartless order, in which there is no place for subjectivity, no place for brotherhood, for awe and wonder, 'Mercy, Pity, Peace, and Love',[50] those qualities which humanize the world in which we live our daily lives.

Blake calls on us to raise the stature of man from a 'passive' mechanism to a 'creative' image of a living God. Instead of reducing the higher to the lower, he calls on us to transform the lower, 'the worm of sixty winters',[51] so that God, Christ, once more can speak in human hearts. The natural mind, Urizen/Satan, can 'reduce' man and universe to a mass of meaningless, dead 'dust';[52] Blake admonishes us to cultivate the living Imagination, intuition, and 'knowledge' of the heart, so that creative and spiritual life can pulsate in universe and man. No matter how precise and far-reaching quantitative scientific research into the nature of universe and man may be, it can never discover the meaning of life — nor life itself — in the 'Void Outside of Existence' of the material universe. Life reveals itself to Imaginative Vision, not to the corporeal eye. An expansion of consciousness is called for, a change in ourselves.

In the following pages the endeavour is made to show how Blake's own perception of the universe, nature and man exercises 'the Divine Arts of Imagination'.[53]

1

BLAKE'S CHRISTIANITY
OF THE FUTURE

Modern Western civilization is established upon the supposition that 'matter' is the 'substance' and foundation of the universe. Earlier civilizations held spirit to be the 'ground' of the universe, including the sense-perceptible phenomena we call 'body' and 'nature'. This is Blake's conviction too. He laboured ceaselessly in the certainty that his conviction would bear fruit for mankind. During his own time and right through the nineteenth century and the first half of our own, his belief found little echo in the hearts and minds of men, immersed as they were — and to a large extent still are — in reductionist modes of thought. But during the last few decades when 'facts' of the spirit are again being 'perceived' as reality and not as fanciful imaginings of a deluded mind, Blake's Imagination, his Vision, is beginning to take on ever greater significance for a growing number of people who recognize the futility and deadendedness of a materialistic conception of man and the universe.

For Blake it is atheism to suppose that nature exists independently 'outside' spirit and the Imagination of God, or Christ, for nothing can exist outside and apart from Him. Atheism is the worship of nature. On one occasion Blake writes: 'There is no such thing as natural piety because the natural man is at enmity with God.'[1] We are reminded here of Paul's words to the Corinthians: 'The Natural Man receiveth not the things of the Spirit of God, for they are foolishness unto him: neither can he know them, because they are spiritually discerned ... he that is spiritual discerneth all things.'[2]

The world with which Blake is primarily concerned is not the world conceived by materialistic science but a spiritual world:

> ... I rest not from my great task!
> To open the Eternal Worlds, to open the Immortal Eyes
> Of man inwards into the Worlds of Thought, into Eternity

Ever expanding in the Bosom of God, the Human Imagination.[3]

For Blake the mind in man is not a mere piece of blotting paper, as Locke and his followers would have us believe; it is not a mere passive recipient of sense-impressions, moulded by them, but an active spiritual agent, continually creative, continually forming and moulding.

The spirit in man creates a universe which, because it is not limited by measurable space and time, but open to immeasurable 'Worlds of Thought', Blake calls 'Eternal'. What Blake strives to show us is of paramount importance for our present and future ages. No matter how significant it may prove to be that we have spent and continue to spend so much time, energy and financial resources on extending our knowledge of outer space, we need to recognize that it is to 'inner space' that we must turn our perception, if human life is not to be passed through in a robot-like 'dread Sleep',[4] in 'darkest night',[5] in a spiritual vacuum, 'Voidness'.[6]

We are living today in an age of materialism, a materialism which seeks to determine and govern all aspects of human life: man's philosophy of life; the very concepts of research; the relations between people. Materialism denies individuals their proper rights; it promotes egotism and impedes brotherhood. Selfless love has no role to play in a world-outlook based on the blind acceptance of matter as being the sole reality, and contends that thought itself has its source in the physical grey mass we call 'brain'.

Blake urges us to recognize that 'We who dwell on Earth can do nothing of ourselves; every thing is conducted by Spirits.'[7] All causation is spiritual not material.[8]

Blake describes a world governed by materialism as a place of man's inhumanity to man, a place of 'cruelties'.[9] It is a world in which 'The Spectres of the Dead', that is, the spiritually lost, 'repent of their human kindness'.[10]

The descent into materialism Blake sees as being only half of the story of human evolution. Moreover, the Logos, Christ Himself, the Creator, sets two limits to the fall into error (see Appendix 2). The other half of the 'story' is the spiritual rebirth, regeneration of man. It is to this 'half' that Blake draws our attention again and again, as we shall see in later chapters.

It is essential to an understanding of Blake that we apprehend the importance he attaches to Christ's, the Imagination's, creative power.

Blake adopted and adapted the teaching of the ante-Nicene Church Fathers (from Justin Martyr to Arius) which stated that the Word, Christ, was the manifestation of the invisible Father and that the biblical theophanies were the appearances of the Son. Blake expresses this belief when he writes of:

> The Holy Word
> That walk'd among the ancient trees,
> Calling the lapsed Soul,
> And weeping in the evening dew.[11]

The 'lapsed Soul' is fallen mankind (and nature). The 'Holy Word' is not the wrathful God of the Old Testament but the sorrowing and merciful Christ, the Divine Logos, whose voice is the forgiveness of sins, errors.[12]

Elsewhere Blake asserts that Christ is the source of everything: 'Around the Throne Heaven is open'd & the Nature of Eternal Things display'd, All Springing from the Divine Humanity. All beams from him.'[13]

'Every thing on earth ... in its essence is God.'[14] Within each 'fallen body', be it the earth, a star, man or worm, there is, invisible to the physical eye, but perceptible to the spiritual eye, the divine essence, a spiritual core:

> ... every Generated Body in its inward form
> Is a garden of delight & building of magnificence.[15]

On earth we dwell in 'fallen' bodies, not in the immortal forms of Eternity, of the spiritual world. Yet the seed of Eternity, the essence of the Divine, spiritual life, is 'within' these bodies.

If there were no essence of the Divine, no spiritual life in fallen, natural man, shrouded though it may be in materialistic, Newtonian sleep, then the second half of the 'story' — regeneration, rebirth — would not be possible.

To natural man — to us — Blake says, as Christ said to Nicodemus (John 3:7): 'Ye must be born again.' Blake sees that spiritual man, real man, lies hidden in the natural man, yet not so concealed and darkened that the Divine Light and Voice cannot radiate and sound through to the spiritual essence in 'cavern'd' man and awaken him to eternal life. There is a limit to the power of Satan (Opacity), but no limit to the creative power of Christ, (Translucence).[16]

Blake's major symbol for Fallen Man is Albion, who is described as

lying asleep on a rock. In one passage in *Jerusalem* he is shown lying cold
on the rock with 'storms & snows' beating around him:

> Howling winds cover him: rearing seas dash furious against him:
> In the deep darkness broad lightnings glare, long thunders roll.[17]

Fallen 'cavern'd' man is in a soulless sea of matter — soulless because
remote from spiritual light. Nature cannot waken him, cannot pierce to
his spiritual core. He remains hard, cold, contracted, opaque, isolated,
miserable, spiritually asleep. As we shall see in the chapter, 'The Rebirth
of Vision', man's spiritual awakening, his new birth, is traced magnifi-
cently in Blake's last epic poem, *Jerusalem*, from which we have just
quoted:

> The Breath Divine Breathed over Albion
>
> ...
>
> The Breath Divine went forth upon the morning hills, Albion mov'd
> Upon the Rock, he open'd his eyelids in pain, in pain he mov'd
> His stony members ... Ah! shall the Dead live again?
> The Breath Divine went forth over the morning hills. Albion rose.[18]

Although these lines and those quoted in the following three passages
will be discussed in detail and quoted again in the later chapter referred to
just now, it is appropriate to bring them to the reader's attention at this
early stage for we may say that the words spoken by Christ and the
questions asked by Albion form the keystone of Blake's philosophy of
life.

To Albion, troubled in conscience and affrighted, Christ says:

> Fear not Albion: unless I die thou canst not live;
> But if I die I shall rise again & thou with me.
> This is Friendship & Brotherhood: without it Man is not.[19]

Albion, still seeking inner certainty, then asks:

> Cannot Man exist without Mysterious
> Offering of Self for Another? is this Friendship & Brotherhood?[20]

Christ's answer rouses Albion's, Man's, spiritual core:

> Wouldst thou love one who never died
> For thee, or ever die for one who had not died for thee?
> And if God dieth not for Man & giveth not himself
> Eternally for Man, Man could not exist; for Man is Love
> As God is Love; every kindness to another is a little Death
> In the Divine Image, nor can Man exist but by Brotherhood.[21]

Here, in a few simple words, Blake expresses the innermost meaning of ultimate human enlightenment, which he calls a Last Judgement. Albion's response is immediate:

> Do I sleep amidst danger to Friends? O my Cities & Counties,
> Do you sleep? rouze up, rouze up! Eternal Death is abroad![22]

Throughout Blake's writings — particularly in *The Four Zoas, Milton* and *Jerusalem* — we find allusions to the story of Job. In the three great epic poems he writes of the Creation, the Fall, suffering, the Apocalypse and redemption. In his *Job* he is concerned, with the exception of the Fall, with the same themes.

In the biblical version of the sufferings of Job we learn that he survives the several tests of his strength of faith and is finally rewarded. He is rewarded, not because he has reached comprehension, but because he has endured. For Blake it is comprehension which is all-important. To him, Job's failure to understand is rooted in an infirmity of vision, of seeing with the inward eye. Part of what Job is made to see is that he has been living by the letter rather than by the spirit of God's law. He must recognize that he has made of religion what Blake means by Mystery: a religion of externalities, rituals and ceremonies rigidly adhered to. But he has to learn more than this. It will only be when Job — man — discovers how to see 'not with but thro' the eye', when he comes to understand the meaning of true spirituality, that he will then be able to achieve the restoration of true happiness. The imprisonment of Job in a 'cavern' (see Chapter 3, blind to the reality of the world of spirit, is at an end when he prays for his 'corporeal' (see p. 347) friends, his accusers.[23] However, in Blake's understanding, Job does not pray for them because he thinks they have sinned, but because it is a joy for him to offer himself for another.

Like all men of true spiritual-imaginative discernment Blake perceives the real man, spiritual man, in natural man. To discern spiritual man is for him the very foundation of a true Christian society, of creative and loving relationships between human beings, and between man and nature. Through imaginative perception man's inner beauty, truth and goodness, become 'Visible'. Imagination is the key to the inner experience of the 'Divine Humanity'.[24] Indeed, Blake tells us time and again: 'The eternal Body of Man is the Imagination, that is, God himself, The Divine Body, Jesus: we are his Members.'[25] 'God is Man & Exists in us & we in him'.[26] We may note here that Blake makes the distinction between

Identity and Essence, the former being what differentiates each indivi-
dual, the latter being what unites all men. Essence is Christ, is God, in
man; is the spiritual, eternal core of man.

Throughout his life Blake can be seen working passionately towards
the realization of the great conception of the Divine Humanity. His
conception of God he expresses in terms of man. He sees man as the crown
of creation, since he is made in the image of the Creator, that is, as
creative, eternal, all-embracing spirit. The image of God is man's
boundless spiritual being, not, of course, Man's transitory physical body.
Man's spiritual essence, which is limitless, is the real man within natural
man, is Christ, the Logos, the Imagination, from which spiritual
knowledge issues — without limitations set by space or time — in
prophetic vision and revealed truth. William Blake describes himself as a
Christian, but it is quite clear that his Christianity is unlike that of
organized religion. Yet the true spirit of the gospels, particularly that of
St John, and of the Epistles of St Paul, is clearly present in his life and
work.

For Blake religion can have no other ground than the spiritual core of
man. This 'ground' Blake calls 'the Divine Humanity', 'Jesus, the
Imagination', which is alike in all men. The Spiritual Son of God, the
Logos, the creative spiritual power dwells in every human soul. Blake
also states his conviction that all religions have their source in the creative
Word, in the Imagination: 'The Religions of all Nations are derived
from each Nation's different reception of the Poetic Genius, which is
every where call'd the Spirit of Prophecy.' And, Blake continues: 'As all
men are alike (tho' infinitely various), So all Religions &, as all similars,
have one source. The True Man is the source, he being the Poetic
Genius.'[27] Blake later uses the word 'Imagination' rather than 'Poetic
Genius'.

True religion is eternal and was manifesting long before Christ
revealed it: 'All had originally one language and one religion: this was the
religion of Jesus, the everlasting Gospel. Antiquity preaches the Gospel of
Jesus.'[28]

At the level of rational argument reconciliation between the various
religions is impossible. At such a level of comprehension truth is seen as
'enclosed' within a set of logical propositions. Divisions of opinion,
irreconcilable with one another, are the inevitable consequence. There is,
however, quite a different approach to truth. It is not against reason as
such, but recognizes that one-sided reason can do no other than bring

about division. This approach is that of the Imagination. Through the Imagination man 'sees' and becomes one with Christ, the Creative Power which is the core of man's being: 'All Things are comprehended in their Eternal Forms in the divine body of the Saviour, the True Vine of Eternity, the Human Imagination.'[29]

Here division has no place. We could say that imaginative consciousness in the Blakean sense is the 'mystical' consciousness, where truth is comprehended as being that which, in any given situation, awakens man to reality. Imaginative consciousness is not a set of concepts arrived at through ratiocination, for they are inevitably 'dead' and quite inadequate to deal with any real-life situation.

In introducing the term 'mystical consciousness' the question arises: Is Blake a mystic? The answer is both 'Yes' and 'No'. He is not a mystic if by that term one has those in mind who suppress sensory experience and seek to lose their individual identities in an undifferentiated Absolute. Blake certainly does not tread the *via negativa*, that is, self-abnegation and detachment from all phenomena in the search for an unnameable God. Our answer would be 'Yes' if we recognize that, in contrast to such 'negative' mysticism there is a Western form of mysticism which glories in sensory images instead of seeking to eliminate them. As Stace expresses it: 'The extrovertive mystic, using his physical senses, perceives the multiplicity of external material objects — the sea, the sky, the houses, the trees — mystically transfigured so that the One, or the Unity, shines through them.'[30] This is just what is described by Blake in a poem he writes in October 1800 beginning with the lines:

> To my Friend Butts I write
> My first Vision of Light.

The poem opens by describing the sun emitting 'His Glorious beams' and goes on to say that he, Blake, was thereby inspired to ride above the temporal and mortal realm of care and desire:

> My Eyes did Expand
> Into regions of air
> Away from all Care,
> Into regions of fire
> Remote from Desire.

Gazing upon an earth lit up by 'jewels of Light' Blake now has a vision of the world as human:

I each particle gazed,
Astonish'd, Amaz'd;
For each was a Man
Human-form'd. Swift I ran,
For they beckon'd to me
Remote by the Sea,
Saying: Each grain of Sand,
Every Stone on the Land,
Each rock & each hill,
Each fountain & rill,
Each herb & each tree,
Mountain, hill, earth & sea,
Cloud, Meteor & Star,
Are Men Seen Afar.[31]

'As a man is, so he Sees.'[32] For him who sees 'not with but thro' the eye' 'Nature is Imagination itself'.[33] He who has twofold vision — that is, sees through the eye — perceives the human values in all things. Then the thistle in the path reveals itself to his 'inward eye' to be 'an old Man grey'[34] and the rising sun to be 'an Innumerable company of the Heavenly host'.[35] Twofold vision is the perception of the human in all things, or, as we hear right at the end of *Jerusalem*:

All Human Forms identified, even Tree, Metal, Earth & Stone ...[36]

Inanimate things have a part in true humanity. They are all created by — and are therefore part of — the Divine Humanity, God, Christ. Nothing exists that, in its essence, is not divine, is not 'human'. Nature, though not created in the image of God is, nevertheless, created from the Divine Substance! Hence, for Blake, 'Every thing that lives is Holy.'[37] God is manifested in all creation: 'Creation is God descending according to the weakness of man, for our Lord is the word of God & every thing on earth is the word of God & in its essence is God.'[38] It follows from this that Blake is convinced of the rightness of the doctrine of apocatastasis (first promulgated by Origen).[39]

Blake's conception of the divinity of all that exists in the universe is in direct contrast to the philosophy of nature of the materialists who assume that the universe operates through natural causes and that the Creator, after the moment of creation, of conception, remains remote, impassive, and inaccessible for evermore. Such a remote Creator Blake calls 'Newton's Pantocrator, weaving the Woof of Locke'.[40] Such a Creator is an 'impossible absurdity',[41] for the creative principle, the Logos, exists actively and creatively in our own bosoms. We have forgotten that each one of us possesses Poetic Genius, Imagination, a creative spirit.[42]

From what has already been indicated, it is clear that for Blake it is Imagination, not Reason, which is man's supreme faculty. Creative Imagination is the true fount of man's being.

Blake sees clearly that any materialistic, mechanistic world-view — such as that which has been prevalent since Newton — allows no place for a living God, a creative spirit, in man and universe. Such a world-view cannot accept that 'every Natural Effect has a Spiritual Cause, and Not/ A Natural'.[43] All mechanistic, materialistic conceptions of man and the universe are inevitably totally blind to the deeper, spiritual life. For such conception the quantitative world is the sum total of everything. Or, as Blake puts it in *Milton*:

> To Mortals thy Mills seem everything.[44]

In *Jerusalem*, fallen Albion, Fallen Man, under the dominion of materialism utters these words of despair:

> God in the dreary Void
> Dwells from Eternity, wide separated from the Human Soul.[45]

Loss of the inward vision, revealed in *Jerusalem* as the key to Albion's decline, is seen by Blake as a universal human phenomon. Loss of the inward vision of the Divine within can do no other than lead to the view:

> O I am nothing, & to nothing must return again.[46]

In a world devoid of living, creative spiritual powers, human beings themselves lose everything but their quantitative aspects. They become:

> ... Shapeless Rocks
> Retaining only Satan's Mathematic Holiness, Length, Bredth & Highth,
> Calling the Human Imagination, which is the Divine Vision & Fruition
> In which Man liveth eternally, madness & blasphemy against
> Its own Qualities ...[47]

In the view of the materialist, living experience is purely subjective and therefore irrelevant, or, as Blake expresses it, 'blasphemy' against the so-called objective maxims of lifeless thinking (science).

For Blake those under the domination of any form of materialistic philosophy are 'cavern'd' men. They are like the cave-dwellers in Plato's *Republic* (Book vii) who, never having seen the light of spiritual or real existence, live always in a world of darkness and see themselves as mere shadows thrown upon the cavern wall by a fire which they cannot see. They lead a spiritually unenlightened life and therefore take these shadows for realities. The materialist confines himself to the physical, the sense-perceptible world. He closes 'himself up, till he sees all things thro' narrow chinks of his cavern'.[48] In *Jerusalem* Blake describes, with compassion, the forlorn state of the 'cavern'd' man:

> Ah! weak & wide astray! Ah! shut in narrow doleful form!
> Creeping in reptile flesh upon the bosom of the ground!
> The Eye of Man, a little narrow orb, clos'd up & dark,
> Scarcely beholding the Great Light, conversing with the ground:
> The Ear, a little shell, in small volutions shutting out
> True Harmonies & comprehending great as very small. ...
> The Nostrils, bent down to the earth & clos'd with senseless flesh
> That odours cannot them expand, nor joy on them exult ...[49]

A very similar passage occurs in *Milton* where, moreover, the 'cavern'd' man is described as 'conversing with the Void',[50] the term 'Void' being used as an equivalent of the state of total error, the deadly sleep of the spirit, the mode of life which rejects spiritual vision, which Blake calls Ulro.

Clearly those who are under the domination of any materialist philosophy and thus turn their backs 'to the Divine Vision', attempt to impose quantitative criteria upon living experience. But life and experience (consciousness) cannot be measured and weighed in terms of inches and ounces. A feeling of joy or sorrow, love or hate, cannot be expressed in a concise mathematical formula; an idea cannot be explained and expressed by a chemical change in a physical brain-cell, and so on.

Through the dominance of fallen reason, of brain- and sense-bound knowledge, man has lost the living experience and perception of the spiritual worlds. Our vision has become 'single', Newtonian, 'Spectrous'; it has narrowed to such an extent that we stand outside, apart from things. We have become lifeless, feelingless observers and confine ourselves, as mere observers, to analysis. In the words of William Wordsworth:

> Our meddling intellect
> Destroys the beautous form of things
> We murder to dissect. (From the sonnet 'The World')

The voice of materialism, of the 'Spectre' (see p. 74), is heard in *Jerusalem*:

I am your Rational Power, O Albion, & that Human Form
You call Divine is but a Worm seventy inches long
That creeps forth in a night & is dried in the morning sun.[51]

The Spectre's statement is the logical conclusion of a materialistic belief which, antagonistic to spiritual vision, analyses experiences, murders them by dissection, instead of unifying them into a spiritual harmony. Discursive reason can give us both necessary and wonderful information about isolated details, but can know nothing of the inner essence, the 'being' of the whole. The comprehension of and inner uniting with the life of the whole, with the eternal, spiritual core of any living thing, can only be attained through subtler modes of perception and intuitive imagination.

To Blake the cold, analytical 'spectator consciousness' is a state of spiritual sleep:

May God us keep
From Single vision & Newton's sleep![52]

Single vision is not properly 'vision' at all. It is merely seeing the physical phenomena with the physical eye.

We have previously discussed Blake's conception of man's boundless spiritual being as being the image of God. The Real Man in every man is one in essence with the Real Man in all men. The spirit in man, the Divine in man, recognizes the spirit, the Christ, in other men, for, 'We are all co-existent with God — members of the Divine Body. We are all partakers of the Divine Nature.'[53]

For Blake the work and ministry of Christ is to show man the way to the gaining of insight into his essential divinity. The first step towards this realization is to arouse natural man from spiritual sleep. Blake asks us to arouse ourselves out of indoctrination into conscious spiritual awareness. Already within a generation or so of Christ's death, resurrection and ascension, spiritual awakening gave place to indoctrination. Christianity became a reflection of man's propensity to intellectualize truth. The sacred writing soon became objects for study and the source of theological definitions and dogma. Christ was no longer experienced 'within', but became an impersonal abstraction. God was 'out there'. For Blake, the God of institutional Christianity has become an abstraction and, as such, hostile to man's true humanity, to the Divinity within him. Abstractions are the inventions of reasoning logic. Urizen (your reason) is the great abstractor![54] He is the moral tyrant of Blake's prophetic books, whose religion and laws prevail in a world which has forgotten its spiritual origin.[55]

The creative, intuitive imagination, 'works' in quite the opposite way to discursive reason. In *Jerusalem*, Los, the Imagination and 'guardian of the Divine Vision', reveals:

> When in Eternity Man converses with Man, they enter
> Into each other's Bosom.[56]

Eternity, of course, for the Creative Imagination, is here and now! We may therefore say that when man, through the intuitive imagination, meets his fellow men he does not experience himself as being 'outside' them, but 'within', at one with them. Here we can take up the theme again of mysticism in relation to Blake. For him real man, 'true man', the man of intuitive imagination, not only seeks union with the Divine, Christ consciousness, but with the divine in every man and woman and child. 'Annihilation' of the blinkered self-centredness of natural man, of the selfhood; not possible for those who remain detached spectators, leads to the 'mystical' unitive experience with someone (or something) other than oneself. The barrier between 'mortal frames' dissolves; spiritual union with the reality is born and grows. It is such a unitive experience which Blake describes in the poem to Butts referred to earlier on; it is what he means by the 'One Man', the Christ, 'infolding' him and freeing his mortal body:

> Till the Jewels of Light
> Heavenly Men beaming bright
> Appear'd as One Man
> Who Complacent began
> My limbs to infold
> In his beams of bright gold;
> Like dross purg'd away
> All mire & my clay.[57]

By cleansing our organs of perception any distinction between object and subject is abolished — such is the essence of intuitive imagination.

True fellowship and selfless love flourish in the interpenetration and flowing together of human spirits. Man has within himself the seeds of spiritual growth. When he becomes conscious of the Real Man within himself and within others then he 'flows' into, enters the bosoms of other spirits and yet retains his true identity. Fallen man, in the thraldom of his analytical reasoning power, has lost this power to live in his brother's bosom. He is too 'opaque' and becomes hard and exclusive, isolated and contracted, in selfhood. In inwardly perceptive, balanced man, imagination and reason work in harmony as stimulating contraries. In Fallen Man who relies solely on his rational power, intuitive imagination is destroyed.

Having lost the divine vision and, in consequence, faith — that is, having experienced the opening of the eyes and ears to self-evident truths (see p. 43), the man of reason can do no other than live by his five physical senses. These are all that is left to inform and teach him. He is, therefore, compelled to live in a 'contracted' world. 'Contracted', Urizenic man, without faith, lives in 'a state of constant distrust with suspension of judgement, in the absence of indubitable proof'.[58]

The five physical senses can only give us information of 'appearance', not 'reality'. Locke's rational philosophy of the five senses posits a world outside the perceiver, or, in Blakean terms, the mind of the 'ratio', fallen reason, creates a finite world, 'outside existence', a world devoid of life. Reason can only perceive the 'worm of seventy inches',[59] can only concern itself with 'Vegetable Mortal Bodies'.[60] But through the inner creative power of intuitive imagination man can experience 'the real & eternal world of which this Vegetable Universe is but a faint shadow'.[61] The man of 'Ratio'.[62] of fallen reason and fallen perception, exists in a spiritual vacuum, in a 'Void Outside of Existence'. However, as Blake shows us in, or instance, *The Four Zoas, Milton* and *Jerusalem*, Urizen, the man of 'Ratio', can be regenerated and then he can take his rightful place in the mental, spiritual life of the Real Man. Even the most Urizenic of men cannot rest satisfied, for hidden within him is the Real Man, his spiritual, eternal essence, which, though bound and inarticulate, vaguely remembers happier times:

> O what a world is here, unlike those climes of bliss
> ... O, thou poor ruin'd world!
> Thou horrible ruin! once like me thou wast all glorious,
> And now like me partaking desolate thy master's lot.
> Art thou, O ruin, the once glorious heaven? are these thy rocks
> Where joy sang in the trees & pleasure sported on the rivers,
> And laughter sat beneath the Oaks, & innocence sported round
> Upon the green plains, & sweet friendship met in palaces,
> And books & instruments of song & pictures of delight?[63]

With sorrow, Blake, through Urizen, contrasts the world of quantitative time and space with the world of life. Throughout his creative life Blake strives to open the eyes of his fellow men — now and in the future — to a universe of spiritual life in which,

> ... every thing is Human, mighty! sublime!

And in which:

> In every bosom a Universe expands as wings.[64]

In contrast to those mystics who flee from the world, Blake recognizes that man, in his fallen state, has to go through the 'Void':

> No form was there, no living thing, & yet his way lay thro'
> This dismal world ...[65]

Yet the essence of the creative Logos dwells in 'this dismal world', for there are limits to 'Contraction' and 'Opacity' (see Appendix 2); were it otherwise man would sink into eternal death never to rise again; he would never emerge from his stone 'cavern'. As has already been intimated, even the most Urizenic of men has within him spiritual essence — otherwise he would not even have been born (whether he realizes this fact or not). This spiritual essence, this spark of divinity, gives every human being the possibility to awaken from 'Newton's sleep', from single vision, and thus to begin to transform within himself the 'abominable Void'.[66] He then takes on the task which Blake set himself: 'To open the immortal Eyes ... into Eternity'.

It is clear from the few remarks already made — and it will become more apparent as we progress — that Blake is a very religious man. It is true, of course, that his criticism of institutional Christianity is vehement, but this does not render him a non-Christian. We shall, in fact, see that what he says of himself is very true: 'I still & shall to Eternity Embrace Christianity and Adore him who is the Express image of God.'[67]

Blake finds — as do an increasing number of people today who are seeking spiritual reality — that, on the one hand, the Gospel is intellectualized in dogmatic terms, and, on the other, that a sentimental evangelism is focused on the historical personality of Jesus. What Blake urges us to do is to make the transition from an external devotion to a remote God (first cause) of a material universe, to an interior awareness of an eternally present spiritual reality continually creating. Only then can the true Christ nature within, the 'indwelling Christ' (St Paul), be released and realized; only then can true self-realization begin to emerge from the 'cavern'.

Blake has immediate, intuitive knowledge of the Divinity Within. This is the God he worships. When he speaks of his worship of 'him who is the Express Image of God' he is not speaking of the historical personality of Jesus, but of the universal Divine Humanity. Spiritual perception, intuitive knowledge, comes to birth in man with the awakening of the heart, of true, selfless love.

In *Jerusalem*,[68] in the lines already quoted (see p. 26), Blake confronts us with the course of conscious spiritual birth. Here he reveals what he means by the annihilation of the selfhood in selfless love and the birth of the true Self, of the 'indwelling Christ' — a repeated and continual process in the spiritual life in every 'member' of Christ.[69] Christ is 'born' with every member of mankind. He is humanity itself, the Divine Image which in every one of us experiences the journey of life from birth to death. Each individual is a unique incarnation of the Divine Humanity:

> The Divine Vision still was seen,
> Still was the Human Form Divine,
> Weeping in weak & mortal clay,
> O Jesus, still the Form was thine.

> And thine the Human Face, & thine
> The Human Hands & Feet & Breath,
> Entering thro' the Gates of Birth
> And passing thro' the Gates of Death.

> … Create my Spirit to thy love …[70]

Blake calls Christ the 'Saviour' and the 'Redeemer' in particular when he is considering the Divine Humanity as man's guide — and friend — in the trials and tribulations of the journey through life, through what he calls 'States' (see pp. 103–5).

As we shall see later, particularly in Chapters 7–9, devoted to the last three Nights of *The Four Zoas*, human relationships (in all spheres of life) were, in Blake's day, and, we must admit, still are today, governed by the abstract philosophy of the Age of Reason and the laws of natural religion. The laws of natural religion are imposed on man from without. They are cruel and hostile to creative life, non-human, which, in Blake's writings, is usually denoted by the term 'abstract'.

Time and again Blake expresses his detestation of the basic idea of the Decalogue. The Ten Commandments were negative generalizations which were devised without any regard to the individual. They were justice without mercy, that is, they were devoid of the love of Christ.

Blake is emphatic that the individual should always be considered first and should never be subjected to lifeless traditions and customs of the past, or treated as though he or she were nothing more than one of a multitude of identical nonentities. One-sided, limited rational man, Urizen, would standardize everything under 'One King, one God, one Law'.[71] But for Blake, 'One law for the Lion & Ox is Opression.'[72] Urizen/Satan was the inventor of the Ten Commandments[73] of which Christ says:

> No individual can keep these Laws, for they are death
> To every energy of man and forbid the springs of life.
> ... I go forth to ... deliver Individuals evermore![74]

In Blake's spiritual religion, 'the religion of Jesus', energy and active life are seen through transparent organs of perception as being infinite and holy. But, under the domination of Urizen, the man of orthodoxy 'sees all things thro' narrow chinks of his cavern',[75] and thus sees energy not merely as finite but also as infernal, and therefore forbids 'the springs of life', decreeing that they are sinful.

For Blake creative and imaginative energy is holy. It is holy because it is that element in man which is at the foundation of his creative activity. The very dignity of man depends on his imaginative creative energy. Without it he would be a degenerate brute, an 'Abomination of Desolation'.[76]

The religion of Satan, the 'God of this World',[77] is antagonistic to energy and Imagination, to Christ. 'State Religion, which is the source of all Cruelty'[78] is the enemy of 'holy Generation ... Birthplace of the Lamb of God'.[79] Those who have lost the vision of Eternity become 'dishumaniz'd men',[80] mere human animals.

It is axiomatic that a religion which is governed by 'natural', 'fallen' reason and therefore can have no experience of or 'faith' in the reality of the spiritual world, the Kingdom of Imagination, of Christ (whose kingdom is not of this world), can neither conceive nor perceive the spirituality of Christ Himself. 'State Religion', natural religion, with its rationalistic doubt and its empirical visionless materialism, is a cruel delusion separating man from man, and mankind from Christ. It leads man inevitably to conflicts and wars of self-preservation, it is, Blake says, conceived by the selfhood, which has no vision of universal brotherhood. Natural religion and 'war' Blake sees as manifestations of the selfhood, of self-centredness, which bars the way to unity with Divinity. As we shall discuss later, it is only when we 'arise from Self/By Self Annihilation' that we can enter 'Jerusalem's Courts',[81] that we can attain spiritual liberty, experience inner resurrection, regeneration, and thus create the invisible, free-flowing bonds which form the very essence of true universal brotherhood.

The prophetic, creative imagination, Blake shows us, can bring a cure to the ills in the world caused by the selfhood. Hence, after the last verse of the lines which we know as the 'Song of Jerusalem' —

> I will not cease from Mental Fight,
> Nor shall my Sword sleep in my hand
> Till we have built Jerusalem
> In England's green & pleasant Land.[82]

— Blake quotes the words of Moses: 'Would to God that all the Lord's people were Prophets'.[83]

The laws of the natural world and of natural religion are imposed on man from without; those of the Imagination, of 'Mental Fight', are created within, and are in harmony with the Divine Vision. The new 'Law' given by Christ, Who is the Imagination, is the 'law' of imagination: 'no virtue can exist, without breaking these ten commandments. Jesus was all virtue, and acted from impulse, not from rules.'[84]

Laws devised by rationalism, devoid of 'heart-understanding' for the individual, divorced from inner experience, and treating men and women as 'outside' objects, are inhuman. Imagination, Christ, Blake maintains time and again, acts with love and compassion, overcomes alienation, whereas the moral laws of State religion, invented by the selfhood, by Satan the Accuser, are remote from and destructive of creative life.

Blake is Pauline in his rejection of the Decalogue, the letter that killeth, 'the ministration of death, written and engraven in stones'. Blake's 'Accuser' is Jehovah in his fallen or Urizenic form. He is forever re-writing the stony law of death in a forlorn attempt to satisfy a morality of guilt.[85] With St Paul, Blake agreed that 'Christ hath redeemed us from the curse of the Law'. (Galatians 3:13). Christ does away with the curses of the moral law, the contentions of 'good' and 'evil'. He breaks the Commandments. Christ's love and forgiveness — the Everlasting Gospel — is shown clearly in his treatment of the woman who was found in adultery and condemned by the law of Jehovah to be stoned to death.[86] We could easily be misled here into thinking that Blake is an advocate of promiscuity. In *Visions of the Daughters of Albion* (1793) there are certainly intimations of such advocacy. But a closer 'look' at Blake's lifelong message reveals that this theme is Forgiveness, not indulgence.

Blake sees the moral code, as laid down by the reason-bound ego, as a direct consequence of blindness to the spiritual, eternal core in man. The morality preached by 'natural religion', can only be relevant to 'natural' man and can have no relevance to Spiritual Man. It is to such blind morality that Blake is vehemently opposed. What he fights to establish is a morality born from within man's spiritual insight, his intuitive imagination.

It is not surprising to find that Blake is so forcefully anti-clerical, anti-priesthood, for he sees in the Church a worship of 'outer forms' and the moral Christianity of the selfhood, Satan. Of the outer forms he writes: 'outward Ceremony is Anti-Christ'.[87] In *Jerusalem* the following lines may be understood to be a deep-felt criticism of natural religion, of the power of Church and State — both of which, as agents of the 'God of this World', Satan, 'Consider'd as Nothing' Vision and Imagination:[88]

O Polypus of Death! O Spectre over Europe and Asia,
Withering the Human Form by Laws of Sacrifice for Sin!
By Laws of Chastity & Abhorrence I am wither'd up:
Striving to Create a Heaven in which all shall be pure & holy
In their own Selfhoods: in Natural Selfish Chastity to banish Pity
And dear Mutual Forgiveness, & to become One Great Satan
Inslav'd to the most powerful Selfhood: to murder the Divine Humanity.[89]

We shall consider a number of points raised in this passage in more detail in later chapters. In our present context we may comment that the morality expressed in these lines contradicts flatly Blake's conception that God is Love, and the Forgiveness of Sins his basic ethic. The religion of guilt and sin turns its back on the Divine Vision. Those who promulgate such a morality and thus 'murder the Divine Humanity', for they are focused on the 'natural' and have no experience of the spiritual in man, are in the state of Hell. They negate the Imagination, 'Which is the Lord'.[90] Real Hell is 'Eternal Death', the state of being cut off from the eternal spiritual world, Eternity.

However, just as Los, the creative imagination in man, dissipates 'the rocky forms of Death'[91] to save those whom Satan/Urizen has set up 'in Holiness of Natural Religion'[92] from Eternal Death, so also the Divine Mercy, Christ, saves those who are under the dominion of Abstract Philosophy, the denial of 'Spiritual or Imaginative Vision'[93] and do not 'see' that 'the Natural Body is an Obstruction to the Soul or Spiritual Body'.[94]

In *Jerusalem* — in the address 'To the Christians' — Blake speaks of sin as a 'spiritual disease, cured by the Great Healer's, Christ's, Forgiveness of Sins':

> Go therefore, cast out devils in Christ's name;
> Heal thou the sick of spiritual disease;
> Pity the evil, for thou art not sent
> To smite with terror & with punishments
> Those who are sick, like to the Pharisees.[95]

This expression of the 'religion of Jesus', of spiritual religion, is quite the opposite to that of natural religion, whose agents are in the state of Hell:

In Hell all is Self Righteousness; there is no such thing there as Forgiveness of Sin; he who does Forgive Sin is Crucified as an Abettor of Criminals, & he who performs Works of Mercy in Any shape whatever is punish'd &, if possible destroy'd, not thro' envy or Hatred or Malice, but thro' Self Righteousness that thinks it does God service, which God is Satan.[96]

In his vision of the future of mankind, Blake sees no place for institutional religion. Speaking through Los he cries:

> Go to these Fiends of Righteousness,
> Tell them to obey their Humanities & not pretend Holiness
> When they are murderers.[97]

For Blake, self-righteousness is the greatest of sins. It renders man more impervious to Spiritual Light than any other, because it strengthens natural man's empirical ego in its self-made belief in itself. Through self-righteousness the selfhood becomes even more self-assertive and alienated from others. It is natural man's self-centred ego which 'invents' moral laws to which others are then subjected and found wanting. The man of Imagination, Spiritual Man, obeys the laws which are revealed to him through his creative, intuitive imagination, but just because they are valid for him, he does not contend that they should also be so for others. He takes guidance from his intuition, just as animals live in accordance with their innate instincts. In making this comparison between man and animal, however, we should bear in mind that the animal can do no other than follow his instincts. We could say, for instance, that a weaver bird is 'forced' to weave its nest in such and such a way. Spiritual Man, on the other hand, is not 'forced' to follow the revelation of his intuitive imagination. He follows it because he loves it. Christ, the inspiring Spirit within man, is the God of Compassion and Mercy. He is also the fountainhead of love. It is worth commenting here, in passing, that 'instinct' and 'intuition' are fundamentally different. In man psychic awareness is an atavistic instinctual activity, a residue from an earlier phase in the evolution of man. Spiritual perception, on the other hand, is an intuitive knowledge which comes to birth in man with the awakening of the heart, of selfless love. We could say that intuition is the channel through which the Spirit of Truth, the Holy Ghost — sent by Christ — is active.[98]

Natural Man, shutting himself off from the indwelling spirit, Christ, clearly has to invent laws, because the living presence of the spirit, which is in every man, is not perceived by the selfhood. Therefore the impulses which are inspired by the 'God Within' are condemned as morally sinful[99] by the selfhood when they fail to conform to the ego-made moral laws. The impulses of Spiritual Man, of intuitive imagination, follow laws of an inner spiritual life which are both invisible and incomprehensible to the selfhood, the Spectre, in Fallen Man. It is invisible to 'Single vision', Newtonian vision, incomprehensible to a Lockian philosophy of the five physical senses, and excluded from Baconian science. The mechanistic universe of Newton, the mechanistic psychology of Locke, and the inductive science of Bacon, exclude spiritual 'Intelligences'. God is left out, which, according to Blake, means that Real Man, life itself, and all true human values, are left out. The universe which survives after these exclusions is a spiritual vacuum, a 'Satanic Void'.[100]

The Spectre, selfhood, speaking in frosty triumph, reveals his identity as the Urizenic rational power:

> '... I am God, O Sons of Men! I am your Rational Power!
> Am I not Bacon & Locke* who teach Humility to Man,
> Who teach Doubt & Experiment?'

The Spectre then goes on to ask:

*Bacon, Newton and Locke are but the names under which Blake denounces the materialistic philosophy which continues to dominate the modern West.

'Where is that Friend of Sinners? that Rebel against my Laws
Who teaches Belief to the Nations & an unknown Eternal Life?
...
Vain Foolish Man! wilt thou believe without Experiment
And build a World of Phantasy upon my Great Abyss ...?'
So spoke the hard cold constrictive Spectre ...[101]

Indeed, 'that Friend of Sinners' and the rebel against 'cold & scientific'
Urizen,[102] does not teach doubt and experiment.

Not only doubt and experiment, but humility, too, is taught by the
'Reasoning Power', fallen Urizen who, before he fell, 'was Faith & cer-
tainty', but, in his fallen state, 'is chang'd to Doubt'.[103] In *The Everlasting
Gospel* Blake writes:

> Humility is only doubt,
> And does the Sun & Moon blot out.[104]

Elsewhere he states:

> He who Doubts from what he sees
> Will ne'er Believe, do what you Please.
> If the Sun & Moon should doubt,
> They'd immediately Go out.[105]

What Blake states poetically in these four lines he restates in another of his
objections to Bacon: 'Self Evident Truth is one Thing and Truth the
result of Reasoning is another Thing. Rational Truth is not the Truth of
Christ but of Pilate.'[106] We can gain some understanding of what Blake
means by 'Self Evident Truth' from his comment:

The Man who pretends to be a modest enquirer into the truth of a self evident
thing is a Knave. The truth & certainty of Virtue & Honesty, i.e. Inspiration,
needs no one to prove it; it is Evident as the Sun & Moon. He who stands doubt-
ing of what he intends, whether it is Virtuous or Vicious, knows not what
Virtue means. No man can do a Vicious action & think it to be Virtuous. No Man
can take darkness for light. He may pretend to do so & may pretend to be a
modest Enquirer, but he is a Knave.[107]

Truth is an inner experience, not something which can be imposed from
without. True knowledge, spiritual knowledge, is an inner experience,
or, in Blakean terms, a 'belief':

Truth can never be told so as to be understood, and not be believed.[108]

Real faith is the opening of the inner 'eye' to self-evident truths. This is
the 'Truth of Christ', of the Imagination, not of Pilate.

Pilate and Caiaphas[109] — or 'Caiphas', as Blake often spells it — represent the twin evils of State and Church. Founded upon the morality of natural religion, their principles are contrary to those of Christ.[110] Blake gives expression to this conviction in *The Everlasting Gospel*:

> If Moral Virtue was Christianity,
> Christ's Pretensions were all Vanity,
> And Caiphas & Pilate, Men
> Praise Worthy __[111]

When Christ pronounced the forgiveness of sins, upon which the brotherhood of man is founded, Pilate and Caiaphas, representing State and Church, protested:

> Loud Pilate Howl'd, loud Caiphas yell'd,
> When they the Gospel Light beheld.[112]

They were spiritually 'blind' in the darkness of single vision and quite devoid of Imagination, of the Spirit of Christ and could not perceive 'Self Evident Truth'.

In *A Vision of the Last Judgement* Blake describes these two Urizenic figures, Pilate and Caiaphas, as 'Two States where all those reside who Calumniate & Murder under Pretence of Holiness & Justice'.[113] The moral virtues of natural religion, of which Pilate and Caiaphas are both representative, can be no other than destructive of Christ's spiritual religion:

> And the Accuser standing by
> Cried out, 'Crucify! Crucify!
> Our Moral Virtues ne'er can be.
> Nor Warlike pomp & Majesty;
> For Moral Virtues all begin
> In the Accusations of Sin,
> And [Moral *del.*] all the Heroic Virtues End
> In destroying the Sinners' Friend'.[114]

Christ repelled, 'Imagination Denied', says Blake, leads to 'War and Dominion'.[115] Christ's 'Works were destroyed by ... Antichrist Science'.[116]

Earlier we saw that the 'Reasoning Power', institutional religion, teaches humility. Humility is considered a great virtue in all authoritarian religions. Fundamentally, it means submission to a higher authority. Not surprisingly, Blake, the defender of individual initiative and freedom,

distrusts this highly estimated virtue. The Living God 'within' does not
ask humility from man. What he does ask is that man should recognize
the divine in the truly Human and the human in the Divine:

> If thou humblest thyself, thou humblest me
> Thou also dwellest in Eternity.
> Thou art a Man, God is no more,
> Thy own humanity learn to adore,
> For that is my Spirit of Life.[117]

Humanity, not humility, is God's 'Spirit of Life'. Humility implies a
failure to recognize one's own eternal identity and so leads to doubt (see
p. 56).
Forced humility — imposed from without — is the teaching of the
Spectre, the spiritless and lifeless teaching of 'Bacon & Newton & Locke'
It is an instrument in the hands of Urizenic Man used to oppress man and
it leads to moral cruelty:

> Then cruelty knits a snare
> And spreads his baits with care.
> ...
> Then humility takes its root
> Underneath his [Urizen's] foot.[118]

Real humility, for Blake, is modesty at the revelation of one's own acts
of selfless love[119] of which the man of imagination reads in the open Book
of Life at the Last Judgement:

On the Cloud are open'd the Books of Remembrance of Life & of Death: before
that of Life, on the Right, some figures bow in humiliation; before that of
Death, on the Left, the Pharisees are pleading their own Righteousness; the one
shines with beams of Light, the other utters Lightnings & tempests.[120]

Those on the right of Christ, reading the Book of Life, of Spiritual Life,
have experienced 'within' the 'Gospel Light' at the sight of which 'Pilate
Howl'd' and 'Caiphas yell'd'. They have experienced 'within' Christ's
Gospel of the Forgiveness of Sins and Selfless Love; they have experienced
the inner, spiritual resurrection and regeneration, the 'Not I but Christ in
Me' (Paul).[121] The Book of Life cannot be read by Natural Man, only by
Spiritual Man, who perceives the Divine Identity as the source of all true
being. In the Son of Man, Christ, Blake sees the conscious realization of
man completely attuned and related to this source within himself. It is

only through the discovery of an 'I am' consciousness that man can come to the source, the 'indwelling Christ'.

In *A Vision of the Last Judgment* Blake writes:

All Life consists of these Two, Throwing off Error & Knaves from our company continually & Recieving Truth or Wise Men into our Company continually. He who is out of the Church & opposes it is no less an Agent of Religion than he who is in it; to be an Error & to be Cast out is part of God's design ... Whenever any Individual Rejects Error & Embraces Truth, a Last Judgement passes upon that Individual.[122]

In *Jerusalem*, Los, recognized by awakened Albion as being the 'likeness & similitude'[123] of Christ, the Imagination, gives a form, 'a body to Falsehood that it may be cast off for ever'.[124] Only by conscious confrontation (creation) 'within' can an error be recognized, limited and finally annihilated. That which remains formless and indefinite festers 'black & deadly' in the human soul. To such a condition Blake gives the name 'Udan-Adan'. It is a state of non-visionary existence (if 'existence' it may be called) in which there is unquestioning reliance on fallen reason, resulting in the major errors: materialism and restrictive morality.

In *The Four Zoas*, Udan-Adan is described as a lake,

... form'd from the tears & sighs & death sweat of the Victims
Of Urizen's laws, to irrigate the roots of the tree of Mystery.[125]

The 'tree of Mystery' is the contrary to the Tree of Life. It is the Tree of Death, the system of Urizenic morality. The Tree of Life, whose 'leaves ... were for the healing of the Nations',[126] is the Tree of the Forgiveness of Sins.

We can see clearly the close association between the Book of Life and the Tree of Life, on the one hand, and the Book of the Law and the Tree of Death (Mystery) on the other.

The Book of the Law and the Tree of Death both preach vengeance and punishment for sin, whereas the Book of Life and the Tree of Life proclaim the 'Gospel of Jesus', Forgiveness of Sins. The God of the Book of the Law, the Angry God, is, as we have seen already, an abstraction. He does not dwell 'within' man's heart, is not experienced, but 'floats' somewhere in an abstract 'unknownness'. Moreover,

... he is Righteous, he is not a Being of Pity & Compassion,
He cannot feel Distress, he feeds on Sacrifice & Offering,
Delighting in cries & tears & clothed in holiness & solitude.[127]

He is inhuman. No brotherhood can exist on the basis of such a religion.

He can never be a Friend to the Human Race who is the Preacher of Natural Morality or Natural Religion.

...

Every Religion that Preaches Vengeance for Sin is the Religion of the Enemy & Avenger and not of the Forgiver of Sin, and their God is Satan, Named by the Divine Name. Your Religion, O Deists! Deism, is the Worship of the God of this World by the means of what you call Natural Religion and Natural Philosophy, and of Natural Morality or Self-Righteousness, the Selfish Virtues of the Natural Heart. This was the Religion of the Pharisees who murder'd Jesus.

...

Those who Martyr others or who cause War are Deists, but never can be Forgivers of Sin. The Glory of Christianity is to Conquer by Forgiveness. All the Destruction, therefore, in Christian Europe has arisen from Deism, which is Natural Religion.[128]

Deism, natural religion, Newtonian science, Lockian philosophy, Baconian experimental method, in short, 'Serpent Reasoning', all constitute the Tree of Death. Christ, Creative Imagination, 'is the Tree of Life'.[129] The world-picture of the Creative Imagination includes the recognition and experience of spiritual beings and forces at work 'within' nature and 'within' the human breast. In the materialistic conception of the world, which is supposed to be scientifically founded, and which even in the Churches has been accepted as the foundation of life, man has been seduced into accepting the 'outside' of the world as being the sole reality. But, with Blake, we would say that every physical, natural, 'outside' has a spiritual 'within'. It is not physical, natural man, who creates, thinks, acts, feels, but Spiritual Man. To envisage Natural Man as a creator is an illusion, a lie. It is Spiritual Man, the man imbued with Christ, Imagination, who is the creator. A world-picture which excludes spiritual reality is a lie. As we have just seen from the last quotation from *Jerusalem*, Blake states quite categorically that a religion which is devoid of supersensible, spiritual reality, cannot be other than destructive and, we should add, fragmentative. In a society in which human beings are being forced more and more into collective, streamlined systems, all devised according to the principles of mechanized expediency (the 'total state', etc.), human life loses its real value. It is not even noticed when life, true life, is destroyed, for man, enmeshed in the web of materialism, can 'sense' no further than the limitations of his five senses permit. Expressed in the language of The Revelation to St John we could say that the world-conception of materialism is itself the image of the two-horned Beast, because it regards man himself as an animal. In such a world-conception it is apparent that man is alienated from his true being, his spiritual essence, the 'indwelling Christ'.

A few more words need to be said here about the Tree of Death before moving on to a discussion of Blake's conception of the Last Judgement.

The Tree of Mystery, the Tree of Death, the forbidden Tree of the knowledge of good and evil, whose fatal fruit brings spiritual death, is described in *Jerusalem* in such terms as the following. It is:

> ... Moral Virtue and the Law
> Of God [Jehovah] who dwells in Chaos hidden from the human sight.[130]

This 'deadly and poisonous, unimaginative'[131] Tree enroots itself 'into many a Tree, and endless labyrinth of woe'.[132] It has grown from the discursive reasoning power of the human mind. It is a Urizenic contrivance:

> The Gods of the Earth & Sea
> Sought thro' nature to find this tree;
> But their search was all in vain:
> [Till they sought in the human brain. *del.*]
> There grows one in the human brain.[133]

In *A Vision of the Last Judgment*, the inhabitants of Paradise (placed by Blake in the human heart)[134] are said to be:

> ... no longer talking of what is Good & Evil, or what is Right or Wrong, & puzzling themselves in Satan's Labyrinth, But are Conversing with Eternal Realities as they Exist in the Human Imagination.[135]

According to orthodox Christianity the Last Judgement will not occur until the end of the world; then Christ will return and judge all mankind, living and dead — separating the good sheep from the evil goats. The saved will be rewarded with everlasting bliss, the damned punished with everlasting torture.

Such a conception is anathema to Blake. It is the direct opposite of his belief in the character and teaching of Christ. It contradicts both Infinite Mercy and the Forgiveness of Sins. For Blake the Last Judgement has quite a different meaning. It can occur at any time during the life of the individual man or woman (as, for instance, for Job)[136] and at any time for the world as a whole.[137] In the individual, we can speak of the Last Judgement in Blakean terms as a moment of crisis, of decision. Significantly, in Chapter 14 of John's Revelation, the Angel with the *evangelium aeternum*, the Everlasting Gospel, in his hands cries: 'The hour of crisis is come'. In the Authorized Version this has been rendered: 'The hour of his judgement is come', but the Greek word used is, in fact, 'krisis'. The crisis, the critical decision-making point, may come at any moment in human life. If we express the critical point in both Blakean and biblical terms we could say that the decision one has to make is this: Does one work towards the creation of the New Jerusalem, the City of Spiritual Love, Brotherhood and Spiritual Freedom, or towards the establishment of the City of the Whore of Babylon, of a society of men and women who have completely abandoned themselves to self-centred materialism; towards the realization on earth of the reality of the spiritual 'within', or the illusory rule of the physical 'without'; inner spiritual reality, or outer physical appearance? At any moment in our lives the opportunity is given to us to read either from the Book of Life, or from the Book of Death. Do we open ourselves to the Spiritual Light of the Tree of Life, or enmesh ourselves ever more deeply in the dark roots of the Tree of Death (Mystery)? Do we render ourselves increasingly alive to the Spiritual Laws of the Forgiveness of Sin and Universal Brotherhood, or do we continue to harden in egoism, self-centredness, and nourish the Tree of Mystery, the moral law of vengeance and punishment? Do we, in short, cast out error, or allow ourselves to be subjected to it?

All these questions — and many more — are not questions to be answered by us in some distant, nebulous future, but are put to us in the clarity of the present moment — every day, here and now.

When Man surrendered himself to the philosophy and religion of materialism, to the Image of the two-horned Beast, he began to misunderstand his own being. He lost sight of his soul and spirit and he began to conceive of himself as the creation of nature. He became blind to his real humanity.

Blake's vital message to us today — and tomorrow — concerns the awakening of Albion, the opening of the Spiritual Eye of every man and woman. It also concerns the transformation of the Spectre, the 'Reasoning Power', so that it works for us, for our Divinity, and not against it. When reason, the Spectre, is embraced and inspired by Imagination as a brother, it is transformed into Winged Intellect.[138] It is in Natural Man that imagination and abstract reason are at 'war' with each other to the detriment of both. In Real Man, inspired by Imagination, by Los, reason is delivered from abstraction. The imaginative, intuitive intellect then informs our affections and emotions. We then no longer live for ourselves alone, as 'selfhoods', but for our fellow men. Selfless love, sacrificial love, the Christ 'within', creates bonds of brotherhood which are 'cemented' by the invisible fire of spirit, spiritual love.

The 'inner' Day of Judgement offers man the opportunity to free himself from the selfhood which binds him in a narrow prison. Barriers are then broken down until, one with the pulsing life of the universe and with the Humanity Divine, man embraces spiritual liberty. The Book of Life is open to him and he can contribute to the building of the New Jerusalem. The selfless love of men and women permeates and warms, enlivens, the universe. The love of man, aware of the Divine 'within', is a cosmic force.

He who has experienced the Day of Judgement 'within' is — to put it in simple terms — a sociable being. From him flows forth a stream of brotherly love. He loves his fellow men according to the measure of *their* receptivity.[139] No longer does he 'plant' his 'Family alone/Destroying all the World beside'.[140] Resurrected Man, he who reads the Book of Life, sees society and humanity as an organic whole. From him flows a healing power who has the experience of his own essential wholeness, perceived in terms of wholeness of Spiritual Life. He who is dominated by abstract reason can only 'see' in terms of fragmentation, separateness, physical death.

In *Jerusalem*, Los, the creative imagination, asks:

> When Souls mingle & join thro' all the Fibres of Brotherhood
> Can there be any secret joy on Earth greater than this?[141]

Here speaks true humanity, the 'image of God', in man. Souls absorbed in materialism cannot see Christ, the Divine Humanity, no matter how near He may be. They are spiritually blind and groping in darkness. Urizenic 'cavern'd' man, who can see with and not 'thro' the eyes', is without light because, like the Foolish Virgins, his lamp lacks oil.[142] Lacking light, the addicts of materialism, in self-defence, mock those who are 'ever expanding in the Bosom of God, the Human Imagination'[143] and judge that of which they have no experience themselves to be a hallucination and/or a sign of madness.

Up to the first few decades of the eighteenth century, thinkers could advocate a materialist view of life without overwhelming practical consequence for moral conduct. However, in due course, the philosophy of the five senses was bound to become 'practical' in its effects. As we have already noted, the picture of the universe and of man presented by materialistic thought is, in terms of the Apocalypse, 'the Image of the Beast', because it can conceive of man only in terms of nature, or, rather, of his animal nature. Indeed, from Darwin onwards, man is regarded as a 'tailless ape'. Now, as Blake says on more than one occasion, men 'become like what they behold'.[144] In other words, man gradually assumes the stamp and *'character bestiae'*,[145] because he pays homage to a philosophy which understands only his physical, animal nature, and is blind to his real humanity, his spiritual, divine essence. Materialism, natural religion, deism, Blake sees as a spiritual disease. In his 'Address to the Christians', Blake exhorts all true Christians to

> ... cast out devils in Christ's name,
> Heal thou the sick of spiritual disease.[146]

The decision lies with us. Do we, or do we not, accept the 'Gifts of the Spirit',[147] reject Error,[148] and thus heal, not merely ourselves, but make ourselves worthy to heal others who are 'sick of spiritual disease', enmeshed in the philosophy and religion of the Antichrist?[149]

The decision which each man and woman makes is vital for the future of mankind and the earth. He who heals himself, and others, of 'spiritual disease' will be able to speak with the Voice of Christ 'within' and say:

> I deliver all the sons of God
> From Bondage of these terrors, & with influences sweet,
> As once in those eternal fields, in brotherhood & Love.[150]

If we continue to worship the 'image of the Beast' we shall continue to degenerate spiritually and sink even deeper into 'Opacity', that is, become more impervious to the Divine Light, than we already are. We would reach a state of existence which we could describe as being a kind of animal kingdom — not, of course, to be considered as identical with the 'innocent' animal kingdom proper. What Blake exhorts us to do is to raise ourselves to the 'Translucence'[151] of the Angel waiting to be released within us. Neglect of the spiritual 'within' enhances the natural 'without'. The essential element in the Human Kingdom, if it lives and moves and has its being in accordance with its divinity, is composed of love and fellowship. Wherever the 'Image of the Beast', that is, of man as a purely natural being, governs the relationship between human beings, social life, love and fellowship decline. Human souls then plunge ever deeper into Urizenic isolation, separation and egoism. In *The Four Zoas*, Urizenic man is described as sinking until he loses his human form and assumes the subhuman form of the Dragon.[152] According to Revelation 17, the Whore of Babylon rides on a beast with seven heads and ten horns. Blake identifies this beast with the Dragon. For Blake the Dragon symbolizes war, conflict and antagonism. Men who have turned their backs on Divine Vision,[153] on their true humanity, and thus have fallen into a subhuman state, live in fear for their very existence. Bitterness and depression, total isolation and haunting fear, are hallmarks of a society devoid of spirituality. The final result will be a war of all against all, unless there are some who can read the Book of Life and radiate the beams of life-giving and creative Love into the Urizenic darkness.[154]

Rational, Spectral/Urizenic Man fears death for he has no knowledge, no experience, of the Eternal. Only 'fallen' man fears death! This fear Blake states, is augmented by orthodox religion:

> Thy purpose & the purpose of thy Priests & of thy Churches
> Is to impress on men the fear of death, to teach
> Trembling & fear, terror, constriction, abject selfishness.

Over and against this teaching, Blake, through Milton, declares:

> Mine is to teach Men to despise death & to go on
> In fearless majesty annihilating Self, laughing to scorn
> Thy Laws & terrors, shaking down thy Synagogues as webs.[155]

We shall return to the Blakean meaning of 'self-annihilation' in a later chapter. For the moment we can confine ourselves to the realization that, for Blake, death is sheer transition: 'I cannot consider death as anything but a removing from one room to another',[156] he said shortly before the 'death' of his own physical body. Death is an episode in life — a state through which one passes, awakening to Eternal Life.[157] He who sees existence in a physical body as the totality of life has turned his back on Divine Vision. The inner being, spiritual essence, of man knows no death. Physical death is an occasion of spiritual joy, not sorrow. When his brother Robert died, Blake saw the released spirit ascend 'clapping its hands for joy'. In a letter to William Hayley we read that the two remained in constant spiritual communion and 'conversation'. Blake writes:

Thirteen years ago I lost a brother & with his spirit I converse daily & hourly in the Spirit & See him in my remembrance in the regions of my Imagination. I hear his advice & even now write from his Dictate.[158]

Death exists only in the thought of those who are empty of Imagination, who have not experienced the Christ 'within'. The Imagination is eternal life, for it is co-existent with God, with Christ — of Whom we are 'Members'.[159] For spiritual discernment: 'All Things Exist in the Human Imagination'.[160]

Only a mechanized universe, perceived with the five physical senses, harbours death, or, we could say, only he who adores the 'God of this World', Satan/Spectre/Urizen, has fear of death. Spirit, 'Mind & Imagination' are living realities which transcend 'Mortal & Perishing Nature'. Death is no more than an illusion of natural religion, materialism. In passing we may note that to enter the world of matter — to materialize — is, in Blake's terminology, to vegetate.

When, with Blake, we perceive all that is 'real & eternal'[161] as existing in the Imagination, in other words, that all real existence is spiritual, not physical (natural), then we are considering a mode of existence and being which does not know death — in which there is no death. Imagination is timeless and limitless. It is immune from the categories of temporal and spatial, limited, existence as we know it as Natural Man: 'What is Mortality but the things relating to the Body which Dies? What is Immortality but the things relating to the Spirit which Lives Eternally?'[162]

Spirit (mind and consciousness) cannot be found in nature, or, perhaps more clearly expressed, spirit in nature remains spirit; it does not become nature. It is spiritual forces which 'breathe' life into nature. But, in the process, they do not lose their spirituality, they do not become 'naturalized'. Nature without spirit is lifeless, just as reason, unless it is bewinged by Imagination, remains divorced from life. Being neither temporal nor spatial Imagination is not subject to the laws of the physical world, of nature. Man, too, in his essential being, his true humanity, is free from the laws which govern his mortal frame — the 'garment' (cf. p. 177–83) as Blake frequently calls it.[163] We are not, then, mere insignificant material specks filling a miniscule volume of three-dimensional physical space in a mechanistic universe, but immaterial spirits in an infinite and eternal world of Life. The 'volume' which true, Real Man, fills is not to be found in a measurable corporeal universe, but in the infinite and eternal 'volume' of Imagination, which is spiritual.

This world of Imagination is the world of Eternity; it is the divine bosom into which we shall all go after the death of the Vegetated body. This World of Imagination is Infinite & Eternal, whereas the world of Generation, or Vegetation, is Finite & ... Temporal.[164]

Because we are dwellers in a spiritual universe, because Christ, the Imagination, dwells in us, the death of the mortal body, the 'Garment', does not in any way change what we really are. The decay of the physical body does not change the reality that in essence we are spiritual, not corporeal, beings.

It will be clear from what has just been said that Blake vehemently rejects the belief:

That an Eternal life awaits the worms* of sixty winters.[165]

A belief in the resurrection of the physical, natural body, if it is held in a concrete, literal sense, is untenable in Blake's view. From our comments above regarding the distinction we need to make between spirit and nature, the meaning of the following statement by Blake is apparent: 'Nature has no Supernatural & dissolves'.[166] By insisting on literal interpretations, rational man kills the real, spiritual meaning. The letter of the Law destroys the spirit of Life.[167] In spite of St Paul's clear statement that it is the 'spiritual body' which is raised at the Resurrection, and not the dead 'natural body', Blake sees that orthodox religion nevertheless insists on the resurrection of the mortal 'natural body'. For Blake, and St Paul, such a belief is fundamentally erroneous. The Church worships death instead of life. For Blake the worship of 'A Vegetated Christ' is 'Blasphemy'.[168]

For the man of fallen reason, limited and governed by his five physical senses, if there is to be any form of resurrection at all, it can, of course, only be a question of a physical resurrection. Since, for him, a 'Spiritual Body' doesn't exist, it is, in Blake's view, unadulterated and hypocritical lip-service to a doctrine, and not an inner experience, when rational, unimaginative, man speaks of the Resurrection.

For the man of Imagination, who experiences the 'indwelling Christ' and is conscious of his own spiritual essence as the eternal reality, the crucified physical body of Christ is still in the sepulchre.[169]

Blake begins a letter to a clergyman, Dr Trusler, with the words: 'I really am sorry that you are fall'n out with the Spiritual World.'[170] The content and purpose of this letter need not concern us here. The significant point to be stressed is that for Blake a 'Spiritual World' is a reality, an experience. The 'Spiritual World' is a matter of inner experience, not of the 'Ratio',[171] for the latter can only conceive of a finite world perceivable to the five limited physical senses.

*i.e. the mortal bodies of men and women.

Blake, in his ceaseless 'Mental Fight', strives to restore to man his true humanity, lost with the supremacy of the 'ratio'. For him, the Gospel teaching that 'the Kingdom of Heaven is within you' is a reality, an inner experience, not an abstract theory. Not only Heaven but also Hell — if they are not to remain mere abstractions — must be experienced within:

> ... in your own Bosom you bear your Heaven
> And Earth & all you behold; tho' it appears Without, it is Within,
> In your Imagination, of which this World of Mortality is but a Shadow.[172]

As we have already seen, the Last Judgement, for Blake, is an event which takes place 'within'. It is not a moral trial imposed from without by a censorious judge, but an inner spiritual awakening. However, although Blake thoroughly rejects the moralistic terms of natural religion, or, in a broader sense, of orthodox Christianity, he does very definitely lay upon each individual man or woman the moral responsibility for the spiritual condition in which he or she goes through life. Man is a free spirit, not a robot. He is free to choose which path he will follow. He can, in Blakean terms, either choose to follow the 'path' of the 'Ratio', of the empirical selfhood, or that of imaginative vision. He can either remain closed up, contracted and opaque, in his 'cavern' of materialism, or expand through 'cleansed' organs of perception. It is given to everyone to 'see' with spiritual eyes, with the Eye of Imagination',[173] but such spiritual sight demands individual effort, strength and courage. 'Why', Los, 'furious, raging', cries out:

> ... Why stand we here trembling around
> Calling on God for help, and not ourselves, in whom God dwells,
> Stretching a hand to save the falling Man?[174]

Do we, or do we not, grasp the outstretched hand of Him who dwells in us? The decision is ours, not that of some remote, abstract God. It is each individual man's and woman's moral responsibility, inwardly experienced, not imposed from without, to overcome the limitations set by 'the Vegetated Mortal Eye's perverted & single vision'.[175] It is the mortal eye of fallen Reason, which, for instance, mistakes our last sleep for literal death:

> ... in the Optic vegetative Nerves, Sleep was transformed
> To Death in old time by Satan the father of Sin & Death.[176]

When fallen Reason persuades us to see 'With, not thro' the Eye',[177] then the senses serve the empirical, encapsulated ego, the selfhood, and not the divine, creative Imagination. By fallen Reason 'We are led to Believe a Lie',[178] to live in a world of illusion.

For Blake, the Last Judgement — a continuous process 'within' — is the opportunity given to man to open the inward sight which enables him to see things as they really are. Every moment of time brings man to stand before the Eternal. For those who persist in following the path of the 'Ratio', who, in other words, choose 'Single vision & Newton's sleep',[179] this ever-present reality will remain hidden until such time as the thick veil of unconsciousness, concealing the spiritual essence within, is rent more and more.[180] This 'veil' is symbolically represented in Blake's poetry by Vala, who, particularly in Nights vi and viii of *The Four Zoas* and in *Jerusalem*, represents the contrary of Jerusalem, being her shadow, Babylon. She represents both rejection of vision and the 'evil' which ensues from such rejection in the sphere of morality. Vala, is the symbol of the illusion that one-sided rational man knows as the physical universe, she is 'our Mother Nature',[181] and, at the same time, she represents the principle of 'evil' or 'error' which causes man to accept the illusion. She personifies, in short, natural religion, natural morality, or what Blake often speaks of as 'Mystery'.[182]

The Last Judgement begins when the 'veil' of deadly sleep, unconsciousness, is rent, or, in the language of St John, the 'cloud' opens and rolls away to reveal the presence of the Divine Human, Christ, that is, the true humanity in man. This is the vision Blake depicts: 'The Cloud that opens, rolling apart before the throne & before the New Heaven & the New Earth'.[183]

It is from 'within', not from 'without', that He shall come. The Resurrection is within ourselves. In this 'regeneration' we see with new eyes, with expanded senses, the 'Eye of Imagination', and become aware that 'the New Heaven & the New Earth' have always been there and that, as long as we allow ourselves to be enclosed 'in the Optic Vegetative Nerves',[184] we are unable to experience them. Against such an inner revelation the usurping self-centred ego — 'Satan, the Selfhood' — fights with all its power, bringing forward one rational argument after another to retain his power over the human soul and enslave Man in a world of lie and deception, doubt and despair.

Any Vision of the 'True Vine of Eternity, The Human Imagination ... throwing off the Temporal that the Eternal might be Established,'[185] is, of course, anathema to the selfhood. Our empirical ego resists it, for it brings about the painful 'fall' of all our self-protective barriers, our self-deceptions, our 'masks' (false personalities) and our carefully constructed self-righteousness.

It is Blake's constant endeavour to reawaken his fellow men to clearer consciousness, to a sense of 'Translucence'. He exhorts them to rise up out of the 'darkened', 'clouded' 'sea of Time & Space'[186] in which 'the five senses whelm'd/ In deluge o'er the earth-born man'.[187]

The Nature of my Work is Visionary or Imaginative; it is an Endeavour to Restore what the Ancients call'd the Golden Age.[188]

Blake calls on us to re-expand our consciousness to embrace spiritual reality, for when 'the Golden Age' came to an end and was succeeded by the Iron Age (see pp. 206–9) then: 'Reality was Forgot & the Vanities of Time & Space only Remember'd & call'd Reality.'[189]

Blake's Judgement, as has been made clear already, is not a Judgement as practised by the Moral Law. Nevertheless, it is a painful experience since it is a judgement by the spiritual reality 'within', our Higher Self, Christ, of all the falsehoods we have 'clothed' ourselves in.

Now, just as the Last Judgement, in the Blakean sense, is an ever-present, continuous process, so also is the Crucifixion. It is continuously re-enacted: we crucify our real selves when we 'harden', 'thicken', the 'veil' and lose consciousness of ourselves as the 'Image of God'. This experience is given expression by Albion, who has fallen into the power of the Satanic Selfhood:

> O Jerusalem. Jerusalem, I have forsaken thy Courts,
> Thy Pillars of ivory & gold, thy Curtains of silk & fine
> Linen, thy Pavements of precious stones, thy Walls of pearl
> And gold, thy Gates of Thanksgiving, thy Windows of Praise,
> Thy Clouds of Blessing, thy Cherubims of Tender-mercy
> Stretching their Wings sublime over the Little-ones of Albion!
> O Human Imagination, O Divine Body I have Crucified,
> I have turned my back upon thee into the Wastes of Moral Law.[190]

Concomitant with our taking up our bows of 'of burning gold' and joining in the 'Mental Flight' to build Jerusalem[191] is the cleansing of our organs of perception, for

The Visions of Eternity, by reason of narrowed perceptions,
Are become weak Visions of Time & Space, fix'd into furrows of death.[192]

The healer of the spiritual disease of the world is the Imagination, Christ, Blake declares:

The Man is himself become
A piteous example of oblivion ...
... however high
Our palaces and cities and however fruitful our fields,
In Selfhood, we are nothing ...
... none but the Lamb of God can heal
This dread disease, none but Jesus.[193]

It is a matter of urgency, Blake says, for Man's, 'Albion's ... death is coming apace'.[194]

Although Blake's prophecies are specifically addressed to the Giant Albion, the English nation, he is clearly concerned about the whole of humanity. He calls every man and woman, whether in England, Russia, North America or elsewhere, to awaken from the 'deadly sleep' of materialism. He calls all 'sleepers' to reawaken to the vision of Eternity.

In his prophetic vision of the future, Blake sees no place for traditional religious bodies, cults and sects. His Christianity is not that of any sect or cult, all of which are to a greater or lesser extent exclusive. Blake seeks to awaken us to the universality of the Everlasting Gospel, to a universal Christianity.

Fear of and servitude to a remote, avenging and wrathful God belong to the past, as also do blind faith and humble filial obedience. We have arrived at a point in man's evolution where he himself has to make a critical decision (see pp. 48–9), for 'Albion's death is coming apace'. Will he choose to read in the Book of Death, or in the Book of Life?

That which is asked of us now, if Albion, man, is not to lie eternally in 'deadly sleep' on the cold rock, is that we commit ourselves to the 'Mental Fight' to build Jerusalem on Earth. An imaginative, spiritual striving is demanded of us, if the Everlasting Gospel, the Gospel of Universal Forgiveness and Divine Selfless Love, incarnate in Christ Himself, is to become a reality. It is up to each and every individual to bring into being the 'Religion of Jesus', the universal religion of spiritual liberty and love, which, in simple terms, may be said to be the religion of mature humanity.

The Everlasting Gospel is not a new book, but a new spiritual revelation of the inner, spiritual sense of the Bible. In the age of maturity, the New Age, man has to find the 'Kingdom of God within'. This awareness of the Divine is not exclusive to any one sect or cult, but universal. We are all members of the Divine Body, Human Imagination, Christ.[195] The Divine Body includes all members of the human race. Christ is the

Universal Self of all mankind. To this religion all men are born: 'Ye are united, O ye Inhabitants of Earth, in One Religion, The Religion of Jesus, the most Ancient, the Eternal & the Everlasting Gospel.'[196]

In the 'age of maturity' all existing forms of worship, ceremonies, rituals, legal and moral codes, will be superfluous (clearly we have a long way to go yet before this will become possible). Instead of appearing as a source from 'without', God, Christ, will be experienced by Man 'within'. Man will be consciously aware of the Divine Source within and there will be no need for any kind of authority imposing itself upon Man from without. Man will then have passed 'through Eternal Death' and awakened to 'Eternal Life';[197] he will have fought, spiritually, through the world of experience, the 'Valley of Death', and arrived at the inner experience of 'self evident Truth' and inner, spiritual liberty, the very essence of spiritual love and universal brotherhood.

2

CREATIVE IMAGINATION, PERCEPTION AND PARTICULARS

For Blake the imaginative life is the only real life. 'All things Exist in the Human Imagination',[1] he states, and 'Mental Things are alone Real ... Where is the Existence Out of Mind or Thought'.[2] The universe is a creation of the imaginative power that is in both God and man, and when man realizes this, then he is on the right path to truth and spiritual regeneration.

Blake rightly points out that we have lost the inner experience and creative use of the imaginative power. Indeed, in addition to 'exposing' the materialism of Newton, Locke and Bacon, Blake could have strengthened his contention by highlighting the statement made by Thomas Hobbes (1588–1679, i.e. before Locke) that all our knowledge originates in what we learn through our physical senses, and that imagination 'is nothing but "decaying sense"'.[3]

It is in such a climate of rationalism and materialism that Blake writes:

The Nature of Visionary Fancy, or Imagination, is very little Known, & the Eternal nature & permanence of its ever Existent Images is consider'd less permanent than the things of Vegetative & Generative Nature ...

But, by a conscious effort, we can regain creative imaginative power. Just as the oak dies but returns through its seed, the acorn, for 'Its Eternal Image & Individuality never dies ...', so

the Imaginative Image returns by the seed of Contemplative Thought; the Writings of the Prophets illustrate these conceptions of the Visionary Fancy by their various sublime & Divine Images as seen in the Worlds of Vision ...

Blake then goes on to say: 'The Nature of my Work is Visionary or Imaginative; it is an Endeavour to Restore what the Ancients call'd the Golden Age.'[4]

In response to Dr Johnson's contention that 'All power or fancy over reason is a degree of insanity,'[5] Blake could have answered: 'Vision or Imagination is a Representation of what Eternally Exists, Really & Unchangeably.'[6] It is 'Forms', Ideas, we could say, spiritual essences, which eternally exist and are real. They are perceived in this phenomenal world as imaginative 'images'. In other words, their reality transcends the realm of 'Vegetative & Generative Nature'. Physical, vegetative oaks sprout, grow old, and eventually die, but their 'Eternal Image & Individuality never dies'.

Blake consistently proclaims that these universal 'images' are not merely deduced, abstracted, from particular sense impressions — such a conclusion can only issue from empiricism. He repeatedly affirms his intuitive knowledge of the existence of a spiritual world,[7] of which the world of empirical perception is but a shadow. One of his many clear statements to this effect runs: 'There Exist in that Eternal World the Permanent Realities of Every Thing which we see reflected in the Vegetable Glass of Nature.'[8]

The forms which are visible to the physical eye and die are the illusory products of creation by a fallen demiurge,[9] whereas the eternal Forms are, literally, timeless, eternal:

> Whatever can be Created can be Annihilated. Forms cannot.
> The Oak is cut down by the Ax, the Lamb falls by the Knife
> But their Forms Eternal Exist, For-ever. Amen. Hallelujah![10]

In such statements as these Blake is not expressing a philosophical hypothesis but what is, for him, an immediate intuition of the truth. For him the main source of insight, 'Vision or Imagination', is the very life of man: 'All that we See is Vision ... Permanent in The Imagination.'[11] Other aspects of experience are no more than temporary 'States', but

The Imagination is not a State: it is the Human Existence itself.[12]

The function of visionary imagination is to reach beyond the images of the ordinary phenomenal world to the true forms in the spiritual world. To imagine, in the sense in which Blake means it, is not to indulge oneself in some airy-fairy and diffuse fancifulness, but to follow a path of considerable clarity and discipline. Indeed, 'He who does not imagine in stronger and better lineaments, and in stronger and better light than his perishing mortal eye can see, does not imagine at all.'[13]

We noted earlier that the universe is a creation of the imaginative power which is common to both God and man. For Blake, it is in Christ that the Imaginations of God and Man become one. Imagination is 'the Divine Humanity',[14] and as 'Man is all Imagination', so also 'God is Man & exists in us & we in him.'[15] Not only is 'The Eternal Body of Man ... The Imagination, that is, God himself', but, more symbolically, the body of man is 'the Divine Body of the Lord Jesus' and 'we are his Members'.[16]

For Blake — as for numerous Romantic thinkers — the Imagination is an energy or force which creates and transforms as it 'perceives'. His concept stresses the active side of the imaginative power, but he also recognizes its contemplative nature. Unlike others (Coleridge, for instance) Blake does not distinguish between different levels of the imaginative power. This is one of the reasons why the word 'Imagination' is so rich and varied in Blake.

The sense of a forming, shaping activity in Blake's conception of the Imagination allows him to liken the creative human mind (spirit) to the forming or plastic spirit which works in God, Christ and the Holy Ghost.[17] Of the Holy Ghost Blake writes: 'Imagination, Art & Science & all intellectual Gifts' are 'the Gifts of the Holy Ghost'.[18] The materialist (e.g. Newton) denies this 'Indwelling of the Holy Ghost'.[19]

In contrast to Wordsworth, Blake emphasizes that the mind alone is creative and that nature, by itself, is not, as Wordsworth implies, 'fitted' to the mind, but is 'fallen' and spiritually lifeless.[20] But, when we 'see' nature with imaginative vision, we bring it to life and redeem it. Moreover, as already indicated, we are then on the way towards the spiritual regeneration of ourselves. He who has a strong imagination and is imbued with creative energy is an enthusiast, is 'possessed' by a god, is 'fired' by inspiration flowing to him from the Divine. Imaginative vision endows us with the greatest power for knowledge, wisdom and understanding. When imaginative, enthusiastic man greets nature he creates it — as well as his own identity (see pp. 96–). For Blake the Divinity is in us.

When Blake says that the Imagination creates reality, he is voicing a similar attitude to that of Keats who remarks that certain ethereal things gain their worth by the 'ardour of mental pursuit' we invest in them. For Keats, 'mental' here means 'imaginative', as it does for Blake, who believes that 'mental pursuit', 'mental fight', redeems the fallen world. Imagination, imaginative art, liberates the mind and in so doing guarantees individual freedom.

The free self — creating the world by its own vision — assimilates the world into itself as a part of itself. Or, differently expressed, the object (the perceived) becomes part of the subject (the perceiver) because the

Imagination makes the object into what it is in the process of perceiving it. However, we must bear in mind here that the 'free' imaginative self does not assimilate the world in an egotistical but in a redemptive sense. Far from being egotistical, the imaginative 'eye' is for Blake always directed outward, away from the selfish. Indeed, Blake conceives of the Imagination and the selfhood as being antithetical. The freedom of the self to create something eternal means the very opposite of self-involvement and self-aggrandizement, which, for Blake, is the worst form of living hell, where the individual psyche splits into spectres and devours itself in self-destructive, Urizenic solipsism.

Nature, including 'Natural' Man, is fallen, that is, it is imperfect — 'but a Shadow' of Eternity — cut off from communion with God. But man's Imagination can regenerate nature and raise transitory forms to the symbolic level of 'ever Existent Images' and ideas.

There is, in Blake, a kind of pre-established harmony between the human soul and nature. This is not to say, of course, that Blake believes in what he called the 'fitted and fitting' of Wordsworth, the equivalency of nature and mind, but rather that the mind has the creative potential to 'mould' nature into something spiritually meaningful. Man's imaginative vision — by referring to a higher spiritual, divine truth — works to create this harmony. The Divine has endowed man with the potential to create harmony of mind and nature. It is in this sense that the harmony is 'pre-established'. Such harmony is destroyed if we fail to engage our creative imagination.

For man's creative energy or imagination to merge with God's through the medium of Nature is to see, according to Blake, that

Nature is a Vision of the Science of the Elohim.[21]

'Science' here can be understood to be the divine knowledge held by the spiritual world, the Eternals. Nature, the world of generation, is a necessary but no more than an interim stage Man has to pass through to reach a higher reality.

When Blake says that 'to the Eyes of the Man of Imagination, Nature is Imagination itself',[22] he is speaking of the forming, shaping energy in the human soul and spirit and in nature alike, an energy at the disposal of man's spiritual enlightenment if only his imagination has the courage to use it. Blake contrasts this idea with the lifeless forms of nature, which he often represents by mechanical or mineral images. What God creates through the Imagination remains part of a great unity. The diversity of

matter, manifestations of the spirit, points back to the one Source. It is
clear that he who is convinced of the reality of the creative Imagination in
nature, man and the Creator, also holds to a panentheistic religion and
cosmology. In his religious views Blake is more a panentheist[23] than an
orthodox Christian (see Appendix 1). He departed from orthodox
Christianity to the extent that he thought it could not express the active
force within an overall cosmological unity. However, for Blake, Christ
remains the central force within this unity. Christ is the imaginative
unifying and all-penetrating force of the 'One and the Many'.

If the universe were divided, split, between the Creator (the One) and
the Creation (the Many), what then forms the ground of their unity? If
nothing, then what is created or 'fallen'[24] from the Divine, from God,
must remain eternally separated from Him. But there is something, Blake
insists. There is in Man a faculty which keeps 'the Divine Vision in time
of trouble'.[25] This faculty, represented by Los, is clearly the Imagination.
Art, therefore, and the creative sound — poetry and music — in par-
ticular, is a regenerative medium given to man as a spiritual bridge by
means of which reunion with the Divine (the unity of subject and object)
can be gained. Blake himself sees it as his task, as poet, to restore this one-
ness with God, 'to Restore ... the Golden Age'[26] which prevailed before
the Fall.

But art, poetry, is not powerful enough on its own to bring into being
the desired reunion of God, man and nature. There is a more powerful
tendency and drive towards union than this: love. Love and Imagination,
love and creative desire, together form the spiritual means by which man
can regain true union in God, in Christ. Indeed, Blake maintains,
Imagination is the power that creates, Love is the force which unites the
creator with his creation.[27] The creative art and love of the human
imagination participates in God's love and deeds of creation. Blake's view
of periods of active creative expansion being rhythmically followed by
periods of rest or contemplation is another way of representing the active
and the loving (passive) aspects of the Imagination.

If we now ask by what specific act of love does God bind Himself to his
own creation, we find the answer, as Blake does, in the Gospel of John:
'God so loved the world, that he gave his only begotten Son, that who-
soever believeth in him should not perish, but have everlasting life.'
Christ is the act of love incarnate, and for Blake He is the Imagination in
divine form. Christ and the Love that is Christ are, for Blake, the
imaginative unifying force of the 'One and the Many'. Christ's Love,

man's love, is more important than the gift of prophecy (1 Cor. 13:2). Christ, for Blake, is the most sublime expression of the creative imagination fired by the all-penetrating bond of love. Alternatively we may say that Blake recognizes Christ's loving power as the highest attainment of the Imagination. Christ is, for him, the symbol of symbols, where Love and Imagination are fused into unity: 'Jesus & his Apostles & Disciples were all Artists.'[28]

Earlier in this chapter we heard Blake saying that 'Mental Things are alone Real'. He continues: 'what is call'd Corporeal, Nobody Knows of its Dwelling Place: it is in Fallacy, & its Existence an Imposture. Where is the Existence Out of Mind or Thought?'[29] Mental, spiritual things alone are real, because reality is spiritual. It follows then that for those who, with Blake, hold this conviction, perception can only be intelligible as a mental or spiritual act. For Blake imagination alone creates a true picture of reality. He insists on the validity of supersensible perception, 'Spiritual sensation', and the falsity of the witness of the limited physical senses. Regenerate man, imaginative man, is not under the abstract domination and rigid rules of the physical space and clock-time, but is free and can be spiritually perceived:

> Creating Space, Creating Time, according to the wonders Divine,
> Of Human Imagination.[30]

In a letter to Dr Trusler (23 August 1799) Blake writes:

What is it sets Homer, Virgil & Milton in so high a rank of Art? Why is the Bible more Entertaining* & Instructive than any other book? Is it not because they are addressed to the Imagination, Which is Spiritual Sensation?[31]

Blake himself strives to revive symbolic poetry in the manner of the Hebrew prophets and St John. To his way of thinking, the faculty of Imagination in man has suffered a general wasting away. It can only be restored to its full power by man's frank use of myth and symbol to represent the psychic states of the individual, current and past social problems and events, cosmological happenings, and causes and effects of religious faith, all transposed into metaphors and symbols as we find them in the Bible. In Blake's view, the 'poetry' we find in the Bible should continue to inspire us; it should not be relegated to the dusty shelves of past history as something no longer relevant. If the Divine lives in human minds and hearts, and if spiritual truths are eternal, then it follows for

---

*Used in the sense of 'affording mental sustenance'.

Blake that truth — and conviction, faith — can be best expressed by man in symbolic art. The kind of spiritual 'sensing', imagination, which inspired the books of Ezekiel or Revelation is the spiritual power Blake exhorts us to find in ourselves again.

In his annotations to George Berkeley's *Siris* (1744) Blake objects to Berkeley's apparent endorsement of a psychology which described reason as acting upon the data of perception. Berkeley's statement runs: 'Reason considers and judges of the Imagination'. Blake's succinct comment is: 'Knowledge is not by deduction but Immediate by Perception or Sense at once. Christ addresses himself to the Man not to his Reason.'[32] Elsewhere Blake writes: 'He who does not Know Truth at Sight is unworthy of Her Notice.'[33] And in response to Reynold's assertion that 'In the midst of the highest flights of fancy or imagination, reason ought to preside from first to last', Blake comments: 'If this is True, it is a devilish Foolish thing to be an Artist.'[34]

'Knowledge is ... immediate by Perception.' We clearly need to distinguish between Blake's understanding of the term 'perception' and that of the empiricists. If we think of perception as involving a confluent mental, spiritual, process, then our understanding of Blake is enhanced. He is, in other words, speaking of intuitive perception: what in German would be called *Anschauung*, the 'looking at', which is usually translated into English as 'intuition', as distinct from *Wahrnehmung*, sense perception. 'Vision' and 'perception' probably express this distinction in Blake most adequately. Clearly 'perception' is necessary and cannot be bypassed, but it is 'blind' unless informed by vision. It is in this sense that we look 'not with but through the eye'.[35] An example of Blake's use of the noun 'sense' where its meaning is clearly that of an organ of perception informed by vision is the following:

The Prophets Isaiah and Ezekiel dined with me, and I asked them how they dared so roundly to assert that God spake to them; and whether they did not think at the time that they would be misunderstood, & so be the cause of imposition. Isaiah answered, 'I saw no God, nor heard any, in a finite organical perception; but my senses discover'd the infinite in everything.'[36]

This view of perception is clearly not that of empiricism. However, Blake does not break entirely with the empiricist. To do so would be to join those who degrade reality into a dark realm of generalizations (abstractions) instead of establishing it in the clear perceptions of particulars. 'What', he asks, 'is General Nature? is there Such a Thing? what is

General Knowledge? is there such a Thing? Strictly Speaking All Knowledge is Particular.'[37] Indeed, 'General Knowledge is Remote Knowledge; it is in Particulars that Wisdom consists & Happiness too.'[38] And he states: 'To Generalize is to be an Idiot. To Particularize is the Alone Distinction of Merit. General Knowledges are those Knowledges that Idiots possess.'[39] And, 'Singular & Particular Detail is the foundation of the Sublime.'[40]

In answer to Reynold's contention that the 'wish of the genuine painter must be more extensive: instead of endeavouring to amuse mankind with the minute neatness of his limitations, he must endeavour to improve them by the grandeur of his ideas', Blake sharply retorts: 'Without Minute Neatness of Execution The Sublime cannot Exist! Grandeur of Ideas is founded on Precision of Ideas.'[41] And, 'All sublimity is founded on Minute Discrimination.'[42] And in regard to Reynolds' attitude which 'will allow a poet to express his meaning, when his meaning is not well known to himself, with a certain degree of obscurity, as it is one source of the sublime', Blake is equally clear: 'Obscurity is Neither the Source of the Sublime nor of any Thing Else.'[43]

Since forms are apprehended by the intellect and since the Imagination sees more sharply than the physical eye, Blake conceives the Forms to be clearly outlined. His doctrine of 'Minute Particulars' is the means of expressing this conception. For example, in *Jerusalem* Los/Blake says that 'he who wishes to see a Vision, a perfect Whole, Must see it in its Minute Particulars, Whole, Organized ...... General Forms have their vitality in Particulars.'[44]

Minute Particulars are, for Blake, the outward expression of the inner, eternal individualities of all things. When, therefore, Reynolds would eradicate the particular and hence also the expression of individuality, Blake's dissent is scathing. In response to Reynold's dictum: 'If you mean to preserve the most perfect beauty in its most perfect state, you cannot express the passions ...', Blake retorts:

What nonsense!
Passion & Expression is Beauty itself. The Face that is Incapable of Passion & Expression is deformity Itself. Let it be Painted & Patch'd & Praised & Advertised for Ever, it will only be admired by Fools.[45]

Ultimately, it is Christ, 'the Divine-Humanity who is the only General and Universal Form,'[46] for He contains all things, including the Universal Forms, the sources of the Particulars. It is in this sense that we should understand Blake's statement that the 'Minute Particulars' of Christ are men:

> ... every
> Particular is a Man, a Divine Member of the Divine Jesus.[47]

Every physical, natural man is a symbol of the ideal, spiritual man. Only the man of vision, be he poet, or philosopher, can apprehend ideal man, the eternal reality. For Blake, Vision is reality itself, which can and must be seen by the artist, if he is to be true to the eternal spiritual essence which is his real self:

A Spirit and a Vision are not, as the modern philosophy [of materialism] supposes, a cloudy vapour, or nothing: they are organized and minutely articulated beyond all that the mortal and perishing nature can produce ... The painter of this work[48] asserts that all his imaginations appear to him infinitely more perfect and minutely organized than anything seen by his mortal eye.[49]

'Vision', Blake reaffirms, 'is Determinate & Perfect'.[50]
Such visions carried Blake into the spiritual realm of eternal principles, of archetypes:

The Artist having been taken in vision into the ancient republics, monarchies, and patriarchates of Asia, has seen those wonderful originals called in the Sacred Scriptures the Cherubim ... being [the] originals from which the Greeks and Hetrurians copied Hercules Farnese, Venus of Medicis, Apollo Belvidere, and all the grand works of ancient art.[51]

The sentences preceding the statement that 'A Spirit and a Vision are not ... a cloudy vapour, a nothing' emphasize Blake's experience that spiritual perception gives 'Immediate Knowledge' of Ideal Forms — that they 'Really Exist':

The connoisseurs and artists who have made objections to Mr B.'s mode of representing spirits with real bodies, would do well to consider that the Venus, the Minerva, the Jupiter, the Apollo, which they admire in Greek statues are all of them representations of spiritual existences, of Gods immortal, to the mortal perishing organ of sight; and yet they are embodied and organized in solid marble. Mr B. requires the same latitude, and all is well. The Prophets describe what they saw in Vision as real and existing men, whom they saw with their imaginative and immortal organs; the Apostles the same; the clearer the organ the more distinct the object.[52]

Clearly, for the man of Vision, of 'Spiritual Perception':[53] 'The Man who never in his Mind & Thoughts travel'd to Heaven Is No Artist.'[54]

And the response of a man of vision to such statements by Reynolds that 'ideal perfection and beauty are not to be sought in the heavens, but upon the earth', for 'they are about us, and upon every side of us', can be no other than that uttered by Blake: 'A Lie! ... A Lie!'[55]

A more measured but no less telling reaction is forthcoming from Blake when Reynolds claims that 'it is from a reiterated experience and a close comparison of the objects in nature, that an artist becomes possessed of the idea of that central form ... from which every deviation is deformity':

One Central Form composed of all other Forms being Granted, it does not therefore follow that all other Forms are Deformity. All Forms are Perfect in the Poet's Mind, but these are not Abstracted nor Compounded from Nature, but are from Imagination.[56]

The clarity and minuteness of details in his visions naturally led Blake to stress the necessity of 'Minute Particulars' in painting. Every detail must be a living outgrowth of the central reality. Each detail is full of meaning:

I entreat, then, that the Spectator will attend to the Hands & Feet, to the Lineaments of the Countenances; they are all descriptive of Character, & not a line is drawn without intention, & that most discriminate & particular[57] ... Painting admits not a Grain of Sand or a Blade of Grass Insignificant.[58]

'Spiritual Perception' is required of the spectator if he is to apprehend the work of a man of vision.

The clarity of detail in Blake's visions led naturally to his stressing the 'Minute Particulars', not only in art, but in other, if not all, spheres of life. 'Minute Particulars' are, indeed, an essential element in his philosophy of life. His insistence on firm outlines follows on quite organically from this 'philosophy':

The great and golden rule of art, as well as of life, is this: That the more distinct, sharp, and wirey the bounding line, the more perfect the work of art ... The want of this determinate and bounding form evidences the want of idea in the artist's mind ... How do we distinguish the oak from the beech, the horse from the ox, but by the bounding outline? ... What is it that distinguishes honesty from knavery, but the hard and wirey line of rectitude and certainty in the actions and intentions? Leave out this line, and you leave out life itself; all is chaos again, and the line of the almighty must be drawn out upon it before man or beast can exist.[59]

Bearing these convictions in mind, we can readily understand Blake's disapproval of what he calls the 'Blots & Blurs'[60] of the artists of Venice and Flanders. He is highly critical of those artists who obliterate the outline and 'lose form':

Such art ... loses all character, and leaves what some people call expression; but this is a false notion of expression; expression cannot exist without character as its stamina; and neither character nor expression can exist without firm and determinate outline.[61]

Since forms can only be clearly apprehended by the imagination, Blake has scant regard for those artists who, lacking in this faculty, 'lose form':

The Venetian and Flemish practice is broken lines, broken masses, and broken colours. Mr B.'s practice is unbroken lines, unbroken masses, and unbroken colours. Their art is to lose form; his art is to find form, and to keep it.[62]

Although the principle of 'Minute Particulars' usually has reference to pictorial art, it has, as already suggested, much wider significance for Blake. For instance, in *Jerusalem*, it has ethical implications:

He who would do good to another must do it in Minute Particulars:
General Good is the plea of the scoundrel, hypocrite & flatterer,
For Art & Science[63] cannot exist but in minutely organized Particulars
And not in generalizing Demonstrations of the Rational Power.
The Infinite alone resides in Definite & Determinate Identity.[64]

In true charity,

All broad & general principles belong to benevolence
Who protects minute particulars every one in their own identity.[65]

And we are admonished to:

Labour well the Minute Particulars, attend to the Little-ones,
And those who are in misery cannot remain so long
If we do but our duty ...[66]

As men are to be seen as the 'Minute Particulars', as Divine Members of Christ,[67] so are the 'Little-ones', the children, to be seen as the 'Minute Particulars' of Man, 'Every Minute Particular is Holy.'[68]

He who does good to another in 'Minute Particulars' acts in accordance with the 'religion of Jesus, the everlasting Gospel',[69] the mutual forgiveness of sins, instead of righteous judgement. Those who are lacking in imaginative vision,

> ... accumulate
> A World in which Man is by his Nature the Enemy of Man,
> In pride of Selfhood unwieldy stretching out into Non Entity
> Generalizing Art & Science till Art & Science is lost.
>
> ...
>
> It is easy to acknowledge a man to be great & good while we
> Derogate from him in the trifles & small articles of that goodness.
> Instead of Albion's lovely mountains & the curtains of Jerusalem,
> I see a Cave, a Rock, a Tree deadly and poisonous, unimaginative.
> Instead of the Mutual Forgiveness, the Minute Particulars, I see
> Bits of bitumen ever burning.[70]

The spiritual perception of 'Minute Particulars', invisible and inaccessible to those who lack imaginative vision, implies here a Religion of Brotherhood, of Christ, for they are the 'Mutual Forgivenesses' (see pp. 41).

Imaginative Man, Los, sees what false science, false art, and false religion, have done to man. In his walk through the city he

> ... saw every Minute Particular of Albion degraded & murder'd,
> ... every minute particular: the jewels of Albion, running down
> The kennels of the streets & lanes as if they were abhorr'd:
> Every Univeral Form was become barren mountains of Moral
> Virtue, and every Minute Particular harden'd into grains of sand.[71]

Without 'the line of the almighty', without Los's creative urge to draw 'a line upon the walls of shining heaven'[72] — and thus instigate the process of regeneration, all is chaos. This chaos will persist until we have learnt to think and to act imaginatively. Then we recognize, with Blake, that the spiritual world, intuitively comprehended, is better 'organized' than the phenomenal, material world. Then we can perceive that the brotherhood of man for which we long on earth already exists in the spiritual world. Then we can experience that Christ, the creative source and sustaining power of brotherhood, is in our breasts too. Only then will life on earth be transformed in all its 'Minute Particulars' from chaos into living existence 'infinitely more perfect and minutely organized than any thing seen by [man's] mortal eye'.[73]

Whereas 'Vision is Determinate & Perfect', is universal truth, the non-visionary state, into which Albion, Man, has fallen, is symbolized by Blake as:

> ... the deeps of Entuthon Benython,[74]
> A dark and unknown night, indefinite, unmeasurable, without end,
> Abstract Philosophy warring in enmity against Imagination.[75]

Blake's conception of truth as perfect and definite, and error, or 'evil', as indefinite, without 'outline', and therefore formless, is expressed repeatedly in his poems.[76] One of the earlier succinct statements made to this effect is found in *The Book of Los* (1795): 'Truth has bounds, Error none.'[77]

The First Book of Urizen (1794) illustrates the importance of this conception to Blake's cosmology. Urizen himself, represents, amongst other things, the material world. His separation from Eternity is the beginning of the descent into formlessness:

> ... Urizen laid in a stony sleep,
> Unorganiz'd, rent from Eternity.[78]

The rational materialist, Urizen, can no longer perceive and intuitively comprehend the perfection of the spiritual world.

A few lines later, Los, the expression in this 'fallen' world of the creative imagination, is described as being

> ... affrighted
> At the formless, unmeasurable death.[79]

Los, we remind ourselves, is the manifestation of one of the Eternals, Urthona, who is the very centre of each individual. In its pure form, as Urthona, Imagination could not be 'affrighted' at death, for in the spiritual world, in Eternity, there is no death, there is no formlessness, but, in its fallen yet still creative form — as Los — Imagination meets an unknown phenomenon, death, and experiences that which is foreign to its own essence, namely, formlessness, for Los is the great 'shaper' and 'embodier' (see Appendix 3).

In the same poem we then hear that other creations in Urizen's material world are formless 'similitudes', that is, only partial life, shadows of Eternity:

> And his world teem'd vast enormities,
> Fright'ning, faithless, fawning
> Portions of life, similitudes.[80]

In relation to the creation of man, we find a very similar idea expressed in *The Book of Los*:

> For as yet were all other parts formless
> Shiv'ring, clinging around like a cloud
> Dim & glutinous as the white Polypus.[81]

In *Jerusalem*, Rahab, one of Albion's 'evil' daughters, refuses to take a 'definite form' and preaches the false doctrine that the definite, the clear outline, is sin:

> And Rahab, like a dismal and indefinite hovering Cloud,
> Refus'd to take a definite form; she hover'd over all the Earth
> Calling the definite, sin, defacing every definite form
> Invisible or Visible ...[82]

Natural Man denies the existence of Spiritual Man. He refuses to accept the truth that the spiritual is the source of the natural, and, lacking in imaginative vision himself, calls the visionary a madman, who ought to be ignored.

Rahab, together with her daughter Tirzah — the 'Mother of my Mortal part'[83] and thus the mother of death — weaves the natural body (as distinct from the Spiritual Body),[84] 'Till the Great Polypus of Generation covered the Earth'.[85]

Here we need to pause for a moment to consider more closely a symbol in Blake which is not mentioned in Chapter 5: the Polypus. This aquatic creature with tentacles (e.g. cuttlefish, octopus, squid) is a rich symbol. For instance, (1) it represents the fragmentation of the world of generation in contrast to the unity of the world of eternity, of the spiritual world, and (2) it symbolizes divided human society in this world of spiritual death and false religion, that is to say, it symbolizes a world-view and religion based on materialism. In *The Four Zoas* we hear that the source of the Polypus is the 'corse' (corpse) of fallen Albion:

> ... as a Polypus
> That vegetates beneath the Sea, the limbs of Man vegetated
> In monstrous forms of Death, a Human polypus of Death.[86]

When, in *Jerusalem*, Blake describes 'a Polypus of Roots, of Reasoning, Doubt, Despair & Death' (all characteristics of a Urizenic society), as 'a ravening eating Cancer',[87] it would appear that he had in mind tumorous growths (polypi) which, with their ramifications, tentacles, lead to the destruction of life. One-sided rationalism and materialism are, for Blake, tumorous growths; they destroy spiritual life. Such a worldly society, devoted to materialism, is the antithesis of the brotherhood of man:

> By Invisible Hatreds adjoin'd, they seem remote and separate
> From each other, and yet are a Mighty Polypus in the Deep!
> ...
> He who will not comingle in Love must be adjoin'd in Hate.[88]

True Brotherhood is expressed when, in Love, 'every Minute Particular is "holy"' and:

> Embraces are Cominglings from the Head even to the Feet.[89]

In true spiritual love — be it in Eternity or as an experience of Eternity in a moment of inspiration on earth — perfection, unity, ideal Form, is achieved:

> In Great Eternity every particular Form gives forth or Emanates
> Its own peculiar Light & the Form is the Divine Vision.[90]

But on his descent into the material life man gradually becomes more and more formless, a mere 'Spectre' or 'Shadow':

> ... Albion fell down, a Rocky fragment from Eternity hurl'd
> By his own Spectre, who is the Reasoning Power in every Man,
> Into his own Chaos ...[91]

In these three lines Blake epitomizes his reaction against rationalism, defining the Spectre, the 'spectrous' (formless, indefinite) as 'the Reasoning Power', which, for him, always stands in enmity towards intuitive or visionary power, the power of creative and imaginative man.

'The Reasoning Power' can know no other world than that of time and space, that is, the material world — often described by Blake as the 'Sea of Time and Space',[92] which gives us the clue that, seen from a higher, spiritual viewpoint, both time and space share with natural man those aspects of 'evil' we have heard Blake describing as formlessness and indefiniteness.

In *The Four Zoas* Urizen is pictured in 'fear & pale dismay' when

> He saw the indefinite space beneath & his soul shrunk with horror,
> His feet upon the verge of Non Existence.[93]

Eternal Man, Albion, threatens Urizen that if he does not 'come forth from Slumbers of ... cold abstraction',[94] he will be cast 'out into the indefinite/Where nothing lives'.[95] There:

> Thy self-destroying, beast form'd Science shall be thy eternal lot.[96]

Both time and space represent the fragmentation of Divine Unity and their usefulness is, therefore, restricted to the 'part', that is, to reasoning man. They have no significance for 'the Divine Humanity',[97] 'the Eternal Body of Man', 'the Divine Body, Jesus',[98] for the all-comprehending Whole, the Divine Imagination.

By means of vision or Divine Imagination man can apprehend the forms of things. All transitory, phenomenal objects in the 'sea of Time and Space' are perceived as symbols of the ideal and eternal. This Blake strives consistently to convey to us. In *Milton* he writes:

> Some Sons of Los surround the Passions with porches of iron & silver,
> Creating form & beauty around the dark regions of sorrow,
> Giving to airy nothing a name and a habitation[99]
> Delightful, with bounds to the Infinite putting off the Indefinite
> Into most holy forms of Thought; such is the power of inspiration.[100]

Although Blake is here speaking of 'Sons of Los', that is, poets, spirits of prophecy, we can understand him in a broader sense: all who contemplate and concentrate on spiritual values can transform the indefiniteness of the phenomenal world — which is 'but a shadow of Heav'n' — and, through the process of transformation, create the definite 'outlines' of the ideal forms of things in the world of Imagination. This transformation can only be brought about, in Blake's view, through ceaseless 'Mental Fight', through a constant search for the spiritual in the corporeal forms.

A powerful illustration of such a 'Mental Fight' is contained in some lines in *The Four Zoas* which describe the struggle of Los, the creative imagination, with the refractory matter of the phenomenal world of 'doubt & reasoning' created by Bacon, Locke and Newton, by the science and philosophy of empiricism:

> Los siez'd his Hammer & Tongs; he labour'd at his resolute Anvil
> Among indefinite Druid rocks & snows of doubt & reasoning.
> Refusing all Definite Form, the Abstract Horror roof'd, stony hard.[101]

Like Blake, Los does not rest from the great task of opening the immortal eyes of man:

> ... inwards into the Worlds of Thought, into Eternity
> Ever expanding in the Bosom of God, the Human Imagination.[102]

Blake is well aware of the gigantic proportions of the task and of the obstacles in the way of opening the immortal Eyes and revealing the Eternal Worlds. In one of his last letters he writes: 'I know too well that a great majority of Englishmen are fond of The Indefinite which they measure by Newton's Doctrine of the Fluxions of an Atom, A Thing that does not Exist.'[103]

The first book of *Milton* ends with a vision of time and space as they are re-created by the Imagination, Los and his sons. We are given a description of time seen through the eyes of Eternity. The eternal moment — between two pulses — is equated with the whole of time (supposed in Blake's day to have lasted 6,000 years). It is the eternal moment which is the 'time' of inspiration:

> Every Time less than a pulsation of the artery
> Is equal in its period & value to Six Thousand Years,
> For in this Period the Poet's Work is Done: and all the Great
> Events of Time start forth & are conceiv'd in such a Period,
> Within a Moment, a Pulsation of the Artery.[104]

To such an imaginative view of time, in which momentous matters take place 'between two moments',[105] the Newtonian Universe, with its constructed time-scales, is of little, if any, relevance. The same is true of space. The vastness of the universe — distance of galaxies, and so forth — is of less significance than the quality of life which each man creates in whatever situation he finds himself. For just as 'Space' is created by Los and his Emanation, Enitharmon (see p. 247), so each man of imagination creates his own universe, beginning at and expanding from the point where he is 'now':

> The Sky is an immortal Tent built by the Sons of Los:
> And every Space that a Man views around his dwelling-place
> Standing on his own roof or in his garden on a mount
> Of twenty-five cubits in height, such space is his Universe:
> And on its verge the Sun rises & sets, the Clouds bow
> To meet the flat Earth & the Sea in such an order'd Space:
> The Starry heavens reach no further, but here bend and set
> On all sides, & the two Poles turn on their valves of gold;
> And if he move his dwelling-place, his heavens also move
> Where'er he goes, & all his neighbourhood bewail his loss.[106]

The imagination within each one of us responds to the Imagination, Los,[107] who creates the form of the universe as a whole:

> As to that false appearance that appears to the reasoner
> As of a Globe rolling thro' Voidness, it is a delusion of Ulro.
> The Microscope knows not of this nor the Telescope: they alter
> The ratio of the Spectator's Organs, but leave Objects untouch'd.

For every Space larger than a red Globule of Man's blood
Is visionary, and is created by the Hammer of Los:
And every Space smaller than a Globule of Man's blood opens
Into Eternity of which this vegetable Earth is but a shadow.
The red Globule is the unwearied Sun by Los created
To measure Time and Space to mortal Men every morning.[108]

Blake's humanized universe exists between two poles, 'valves': the globule of blood which beats within each one of us and the universal pulsation of energy through which 'the unwearied Sun' gives light and warmth to earth and man each and every day. Eternity is at the centre, the heart, of each of these poles. The 'red Globule' pulsating within us is the inward sun, it is the flame of energy without which we could not live, microcosm of the rhythmically beating outward centre of the universe.

The 'delusion of Ulro', of Urizenic man, makes a man a point 'rolling thro' Voidness', but such a globe is a 'false appearance', non-existent, just as the abstract scientific view and explanation of the sun is mere illusion.

In the second Book of *Milton* there are two passages which are like an answering chorus to this vision of the world of Imagination, of Los. They must be quoted in full, for they are some of the most beautiful lines in English poetry:

Thou hearest the Nightingale begin the Song of Spring.
The Lark sitting upon his earthy bed, just as the morn
Appears, listens silent; then springing from the waving Cornfield loud
He leads the Choir of Day: trill, trill, trill, trill,
Mounting upon the wings of light into the Great Expanse,
Reecchoing against the lovely blue & shining heavenly Shell,
His little throat labours with inspiration; every feather
On throat & breast & wings vibrates with the effluence Divine.
All Nature listens silent to him, & the awful Sun
Stands still upon the Mountain looking on this little Bird
With eyes of soft humility & wonder, love and awe.
Then loud from their green covert all the Birds begin their Song:
The Thrush, the Linnet, & the Goldfinch, Robin & the Wren
Awake the Sun from his sweet reverie upon the Mountain.
The Nightingale again assays his song, & thro' the day
And thro' the night warbles luxuriant, every Bird of Song
Attending his loud harmony with admiration & love.
...

Thou perceivest the Flowers put forth their precious Odours,
And none can tell how from so small a center comes such sweets,
Forgetting that within that Center Eternity expands
Its ever during doors that Og & Anak[109] fiercely guard.
First, e'er the morning breaks, joy opens in the flowery bosoms,
Joy even to tears, which the sun rising dries; first the Wild Thyme
And Meadow-sweet, downy & soft waving among the reeds,
Light springing on the air, lead the sweet Dance: they wake
The Honeysuckle sleeping on the Oak; the flaunting beauty
Revels along upon the wind; the White-thorn, lovely May,
Opens her many lovely eyes listening; the Rose still sleeps,
None dare to wake her; soon she bursts her crimson curtain'd Bed
And comes forth in the majesty of beauty; every Flower,
The Pink, the Jessamine, the Wall-flower, the Carnation,
The Jonquil, the mild Lilly, opes her heavens; every Tree
And Flower & Herb soon fill the air with an innumerable Dance,
Yet all in order sweet & lovely. Men are sick with love.[110]

In these two great passages of poetry in which imaginative vision re-
creates nature Blake is telling us that the experiences we have of beauty
are momentary visions of the greater reality of Eternity. The creativity of
the imagination is enhanced here by the presence and activity of the lark
and the wild thyme. The lark, rising at the break of day, and the flower,
opening to the rising sun, are two of Blake's finest symbols of the relation
between time and Eternity. Both represent a living response to the spiri-
tual light — but in opposite forms: the soaring lark expresses the rising of
the human spirit beyond the limits of the finite universe; the opening
flower expresses the presence of Infinity and Eternity within the smallest,
hardly measurable space. The thyme focuses human vision on the minute
particularity of its joyous beauty. At any instant — 'between two
moments' — human vision may focus on a particular object, a grain of
sand or a minute wild flower, and find in it a comprehensive emblem of
the infinite; at any instant the activity of his own creative energy may
raise man into a state which is both expansive and timeless — he can
become the soaring morning lark filling the universe with its song.

Both the lark and the wild thyme are messengers of Los;[111] they are the
'natural' signs that his visions are soon to be apparent. In *Milton* the lark is
described as 'a mighty Angel',[112] and elsewhere as 'an Angel on the
Wing'.[113] Symbolically, the lark is the new idea which inspires a whole
poem, *Milton*.[114] Such flashes of inspiration, of a new dawn, occur simul-

taneously with moments of psychic transformation.[115] The magic moment of a new dawn, is for Blake, [116] particularly significant as a time of spiritual illumination. It is the

> Moment in each Day that Satan cannot find,
> Nor can his Watch Fiends find it;[117] but the Industrious find
> This Moment & its multiply, & when it once is found
> It renovates every Moment of the Day if rightly placed.[118]

One moment of vision, of inspiration, can fill the day, can fill Eternity, so that 'the awful Sun' itself 'stands still upon the Mountain looking on this little Bird' — the lark — 'with eyes of soft humility & wonder, love & awe'. The wild thyme and the throat of the lark are 'small centers'. The one fills the air with an exquisite aroma, the other with enchanting sound 'reecchoing against the lovely blue & shining heavenly Shell'. But, says Blake, we have forgotten that from 'within' the 'Center Eternity expands'.

Blake's symbolism of the 'centre' must now engage our attention.

The 'above' of orthodox religious imagery is Blake's 'within'. For him the portal of Eternity is not to be found 'in the sky' but 'within' man himself. Blake uses the image of an expanding circumference to suggest the imaginative space within man. The goal of such expansion is, of course, Eternity. 'Center' and 'within' are not synonymous, however, because man's spiritual essence, his 'within', cannot be moved outside him, no matter how limitless the process of expansion may be, whereas man can 'move' his 'Center' elsewhere and, as a consequence, be estranged from himself. The Blakean symbol of the centre is, therefore, not as completely positive as it is generally represented as being in myth.[119] For instance, Los's city of 'Art & Manufacture',[120] Golgonooza, is built at the centre; but we also learn that 'All fell towards the Center in dire ruin sinking down'.[121] The Fall is not away from the centre but towards it; it is the point towards which those hasten who lack Imagination, who are spiritually blind; on the other hand, it is also the point from which the visionary proceeds. It is the point at which the 'fault' in the cosmos, created by the Fall, and the archetype of the Sacred City are, paradoxically, coincident.

The 'Center' can either be 'within' or 'without'. When it is 'within', it is visionary; when 'without' it is fallen.

It is from the 'Center' 'within' that Eternity expands outwards:

> And none can tell how from so small a center come such sweets,
> Forgetting that from within that Center Eternity expands.[122]

And in *Jerusalem* Blake writes:

> The Vegetative Universe opens like a flower from the Earth's center
> In which is Eternity. It expands in Stars to the Mundane Shell
> And there it meets Eternity again, both within and without.[123]

Also in *Jerusalem* we hear that:

> Wonder siez'd all in Eternity, to behold the Divine Vision* open
> The Center into an Expanse, & the Center rolled out into an Expanse.[124]

When the 'Center' rolls out into an Expanse and opens itself it is a source of regeneration. When the 'Center' of man is 'within', Eternity is there too.

To have one's centre within oneself is, in Blakean psychology, quite clearly not the same as being selfish. On the contrary, it is 'without' that 'is formed the Selfish Center.'[125] But when man has his centre 'within' himself, then, as already seen, its circumference expands into Eternity to include others, to include the whole of mankind:

> ... the Sanctuary of Eden is ... in the Outline,
> In the Circumference ...[126]

It is clear that 'within' is not to be mistaken for the mystic's inclination towards total withdrawal from the phenomenal, sensory world. Indeed, Blake's positive emphasis on the 'within' implies just the opposite. The 'within', or Imagination, is the very means of joining man to man, of bringing universal brotherhood into creative being. Time and again we find Blake speaking of 'being in one another'. For instance, Christ declares to all humanity:

> I am in you and you in me, mutual love divine ...
> I am not a God afar off, I am a brother and a friend;
> Within your bosoms I reside, and you reside in me:
> Lo! we are One ...[127]

When, on the other hand, man is self-centred, i.e. selfish, he is 'contracted' and, in his lack of selfless, imaginative love, he is 'outside', not only of others, but also of himself. In other words, to 'contract', to

*That is, Christ.

'shrink', is not only to lose all relationship with others, but also to lose the ability of perceiving in imagination of the oneness of all things. To 'contract', to 'shrink',[128] is to become increasingly blind to spiritual reality, to Eternity; it is to lose all ability of seeing the imaginative identity of all things. If the states of 'contraction' and 'opacity' were to become permanent — and they would do, were Urizenic rationalism able to eradicate Imagination (Los) — if they were to become permanent, absolute, then the light of Eternity would never be able to penetrate and illuminate man's organs of perception. Therefore, limits are set on contraction and opacity (see Appendix 2).

Christ, in His Divine Mercy, takes on the Limit of Contraction Himself [129] and thenceforth works from 'within' to expand man's circumference outward again, to expand 'forward to Eternity'. Regeneration is the opening of man's centre into an expanding circumference, 'ever expanding in the Bosom of God, the Human Imagination'.[130] Unregenerate Man, man in his spectral body of self-love, self-righteousness and inveterate self-consciousness, is a totally closed 'centre', is a 'without' onlooker; 'Beyond the bounds of their own self their senses cannot penetrate'.[131]

The 'Sanctuary of Eden' is in the circumference, and the 'outline' signifies the wholeness and unique identity of a goal achieved — 'every Minute Particular is Holy'. But the fixed, inflexible and isolated 'centre' — the mental and emotional viewpoint of self-bound man — Blake describes in the following image as an emptiness:

> A Void immense, wild dark & deep,
> Where nothing was ...[132]

It is a petrified state of non-identity, devoid of achievement and self-renewal:

> There is an Outside spread Without & an Outside spread Within,
> Beyond the Outline of Identity both ways, which meet in One,
> An orbed Void of doubt, despair, hunger & thirst & sorrow.[133]

Here Blake is saying that the 'center' is the meeting point of two 'outsides', of the fallen mind with the fallen body. As Blake places all the deities, whom we conventionally locate up in the heavens, inside the human breast,[134] so he finds the 'Outline of Identity' within the centre. Elsewhere he writes:

> What is Above is Within, for every-thing in Eternity is translucent:
> The Circumference is Within, Without is formed the Selfish Center.[135]

The 'Within' Blake is speaking of here is clearly directly opposed to the 'Outside spread Within' in which Urizen wanders. It is the imaginative vision as opposed to abstract reason.

Abstract reason sees the source of any object — for example, the lark or the wild thyme — as being in the material world, but, as is stated more than once in these pages, the imagination recognizes that 'every Natural Effect has a Spiritual Cause'. Similarly, whereas reason would claim that the physical lark or wild thyme is the reality, the Imagination perceives the physical as being a shadow of reality. The real flower, the real bird, is in Eternity, for 'This world is too poor to produce one seed.'[136] The spiritual is always the true reality; 'the natural power of itself continually seeks & tends to Destruction.'[137] Similarly, the natural world is too 'poor' to accommodate the full growth of Spiritual Man, for the rich world of the Imagination is not accessible to our five senses.

In Blake's cosmology Ulro — or Chaos, the sphere of formlessness and non-entity — is furthest of all from Eden (Heaven). But Eden cares for Ulro and Los is set there, constantly building and rebuilding the beautiful city of Golgonooza, which guards against Chaos and is a refuge for souls escaping from its void. Now, though the 'outside' is usually negatively treated, it is not a 'space' of hopelessness. Indeed, in Blake's cosmology the creation of any kind of space is an act of mercy. Even Ulro, this material, spirit-blinded world, is a space created to prevent man falling into 'Eternal Death'.[138] The creation of definite spaces is a necessary activity to counteract any trend towards 'indefiniteness'; the indefinite being for Blake the horror of horrors 'where nothing lives'.[139]

The opening quatrain of 'Auguries of Innocence' encapsulates essential Blakean responses to empiricist philosophy:

> To see a World in a Grain of Sand
> And a Heaven in a Wild Flower,
> Hold Infinity in the palm of your hand
> And Eternity in an hour.[140]

A basic assumption of empiricist philosophy is the limitation of human understanding,[141] for man is confined to an insignificant spot in a vast universe. In contrast to this seemingly reasonable viewpoint Blake proclaims that infinity is present in a point and eternity in a moment. What he would have us arrive at is the same insight which Urizen finally gains in *The Four Zoas* (Night ix), namely, that whereas the physical eye is incapable of taking in the infinite, conceived spatially, true human Vision recognizes the infinite as part of its own essence. When Blake uses the term 'infinite' with reference to Imagination, he is speaking of the unlimited possibilities inherent in any and every 'Minute Particular'. What empirical science regards as infinity, Blake regards as chaos. His entire 'philosophy', like his aesthetics (as we have seen already earlier in this chapter) is based on the idea of coherent form or 'limit', the 'hard and wirey line' which separates reality from chaos. According to Blake, the generally accepted spatial metaphors are mistaken: time is not a 'line' stretching out indefinitely, nor is space indefinite extension, for 'What is Above is Within'.[142] From our discussion hitherto it is apparent that what Blake means here is that eternity and infinity are both comprehended within the human imagination. In *The Marriage of Heaven and Hell* there is a passage which can help us clarify this point. The eagle, symbol of inspiration, 'caused the inside of the cave to be infinite'.[143] Here Blake is saying that the 'cave' can 'open out' — we could also say 'open in' — into infinity, and therefore the 'Grain of Sand', like the tiniest particles of the atomists, contains the World within itself.[144]

On more than one occasion we have noted that Blake is not a mystic in the generally accepted sense of the term. He does not suggest that we escape from living in a temporo-spatial world; on the contrary, he urges us to live more fully in this world, and we can achieve this when we transform it imaginatively and, in so doing, attain liberation from the domination of the fallen world of indefinite time and space. In a world perceived with imaginative vision the 'Grain of Sand', because it contains the infinite within itself, is also symbolic of liberation from 'indefiniteness' and 'formlessness'. However, as so often with Blake's symbols, the 'Grain of Sand' can be representative of something quite other, for it is equally suited to symbolize the separateness of the isolated selfhood. In other words, it is always open to the mockery — just as spiritual freedom is — of the nihilistic rationalist.

A poem which can illustrate the two contrasting symbolic values under consideration is one Blake wrote sometime during the years 1800–1803:

> Mock on, Mock on Voltaire, Rousseau:
> Mock on, Mock on: 'tis all in vain!
> You throw the sand against the wind,
> And the wind blows it back again.
>
> And every sand becomes a Gem
> Reflected in the beams divine;

Blown back they blind the mocking Eye,
But still in Israel's path they shine.
The Atoms of Democritus
And Newton's Particles of light
Are sands upon the Red sea shore,
Where Israel's tents do shine so bright.[145]

To the 'fallen' eye, the eye of materialism, the grains of sand are like the atoms or light corpuscles of physics; individuality is reduced to 'sameness', since, according to Newton, the rays of light no more differ from each other than the sands on the shore. Blake is scornful of Democritus' theory of random atoms raining through the void, irreversibly and without meaning — what he, in *Jerusalem*, calls 'fortuitous concourse'.[146] Atomism, we may remind ourselves, is the belief in an unperceived unit of the sense-perceptible world, the belief, in short, which, Blake writes, is 'fond of The Indefinite' and is 'measured' 'by Newton's Doctrine of the Fluxions of an Atom, A Thing that does not Exist'.[147] Atomism, Blake sees, is a rationalist attempt to annihilate the perceived differences in forms by the abstract assertion that they have all been constructed out of similar units of 'matter'. If, then, as materialists, we look for an image of a universe which is made up of atoms in 'fortuitous concourse', a sandstorm, in which the wind blows sand grains hither and thither, could hardly be improved upon. A sandstorm, seen in this way, is a telling symbol of generalization, of the non-recognition of 'Minute Particulars', of a 'Spectrous Chaos'.[148] The 'fallen' eye sees the sand as a symbol of Ulro deadness. To the imaginative eye it shines in the sunlight, 'the beams divine, like jewels'. The mocking of Voltaire and Rousseau is analogous to throwing sand against the wind; the sand being blown back, blinding 'the mocking Eye', indicates that such mocking is of no avail and to no purpose.[149] As one Blake scholar acutely observes, the sand is no commonplace image, for, in the second quatrain, the grains of sand undergo a transformation which gives them a twofold function: a punitive, retributive function, and an imaginative, redemptive function. In the first instance, the grains of sand blind the mocking eye of the anti-imaginative philosopher; in the second, imaginative beams provide a redemptive transformation of dead (Ulro) matter into light-giving gems, the grains of sand shine in Israel's path and lead through the wilderness. That is, they symbolize the imaginative Exodus which will culminate in the arrival at the Promised Land, or, differently expressed, in a condition of achieved vision.[150]

What must not be negated by rationalism is the divinity of the creative individual. What we must acknowledge, Blake declares in his tractate 'All Religions are One', is that 'all men are alike (tho' infinitely various)', both in outward form and 'in the poetic Genius', which, he states, in his annotations to Swedenborg's *Wisdom of Angels Concerning Divine Love and Divine Wisdom*, 'is the Lord'.[151] And it is the Poetic Genius, the Imagination, in every man which can see both these aspects of every other man, the outward likeness and variety and the inward likeness and variety. To accept Lockian psychology is to see only the likenesses, the 'sameness'. The Newtonian universe, conceived in such terms, would be, though physically vast, no more than 'the same dull round ... a mill with complicated wheels'.[152] However, to see only the varieties is to be Quid, the Cynic, who sees men as 'Goats' and 'Tygers' and 'fleas'.[153] The man of imagination must restore a vision of men's shared humanity as well as their infinite variety.

The point was made earlier that the grain of sand can be seen to be a symbol of liberation as well as symbolizing the separateness of the isolated selfhood; to be a symbol of spiritual freedom as well as the threat to such freedom by nihilistic atomism. In *Jerusalem* Blake draws our attention to the latter alternative in a larger context:

> Fearing that Albion should turn his back against the Divine Vision,
> Los took his glob of fire to search the interiors of Albion's Bosom ...
>
> And saw every Minute Particular of Albion degraded & murder'd ...

Then Los sees men's souls being moulded, baked and pressed into inert bricks to build the pyramids of Egyptian tyranny;[154] and in London he:

> ... saw every minute particular: the jewels of Albion running down
> The kennels of the streets & lanes as if they were abhorr'd ...

That is, should the 'bricks' disintegrate then individual souls would flow into the open drains like so much dirt.

> Every Universal Form was become barren mountains of Moral
> Virtue, and every Minute Particular harden'd into grains of sand ...[155]

Barren 'mountains of Moral Virtue' represent the false universal of abstract, Urizenic-Satanic generality. 'Minute Particulars' can only sustain their living identity (as opposed to their isolated selfhoods) in Christ who is 'the only General and Universal Form'.[156]

Whenever Blake deals with the age-old problem of particulars and universals, he asserts that the two are reconciled in and through Christ. All particulars, he says, are subsumed in one loving Universal:

> General Forms have their vitality in particulars, & every
> Particular is a Man, a Divine Member of the Divine Jesus.[157]

He disagreed with the view which considered the forms to be general and assumed they were multiple.[158] In *Jerusalem* he says, through Los, the imaginative power:

> Swell'd & bloated General Forms repugnant to the Divine-
> Humanity who is the Only General and Universal Form,
> To which all Lineaments tend & seek with love & sympathy.
> All broad & general principles belong to benevolence
> Who protects minute particulars every one in their own identity ...[159]

For Blake Christ is Himself the ultimate ground, in which all 'otherness' is unity and all diversity is identity.

Blake attaches great importance to individuality. Nevertheless, he sees this individuality as being subsumed in the Universal Divine-Humanity, which — in his later works — he identifies with Christ. The individual is subsumed in humanity, but in this subsumption does not lose his individuality. There is an entire heaven in every man, which yet corresponds to each man's 'particularity'. And what each man 'particularly' has is a flow of creative energy which must not be restrained, for the spiritual life of the body is 'fire', 'the God of Fire and Lord of Love', Christ.[160]

An important conclusion in regard to the limit of knowledge can be drawn from this: if all forms are united in God, in Christ, 'the Only General and Universal Form', then it follows that individual man on earth, as a 'particular', is not precluded from gaining knowledge of either humanity, or the invisible, spiritual universal.

Through the Fall into Urizenic rationalism, man has spiritually contracted into 'Newton's sleep' and separated himself from the universal, from the Divine Humanity. But through the Intellect, through the Imagination, he can 'expand' again to apprehend the infinite and the universal. Blake always maintains that fourfold vision — purged of 'Single vision & Newton's sleep' — can attain direct, intuitive apprehension of truth.

3

'CAVERN'D MAN' AND THE SANCTITY OF TRUE INDIVIDUALITY

Five windows light the cavern'd Man: thro' one he breathes the air;
Thro' one hears music of the spheres; thro' one the eternal vine
Flourishes, that he may recieve the grapes; thro' one can look
And see small portions of the eternal world that ever groweth;
Thro' one himself pass out what time he please; but he will not,
For stolen joys are sweet & bread eaten in secret pleasant.[1]

In this description of man's fallen perception, 'True Man'[2] is a prisoner in the cavern of his skull — or body, or physical world as a whole. The 'five windows' are the outlets of the five senses: nose, ears, tongue, eyes, and the whole physical body with its sensitivity to touch. Creature rather than creator, 'cavern'd Man' is a *tabula rasa* (see p. 24) inscribed by the impressionists which enter his five senses. He is a passive recipient of his life. Passivity also characterizes his perception. However, as Blake shows us in the lines just quoted, each sense intimates apocalyptic opportunities — for instance, the fifth, the sense of touch, offers the possibility of passing 'out what time he please', that is, it offers complete liberation from limited, inactive existence, but 'cavern'd Man' refuses eternal, spiritual pleasures and indulges in 'stolen', 'secret', earthly substitutes.[3]

The cognitive processes of the 'cavern'd Man', Urizenic Man, are marked by the same passivity. For Blake, the Urizenic mind is analogous to a reflector, to a large 'eye' which passively receives impressions from the external world and mistakes the physical reflection for the spiritual reality behind appearances. The mortal eye of reason can only apprehend appearances and cannot perceive spiritual 'essences', and, for instance, therefore mistakes our last sleep on earth for literal death:

... in the Optic vegetative Nerves, Sleep was transformed
To Death in old time by Satan the Father of Sin & Death.[4]

Urizen's (Reason's) sense is that of 'sight'. Like the physical eye, reason — to function properly, has to focus and isolate. It first has to sunder experience into fragments. Then, to complete the process of cognition, it assembles the fragments into a 'picture'. In such a process, knowledge is neither direct nor immediate. Perception is sundered into a twofold process: first, sensation; and second, synthesis. Whenever an 'object' enters the sensory field of 'cavern'd Man' the impression is at first registered and then the process of explanation, or identification, can take place. As long as man's visionary capacity remains imprisoned it is only by means of this two-stage mediation that he can gain any knowledge at all. For the 'Eyes of the Man of Imagination',[5] for true vision, on the other hand, perception and cognition are one process. Intuitive knowledge is immediate. When cognition follows on after the act of perception, it is necessarily based on sensations which are past, in other words, its operation is dependent on memory. Fallen 'cavern'd Man' is rigidified into habitual mental operations which are grounded in memory, in recollection. He is a slave to the past, to memory. Lacking in creative and intuitive imagination all 'cavern'd Man' can do is assimilate current sensations to past patterns of experience. Growth, inner, spiritual growth, is inhibited. For Blake any dependence upon the past in order to know — and to act — is a living in the past, is a refusal on the part of man to undertake the 'Mental Fight'[6] to free himself from limited, earthbound existence. In his great myth of the awakening of Albion, man is shown to gain nothing by repeatedly re-experiencing his nightmares; on the contrary, he glides deeper into spiritual sleep with each recollection.

For the empiricists, the materialists, man is nothing other than a product of nature and all knowledge is obtained by his experience of the natural world. Such 'naturalism' is, to Blake, the most dangerous betrayal of man's true self. It is the latest of a series of self-betrayals which originated in the nature-worship of the Druids. The 'naturalist' is a 'cavern'd Man'. The image of the cavern applies to any assertion of man's passive dependence on nature, to any concept of man as being, in essence, a natural being.

By extension, the Mundane Shell (see pp. 191–4) is full of 'caverns',[7] closed off by horizons (Urizen) and surrounded by a void. Such, for Blake, is the Urizenic, Newtonian world — closed and fettered. A Newtonian world is an unfree, predestined world for it is organized by mechanical laws set in perpetual, unchangeable motion at its inception. In such a world man, too, is fettered. In *Jerusalem* Blake describes such a world as a cruel mechanism.[8] Presiding over the machine is Urizen. Urizen decrees limits to thought and perception and he seeks to 'bound' energy and imagination. He sets limits. Rational, Urizenic man does not seek beyond what is habitual, natural and reasonable.

The hidden, remote deity of natural religion and of orthodoxy governs a universe of fearsome time and distance. Hence the experience of 'cavern'd Man' is characterized by the remoteness of the objects of perception. We, as 'cavern'd' men and women, are surrounded by secret and mysterious unknown 'spaces' — including those of time and those of our fellow men. Wherever and whenever Urizen governs, things and people become remote and obscure. Alienation rules!

In the poem 'To Nobodaddy', who largely resembles Urizen, the secretive nature of such a God is characterized:

> Why art thou silent & invisible
> [Man *del.*] Father of Jealousy?
> Why dost thou hide thyself in clouds
> From every searching Eye?

> Why darkness & obscurity
> In all thy words & laws,
> That none dare eat the fruit but from
> The wily serpents jaws?[9]

Urizenic man, 'reasonable' man, is a fettered prisoner who either peeps 'thro' narrow chinks'[10] or turns away from them and peers into his own darkness, thus losing himself in apathy and desolation.

But the condition of 'cavern'd Man' is nevertheless not irrevocable. Though it may be dim, there is in him a sense of something more than the limited world in which he physically exists. Within man there is frequently a feeling of an upsurge of energy which impels him to endeavour to break out from the confines set round him. This energy, a titanic force, Blake calls Orc, who is also the power of social revolution, of rebellion against rigidity, habit and convention. Orc is the sense that a caverned existence does not suffice for our energy, our creativity. He is the sense that the Lockian philosophy of five senses does not comprehend all that we experience, and that the set limits are not, in fact, definitive, but merely arbitrary. Blake expresses this thought in *Visions of the Daughters of Albion*. Oothoon[11] laments:

They told me that the night and day were all that I could see;
They told me that I had five senses to inclose me up,
And they inclos'd my infinite brain into a narrow circle,
And sunk my heart into the Abyss, a red, round globe, hot burning,
Till all from life I was obliterated and erased.
Instead of morn arises a bright shadow, like an eye
In the eastern cloud;...[12]

The earth- and brainbound, 'cavern'd' eye of man can see only the physical appearance of the sun. It cannot experience the full spiritual joy of dawn.

Sensing that to limit cognition to impressions received through the five physical senses is both arbitrary and inadequate, Oothoon, described as being 'the soft soul of America'[13] (she can therefore be seen as the ideal of physical freedom), asks:

With what sense is it that the chicken shuns the ravenous hawk?
With what sense does the tame pigeon measure out the expanse?
With what sense does the bee form cells? have not the mouse & frog
Eyes and ears and sense of touch? yet are their habitations
And their pursuits as different as their forms and as their joys[14]

Here Oothoon expresses the idea that each individuality has perceptual possibilities peculiar to itself. She emphasizes the right of the individual to fulfil his or her own potentialities and impulses. In contrast to this ideal of freedom, Bromion, resembling Urizen in 'loving Science',[15] insists on 'one law for both the lion and the ox'[16] and thus defends the concept of a standardized sensory system — and, hence, a uniform world of valid appearances beyond which man should not seek. Man should stay with what he knows, not seek beyond the surface of things. There are, Bromion/Urizen admits, unknown things but this is because our five senses are weak. The unknown will become known, rational, reasonable man contends, once we learn to extend our senses mechanically. But the vision Oothoon speaks of is not to be gained by such extension. To gain expanded vision the very nature and structure of 'cavern'd' perception must first be transformed:

The Microscope knows not of this nor the Telescope: they alter
The ratio of the Spectator's Organs, but leave Objects untouch'd.
For every Space larger than a red Globule of Man's blood
Is visionary, and is created by the Hammer of Los:
And every Space smaller than a Globule of Man's blood opens

Into Eternity of which this vegetable Earth is but a shadow.[17]

The real, 'true Man' within us is liberated through the dissolution of the cave in which we have been imprisoned by one-sided rationalism and materialism.

To five-sense perception, to the 'cavern'd Man', the physical body is no more than an external object, is part of the external world, and is itself known through its own 'narrow chinks'.[18] To Blake, on the other hand, the body is the perceptible 'portion' of the soul.

Here we can look more closely at the statement in *The Marriage of Heaven and Hell* that 'Man has no Body distinct from his Soul', for we could well misunderstand Blake and consider him to be adopting a materialist's position, whereas, as we have seen earlier, Blake is strongly convinced of the reality of the spiritual being of man. The statement in its entirety runs as follows:

(1) Man has no Body distinct from his Soul; for that call'd Body is a portion of the Soul discern'd by the five Senses, the chief inlets of Soul *in this age*.*
(2) Energy is the only life, and is from the Body; and Reason is bound or outward circumference of Energy.[19]

Blake is not saying that the soul is part of the body, but that the body is the 'outward' circumference (or boundary) of the soul; the 'inner' circumference, the centre, of the soul is infinite and eternal.[20]

In saying that the five senses are 'the chief inlets of Soul in this age' Blake implies that in former ages man had not only more numerous but also 'expanded' senses and that they were able, therefore, to discern a greater 'portion' of the soul than the limited imprisoned five senses of modern men and women are able to do. What *can* be discerned by the soul *now* is chiefly its materialized aspect, the physical body.[21] Blake hints at the unity of the body and soul already in his tractate *All Religions are One* (1788) where he writes: 'the body or outward form of Man is derived from the Poetic Genius'.[22] Body is one aspect of the wholeness which includes all the perceptual and conceptual capacities of man. Blake includes body within his soul concept and, we may add, the spiritual nature of man is also a 'part' of this expanded concept of the soul.

An interesting comment of approbation in one of Blake's annotations to Swedenborg's *Wisdom of Angel's Concerning Divine Love and Divine Wisdom* is relevant here. Swedenborg writes:

*My italics.

When Love is in Wisdom then it existeth. These two are such a One, that they may be distinguished indeed in thought, but not in Act.

Blake's comment is:

Thought without affection makes a distinction between Love & Wisdom, as it does between body & Spirit.[23]

Towards the end of his life, after a serious illness, Blake wrote to George Cumberland:

I have been very near the Gates of Death & have returned very weak & an Old Man feeble & tottering, but not in Spirit & Life, not in The Real Man The Imagination which Liveth for Ever. In that I am stronger & stronger as this Foolish Body decays.[24]

In the process of the body weakening and the spirit growing in strength we can see that the body — as the 'boundary' of the soul, spirit, Imagination — expands, as it were. It loosens its rigidifying and circumscribing power; the 'chinks' become larger and larger; the dark cavern of naturalistic perception is transformed into the light of spiritual, intuitive-imaginative vision, reaching out into Eternity, to the spiritual sun.

Casting out the Urizenic error of considering mortality as a reality means, for Blake, among other things, eliminating the consciousness of the body as being solely a natural object in three-dimesional space and also the brain-bound conception that our faculties of conception are bound to, limited by, the five natural senses. The Apocalypse, Blake says, will occur in life on this earth when 'all those are Cast away who trouble Religion with Questions concerning Good & Evil or Eating of the Tree of those Knowledges or Reasonings which hinder the Vision of God'.[25]

All those who continue to 'eat' of the Tree of 'Reasonings' see all things 'thro' narrow chinks' of their 'caverns'. They are, in short, ensnared in the net of materialism. The vision of the Divine will be achieved when 'the doors of perception' are cleansed, for then every thing will 'appear to man as it is, infinite'.[26] Then error (evil) will be cast out and truth (good) embraced.

For Imaginative Man, the man of Vision, an ethic of responsibility comes into being which is the counter of 'cavern'd' man's apathy. In response to 'cavern'd' man's plea,

O God of Albion! deliver Jerusalem from the Oaken Groves![27]

Los, the creative imagination, responds, furiously:

Why stand we here trembling around
Calling on God for help, and not ourselves, in whom God dwells,
Stretching a hand to save the falling Man?[28]

In general terms, freedom is, 'the liberty both of body & mind to
exercise the Divine Arts of Imagination'.[29] The kind of cognition of
which Blake speaks is one in which our experience is made whole by ceas-
ing to departmentalize our awareness into unrelated and often conflicting
components and modes of knowledge. Real knowledge 'is not by
deduction, but Immediate by Perception or Sense at once. Christ addres-
sed himself to the Man, not to his Reason.'[30] We can supplement this
statement with another: 'Self Evident Truth is one Thing and Truth the
result of Reasoning another Thing. Rational Truth is not the Truth of
Christ, but of Pilate. It is the Tree of Knowledge of Good & Evil.'[31]

To gain knowledge of the Tree of Life, which Los sees descending with
the River of Life out of Heaven,[32] our organs of perception must not only
be cleansed,[33] but also become 'all flexible' again so that they can be
expanded, or contracted, at will.[34] Then a visionary knowledge and
experience of wholeness will come about in which alienation between
inner and outer, between the subject (here) and the object (there), dis-
appears.

Immediacy, oneness, wholeness, grounded in creative, intuitive
imagination, which, ultimately, means Christ Himself, is the experience
of the 'Real Man', the Man of the Universal Brotherhood reigning in the
New Jerusalem, the spiritualized society of spiritually free and imagina-
tively creative men and women.

Let us return for a moment to Blake's conception of energy. Blake
conceives of energy as the life-giving force within man's very depths,
springing from a body which is imbued with and embraced by the soul-sp-
iritual. It is the soul-spirit within the natural body which gives it form.
The soul-spiritual, invisible — and non-sensical — to the 'cavern'd
Man', to the five natural senses, has, at its eternal and infinite 'centre', a
dynamic, creative force, which, in incarnate man, has to find expression
through the instrument at its disposal, that is, through the body.

Creative, Imaginative Man perceives, inwardly, an idea, avails himself
of the form- and life-giving energy within and then gives outer expres-
sion to his vision. Without the body there could be no manifestation. For
instance, a painter's inspiration remains unmanifest without the energy

issuing from his soul-spiritually permeated body in freedom of activity in co-operation with the 'body' of brush, medium and canvas. Paradoxically — and Blake states this clearly — essential to this force of energy is the polar but complementary power of reason. Just as molten iron needs a mould in order that it should take on a definite form, so also that which radiates forth from the soul-spiritual centre needs a 'circumference' in order to find form. Here, then, in co-operation with energy, reason plays a vital role:

Reason is the bound or outward circumference of Energy.[35]

Energy needs its contrary, reason. Reason itself is not creative and has itself to be vitalized and balanced by energy. In 'whole' Man there is a dynamic flowing backwards and forwards, a creative interaction, between reason and energy. Urizenic Man and Orcian Man both have to learn, as it were, that enmity between them either leads to a spiritual 'stalemate', or, if the one dominates over the other, to destructive tyranny.

This universe of ours is a unity. In Blake all those things which have for so long been separated by one-sided analytical reason — God and man, man and nature, body and soul, good and evil, all religious, social, political differences — are, at the Last Judgement (see pp.55–7), 'reconciled'. The contraries are essential to each other. They work together in Blake's dynamic universe. This working together finds expression in the visionary and creative artist in man. All men and women have 'energy' within. But as long as they remain prisoners of their five natural senses under the domination of Urizen, *fallen* reason, as long as they remain contracted and rigidified inside their cold and rocky 'caverns', creativity in freedom and love, expansion outward from the 'centre', remains suppressed. Neither love nor life is possible if man remains contracted within his selfhood (see p. 56). The selfhood destroys love. But, as Blake baldly states:

LOVE IS LIFE.[36]

Christ, the Logos, is Life and Love in their most perfect human form. He '& his Apostles & Disciples were all Artists. Their Works were destroyed by the Seven Angels of the Seven Churches in Asia, Antichrist Science.'[37]

All men and women have the artist within them. To a greater or lesser degree Los is active within all of us.

In regard to orthodox Christians Blake is in agreement with St Paul who writes to the Corinthians:

And I, brethren, could not speak unto you as unto spiritual, but as unto carnal, even as unto babes in Christ. I have fed you with milk, and not with meat: for hitherto ye were not able to bear it, neither yet now are ye able. For ye are yet carnal ...[38]

In Blakean terms we may interpret Paul's words as meaning that what the Church sees is not the spiritual essence of man, but merely the outward circumference of spiritual energy provided by fallen reason. As we have seen already, Blake contends that the true soul-spiritual is revealed through the body by its creative energies. To 'cavern'd Man' fallen reason appears superior to these creative energies. But once man becomes aware that the soul- and spirit-imbued body is not bounded by perception which is restricted to the limitations imposed by the five natural senses of one-sided rational man, once the organs of perception have been 'cleansed', then we shall see that the soul-spiritual is a more splendid form of energy and is 'Eternal Delight'.[39]

It is not only in man but also in the cosmos that we find this opposition between fallen Reason and energy. As others before him (Swedenborg, for instance) Blake distinguishes between the material sun and the spiritual sun (see p. 132). He identifies them, respectively, with fallen Reason and Imagination.[40] In the heavenly state (as described in the Book of Revelation), that is, illumined by the Light of Fourfold Vision, the sun appears in its true, spiritual form.[41] For the man of intuitive imagination the spiritual sun is the 'home' of Los/Christ, who is the creator of the material sun. As distinct from the material sun, the energy of the spiritual sun is not 'contained' in a finite orb, 'bounded' by a limited horizon (reason), but is infinite and permeates the whole cosmos as living, creative spiritual forces, every force being active in harmony with others in love and brotherhood.

The struggle between fallen reason and creative energy among men and women — only to be resolved by the attainment of Fourfold Vision — Blake also sees reflected in the heavens, where the opposition between void and energy is strengthened by rational man's persistent and one-sided emphasis on the mechanical laws that govern the heavens, by his insistence on reducing the awe-inspiring experience to a mathematical formula. Here we need to note that Blake is not antagonistic to mathematics as such — just as he is not against discursive reason as such. What he decries is the use of mathematics to the exclusion of inner experience, of life itself, for

God is not a Mathematical Diagram.[42]

Instead of experiencing the glory of the sun and of inwardly seeing it as an all-permeating and ever-expanding core of life and energy, rational man enmeshes himself in a 'Net' of mathematical analysis.

In his highest state, the state of Eternal Man, man exercises his imaginative and creative energies to their fullest extent under the supreme light of Vision. We have fallen from this state into the 'cavern', but it is regained by us in moments of inspiration.[43] Such moments cannot be touched by Satan/Urizen.[44]

The ultimate goal — the building of the City of Love and Brotherhood — will be realized when man lives and moves and has his being within the light of True Vision, Fourfold Vision, which contains and reconciles those 'below' it; including the vision of 'cavern'd Man', 'Single Vision & Newton's Sleep'.[45]

Earlier in this chapter mention was made of the right of the individual to fulfil his or her own potentialities and impulses. The sanctity of individuality is central to Blake's philosophy of life. Whereas the mystic would banish individuality, and thus silence its faculties, Blake extols individuality and demands that it reintegrates its faculties. For the mystic, death of self is attained when the last claim of individuality has been annihilated, for Blake the annihilation of selfhood is achieved when the last claim of individuality has been harmoniously fulfilled. The key words being 'harmoniously fulfilled', that is, no faculty should act to the detriment of any other. All self-centred interest of any one faculty is annihilated in the process of reintegration.

Blake exalted the individual identity in such terms as:

Deduct from a rose its redness, from a lilly [sic.] its whiteness, from a diamond its hardness, from a spunge [sic.] its softness, from an oak its heighth [sic.], from a daisy its lowness, & ... we shall return to Chaos.[46]

Every portion of Creation has its own peculiar merit and excellence. A divine principle of order, of individual identity, exists in the universe. In *A Vision of the Last Judgement* Blake writes:

In Eternity one Thing never Changes into another Thing. Each Identity is Eternal ... Lot's Wife being Changed into [a] Pillar of Salt alludes to the Mortal body being render’d a Permanent Statue, but not Changed or Transformed into Another Identity while it retains its own Individuality. A Man can never become Ass nor Horse; some are born with shapes of Men, who may be both, but Eternal Identity is one thing & Corporeal Vegetation is another thing.[47]

Elsewhere Blake says that

The Whole Business of Man Is the Arts, & All Things Common.[48]

To recognize that ‘Each Identity is Eternal’ and to hold ‘All Things Common’ is to acknowledge the liberty of individuality within universal brotherhood.

An essential element of the ‘Mental Fight’ to which Blake dedicates himself, and to which he asks each and everyone of his fellow men to dedicate themselves, may be said to be the bringing about of union between ‘Each Identity is Eternal’ and ‘All Things Common’. If both these are realized, then fulfilled individuality, identity, manifests itself within the widest possible universality. The paradox here between individualism and universalism is that of a democratic society: the right of the individual to develop in spiritual freedom, and the evil of any individual developing at the expense of others. When, in short, is an individual impulse right and good, and when is it mistaken and evil? In Blake’s view, the latter is the case when it separates itself from its co-members to exalt itself above them, when, in other words, it competes with them to their detriment and disadvantage, when it destroys harmonious interaction and co-operation. An individual impulse is good when it strives to re-create the original totality and thus establish a harmony of co-members. Individualism is ‘evil’ when it expresses itself as a will to power, to domination over others; it is good when it manifests itself as a will to harmony. Clearly, the way to achieve the good is through love, forgiveness — mutual understanding and acceptance — and brotherhood.

For many years, starting in the late 1780s, Blake strove to fashion a statement which would clarify the spiritual revolution which he felt man needed to experience in order to arrive at a true spiritual freedom of the individual which would harmonize with, be of the very essence of, universal brotherhood. The process involved in arriving at his ‘revolutionary’ conception is first apparent in a crucial statement Blake makes in the last of his annotations to Lavater’s *Aphorisms of Man*:

There is a strong objection to Lavater’s principles (as I understand them) & that is He makes every thing originate in its accident; he makes the vicious propensity not only a leading feature of the man, but the stamina on which all his virtues grow. But as I understand Vice it is a Negative. It does not signify what the laws of Kings & Priests have call'd Vice; we who are philosophers ought not to call the Staminal Virtues of Humanity by the same name that we call the omissions of intellect springing from poverty.

Every man's leading propensity ought to be call'd his leading Virtue & his Good Angel. But the Philosophy of Causes & Consequences misled Lavater as it has all his Cotemporaries. Each thing is its own cause & its own effect. Accident is the omission of act in self & the hindering of act in another. This is Vice, but all Act is Virtue. To hinder another is not an act; it is the contrary; it is a restraint on action both in ourselves & in the person hinder'd, for he who hinders another omits his own duty at the same time.[49]

Lest we should rush to a false conclusion as to what he means by 'all Act is Virtue' Blake then goes on to say:

Murder is Hindering Another.
Theft is Hindering Another.
Backbiting, Undermining, Circumventing, & whatever is Negative is Vice.

He brings his annotation to an end with the remark:

But the origin of this mistake in Lavater & his Cotemporaries [sic.] is, They suppose that Woman's Love is Sin; in consequence all the Loves & Graces with them are Sin.[50]

Blake here is warning us against confusing repression with virtue. Repression is a form of murder. A Urizenic morality of restraint derives from the error of believing that 'Woman's Love is Sin'. The real Satan is the Urizenic life-denying, energy-denying principle which 'Hinders Another'. Kings and priests and their laws are restraints, of course, but they are not their source; they are representative of a human fallacy which both establishes and tolerates them. What, in other words, Blake is concerned to show is that rulers and laws are not mere external facts, but impulses to which certain aspects of human nature itself have perversely given birth.

We can gain some insight into what Blake means by considering an episode in human history which Blake experienced in his own time — the French Revolution. It was the professed goal of the leaders of the revolution to free man, physical man, from the oppression exerted by an unjust social and legal system, on the one hand, and to deliver the human mind from superstition and ignorance, on the other. Blake clearly favoured both aspects of this goal, but, before the revolution had progressed far, he discovered what, for him, was the true source of both social and mental restraint (injustice), namely, the overdue emphasis on reason. That very aspect of the human soul by means of which the revolutionaries aspired to banish restraint is, when it dominates the other soul faculties, for Blake, the cause of both physical oppression and mental repression. Reason, fallen Reason, imposes restraints or laws which reduce the mind to 'a mill with complicated wheels', a 'dull round' repeated over and over again, denying man 'the Infinite' which he desires.[51] In short, rationalism not only restricts man's knowledge to precedent, but also breeds a restricted, self-satisfied, egotistic, heartless philosophy of life, which ignores the sanctity of individuality. Blake would have agreed with Whitehead who says:

true rationalism must always transcend itself ... A self-satisfied rationalism is in effect a form of anti-rationalism. It means an arbitrary halt at a particular set of abstractions. This was the case with science.[52]

In the third tractate, *All Religions are One*, Blake gives us some insight into what he sees as the true source of knowledge. There he states

That the Poetic Genius is the true Man, and that the body or outward form of Man is derived from the Poetic Genius. Likewise that the forms of all things are derived from their Genius, which by the Ancients was call'd an Angel & Spirit & Demon.[53]

Here we are brought back again to the meaning of the sentence already quoted from Blake's annotations to Lavater's *Aphorisms of Man*: 'Every man's leading propensity ought to be call'd his leading Virtue & his good Angel.' That 'Infinite' which creative, imaginative man desires, and which can only be experienced through his genius, his spiritual being, or, we could also say, through the unhampered exertion of his creative imagination, exists in everything. The infinite — the 'world' or 'heaven' — is in everything, in everyone, but it receives different expressions and it is just in the differences that its true value is perceived by the Imagination, the Poetic Genius. Fallen Reason would reduce all variety to a lowest common denominator, would eliminate all individual characteristics and qualities. It would subject everything, everyone, to 'One Law', whereas the Imagination, the Poetic Genius, not only recognizes but is the very source of individuality:

As all Men are alike (tho' infinitely various), So all Religions &, as all similars, have one source.

The true Man is the source, he being the Poetic Genius.[54]

The source of diversity is the source of individual character. Thus the Poetic Genius, creative, imaginative energy, is the true humanity in man, which, in turn, is, for Blake, the Divine, Christ.

The basic idea running through Blake's work from 1788 onwards is respect and reverence for the spiritual freedom of the individual and its inherent holiness.

Reason, rational man, is quite incompetent to experience the infinite. Or, as Blake expresses it:

As none by travelling over known lands can find out the unknown, so from already acquired knowledge Man could not acquire more: therefore an universal Poetic Genius exists.[55]

'To see a World in a Grain of Sand' or 'Heaven in a Wild Flower'[56] is quite beyond the possibilities of reason; to have such an experience reason is as useless as the most sophisticated instrument ever to be invented by Urizenic Man. Moreover, for reason, since one of its main functions is to analyse, in addition to setting limits and restraints, the very idea of perceiving 'Heaven in a Wild Flower' can be no more than a fleeting fancy of disorientated mind. Reason would destroy the indestructible, the spiritual essence, the individuality, which can neither be governed by rational law, imposed restraints, nor subjected to the 'wheels' and 'cogs' of satanic mills; though it can, of course, deprive Man of the means — the freedom — to give expression to this spiritual essence. This Urizen can do, for instance, by subjecting the growing human being to a form of education which is devoid of imagination and, then, having restricted the mind of the child, by the indoctrination of a religion without a true spiritual content. Such an education, devoid of imagination, also preaches 'One Law for the Lion & Ox'[57] and does not take individual characteristics and qualities into consideration. Indeed, as far as the latter are concerned, they do not figure in the curriculum at all. Just as law and anarchy are irreconcilable, so also are fallen Reason and spiritual freedom. Here, incidentally, we need to remind ourselves that Blake is not advocating a lawless society, for

> Murder is Hindering Another.
> Theft is Hindering another.

What he does do, however, is to assert the integrity of the individual man and his need to express, unhampered, his genius, his energy and his talent — though always with the important proviso that his expression does not 'Hinder another'!

It is in *Tiriel*,[58] written very shortly after the three short tractates to which reference has already been made in this chapter, that Blake puts into a symbolic narrative his conception of the spiritual revolution which has to be undergone in order that man may attain true spiritual freedom.

Tiriel, the king of the West, is representative of outworn authority or dogma. We need not consider the whole poem here, nor the various stages in the process of degradation it depicts, but simply note that during the course of his wanderings he has cursed all his offspring (see p. 236) and finally asks his daughter, Hela, to lead him — for he is blind — back to the realm of his parents, Har and Heva, who are described as sleeping 'fearless as babes on loving breasts'.[59] That is, Tiriel hopes to attain to the pastoral pleasures of the world of innocence through that which he represents: judgement and repression. This is his error. He does not recognize, until some moments before his death, that the rule of dogma and oppression, which we recognize now as the rule of Urizenic, 'fallen Reason', has degraded such pleasures. When he does finally recognize his error he exclaims:

> Why is one law given to the lion & the patient Ox?
> Dost thou not see that men cannot be formed all alike?[60]

He has understood the error which originated with him and which he has imposed upon others like a father who 'scourges off all youthful fancies from the new-born man';[61]

> ... Such was Tiriel,
> Compell'd to pray repugnant & to humble the immortal spirit
> Till I am subtil as a serpent in a paradise,
> Consuming all, both flowers & fruits, insects & warbling bird.
> And now my paradise is fall'n & a drear sandy plain
> Returns my thirsty hissings in a curse on thee, O Har.[62]

The king, reason, exalts himself by humbling 'the immortal spirit', the infinite creative energy, of his subjects. He does this by enmeshing them in a 'Net' of divisive judgement and stricture. But, as Tiriel realizes at the end, amid an all-permeating and contagious decay of life — affecting not only the arts and sciences, but religious dogma and authority, too — reason is finally forced to recognize that its analytical and destructive nature is inimical to life, that its inflexible law betrays the very principle of life. One and the same law cannot apply to both the raging lion and the patient ox, for every individual, every 'Genius', has its own law. When reason, here in the figure of Tiriel, recognizes this fact it dies:

> '... my voice is past'
> He ceast [sic], outstretch'd ... in awful death.[63]

Reason's 'voice is past'. Creative imagination — common to all men, but finding individual expression in each and every one of us — may now be freed. Individual and free expression, which, of its own free will, does not 'hinder another', is the sure foundation and guarantee of the growth of spiritual love and universal brotherhood. The only way to achieve what Tiriel failed to achieve, a new life of innocence, is through selfless, loving acts of imagination.

In *The Four Zoas* — as unfinished as this poem is — Blake reveals to us a marked transition in the development of his thinking. He shifts the main thrust of his visionary insights from the historical to the psychological and spiritual, from the external to the internal, from outer, political revolution to inner, spiritual revolution. In short, from Orc to Los/Christ. Brotherhood cannot be achieved by outer means alone, as thought by the instigators of the French Revolution, for instance (of which Blake is now critical), but above all by the overcoming of the self-hood, by an inner transformation. In Blake's mature conception, the outer transformation follows almost immediately upon the inner, spiritual transformation, but the reverse is not true. The 'inner' does not — as history has shown time and again — follow upon the external changes. Better working conditions, for example, do not of themselves inculcate brotherly love; whereas this love once achieved, devotes itself to the banishment of restrictive practices of every kind. It not only allows, but encourages, creative energy to find free expression.

We find in Blake's later poems — *The Four Zoas, Milton* and *Jerusalem* — two main modes of imagery functioning side by side. On the one hand there is the imagery of industrial, political, religious, and other forms of oppression and repression — the imagery of a disharmonious humanity; on the other hand there is the imagery of pastoral joy, of nature and humanity in harmony.

To illustrate Blake's shift of emphasis, let us take a closer look at Orc's development. In earlier poems, Orc's function is to destroy in order to create. In *The Four Zoas* his function is devoted solely to destruction. He is, as we discuss elsewhere (see p. 231), the son of Los, but, once he is born, he is more closely associated with Luvah, who is in turn associated with Christ (see p. 256). There is, therefore, a close relationship between Orc and Christ, but it is an antithetical relationship. Whereas Orc is anger, passion devoid of love, Christ is love, passion without anger. Whereas Orc destroys what has to be destroyed — false forms of the social order and restraints on individual initiative and creative energy, Christ descends into the soul of man and through the impulse of forgiveness and brotherly love, breaks through the rigid barriers of the selfish heart. In that impulse, both Urizen and Rahab are forgiven.[64] All individuality is finally seen as pure, and is recognized as being distinct from the states of existence into which it has been forced to fall. To destroy a rigid dogma or an outworn social convention, is certainly an essential element in the process of regeneration, but without the opening of the closed heart so that it may grow beyond its self-centredness, such a regeneration — in any sphere of life — is doomed to failure. The process of self-annihilation, of the destruction of self-centred impulses, is the imaginative act which recognizes the integrity of all individuality. It is the imaginative act, too, which is essential if man is to expand 'in the bosom of God', Christ.

> Wonder siez'd all in Eternity, to behold the Divine Vision open
> The Center into an Expanse, & the Center rolled out into an Expanse.[65]

In *Jerusalem* Christ is also shown as removing the 'False Holiness hid within the Center'.[66] Holiness is a term Blake often uses in a pejorative sense — as he does in this instance — to denote the state of mind of the Pharisees, the state of the 'Fiends of Righteousness' who enact and execute cruel laws and repudiate the sanctity of freely creative individuality. Righteousness is opposed to mercy, to Christ Himself.[67] In the opening of the 'Center', which is an act of Divine Mercy, righteousness, the enemy of universal love and brotherhood, is destroyed.

In *The Four Zoas*, Los, addressing his Emanation, Enitharmon, says:

> 'I behold the Divine Vision thro' the broken Gates
> Of thy poor broken heart, astonish'd, melted into Compassion & Love.'
> And Enitharmon said: 'I see the Lamb of God upon Mount Zion.'
> Wondering with love & awe they felt the divine hand upon them.[68]

Once Enitharmon's 'Obdurate heart' is 'broken'[69] she begins to assist Los in his task of imaginative activity, of regeneration. Los, the guardian of imaginative vision, knowing that Christ represents an eternal quality which is indestructible, voices one of Blake's major conceptions: that of the distinction between 'States' and 'Individuals':

> There is a State nam'd Satan; learn distinct to know, O Rahab!
> The difference between States & Individuals of those States.
> The State nam'd Satan never can be redeem'd in all Eternity;
> But when Luvah in Orc became a Serpent, he descended into
> That State call'd Satan.[70]

In this speech Blake gives us his mature conception of evil. The individuality, of which Christ, Who is Love, is the very centre, is pure and eternal. The 'State', into which the restraints of limited perception, prejudice and outworn custom, and so on, constrain the individuality, is represented, in its extreme form, by Satan. We could describe a 'State' as being an external incrustation imposed upon man from which he, as individuality, can free himself. Revolution, for the mature Blake, in its aspect of revengeful violence, hate, or war, is in the 'State' of Satan and, in the end, is self-destructive. The motive of spiritual revolution, Christ, on the other hand, is regenerative and eternal.

Rahab, or the moral virtue of natural religion, is another such 'State'. Los, Imagination, the guardian of the Divine Vision, rejects her; Urizen accepts her and a further 'fall' takes place. He petrifies in the same measure as his true individuality is progressively smothered by his erring selfhood.

In *Milton* we find Blake's elaboration of his ideas of spiritual revolution, not now in terms of a nation or of mankind as a whole, but of an individual — John Milton. Now, it is true that both the Industrial Revolution and the Lockian philosophical revolution took place after John Milton's death, but Blake was of the view that Milton's own errors had contributed to both these great errors. His poem about John Milton is written to show the 'imperfect' poet returning to earth in order to redeem not merely himself but, above all, the erroneous 'State' mankind had fallen into since he was last on earth. Spiritual regeneration has to start within the individual, through individual efforts of will. Milton must, therefore, cast off his rationalism and free his true identity, his essential humanity. He has to do this by bringing all its elements into harmony with one another. In *Milton*, John Milton's own salvation is a dramatization of the salvation of the whole of mankind (as Blake had already shown it operating in *The Four Zoas* in 'Eternal Man', Albion).

The poem *Milton* opens with a summary of action already familiar to the reader: the Fall of Albion, the binding of Urizen, Los's bondage, his separation from his Emanation, Enitharmon, the births of Orc and Satan, and so on.[71] Los, Imagination, attacks Satan, rationalistic error, for his

Urizenic conception of the nature of identity. To correct his error, Satan/Urizen must recognize that:

> Every Man's Wisdom is peculiar to his own Individuality.[72]

He has to learn to differentiate between permanent individuality and the temporary 'incrustation' that forms its fallen, corrupted exterior:

> ... the Divine Humanity & Mercy gave us a Human Form
> Because we were combin'd in Freedom & holy Brotherhood,
> While those combin'd by Satan's Tyranny, first in the blood of War
> And Sacrifice & next in Chains of imprisonment, are Shapeless Rocks
> Retaining only Satan's Mathematic Holiness, Length, Bredth & Highth,
> Calling the Human Imagination, which is the Divine Vision & Fruition
> In which Man liveth eternally, madness & blasphemy against
> Its own Qualities, which are Servants of Humanity, not Gods or Lords.
> Distinguish therefore States from Individuals in those States.
> States change, but Individual Identities never change nor cease.
> You cannot go to Eternal Death in that which can never Die.
> Satan & Adam are States ...
> And thou, O Milton, art a State about to be Created,
> Called Eternal Annihilation, that none but the Living shall
> Dare to Enter, & they shall enter triumphant over Death.
> And Hell & the Grave: States that are not, but ah! Seem to be.[73]

In our present context the critical lines in this passage are 22–3. Blake is seeking to find a way to condemn sin but not the sinner. An evil act is perpetrated by a man who is 'in a state' of sin — of Satan. When such an evil man is redeemed, it is his sinful nature which is destroyed, not the 'true Man' within, his individual identity. While man is in a state of sin, his personality is subjected to Satan, to sin. And Satan, we recollect, is fallen Lucifer. He is the immortal Lucifer in a sinful 'State'. When sin is destroyed, Satan ceases to be in a state of sin, but he does not cease to exist. He 'puts off' the State and is then revealed in his true, unfallen form, as Lucifer.

The idea of 'States' is important to Blake, for he is convinced of the reality of the individual as an immortal soul. States are essentially 'unreal'; only the true inner individuality is 'real'.

In his address 'To the Deists'[74] Blake attacks the deistic view of human self-sufficiency and the attempt to reduce religion to 'Natural Morality or Self-Righteousness'. Self-righteousness has 'accursed consequence to

Man', for it creates rigid law, which ignores the sacred individual iden-
tity. Brotherhood cannot be achieved until self-righteousness is inwardly
denied. He who perpetuates 'Tyrant Pride & the Laws of ... Babylon ... is
in the State named Rahab, which State must be put off before he can be
the Friend of Man.'[75]

In the third chapter of *Jerusalem* the 'accursed consequence to Man' is
depicted:

> In Great Eternity every particular Form gives forth or Emanates
> Its own peculiar Light, & the Form is the Divine Vision
> And the light is his Garment. This is Jerusalem in every Man,
> A Tent & Tabernacle of Mutual Forgiveness, Male & Female Clothings.
> And Jerusalem is called Liberty among the children of Albion.
> But Albion fell down, a Rocky fragment from Eternity hurl'd
> By his own Spectre, who is the Reasoning Power in every Man,
> Into his own Chaos, ...[76]

In its pure uncorrupted form, each individual thing differs, it has 'Its
own peculiar Light'. The recognition of this spiritual light is in itself a
free act, is liberty, we could say. Urizenic law, reason, kills such dis-
tinctiveness. When distinctiveness between human beings is lost, then
not only individuality, but also liberty, is repressed, lost. The agent in
such destructive repression is the 'unreal' Spectre, the power which
denies individual impulse and energy.

Blake criticizes the rationalism of the bourgeois revolutions because it
proves to be the agent not of freedom but of renewed tyrannies. Equality
and liberty must be granted not only to all men in a social, political
context, but to all 'parts' of Man. They must be granted to the whole
man, not solely to his reason, but to all his faculties, including his
individual creative energy. If liberty is granted to only a 'part' of Man,
then that 'part' will dominate his other faculties and subject them to his
tyranny. This is what Blake saw happening in his own day and what he
would see happening today: liberty of rationalism and subjugation of
individual creative imagination and energy. The head rules and inhibits
both heart and hand! True liberty, fraternity and equality, can only exist,
in both individual man and in society, when every faculty, every indivi-
dual, acts freely in harmony and brotherhood with all other faculties,
individuals. Liberty which is enjoyed only by a privileged few, is a false
liberty, for it exists without a true universal social conscience. Concepts
of power breed practices of power, manifestations of tyranny. When

universal brotherhood reigns, that is, when Christ, the Creative Word, Imagination, resides in the human breast, then

> Superior, none we know; inferior, none: all equal share
> Divine Benevolence & joy; for the Eternal Man
> Walketh among us, calling us his Brothers & his Friends.[77]
> ...
> Let the Human Organs be kept in their perfect Integrity,
> ...
> Every one knows we are One Family, One Man blessed for ever.[78]

Here is expressed the innocence of love which exists before the Fall into experience and the wisdom and love of innocence which is born after the reintegration and regeneration of Man. From this new-born wisdom imbued with love, gained in spiritual freedom in the world of experience, issues the insight that

> ... It is better to prevent misery than to release from misery:
> It is better to prevent error than to forgive the criminal.
> ... those who are in misery cannot remain so long
> If we do but our duty ...[79]

Duty here is born of love, not of law. Duty which is performed because it is laid down by dogma and law can only fetter and bind the performer and the object of his deed; duty born of love of one's fellow men is freely given and frees both the giver and the receiver. True Man, the eternal individuality, does not come to expression under the stricture of being 'bound by law'; it comes to free expression when an act is born through the individual recognition of the need of every other individual to be himself. Such a recognition is founded in the repudiation of selfish individualism. It is an act of Imagination and Love which breaks down all barriers between men. This is true brotherhood. Without the imaginative act, without, in our present context, love for duty, love itself is a mere 'State', the 'Cruelty & Pride'.[80] 'Without Forgiveness of Sin, Love is Itself Eternal Death.'[81]

Of the three ideals of the French Revolution, liberty, equality and fraternity, only the first was partially realized. The nineteenth century ushered in the most tyrannical development of individualism (egoism) in recent history. In that century, liberty — false though it may have been — was the privilege of one class. And so it remains today, albeit in a modified form. One of Blake's annotations for this class is the 'Monopolizing Trader'.[82] We clearly have to distinguish between the 'true

Man', the individuality aware of his 'own peculiar Light' and the 'peculiar lights' of his fellow men, between the spiritual and unique essence of individual identity, on the one hand, and the self-centred, egotistic individualism, on the other. It is the latter which is the hallmark of 'the Monopolizing Trader'. He is the Urizenic Man who thinks, acts, and lives, in such a way that the selfhood, the Spectral Power, becomes more and more deeply entrenched, thus vitiating every impulse towards brotherhood. What he fears more than anything else is that the souls of men he 'trades' in and 'bargains' with should wake up from their 'Newtonian Sleep'. His aim is, on the contrary, to perpetuate

... monstrous forms of Death, a Human Polypus of Death,[83]

a cancerous, life-destroying growth.[84]

Blake would have us sweep away all barriers to individual freedom (with the proviso mentioned earlier). This is at the root of his basic objection to the revolutionary doctrine of rationalism, of his rejection of reason as the hope for man's salvation. This rejection includes the entire Urizenic conception of sense, reason, logic and science. His rejection of experimental science and demonstration as a means to any kind of true knowledge is all of a piece with his exaltation of the genius of the individual, of man's identity. When the genius of the individual, the imaginative and creative impulse, is free to achieve what it knows to be its own need and the need of others, then it retains its purity and its power. When it has this freedom, the genius of the individual has intuitive perceptions of the meaning and matter of life which are superior to empirical, scientific knowledge. When Blake asks, 'What is the Life of Man but Art & Science?'[85] he has in mind, not experimental science, but another kind of science, namely wisdom. On one occasion he distinguishes this 'sweet science' (see pp. 331–7)[86] from materialistic, experimental, science by examining the word 'conscience'. In his counter-attack against Locke's theory of innate ideas Blake splits the word into its two component parts: 'Con-Science'. Now, Locke, we remember, denies any innate knowledge or intuition. A newborn baby, he maintains, is born with a brain like a blank slate; he learns only through his five senses and the use of his reasoning power. Over and against this theory — which could only have been devised by 'cavern'd Man' — Blake protests:

Innate Ideas are in Every Man, Born with him; they are truly Himself. The Man who says that we have no Innate Ideas must be a Fool & Knave, Having No Con-Science or Innate Science.[87]

This is wisdom, the knowledge that is the individual's own. Blake is here stressing that every man's wisdom is peculiar to his own individuality.

Any power which prevents an individual from expressing the particular potentialities with which he is born, and which make him unique, is tyrannical, no matter whether this power is in the mind or external to it.

A prerequisite for the manifestions of the integrated society is a progressive and deepening integration and harmonious working together of the various soul faculties within the freely creative individual. Just as no one faculty has the divine right to rule over the others, so also no one human being has that right to act as a 'Monopolizing Trader'.

Blake's vision of the integrated man is symbolized by Christ, Who is the core and fountainhead of universal brotherhood.

In an advertisement of an exhibition of some of his works Blake writes: 'Genius and Inspiration are the Great Origin and Bond of Society.'[88] Here he is sharing with us his conviction that brotherhood, spiritual communion, is an original mode of relationship.

From this original brotherhood, through historical time, the Fall into self-centredness and isolation has increasingly rigidified. Through Imagination, through identification with Christ — 'Not I, but Christ in me' — brotherhood can be experienced again. But this goal can only be achieved through freely exercised and uncompromised uniqueness of individual creative perception. In short, Blake gives us 'the end of a golden string' and exhorts us to 'wind it into a ball',

> It will lead you in at Heaven's gate
> Built in Jerusalem's wall.[89]

He exhorts us to cleanse our organs of perception so that we can see beyond the generally accepted dualism of brotherhood, on the one hand, and individualism, on the other. Blake himself gives us two living examples, at the end of The Four Zoas and of Jerusalem, of how the individual discovers both a full sense of brotherhood and a full sense of particularity, individuality, at one and the same time.

To lose one's individuality is tantamount to losing one's integrity — and brotherhood then dissolves. Brotherhood has its vitality in the imaginative creativity of the individualities of whom it is formed. For Blake the integrity of the whole depends on the integrity of each of its individual parts.

4

UNIVERSAL
BROTHERHOOD AND
OUR SOCIAL
CONSCIENCE

We are fully justified in giving a metaphysical and apocalyptic interpretation to the works of William Blake, but we would be doing him an injustice if we were to abstract them from their humane and social context. He 'uses' his poetry and art — in varying degrees — as a means to bring about in the souls of his fellow men a living and imaginative response to the evil social conditions and 'spiritless' human relationships he sees men and women passing through in their lives on earth.

Geoffrey Keynes, commenting on Blake's poem, *Visions of the Daughters of Albion*, makes an interesting statement, which, though uttered in a different context from that presently under discussion, is highly relevant:

The theme of this poem has been related by some writers to crises in Blake's own life, such as his realization that he was tied legally and morally to a barren wife. But this is pure conjecture, and it is better to regard the book as a poet's view of the evils of organized religion, compulsory morals, oppressed womanhood, and, in addition, of slavery ...[1]

Blake was fully aware of the iniquity of the social structure of his day — we might ask: would his views have altered much if he were alive today? — and, as already stated, he 'uses' his poetry and art as a means of social criticism. He was, of course, not alone in this. R. W. Harris writes: 'It is sometimes suggested that the Romantics were social misfits, weak and vapid in their idealism, beautiful and ineffectual angels, beating in the void, their luminous wings in vain'. Such a suggestion is, he goes on to say, 'both inaccurate and an uncharitable judgement'.[2]

Blakean man lives consciously in the spiritual world *and* in the phenomenal world. He perceives the conditions of the society in which he lives, and the trials and tribulations of his fellow men, from both an eternal, spiritual viewpoint, and in the light of a temporal, material perspective.

Blakean man's visionary world encompasses man's eternal as well as his transitory life, deeds and thoughts. He is a man of the present, alert to the aspirations and needs of his spiritual brothers and sisters. He is a man with a holistic world-view; he is imbued with a loving social conscience and a passion to work constructively towards bringing into living and creative existence that which is true, beautiful and good in his fellow sojourners on earth — and in himself. At the very foundation, or rather, at the very core of the life of Blakean man, of his thinking, feeling and willing, is the creative imagination. Here lies what can be expressed in religious terms as Christ, *the* Imagination.

Creative imaginative man is not one who lives in Cloud-cuckoo-land and hankers after an unrealizable Utopia. On the contrary, living fully in the eternity of the present, he strives towards the realization of an ideal which, he sees, already potentially exists and is 'waiting' on man, to find manifestation and growth.

Blake sees that this potentiality is threatened with extinction. He sees that man's true humanity, the divine in him, his spirituality, either does not come to expression in, for instance, the Urizenic Oppressor, or that every obstacle — religious, philosophical, psychological, political, social, and so on — is placed in the way of others, the oppressed, who would give expression to their creative energy and imagination, that is, to their true humanity.

When, in *Milton*, Blake speaks of the 'dark Satanic Mills'[3] he conjures up before our inner eye and ear not merely the enormous 'inhuman' mills of the Industrial Revolution, but also the 'inhuman' Urizenic systems under which the people of England suffer.

We need to emphasize here that Blake's spiritual vision is harmoniously harnessed with a 'down-to-earth' approach to human life. In his poem 'London'[4] his practical everyday experience of life in London gives him a clear insight into the havoc commercial interests have wrought in the lives of his fellow men. He is clearly opposed to the injustices he sees perpetrated in the interests of those in power and we could easily draw the conclusion that he is antagonistic to commerce — and to industry — as such. However, it is not against commerce and industry that he protests so much as against the motives behind them and the use to which they are put by the Urizenic wielders of power. Indeed, Blake sees that a people who have not turned their backs on Vision, who have not forsaken the 'Courts' of Jerusalem, who, in other words, live in spiritual freedom, can walk 'In the Exchanges of London' 'mutual in love & harmony'[5] and demonstrate the true spirit of brotherhood.

In short, Blake does not rebel against industrialization as such but against the industrial exploitation of man. Similarly, he is not critical of the rich and privileged because they constitute the nobility, landed gentry, and industrialists, but because, as he writes in a very early poem:

> The Nobles of the Land did feed
> Upon the hungry Poor;
> They tear the poor man's lamb, and drive
> The needy from their door![6]

Throughout his lifetime Blake saw that Parliament failed to take any real measures to improve the conditions of the 'hungry poor'. The Law of the Establishment was rigid and inhumane, protecting only the interests of the privileged to the detriment of the poor. His 'London' poem in the *Songs of Experience* is one of many expressions of his reaction to the injustices and misery suffered by the voiceless majority:

> I wander thro' each charter'd street,
> Near where the charter'd Thames does flow,
> And mark in every face I meet
> Marks of weakness, marks of woe.
>
> In every cry of every Man,
> In every Infant's cry of fear,
> In every voice, in every ban,
> The mind-forg'd manacles I hear.
>
> How the chimney-sweeper's cry
> Every black'ning Church appalls;
> And the hapless Soldier's sigh
> Runs in blood down Palace walls.
>
> But most thro' midnight streets I hear
> How the youthful Harlot's curse
> Blasts the new born Infant's tear,
> And blights with plagues the Marriage hearse.[7]

These sixteen lines are a succinct social history of Blake's time. Indeed, in spite of obvious improvement in many respects, they can be accepted as a general picture of man's inhumanity to man in the twentieth century. The 'mind-forged manacles' of the second stanza show that Blake is concerned with a mental state symbolized by the social injustices we can see every day in a society which is dominated by financial interests of a privileged few — be they individuals or monopolies. The term 'charter'd' here applies specifically to the streets and the Thames signifying the restrictive, suppressive and exploitative effects of the charters and corporations of the world of high finance upon the individual. In more general terms Blake is also saying that the 'streets', or rather, the man in the street, is 'chartered' by laws and social attitudes and conventions which function in such a one-sided way as to stifle and manacle individual and original action and thought. The image of the child chimney sweep is called upon to illustrate social evils condoned by the Establishment, here depicted as the Church, and the soldier's unfortunate lot is invoked as blood streaming down the walls of the Palace, that is, the State. In the final stanza the fettered, Urizenic mind even converts the marriage bed into a place of death — neither partner giving love freely, but bound to each other by a rigid contract.

Social inequality of inhuman proportions forced poor parents to sell their young children's labour. They were of course, cheap labour. They could easily be replaced and were constantly exploited. It is true that today parents in the so-called 'advanced' countries no longer sell their children, but the exploitation of children as cheap labour is still rife. The provisions in the 1973 Employment of Children Act for a nationwide scheme in regard to child labour have still not been implemented. A survey carried out by the Low Pay Unit as recently as 1984 mentions, among many other examples, a 14-year-old London boy who worked for 36 hours a week in a shop for 17p an hour (*Daily Telegraph*, 17 January, 1985). Blake's poem 'London' — one of his most outspoken protests against the evil effects of industrial (commercial) civilization upon the life of the individual — is as relevant today, in a modified form, as it was when he wrote it nearly 200 years ago.

In 'The Chimney Sweeper' the small boy tells of his exploitation by his parents, who imagine they are not wronging him because his spirit is not completely subdued:

> A little black thing among the snow,
> Crying ''weep! 'weep!' in notes of woe!
> 'Where are thy father & mother? say?'
> 'They are both gone up to church to pray.
>
> 'Because I was happy upon the heath,

'And smil'd among the winter's snow,
'They clothed me in the clothes of death,
'And taught me to sing the notes of woe.

'And because I am happy & dance & sing,
'They think they have done me no injury,
'And are gone to praise God & his Priest & King,
'Who make up a heaven of our misery.'[8]

The parents are appropriately spoken of as being in church, for, in Blake's view, the Church condoned a society in which such cruelty could be inflicted on an innocent child. In Blake's view, God, that is, a Urizenic/Satanic God and his 'Priest & King' are responsible, are the cause of social injustice and misery.

Throughout Blake's life — and for decades after his death in 1827 — the rural and urban poor held no offices. Being uneducated and illiterate they were unable to give written expression to their plight. They were the 'faceless' and 'voiceless' ones and probably made up three-quarters of the population of England.[9] They were unable to tell their fellow men what they experienced, felt and thought. Others had to speak for them. Blake is one of those who spoke up on their behalf. Throughout his life Blake strove to defend human values against a social order which was founded on inequality, human suffering and misery.

Though varying in degree of intensity — and more obvious in some of his writings than in others — Blake's criticism of philosophical, scientific and religious thought is closely bound up with his social criticism. He recognized that the intellectual and philosophical climate of the eighteenth century reinforced social structures which allowed unjust and inhuman conditions to prevail. Locke's philosophy of the five senses denying the existence of innate ideas, though postulating that man also learns through the use of reason, placed man, or, rather, 'primitive' man, that is, the peasant, the factory worker, and so on, at a level little higher than that of an animal, a being who was a creature of nature, without spiritual life and individual desires and initiatives. For Blake, a defender of the spirit, creative energy and imagination, such a philosophy was clearly inimical to all true human values. His attitude towards the Newtonian world-view was obviously as critical. He saw that Newton's mechanical laws of the universe had also found relevance to every aspect of social life. Newtonian principles were applied to the art of government. The social constitution had to function, on a smaller scale, in similar fashion to the clockwork of the universe as a whole. Religion, politics, ethics, law and art were all based on nature. Social relationships had to conform to the universal system in which each planet and star had its fixed and proper place. The great clockmaker, God, had created a balanced and well-oiled universe and given it to man in perfect working order. Church and State saw it as their task to keep the mechanism working perfectly by respecting and practising its laws. As Blake consistently points out it was in their own self-interest that the social structure should function in accordance with such a 'natural' and mechanistic model; it had to work by the same rigidly determined laws as the 'Great Machine', the universe itself.

Blake's 'dark Satanic Mills' are a symbol of this mechanical social order where each institution such as Church, university and factory is like a 'mill' within the Urizenic mechanical social system which suppresses and deprives man of the possibility to exercise his creative and imaginative energy. While Newton's mechanical laws of the universe 'naturalized' the social order, orthodox religion was served by Locke's philosophy under the name of deism. Orthodox religion saw and interpreted social events and changes in terms of Divine Providence, and natural religion saw them in terms of a nature discoverable by reason. Everyone had an assigned and fixed place; everyone was born into his predestined position as are the stars in the sky. By divine decree the poor were placed under the leadership and patronage of the privileged few. For their part, the few were charged by 'natural' providence with the care of the many, the poor.

Blake, in a dramatic fragment called 'King Edward the Third' satirizes this rationalized mechanical system:

> ... Our names are written equal
> In fame's wide trophied hall; 'tis ours to gild
> The letters, and to make them shine with gold
> That never tarnishes: whether Third Edward,
> Or the Prince of Wales, or Montacute, or Mortimer,
> Or ev'n the least by birth, shall gain the brightest fame,
> Is in his hand to whom all men are equal.
> The world of men are like the num'rous stars,
> That beam and twinkle in the depth of night,
> Each clad in glory according to his sphere ...[10]

As well as against the mechanistic and deistic, materialism and natural religion, Blake also fought against self-interest and abstract moral law. In *The Four Zoas* he writes:

> It is an easy thing to talk of patience to the afflicted,
> To speak the laws of prudence to the houseless wanderer,
> To listen to the hungry raven's cry in wintry season
> When the red blood is fill'd with wine & with the marrow of lambs.[11]

He who enjoys a cornucopia of earthly goods and preaches 'patience' and 'prudence' to those who can scarcely eke out an existence worthy of the least degree of human dignity is, in Blake's view, a hypocrite blinded by Urizenic abstract moral law rooted in self-interest. Such moral law — supported by natural religion, a religion devoid of spiritual reality — is an evil in the structure of society which must be overcome.

Blake sympathized with such humanitarian and religious thinkers as Johann Kaspar Lavater,[12] the Zurich preacher, and revolutionary thinkers like Thomas Paine.[13] To Blake, who believed in universal brotherhood and equality and considered this to be true Christian philosophy, such characteristic utterances of Lavater as the following rang true:

Know, in the first place, that mankind agree in essence, as they do in limbs and senses.

Mankind differ as much in essence as they do in form, limbs, and senses — and only so, and not more.

In response to these two statements Blake comments: 'This is true Christian philosophy far above all abstraction.'[14]

Looking back over his comments, and regarding Lavater's aphorisms with which he did not agree, Blake writes:

I hope no one will call what I have written cavilling because he may think my remarks of small consequence. For I write from the warmth of my heart, & cannot resist the impulse I feel to rectify what I think false in a book I love so much & approve so generally.

He then makes a number of statements which give us a few stimulating insights into his philosophy of life and his vision of universal brotherhood:

Man is bad or good as he unites himself with bad or good spirits: tell me with whom you go & I'll tell you what you do.

As we cannot experience pleasure but by means of others, who experience either pleasure or pain thro' us, And as all of us on earth are united in thought ... so it is impossible to know God or heavenly things without conjunction with those who know God & heavenly things; therefore all who converse in the spirit, converse with spirits. [& they converse with the spirit of God. *del.*][15]

Blake had a particular empathy with those who suffered:

> Can I see another's woe
> And not be in sorrow too?
> Can I see another's grief,
> And not seek for kind relief?[16]

He was particularly concerned for those who found no outlet for their innate energy, for he knew that he who can give expression to his own energy of body and mind does not dwell on unhappiness.

> The busy bee has no time for sorrow.[17]

Let us now consider a few more of Blake's poems in *Songs of Innocence and Experience* in the light of his thoughts on the social life of man.

Innocence and experience are 'Two Contrary States of the Human Soul'.[18] The state of true innocence is selfless, that of experience selfish; the former opens itself to the service of all men, the latter has a devouring character which seeks to serve only itself.

We can gain some living idea of true innocence by contrasting the 'Lamb'[19] with the 'Tyger'.[20] Clearly an attempt to do justice to Blake here would need a lengthy discussion of many pages. All we need say here is that we can recognize the lamb as representing selflessness and the 'tyger' self-centred and destructive individualism, selfhood. The 'tyger' is a terrifying, rapacious beast with tremendous natural energy. Like Urizen, the social tyrant, the 'tyger' has devouring power.[21] Both are fallen because of their individualistic selfishness which has divided them from others. Both indulge their own limited, selfish and 'devouring' interests by turning against others. The lamb, on the other hand, sacrifices his selfhood for others. The power of the lamb, symbolic of the Christ, the Imagination, emanates from his selfless and loving relationship with others; a relationship which brings joy, not fear, to the world, makes 'all the vales rejoice'.[22] The social tyrant, Urizen, shares with the 'tyger' a devouring power which would destroy the lamb. True innocence is nurtured by the freely creative imagination; it is destroyed by Urizenic power.

The 'tyger' is representative of a society based on 'nature'. His is a jungle-like society, where the meek are the prey of the powerful. Blake, as a true prophet, sees that in the future the earth will rise and see her 'maker meek', the creative man:

> In futurity
> I prophetic see
> That the earth from sleep
> (Grave the sentence deep)
>
> Shall arise and seek
> For her maker meek;
> And the desart wild
> Become a garden mild.[23]

The lamb represents the selfless state of the human soul:

> Little Lamb I'll tell thee:
> He is called by thy name,
> For he calls himself a Lamb.
> He is meek & he is mild;
>
> He became a little child.
> I a child, & thou a lamb,
> We are called by his name.[24]

The divine and the human are one. Man in his creative and selfless 'Lamb' state is one with Christ. The 'child' represents true innocence, which is selfless and free — two fundamental elements without which universal humanity, universal brotherhood cannot come into being.

Without Imagination, without becoming one with the Lamb, the Divine, there can be no true innocence. Imagination can 'see' all men, all children of God; it can encompass the whole of humanity. Blake — 'I a child' — wrote his 'happy songs' that 'Every child may joy to hear'.[25] The voice of Imagination, of the true prophet, has a unifying and universalizing force.

In *The Marriage of Heaven and Hell* Blake sees the original, imaginative relationship among men as similar to that which he shows us in 'The Lamb', but in the former the meek and mild, the true innocents, are driven into 'barren climes', into division, by the selfhood, by the Urizenic character, Rintrah, the false prophet:

> Rintrah roars & shakes his fires in the burden'd air;
> ...
> Once meek, and in a perilous path,

> The just man kept his course along
> The vale of death.
> Roses are planted where thorns grow,
> And on the barren heath
> Sing the honey bees.
>
> Till the villain left the paths of ease,
> To walk in perilous paths, and drive
> The just man into barren climes.[26]

We need to note here that Blake's characters often take on different 'natures' according to their relationship with others. Rintrah, for instance, is a dual character. In this poem he is the false prophet, the Urizenic character. Elsewhere we find him spoken of as the true prophet. In *Milton*, for instance, he 'is of the reprobate'.[27] For Blake the transgressors and reprobates are the saviours of mankind. The greatest of the transgressors was Christ.[28]

It is the false prophet and spiritually barren relationships among human beings, the Urizenic conception of life, which Blake criticizes in the *Songs of Experience*. In *Songs of Innocence* the poem 'Holy Thursday' has clear satirical overtones. In *Songs of Experience*, in the poem with the same title, Blake is emphatically and overtly critical of Urizenic social relationships and conditions, supported and hypocritically justified by a Urizenic philosophy of life and orthodoxy:

> Is this a holy thing to see
> In a rich and fruitful land,
> Babes reduc'd to misery,
> Fed with cold and usurous hand?
>
> Is that trembling cry a song?
> Can it be a song of joy?
> And so many children poor?
> It is a land of poverty!
>
> And their sun does never shine,
> And their fields are bleak & bare,
> And their ways are fill'd with thorns:
> It is eternal winter there.
>
> For where-e'er the sun does shine,
> And where-e'er the rain does fall,
> Babe can never hunger there,
> Nor poverty the mind appall.[29]

'Holy Thursday' in *Songs of Innocence* can be understood to be a satire on an annual event in St Paul's Cathedral. This 'event' was the marching of about six thousand of the poorest children from the charity schools in London into St Paul's, led by their parish officers (beadles), for a compulsory showing of their piety and gratitude to their patrons. In the poem just quoted, Blake expresses his true feelings. Here he roundly condemns the social injustice of poverty and charity. The spiritual state of such a country in which such injustice prevails and is condoned is eternal winter — symbolic of spiritual death, of the rule of Satan/Urizen, and stands in complete contrast to the life-endowing sunshine which, in a just society, would be enjoyed by all. Such a society is 'shone upon' by the life-giving and enspiriting power of the creative imagination which has its source in the love of Christ, the Imagination.

In 'The Human Abstract' Blake tells us that it is false pity and mercy which we, as Urizenic holders of power — be it in the social, religious, or any other sphere — shower on those who are the victims of the very tyranny we ourselves exert. Such pity and mercy are hypocritical. Evil, perpetrated by us, gives us the opportunity to show ourselves in a 'good' light, to be seen to 'do good'. All we are actually doing, in fact, is playing the role we have allocated to ourselves in a Newtonian and Lockian social structure:

> Pity would be no more
> If we did not make somebody Poor;
> And Mercy no more could be
> If all were as happy as we.
>
> And *mutual fear brings peace*,[30]
> Till the selfish loves increase:
> Then Cruelty knits a snare,
> And spreads his baits with care.
>
> He sits down with holy fears,
> And waters the ground with tears;
> Then Humility takes its root
> Underneath his foot.
>
> Soon spreads the dismal shade
> Of Mystery over his head;
> And the Catterpiller and Fly
> Feed on the Mystery.
>
> And it bears the fruit of Deceit,
> Ruddy and sweet to eat;

And the Raven his nest has made
In its thickest shade.

The Gods of the earth and sea
Sought thro' Nature to find this Tree;
But their search was all in vain:
There grows one in the Human Brain.[31]

False virtues arise not only from selfishness, but also from fear and weakness. The Tree of Mystery is, as elsewhere in Blake, the contrary of the Tree of Life, of Christ. It is the Urizenic, Satanic Tree of Death, the fruits of which bring spiritual death. It is the system of the false, Urizenic morality, the false Church of Mystery. The Raven of the fifth stanza is the symbol of the Fear of Death which has been inculcated into the soul of man by Urizen/Satan. The last stanza states that nature does not know of this Tree; it has grown from the reasoning powers of the human mind.[32]

The Poetic Genius, Imagination, sees and experiences that those who preach love and look upon themselves as 'Fathers' and guardians are, in reality, both selfish and cruel. Whenever Blake speaks disparagingly of the father figure he is, primarily, attacking dogmatic authoritarianism — the Church and State, ruling interests — which teach abstract moral laws but, in practice, are inhuman in their relationships with others. True innocence and imagination see that such a social system and cultural authority — represented by the 'Father', that is, God (Satan/Urizen), Priest and King — are the causes of evil and, consequently of human misery. One example of Blake's attack is found in 'The Chimney Sweeper' in *Songs of Innocence*:

When my mother died I was very young,
And my Father sold me while yet my tongue
Could scarcely cry ''weep! 'weep! 'weep!'[33]

The natural 'father' is not to be mistaken for the 'Father'. It is true that he it is who actually sells his son, but it is the Establishment which is to blame for allowing the conditions to exist which make such a deed possible. As we read on in this poem it becomes clear where the blame lies:

As Tom was a-sleeping, he had such a sight!
That thousands of sweepers, Dick, Joe, Ned, & Jack,
Were all of them lock'd up in coffins of black.

And by came an Angel who had a bright key,
And open'd the coffins & set them all free;

...

> Then naked & white, all their bags left behind,
> They rise upon clouds and sport in the wind;
> And the Angel told Tom, if he'd be a good boy,
> He'd have God for his father, & never want joy.[34]

This is a striking depiction of the abstract hope and vision that the Urizenic Church, the 'Father' teaches.

In the corresponding poem, with the same title, in *Songs of Experience*, to which reference has already been made, the experience of Poetic Genius, of Imagination, reveals the deception and accuses 'God & Priest & King' of making 'up a heaven' of others' misery.

In these two poems Blake depicts the contrast between what the ruling interests — Church and Ruler — preach and what they practise.

The vision of creative imagination unveils the fact that those who set themselves up as leaders above others are themselves entrapped in their own 'nets' of deceit and hypocrisy,[35] or, as Blake expresses it in 'The Voice of the Ancient Bard', they stumble 'over bones of the dead'. In this poem imagination highlights the inherent and inevitable wrongfulness and, in the final analysis, inability of the one-sided rationalist, Urizenic man, to set himself up as a leader of his fellow men:

> Youth of delight, come hither,
> And see this opening morn,
> Image of truth new born.
> Doubt is fled & clouds of reason,
> Dark disputes & artful teazing.
> Folly is an endless maze,
> Tangled roots perplex her ways.
> How many have fallen there!
> They stumble all night over bones of the dead,
> And feel they know not what but care,
> And wish to lead others, when they should be led.[36]

Imagination and true innocence are here in revolt against the self-centred righteousness of Church, Father and King. Creative imagination is free from the 'natural' and from the limitations, the imprisonment and subjection, imposed by Urizenic religion, social structure and philosophy of life. The 'Human Soul' — the poet, Blake — saves his imagination by not being enslav'd by another Man's.

> I must Create a System or be enslav'd by another Man's.
> I will not Reason & Compare: my business is to Create.[37]

Being free from the 'natural', from the changeable and transitory, and being conscious of the difference between the eternal and the transitory, Imagination can speak freely and see clearly. Arising out of this consciousness an 'Image of truth' is born. The vision of this 'truth new born' disperses the Urizenic 'Doubt' and 'clouds of reason'. New poetic, creative energy is born of the vision of this truth. The 'Human Soul' is endowed with the energy to expose to creative insight the fallacy and untenability of the outworn and hoary wisdom and power of the selfish Urizenic father figure. His power inculcates, and is supported by, paralysing fear and inhibitive restraint. His wisdom is grounded in the 'bones of the dead'. Both Urizenic 'wisdom' and 'power' are restrictive and abstract, divorced from living reality, depriving man of free creative activity.

In his 'Introduction' to the *Songs of Experience* the poet calls upon mankind, the 'Earth', to rise and liberate itself from the chains by which it has been bound by the

> Selfish father of men!
> Cruel, jealous, selfish fear![38]

By, in short, Urizenic 'Error'. For imaginative vision, 'Error is created. Truth is Eternal.'[39]

The Call of the Bard, of Imagination, is answered by Earth, 'her locks cover'd with grey despair'. She bemoans her state as a prisoner of reason and of the jealous creator of the phenomenal world, Urizen. She is

> Prison'd on wat'ry shore,
> Starry Jealousy does keep my den:
> Cold and hoar,
> Weeping o'er,
> I hear the Father of the ancient men.[40]

And she calls on the Bard, on the creative imagination, to

> Break this heavy chain
> That does freeze my bones around.
> Selfish! vain!
> Eternal bane![41]

Earth, mankind, calls on imaginative man to break the chain which, with the Urizenic fall of man,

> ... free Love with bondage bound.[42]

Blake is not advocating promiscuity, but love given freely in true brotherhood; such love unifies mankind. Such love typifies the freedom lost by the Fall into a Urizenic world.

The 'heavy chain', the Error, is created by the selfish father who lives at the expense of the spiritual life of his children, the 'virgins of youth'.[43] At the foot of the decorations to this poem Blake has depicted a serpent immediately under the line 'That free Love with bondage bound'. It symbolizes here the priesthood with their denial of freedom for creative energies. The 'Father' binds the universal love, which is inherent in man and longing to burst forth, by his selfish, restrictive and limited love.

True 'free' love is characterized by Blake in the poem 'The Clod & the Pebble' which follows on immediately after 'Earth's Answer':

> 'Love seeketh not Itself to please,
> Nor for itself hath any care,
> But for another gives its ease,
> And builds a Heaven in Hell's despair.'
>
> So sang a little Clod of Clay.
> Trodden with the cattle's feet.[44]

This is Blake's 'true religion' and stands in contrast to the religion of the Church, which, in his view, represents false religion.

It is worth stressing the point here that it is a mistake to interpret Blake's opposition to Priest and Church as being opposition to religion as such, or his criticism of the annointed king as being opposition to royalty. What he is clearly attacking is not Priest and Church, but the fact that the religion they propound is divorced from true humanity and the everyday life of human beings. Again it is not the King as such, but the selfish ruling interests, the human interests of trade and commerce, of which he, as ruler, is symbolic, which Blake confronts with his criticism.[45]

False religion is represented in the present poem by the hard pebble. In direct contrast to the soft and pliable clay, whose song is of unselfish love (thus building a Heaven to the despair of the Hell of unselfishness), the hard pebble, lying rigid in the waters of materialism (see pp. 163–5) symbolizes the contrary state of selfishness and rational materialism. It sings a song of selfish love and the building of a Hell in spite of Heaven:

> But a Pebble of the brook
> Warbled out these metres meet:

'Love seeketh only Self to please,
To bind another to Its delight,
Joys in another's loss of ease,
And builds a Hell in Heaven's despite'.[46]

The 'love' which 'seeketh only Self to please', the 'love' which, in other words, lives as a parasite, which reduces men to a state of misery and poverty by building a 'Hell in Heaven's despite', is destructive. The limited and devouring nature of such love is opposed to universal 'free love', and makes every effort to combat and destroy a true social conscience and hence also the coming into being of universal brotherhood.

As often remarked in these pages, Blake opposes passivity, non-creativity and abstraction. For him, 'He who desires but acts not, breeds pestilence.'[47] He who preaches love and brotherhood but does not put them into practice in everyday life creates a sick society. In such a society the very words we speak lose their true meaning, and reality is ousted by abstraction. Blake shows this contrast in the two poems 'The Divine Image'[48] and 'The Human Abstract'.[49] In the latter the Church is seen creating the 'Poor' and, at the same time, offering 'Pity' and 'Mercy' to its own creation! But in 'The Divine Image', 'Mercy, Pity, Peace and Love' are integral elements of a unified human society in which

... all must love the human form,
In heathen, turk, or jew;
Where Mercy, Love, & Pity dwell
There God is dwelling too.[50]

In such a society universal brotherhood reigns. In a selfless society, God, Christ dwells in every human heart. In this poem Blake gives expression to one of his ardently felt convictions — the identification of true man with the Divine. Throughout his writings we find expressions of his belief in the divinity of man. God has revealed Himself in Christ as a man. Among the many variations of expression of this conviction are the following:

Human Nature is the image of God.[51]

God is Man & exists in us & we in him.[52]

Crabb Robinson records Blake as stating: 'We are all co-existent with God — members of the Divine body. We are all partakers of the Divine nature.'[53]

Blake did not distinguish between the two natures of Christ as defined in the Prayer Book: the Divine and the truly human were identical to Him. Because he is truly human, he is Divine.[54]

God, Christ and man are inseparable in a true, human society. It is for the creation of such a society, universal brotherhood, that the Word was made flesh. Such a creation, in which man is an active co-creator with God, with Christ, who is the Imagination, is a continuous process. The incarnation of Christ is likewise a continuous process: 'God becomes as we are, that we may be as he is.'[55]

Berkeley stated that Plato and Aristotle considered God 'as abstracted or distinct from the natural world. But the Aegyptians considered God and nature as making one whole, or all things together as making one universe.' Blake writes that Plato and Aristotle

also consider'd God as abstracted or distinct from the Imaginative World, but Jesus, as also Abraham & David, consider'd God as a Man in the Spiritual or Imaginative Vision. Jesus consider'd Imagination to be the Real Man.[56]

Real Man 'is All Imagination'.[57] And 'What Jesus came to Remove was the Heathen or Platonic Philosophy which blinds the Eye of Imagination, The Real Man.'[58]

For Blake the words of Christ in His answer to the Jews, who accused Him of setting Himself up a God (John 10:33), are a reality: 'Ye are all gods, and all of you are children of the most high.'[59]

The God of the Anglican Prayer Book 'without passion or parts' is, for Blake, a mere abstraction. A God who dwells solely in heaven and not in the human breast is outside of human experience and is, therefore, a false God. In the poem 'The Divine Image' Blake universalizes the 'human form divine' and sees God in human unity and selflessness.

Imagination, the creative energy in Man, is the true God who 'only Acts & Is, in existing beings or Men'.[60] Man 'falls' from this divine, creative state when he uses his energy against humanity, when he uses it for selfish and limited, Urizenic ends.

In a society where social conscience and imagination are vibrant with loving creative force, each individual is esteemed for what he really is. The spiritual in man is perceived as the Real Man; the eternal in man, not the transitory, is the criterion by which each individual is justly esteemed by his fellow men: 'The Worship of God is: Honouring his gifts in other men ... and loving the greatest men best: those who envy or calumniate great men hate God; for there is no other God.'[61] By the 'greatest men'

Blake does not mean those who are famous and have power (though, of course, they could qualify). Seen from the viewpoint Blake is putting forward, the chimney sweep could be a Real Man and be far greater than any reigning monarch.

Elsewhere (pp. 105–6) we discuss in greater detail Blake's theme that 'Every Man's Wisdom is peculiar to his own Individuality.'[62] Each individuality is unique and eternal; it is the indestructible spirit of each one of us. Each individual is sacred. His special genius is 'the Holy Ghost in Man'.[63] As we are all different, 'One Law for the Lion & Ox is Oppression.'[64] One Urizenic law could not exist if man's social conscience were spiritually alive to the needs, strengths and weaknesses, of his individual fellow men — if the creative imagination were constantly active.

The ideal of the creative individual is spiritual freedom, liberty, Jerusalem.[65]

He who violates the individuality of another person, who acts against the ideal, liberty, has sullied, rendered ugly, his own individuality. It is his self-centred selfhood which directs his energy against others and, as a result, Poetic Genius, Imagination, loses its divine creativity and strength. Such a loss is inevitable if an individual separates himself from universal humanity.

Time and again Blake rejects both the negative attitude to the phenomenal world and man's subjection to it. Both lead to egotism, selfish individualism, and, consequently, to separation from others.

In the poem 'The Garden of Love' the Priest negates selfless love of the world:

> I went to the Garden of Love,
> And saw what I had never seen:
> A Chapel was built in the midst,
> Where I used to play on the green.
>
> And the gates of this Chapel were shut,
> And 'Thou shalt not' writ over the door;
> So I turn'd to the Garden of Love
> That so many sweet flowers bore.
>
> And I saw it was filled with graves,
> And tomb-stones where flowers should be;
> And Priests in black gowns were walking their rounds,
> And binding with briars my joys & desires.[66]

The garden where the child — Blake, you and I — had played in a state of innocence is now usurped by the Chapel of negation. By his negative instruction, 'Thou shalt not', Urizenic Man restrains joys and energies in others, and in doing so he kills the soul — and love, and turns human life into a state of death, a graveyard, 'where flowers should be'. The Priest of organized religion is here seen as the agent of repression. He is symbolic of the Urizenic power, which fetters man's creative energy in 'mind forg'd manacles'[67] and is devoid of the imaginative social conscience necessary to found the New Jerusalem. In the illustration he is seen instructing a boy and a girl in his limited, fettering systems and doctrines. At the foot of the page the grave-mound of 'joys & desires' is seen bound with briars. Blake sees organized religion constantly crowning Christ's head with thorns; constantly killing Imagination, the 'Divine Humanity'.[68] By negating 'joys & desires' the priest also negates Imagination without which the phenomenal world cannot evolve into the 'Garden of Love'. Imagination needs the experience of the phenomenal world, needs to be freely creative through love, 'joys & desires', in this world in order to be able to effect the spiritual transmutation necessary for the bringing into being the ideal, the 'Garden of Love' in which all the fruits are from the Tree of Life.

Imagination needs to be able to make full 'use', in love, of the phenomenal world, for, Blake contends: 'Energy is the only life, and is from the Body.'[69] Imagination withers, either because man negates the phenomenal world, the world of the five senses, or because he subjects himself to that world — as the rational materialist does.[70]

In his Notebook, immediately following on after a draft of 'The Garden of Love', Blake writes the poem 'Chapel of Gold':

> I saw a chapel all of gold
> That none did dare to enter in,
> And many weeping stood without,
> Weeping, mourning, worshipping.
>
> I saw a serpent rise between
> The white pillars of the door,
> And he forc'd & forc'd & forc'd,
> Down the golden hinges tore.
>
> And along the pavement sweet,
> Set with pearls & rubies bright,
> All his slimy length he drew,
> Till upon the altar white.

Vomiting his poison out
On the bread & on the wine.
So I turn'd into a sty
And laid me down among the swine.[71]

The imagery of 'The Garden of Love' suggests that we may interpret the 'chapel of gold' in this poem as being the temple of innocent and imaginative love, sullied and defiled by the repressing Urizen/Satanic power Blake describes in the earlier poem. In this poem love is seen as being perverted into something nauseating and monstrous. The sight revolts the imaginative, creative poet and he finds comfort 'among the swine'.

Freedom of the Imagination depends, in part, on the freedom of the senses from Urizenic 'slavery', 'doubt' and 'fear', but this is not to suggest that we should worship nature, for it is the serpent who not only symbolizes evil, but also the worship of nature. His church is serpent-shaped and the priest is also serpentine.[72] The Church is the servant of Urizen. It belongs to him:

Plac'd in the order of the stars, when the five senses whelm'd
In deluge o'er the earth-born man: ...
Thought chang'd the infinite to a serpent, that which pitieth
To a devouring flame ...
Then was the serpent temple form'd, image of infinite
Shut up in finite revolutions, ...[73]

Coiled and threatening, the serpent occupies the title page of *Europe, a Prophecy* (1794). Its coils represent the dull rounds and repetitions of world dominated by reason, by Urizen. Some six years earlier Blake had written:

If it were not for the Poetic or Prophetic character the Philosophic & Experimental would soon be at the ratio of all things, & stand still, unable to do other than repeat the same dull round over again.[74]

As nature offers us the temptation of material wealth, so the serpent is described — in the 'Chapel of Gold' poem, for instance — as being of precious stones.

In his 'Introduction' to the *Songs of Experience* we have seen that the voice of the Bard calls upon 'Earth', that is, Fallen Man, 'the lapsed soul', to rise and gain freedom from the tyranny of the Urizenic Father. He is called upon to regain his rightful place in the universe, lost when he adopted reason, the 'starry pole', as the sole judge of the nature of reality, to the exclusion of imagination. Man is summoned to awake from materialism, from spiritual sleep, and to turn again to the free and creative life of the imagination. The 'starry floor' of reason and the 'wat'ry shore' of the Sea of Time and Space — the edge of materialism — are there only till 'the break of day', if man would but consent to leave 'the slumberous mass'.

In *Jerusalem*, the Bard, Blake, calls in similar vein to 'the lapsed Soul':

> I see the Past, Present & Future existing all at once
> Before me. O Divine Spirit, sustain me on thy wings,
> That I may wake Albion from his long & cold repose;
> For Bacon & Newton, sheath'd in dismal steel, their terrors hang
> Like iron scourges over Albion: Reasonings like vast Serpents
> Infold around my limbs, bruising my minute articulations.
>
> I turn my eyes to the Schools & Universities of Europe
> And there behold the Loom of Locke, whose Woof rages dire,
> Wash'd by the Water-wheels of Newton: black the cloth
> In heavy wreathes folds over every Nation: cruel Works
> Of many Wheels I view, wheel without wheel, with cogs tyrannic
> Moving by compulsion each other, not as those in Eden, which,
> Wheel within wheel, in freedom revolve in harmony & peace.[75]

These are discussed at some length elsewhere (see pp. 165–6). Here we confine ourselves to noting that the 'reasonings' of Locke and Newton imprison man with sheaths of steel 'like vast serpents'. Urizenic rationalism chains Imagination. Rational logic, like 'cogs tyrannic' moves, and is moved, by rigid, binding, blind laws, inhibiting free creativity, in contrast to the free, creative 'laws' of Imagination which in 'freedom revolve in harmony & peace'.[76]

In commenting on 'the Schools & Universities', seeing those impregnated with the rationalism of Locke and Newton, Blake again draws our attention to the fact that the freedom of the Imagination is eradicated, is enslaved by a world conception relying entirely on the limitations of the five physical senses. Blake has already touched on this in his poem 'The School Boy' who asks:

> How can the bird that is born for joy
> Sit in a cage and sing?
> How can a child, when fears annoy,
> But drop his tender wing,
> And forget his youthful spring?

> O! father & mother, if buds are nip'd
> And blossoms blown away,
> And if the tender plants are strip'd
> Of their joy in the springing day,
> By sorrow and care's dismay,
>
> How shall the summer arise in joy,
> Or the summer fruits appear?
> Or how shall we gather what griefs destroy,
> Or bless the mellowing year,
> When the blasts of winter appear?[77]

Throughout Blake's works, wherever Imagination is struggling for freedom, there the voice of true innocence is heard. In 'The School Boy' — as in 'A Little Boy Lost'[78] — Blake issues a sustained protest against the destruction of innocence and creative joy in life by the 'cruel eye outworn', by the Urizenic dreary, lifeless round of school founded on the past, on 'memory' and not on Imagination. Such an education is not for living but for dying. The spirit, the creative mind, is destroyed, is 'brushed away' by 'some blind' and 'thoughtless hand'[79] that is, by Urizenic selfish dogmatism which has no insight into the inner life of others. Rational, 'natural' man inhibits the growth of imaginative, spiritual man. Fear, dismay, grief — all deathlike states — are planted in the human soul, which, together with rigid formulae, definitions and sense-bound thinking, inhibit, 'nip' the imaginative creativity of the growing human being in the bud. No individual can blossom under such a regime in any sphere of life.

In *The Gates of Paradise* (first engraved in 1793), the eleventh of a sequence of sixteen pictures is entitled 'Aged Ignorance'. It shows an aged, bespectacled and white-bearded man sitting under a dead branch of a tree. He is clipping a wing of a fleeing infant cherub.[80] Blake's written commentary to this picture runs:

> In Aged Ignorance profound,
> Holy & cold I clip'd the Wings
> Of all Sublunary Things . . .[81]

In the inscription Blake has written:

> Perceptive Organs closed, their Objects close.[82]

This echoes the inscription under the frontispiece:

> The Sun's Light when he unfolds it
> Depends on the Organ that beholds it.[83]

Which, again, echoes Blake's answer to the question whether, when the sun rises, he does not see a round disc like a guinea in appearance:

O no, no, I see an Innumerable company of the Heavenly host crying 'Holy, Holy, Holy is the Lord God Almighty.' I question not my Corporeal or Vegetative Eye any more than I would Question a Window concerning a Sight. I look thro' it and not with it.[84]

Seeing *with* and not *through* the eye means that man relies exclusively on the physical sense organs for his 'picture', his conception of the world, and, by implication, limits himself unduly and restricts his breadth and height of consciousness. He is like the man who

has closed himself up, till he sees all things thro' the narrow chinks of his cavern.

He has not realized that

If the doors of perception were cleansed everything would appear to man as it is, infinite.[85]

Nor has he realized that

> This Life's dim Windows of the Soul
> Distorts the Heavens from Pole to Pole
> And leads you to Believe a Lie
> When you see with, not thro' the Eye.[86]

'Aged Ignorance' and the various passages just quoted all refer to the tendency to try to explain everything in life by the known, to reduce everything to fit in with a preconceived idea or formula — a characteristic Urizenic tendency. But if — as 'The School Boy' also says in essence — everything inexplicable is rejected, if the new, the adventurous, possibly disturbing and challenging, has no place in life, then life itself 'dies'. Life itself, and what it holds in the future, is unknown. Life which is 'alive' is an ongoing process of birth, of rebirth. The future is being born in the present. Whereas reason deals with the present in terms of the 'dead' past and can have no vision of the future, Imagination, 'the Poetic Genius, which is every where call'd the Spirit of Prophecy',[87] sees the future in the 'living' present in which the past itself is transformed and given new life flowing towards it from the future. To overvalue rational and moral perfection, based on the known past, leads, not to the full realization of one's potential, but rather to a state of stagnation and, in its effect on relationships with others, to a state of unrelatedness, of isolation in selfhood. Overvaluation of rationalism and materialism and reliance on precedent precludes a living and relevant social conscience, for the spirit 'within' is silenced.

The picture of 'Aged Ignorance' and the statements in *The Marriage of Heaven and Hell* and *The Everlasting Gospel* all indicate the road which leads to what Blake calls the Limit of Opacity, Satan. This is a state in which all creative imagination and all sensibility, all those stirrings of the heart, all comprehension which springs from the heart, all feelings of love, compassion and sympathy, are non-existent. In the state of Satan, that is, at the Limit of Opacity, imagination, empathy (relatedness), insight and vision, are all lacking. At the Limit of Opacity, in the spiritual darkness of one-sided rationalism, we can have no understanding for true innocence and we are completely shut off from our fellow men. Social conscience, fellowship and brotherhood are no more than empty, meaningless and lifeless words, if they issue from the mouth of abstract rationalism. Ignorance, we may learn from Blake, is the attempt to explain rationally a totality in terms of its fragments, of its constituent parts, instead of, through the creative imagination and the cleansed organs of perception, perceiving the fragments in terms of the totality.

As we have discussed on several occasions already, Blake is constantly opposing rationalism and natural religion, deism. He sees in these the worst manifestations of man's faculty of thinking functioning in its most limited ways. Rationalism, materialism excludes everything which cannot be calculated (weighed and measured), and deism attempts to explain everything in relation to logical thought processes. It is the danger inherent in the exclusive application of such one-sided attitudes against which Blake protests so vehemently. He is not, of course, suggesting that we should no longer use our faculty of logical thought. But unless it is harmoniously harnessed with creative energy and imagination, its power and sagacity can but lead to destruction of the totality of the human soul. In itself, fallen reason, rationalism, can only deal with and grasp the lifeless; to comprehend life requires an inner 'moving' and 'growing' activity, an 'artistic poetic creativity'. Without this creativity a true social conscience is impossible.

The birth of true, living fellowship and brotherhood will not come into being on earth through the intervention of some divine power or other; man needs to be co-creator with the Divine in the manifestation of the ideal; he must assume responsibility for the future and for his fellow men. Once this conscious decision is taken, once we have responded to the call of Imagination, of Los, who asks,

> Why stand we here trembling around
> Calling on God for help, and not ourselves, in whom God dwells,
> Stretching a hand to save the Falling Man?[88]

— once we have responded with our creative imagination, then the influx from the Divine Imagination, from Christ, begins to inspire us; the divine in us, the 'Gifts of the Holy Ghost', that is, 'Imagination, Art & [true] Science & all Intellectual Gifts'[89] begin to 'speak' in and through us. We think, feel and act out of a living and enspirited social conscience. Then All are known as 'my Friends & Brothers . . . my beloved Companions';[90] then the New Jerusalem, true Liberty, can come on Earth, for we are then one with Christ, the Imagination, Who has never left us 'comfortless' (John 14:19). The words 'I live; yet not I, but Christ liveth in me' (Galatians 2:20) and 'I am the way, the truth, and the life' (John 14:6) will then no longer be mere words, but a living, imaginative experience.

We have seen that man must become co-creator with the Divine, with the Creative Word, Christ. Christ, the Creator, is the True Man, the Imagination. We, as men of the Imagination, 'are his Members'.[91] As we have seen, the Imagination is, for Blake, the central faculty of both Christ and man. In the tractate 'All Religions are One' (1788) we recall Blake's statement that 'the Poetic Genius is the True Man'.[92] True Man works and lives in and through the Imagination. He is an artist.[93] By 'Artist' Blake is clearly not thinking solely of practising poets, painters, or composers. He is thinking in more profound, yet immediate, terms than this. The term 'Artists' includes all men who could be described as men of visible love. They endeavour, through deeds of love, to make visible the invisible. A true man, an 'artist', is the man who lives in and perceives the spiritual world, the true, real world — a world which is Man's true home — and endeavours to make that world visible to others. Imaginative Man, the Artist in Man, makes visible and concrete a hidden creative power. He 'repeats' in his individual yet universal way, the Incarnation, the manifestation of the Creative Word in a visible human body. It is the task of all who would live according to 'the religion of Jesus, the everlasting Gospel'[94] — and thereby achieve brotherhood — to 'engage himself openly & publicly before all the World in some Mental pursuit for the Building up of Jerusalem.'[95] In the same address 'To the Christians' in which these words occur, Blake also writes: 'I know of no other Christianity and of no other Gospel than the liberty of body & mind to exercise the Divine Arts of Imagination.'[96]

To exercise 'the Divine Arts of Imagination' is to be an artist in the sense to which attention has just been drawn. It is the artist, the man of creative imagination, who makes the invisible visible, who works on the 'Building up of Jerusalem', on the creation of liberty and the City of Peace, the perfect society, universal brotherhood.

Jerusalem is the symbol of the community men and women could establish as a reality, if they were to live life in and through the Divine Imagination, if they were all to become 'artists'. All life aspires to the condition of art which — for Blakean man — is the highest and most unitive activity of the creative mind.

Liberty, both spiritual and physical, is not a special privilege of the 'Elect'; it is a need of every man and woman. 'What is Liberty without Universal Toleration?'[97] asks Blake.

Liberty is the ideal for the individual and for society as a whole, for on liberty is founded the brotherhood of man, without which men and women cannot exist as true human beings. Liberty, in the Blakean sense, is 'the Divine Appearance' which is brotherhood.[98] In a society in which life is lived in and through the Divine Imagination, brotherhood and an imaginative and love-filled social conscience would find expression in politics!

> Are not Religion & Politics the Same Thing? Brotherhood is
> Religion,
> O Demonstrations of Reason Dividing Families in Cruelty & Pride![99]

The 'Politics' Blake here has in mind is not that which he found in his day — nor that which he would find today. Of such politics he writes:

I am really sorry to see my Countrymen trouble themselves about Politics. If Men were Wise, the Most arbitrary Princes could not hurt them. If they are not wise, the Freest Government is compell'd to be a Tyranny. Princes appear to me to be Fools. Houses of Commons & Houses of Lords appear to be fools; they seem to me to be something Else besides Human Life.[100]

Adherence to any dogmatic political ideology is divorced from the totality of 'Human Life'. If politics are not grounded in 'Human Life' then they must be based on Urizenic self-interest in one form or another. They are based on 'The Great Satan or Reason'. A Satanic social system cannot be overcome by setting one ideology against another. The result can be no other than a further crystallization of Urizenic confrontation and polarization. It is only a holistic and imaginative world-view, through which the creative human imagination, the imaginative individuality, can find expression, that a politics of universal brother-hood can come into existence. Such a politics, it goes without saying, would be imbued with and sustained by a 'holistic' social conscience.

Politics, just as much as education, religion, philosophy, and so forth, must be grounded in the creative imagination, in 'the Divine Humanity'. A political system which is divorced from the totality of 'Human Life' is as abstract as, for instance, a remote and passive God who dwells in a 'Void outside of Existence'.[101] The experience of Christ living and active in the human breast is as essential in politics as it is in true religion.

For Blake, imaginative creative power is a form of active divinity in man — Imagination is the 'Divine Humanity'[102] — and is of a completely different substance and character from the remote and abstract God of Rational Man. To the question: 'Is not God alone the Prolific?' Blake answers: 'God only Acts & Is, in existing beings or Men'.[103] Rational Man, 'false' Man, postulates an abstract God Who is both passive and exterior to human experience. This 'false' God, Urizen, has created a circumscribed world, which is inevitably founded on his finite and limited impressions (Locke, etc.). Urizen has spread his net so widely and woven his web so densely, that 'true' Man, Real Man, the Imagination, has been smothered by abstract teachings, that is, by social theories, political ideologies, schools of psychology, sociology and philosophy, which are all based on the acceptance that the only reality is that which can be perceived by the five senses. Such false Gods

> combine against Man, setting their dominion above
> The Human form Divine, Thrown down from their high station
> In the Eternal heavens of Human Imagination, buried beneath
> In Dark Oblivion, with incessant pangs, ages on ages.[104]

Imagination is the 'Human Form Divine', the 'Divine-Humanity', is Christ. Abstract philosophy and natural religion destroy the living and creative and hence destroy Christ, destroy our humanity which seeks Divinity.[105] Through the cultivation and activity of the Imagination, of Los, the Divine Humanity within us can be awakened. When it wakens, the Spectre, Satan/Urizen, the one-sided, domineering rational power of the divided man, can be cast out. Indeed, Jesus Himself, or, rather, the

Jesus Who is projected, as an idea, by an abstract reasoning Church as being only concerned with those who adhere to a definite set of dogmas, must be cast out. To Blake, a divine, spiritual power, which precludes any soul from the Universal Human Divine, which does not embrace all humanity, is an abstraction and must be cast out. Such an exclusive Jesus is a spiritual falsehood, an Error. To orthodox Christianity Blake could say:

> The Vision of Christ that thou dost see
> Is my Vision's Greatest Enemy ...[106]

For

> ... Publicans & Harlots he
> Selected for his Company,
> And from the Adulteress turn'd away
> God's righteous Law, ...[107]

Los, Imagination, denounces the 'Fiends of Righteousness' and, as we mention elsewhere too (see p. 41), instructs them to

> ... obey their Humanities & not pretend Holiness
> When they are murderers ...[108]

Los, Imagination, urges us to awaken the sleeping humanity, the Divine Humanity, within us. When it awakens then the Spectre — the one-sided rational power — is transmuted, 'rises' to work in harmony with other faculties of the human soul.

The Jesus of orthodoxy is, for Blake, an Error. He is Satan. He is

> ... The Accuser who is
> The God of this World.[109]

Man's idea of God, which he raises on high altars, is only a projection of an isolated part of his total being. It is a mental phenomenon which springs from the rational mind and is limited by that one-sided mind. It is, in Blake's terms, the 'Traveller's Dream'[110] which has led man astray. It is an illusion which denies, negates, a true all-embracing social conscience and universal brotherhood.

Satan, the 'god of this world' (2 Cor 4:4), raised on the high altars of orthodoxy, is the adversary of the Divine Vision, Christ. Satan

> ... created Seven deadly Sins, drawing out his infernal scroll
> Of Moral laws and cruel punishments upon the clouds of Jehovah,
> To pervert the Divine voice in its entrance to the earth
> With thunder of war & trumpet's sound, with armies of disease,
> Punishments & deaths muster'd & number'd, Saying: 'I am God alone:
> There is no other! let all obey my principles of moral individuality.'
> ...
> Thus Satan raged ... & his bosom grew
> Opake against the Divine Vision ...[111]

And:

> ... Los lamented over Satan who triumphant divided the Nations.[112]

The 'individuality' of which Blake is here writing is not to be identified with the unique spiritual essence of each individual but with the selfhood, the Spectre, Satan in man. Blake consistently maintains that the moral code, as promulgated by State religion, is a result of the selfhood. In the lines just quoted Satan is shown creating the moral law. The hint that the moral law is Jehovah's indicates that the selfhood is author of the Ten Commandments, which have been formulated in order to dominate and control others. When, in *Milton*, Blake has Satan call 'the Individual Law Holy'[113] he is saying that the moral law, engendered by the selfhood, has become integrated into the teaching of holiness. Such holiness is both delusive and hypocritical — on a par with Urizen's false pity (see p. 120). Its effect is highlighted when the unformed and unenlightened souls call out to Los and

> ... howl round the Porches of Golgonooza,
> Crying: 'O God deliver us to the Heavens or to the Earths,
> That we may preach righteousness & punish the sinner with death.'[114]

To call out for righteousness and punishment is the moral attitude which is not only delusive but also totally opposed to the 'religion of Jesus',[115] of true, all-embracing, spiritual social conscience and the brotherhood of man. Righteousness and 'Vengeance for Sin'[116] are two major weapons in the 'Religion of Satan',[117] in Urizen's State religion. Through State religion morality is associated with war, 'with thunder of war & trumpet's sound'.

Blake commonly equates Satan with the law-giving God. The opening lines of the quotation above from Plate 9 of *Milton* recapitulate Urizen's actions in *The First Book of Urizen*.[118] Both Satan and Urizen are 'opaque against the Divine Vision', that is, both symbolize spiritual death. Both devise 'Seven deadly Sins' and the rigid 'Moral Laws and cruel punishments' to deal with them. Both accuse and condemn instead of providing the spiritual enlightenment which arises in man when he meets total love and forgiveness. Love gives birth to love when it is given spiritual freedom without any tinge of Urizenic/Satanic possessiveness. Without such love a Christ-filled social conscience cannot function. The so-called conscience of Urizenic Man divides man against man; a true social conscience has both a creative and a unitive force.

In his 'Illustrations to the Book of Job', a sequence of twenty-one engravings with a text commenting on the biblical story of Job, Blake is concerned, amongst other things, with the connections between the Urizenic, authoritarian moral code based on rigid concepts of right and wrong, good and evil, and the disastrous effects which ensue from accusation and condemnation. Plate 10 shows Job's three friends who have come to console him, but who appear in the guise of his accusers. They are certain, in their Urizenism, that the misfortunes which have befallen Job must be due to a 'sinful' life, to his failure to obey the strict laws of morality laid down by Jehovah. As Blake sees it, however, Job's troubles have a totally different source, namely his rigid adherence to an outworn moral code, his self-righteousness, and his consequent lack of humanity and true vision. He had, in other words, grown 'Opake' against the Divine Vision, Christ.[119] This 'opacity' had led him into deep inner conflict with his own true nature.

Metanoia, a 'turning about at the centre', a spiritual and psychological rebirth, is needed to transform 'Opakeness' into 'Translucence' to which there is no limit:

There is a limit of Opakeness and a limit of Contraction
In every Individual Man, and the limit of Opakeness
Is named Satan, and the limit of Contraction is named Adam.
But . . . the Saviour in Mercy takes
Contraction's Limit, and of the Limit he forms Woman, That
Himself may in process of time be born Man to redeem.
But there is no Limit of Expansion; there is no Limit of Translucence
In the bosom of Man for ever from eternity to eternity.
Therefore I break thy bonds of righteousness.[120]

The realization of Jerusalem — Blake's vision of human relationships which need to be created on earth — inevitably means a 'breaking down', a 'casting out', or, rather, a transformation and redemption of an established unjust social system, a rigid and limited rationalism, and a dogmatic, one-sided, religious doctrine. To Blake, the New Jerusalem is not a Utopia or a religious fancy, but an existence man can bring into being, if he will undertake the inner, spiritual transformation necessary. The responsibility lies with each individual person. The spiritual trans-formation and development in Man is the cause of the creation of a just, loving and free community of men. Blakean Man, however, true to his imaginative social conscience and to the ethos of universal brotherhood does not strive egotistically to reach Jerusalem, to gain freedom solely for himself. That is not enough for him. True freedom must exist on a universal level, not solely on a personal level.

It is clear from what has been said so far that Blake is well aware that evil 'forces' are at work within society and that men are agents of evil. In *A Vision of the Last Judgement* (1810) he writes: 'There is not an Error but it has a Man for its ... Agent, ... Good & Evil are Qualities in Every Man.'[121] And Blake begins the epic poem, *The Four Zoas*, by quoting, in Greek, from Ephesians 6:12: 'For we wrestle not against flesh and blood, but against principalities, against powers, against rulers of the darkness of this world, against spiritual wickedness in high places.'

Evil in the world is ultimately to be traced to the corruption of man's spiritual powers by such a spiritual power as Lucifer/Satan/Urizen. True to his conviction that 'every Natural Effect has a Spiritual Cause, and not a Natural'[122] for 'There is no Such Thing as ... a Natural Cause for any Thing in any way',[123] Blake sees certain Principalities and Powers, that is, certain Archai and Exusiai, as being spirits of Evil 'in high places'. They are the spiritual source and causes of evil in the minds and deeds of worldly princes and men of power, that is, men 'in high places'. To ignore the former, the spiritual powers, in our understanding of Blake's meaning here would be to suggest that Blake had not only completely misunder-stood Paul's message, but also to see Blake as little more than a socialist ruled by materialism.

In order to build Jerusalem — the City of Universal Brotherhood — we must rise against a 'class of men whose delight is the destruction of men'.[124] That is, we must rise against Urizenic Man, the Urizenic principle in others as well as within ourselves. Another way of saying this would be: Imagination — the human identity or energy — must combat and overcome abstract philosophy and natural religion, both of which are manifestations of the single vision of Newton, Bacon and Locke, the Satanic trinity (as Blake sees them) and teachers of the atheism of 'unbelief' and materialism. In *A Vision of the Last Judgement* Blake comments:

We do not find any where that Satan is Accused of Sin; he is only accused of Unbelief & thereby drawing Man into Sin that he may accuse him. Such is the Last Judgement — a deliverance from Satan's Accusation. Satan thinks that Sin is displeasing to God; he ought to know that Nothing is displeasing to God but Unbelief & Eating of the Tree of Knowledge of Good & Evil.[125]

A spiritual rebirth — the onset of a spiritual re-education and regeneration — implies conscious confrontation with Error (evil). In his notes on his picture of 'The Last Judgement' (of which only sketches still exist) Blake gives a clear exposition of the principle that, if Error is once seen for what it is, then it can be cast out, or transmuted and transcended.[126] In his poem *Milton* Blake 'brings back' the poet John Milton so that he may redeem his puritanical intransigence and ratiocinative coldness. Blake's Milton realizes that the false tyrant within himself must be cast out. He accepts the teaching of the Bard, 'Who, Present, Past, & Future, sees',[127] that his Spectre, his Satanic reasoning power, his selfhood, has been the source of his error. Milton does not simply accept this fact passively, he actively claims his error:

I in my Selfhood am that Satan: I am that Evil One.[128]

'What', he has just asked himself:

do I here
With the daughters of memory & not with the daughters of inspiration.[129]

The reborn Milton realizes that he himself had strengthened the process of division, of fragmentation through his works. In *Paradise Lost*, in particular, he had created a natural religion which divided God from man, the divine from the human. He had been a false prophet, representing 'natural' as distinct from spiritual truth. When, in Blake's poem, Milton, on his inner spiritual journey, meets Urizen, 'the demon cold', he is baptized with the 'icy fluid' of rational power — a 'baptism' to death, not to life. But now Milton does not surrender to Satan/Urizen. He counters by sculpting Urizen a new body, thus

giving a body to Falsehood that it may be cast off forever.[130]

Milton's redemptive activity is described in the following way:

Silent they met and silent strove among the streams of Arnon
Even to Mahanaim, when with cold hand Urizen stoop'd down
And took up water from the River Jordan, pouring on
To Milton's brain the icy fluid from his broad cold palm.

> But Milton took of the red clay of Succoth, moulding it with care
> Between his palms and filling up the furrows of many years,
> Beginning at the feet of Urizen, and on the bones
> Creating new flesh on the Demon cold and building him
> As with new clay, a Human form in the Valley of Beth Peor.[131]

Urizen strives to petrify, Milton to redeem.

In Blake's illustration of this scene[132] Urizen appears as Moses carrying the Tablets of the Law. He is the false priest of John Milton's natural religion, whom Blake's Milton is striving to overcome and transform. Beneath the illustration Blake has written one all-important line of text:

> Annihilate the Self-hood of Deceit and False Forgiveness.[133]

In his Annotations to Berkeley's *Siris* Blake writes that 'Imagination is the Divine Body in Every Man,' and then states: 'The Divine Image or Imagination [is] The All in Man.'[134]

Imagination represents True Man, Urizen False Man. The struggle between True Man and False Man is cosmological, spiritual and psychological. Imagination, True Man, expresses this opposition in the world in every sphere of life: cultural, social, political and economical. It takes place within society, in everyday life, wherever Urizenic falsehood has taken root and found 'existence'. True social conscience enlightened by the Imagination engages in 'Mental Fight' against Urizenic self-centredness, the 'Self-hood of Deceit'.

In the address to the deists which introduces the third book of *Jerusalem* Blake declares categorically that

... Deism, is the Worship of the God of this World by the means of what you call Natural Religion and Natural Philosophy, and of Natural Morality, or Self-Righteousness, the Selfish Virtues of the Natural Heart. This was the Religion of the Pharisees who murder'd Jesus. Deism is the same & ends the same.[135]

To be moral, for the rationalist, the deist, is nothing other than to fulfil his own 'nature'. The man of reason, who only accepts the 'natural', the physical, as reality and denies the very existence of spirituality as a reality, is like our modern metaphysical or philosophical behaviourist who accepts only physical behaviour for claims about the mental. But, although he concedes that it has some degree of existential reality, nature, the natural, for Blake, is only a quasi-reality, a shadowy existence:

Vala* is but thy Shadow, O thou loveliest among women!
A shadow animated by thy tears, O mournful Jerusalem![136]

Those who worship Vala and do not strive to build Jerusalem are the enemies of Christianity; they are the worshippers of the false god, Satan. They are caught in the 'Net of Urizen'. In this 'Net' there can be no question of free will, of freely acknowledged responsibility for one's fellow men, of true social conscience. In a Urizenic world everything is fixed and predetermined; everything runs in accordance with mechanistic, natural laws. In such a world there can be no forgiveness of sins but only condemnation and vengeance for sin, for he who, like Christ, breaks 'the Coercive Laws of Hell, Moral Hypocrisy'[137] goes against 'the Selfish Virtues of the Natural Heart'.

Brotherhood and selfless, true love, cannot exist in a society ruled by Urizen.

When, in the Address to the Deists, Blake speaks of the deist as being an enemy of 'Universal Nature' he is making the point that he who ignores the spiritual also views nature from too restricted a viewpoint. His vision of the universe is too circumscribed, it is spectral. He who is dominated by his 'Reasoning Power', by his Spectre,

... the Great Selfhood
Satan, Worship'd as God by the Mighty Ones of the Earth[138]

is too blinkered to see the Divine in Man. He sees man as being no more than 'a worm seventy inches long'[139] and 'of sixty winters creeping on the dusky ground'.[140]

All that Urizenic man can perceive and conceive is a fallen state of man and hence also of society. He negates the 'Eternal Man'. Selfhood, rooted in a mentality which can only accept a knowledge of man which is based on the impressions received by the five physical senses, is the enemy of Imagination. Self-centredness, inhibiting the creative imagination, overshadows the inner light of social conscience.

The cultivation of Imagination, of spiritual freedom, is the very foundation and prerequisite for the bringing into being of the living principles of equality in the sphere of social and political life and of fraternity in the economic sphere. We have seen that, for Blake, Jesus Christ is the Imagination, the 'Poetic Genius':

*Vala is the Goddess of Nature.

He who Loves feels love descend into him & if he has wisdom may perceive it is from the Poetic Genius, which is the Lord.[141]

But the tragedy of mankind has been that the Poetic Genius has been suppressed by the influence of abstract philosophies. When Blake attacks abstract philosophy — the philosophy of 'Reason' — he attacks the system which uses religion and reason as a 'Net' for its interests. The reasoner perverts truth by abstract arguments. For Blake truth is concrete and ought to be sought not in abstract ideas but in everyday life, in, for instance, human relationships. Imagination, the Poetic Genius, is 'Truth' and the uniting principle of humanity, but Urizenic reasoning, the 'sting of the serpent',[142] is 'Error', which divides humanity. Urizen propagates Ratio, that is, a limited system, an ideology, and hence division. He moulds minds and limits them to natural impression, to, for instance, a Lockian materialistic universe based on a philosophy of the five senses. Blake regards this 'Reason' as 'Human Illusion':

> Till his Brain in a rock & his Heart
> In a fleshy slough formed four rivers
> Obscuring the immense Orb of fire
> Flowing down into night: till a Form
> Was completed, a Human Illusion
> In darkness and deep clouds involv'd.[143]

Urizenic man, 'Natural Man' — 'clouded' over by his limited impressions and separated from the Totality on his island of self-centredness — cannot know life. To him we could say, with Blake,

> Return, O wanderer, when the day of clouds is o'er.[144]

In a society, in a world, created by Urizen, Man is enmeshed in 'the same dull round over again'[145], in the revolving world of matter with its mechanistic system of cause and effect, in that which Blake, in *The Four Zoas*, calls the 'Circle of Destiny'.[146]

Los, Imagination, sees that

> Sick'ning lies the Fallen Man, his head sick, his heart faint:
> ...
> Refusing to behold the Divine Image which all behold
> And live thereby, he is sunk down into a deadly sleep.
> But we, immortal in our own strength, survive by stern debate
> Till we have drawn the Lamb of God into a mortal form,
> And that he must be born is certain, for One must be All
> And comprehend within himself all things both small & great,

Los then goes on to say:

> Tho' in the Brain of Man we live & in his circling Nerves,
> Tho' this bright world of all our joy is in the Human Brain.[147]

In the Fall, Urizen and 'all his Hosts' have hung 'their immortal lamps'[148] there, that is, 'in the Brain of Man'.

Here Los is claiming that the brain — usually associated with Urizen — really belongs to him. Now, Los is generally spoken of by Blake as a heart-force. Perhaps we may understand what Blake is saying in these three lines somewhat as follows. The 'Brain of Man' in which the heart also speaks is creative and dynamic. It animates, gives life with its joy and energy. Such thinking is alive and in tune with life when it is imbued with forces of the heart, with the energy of Imagination, of, ultimately, Christ. Such living thinking is 'social' thinking. It embraces humanity — 'One must be All'. Thinking imbued with forces of life, with forces of the heart, is the very life's blood of a true social conscience and the creative foundation of universal brotherhood. But, when Urizen hangs his lamps in the brain, abstract and negative teachings of doubt take the life out of thinking, and one dire consequence is that human creativity, human values, human dignity, are underrated, or, rather, suppressed. A lifeless, suppressed form of society then comes into being in which man leads a spiritually static, uncreative form of life. However, Los will 'survive by stern debate', he will take up the challenge and 'not cease from Mental Fight'.[149]

Imagination, true, Real Man, is open to the Infinite. Natural man, False Man, is bound and closed in by the finite, by the ratio. The man of ratio, Natural Man, has fallen from Imagination, turned his back on the Divine Vision. Concerned solely with material things — with power and wealth — he is guided by self-indulgence, by his selfhood, which is opposed to a living community of creative human beings. Natural Man cannot, in his own self-interest, encourage and endorse universal brotherhood. He is opposed to the wider humanity envisaged by Imagination. Social conscience is for him, in the final analysis, no more than an illusory virtue. Concerned only with the physical world he does not recognize the existence of a living, creative soul, of a spiritual essence — either in himself or in others. Hence, for Blake, 'The Natural Body is an Obstruction to the Soul or Spiritual Body.'[150]

In a letter to Dr Trusler, Blake writes:

I know that This World is a World of imagination & Vision. I see Every thing I paint In this World, but Every body does not see alike. To the Eyes of a Miser a Guinea is more beautiful than the Sun, and a bag worn with the use of Money has more beautiful proportions than a Vine filled with Grapes ... As a man is, So He Sees. As the Eye is formed, such are its Powers.[151]

The miser has not only destroyed the Real Man in himself, but, implicitly, through the selfish use of his fortune, also in others. Such a self-centred interest is, in Blake's view, evil. False man, Urizenic man, negates and restrains the desires, will and imagination in his fellow men. The desire and will of false man are evil because they are are directed negatively against others. Urizenic man petrifies 'all the Human Imagination into rock & sand'.[152]

In his *Descriptive Catalogue of Pictures*, written in 1809, Blake speaks of 'The Horse of Intellect' which is 'leaping from the cliffs of Memory and Reasoning; it is a barren Rock; it is also called the Barren Waste of Locke and Newton'.[153] Thus we see Blake again attacking Locke and Newton. Locke's conception of the mind as a *tabula rasa* and Newton's of a mechanical universe both suppress creative imagination. Both Locke and Newton are false, Urizenic men.

All men for Blake are born with imaginative power and are potentially creative. But their imaginative power and potential creativity are 'killed' by the abstract teachings of Urizenic reason.

> The idiot Reasoner laughs at the Man of Imagination.[154]

The 'idiot Reasoner' not only laughs but would suppress the creations of Imagination wherever they may appear. For instance, because Imagination sees human values to be far more important than all abstract moral laws it is regarded as being the enemy of established systems and ruling interests — of King, Church and State.

Blake's Milton, going through the process of regeneration, has gained the insight that annihilation of every aspect of the selfhood is essential if spiritual freedom is to be gained:

> All that can be annihilated must be annihilated
> That the Children of Jerusalem may be saved from slavery.
> There is a Negation, & there is a Contrary:[155]
> The Negation must be destroy'd to redeem the Contraries.
> The Negation is the Spectre, the Reasoning Power in Man:
> This is a false body, an Incrustation over my Immortal
> Spirit, a Selfhood which must be put off & annihilated away.

To cleanse the Face of my Spirit by Self-examination,
To bathe in the Waters of Life, to wash off the Not Human,
I come in Self-annihilation & the grandeur of Inspiration,
To cast off Rational Demonstration by Faith in the Saviour,
To cast off Bacon, Locke & Newton from Albion's covering,
To take off his filthy garments & clothe him with Imagination,
....
To cast off the idiot Questioner who is always questioning
But never capable of answering, who sits with a sly grin
Silent plotting when to question, like a thief in a cave.
Who publishes doubt & calls it knowledge ...[156]

'To cast off Bacon, Locke & Newton' is to become free of 'doubt' and the
'idiot Reasoner', the 'idiot Questioner', the brooder who squats in Ulro,
in the delusions of a Urizenic, rationalistic system and materialistic
science. It is 'the idiot Questioner', always asking but never able to
answer, whose doubtings emasculate creative activity. In these lines
Blake is clearly once again opposing those who base their so-called
'knowledge' solely on their limited natural impressions formed by the
five senses. These natural impressions, which clothe false man, are the
'filthy garments'. We need to note here that Blake does not, of course,
deny the significance of the earth, of the material, phenomenal world. If
he did, he would not have written *Milton*. He has John Milton go through
the process of reincarnation on earth because earth is the only place where
'Heaven' can be actualized. What Blake attacks is the rationalistic
materialist who denies the reality of such a Heaven. Many passages in
Milton show clearly enough that Blake saw the phenomenal world as both
impressive and beautiful. But it must be subservient to man's spiritual
aspirations, not quell them. Real Man, Christ in Man, inspires others by
his own freedom from subservience to that which is transitory, to that
which is 'natural' as distinct from spiritual. The man of one-sided reason
sees only the 'natural' in Nature. Like fallen Albion, seduced by Vala, the
Goddess of Nature, the soul of the rationalist is 'melted away, inwoven
with the Veil' of Vala,[157] he perceives only the veil of matter which covers
all reality. True Man, Imagination, sees through the veil and perceives
the eternal spiritual reality. He receives inspiration for his creative energy
from that reality. Imagination perceives his reality in Nature and in
humanity. It is the creative imagination which animates Nature and
endows it with identity and reality. Indeed 'To the Eyes of the Man of
Imagination, Nature is Imagination itself.'[158]

Imagination in man creates the meadows, the woods, the towns through which he roams and the people he knows and loves.

To the 'Eyes of the Man of Imagination' a true society, a society in which a social conscience born of free will and free love prevails, is also Imagination itself. In a society where there is division between people, where tyranny of any kind rules, there Imagination cannot thrive, there universal brotherhood can find no fertile soil in which to grow.

For Blake it is axiomatic that all men share one great divine gift, the 'Poetic Genius', Imagination, but do not have equally favourable opportunities to develop and live it. This, as we have seen, is not solely due to social conditions, nor indeed to lack of material resources, but, above all, to a system of philosophical thought and religious dogma, which deprives man of his inner creative energy and makes him less than man. Falsehood breeds falsehood. Neither tyrant nor slave live as true men. To mould others in accordance with one's own principles is to act and think in accordance with the Urizenic principle, which 'unknown, abstracted,/Brooding, secret'[159] decrees:

> One command, one joy, one desire,
> One curse, one weight, one measure,
> One King, one God, one Law.[160]

A formula which allows for no free expression and development of the 'Poetic Genius' within each and every human being.

In *An Island In The Moon*,[161] one of Blake's most satirical works, he expresses his concern in regard to the spiritual and material poverty of his fellow men — 'The hungry poor enter'd the hall'.[162] He attacks clerical authority — 'a person may be as good at home';[163] war —

> A crowned king
> On a white horse sitting,
> With his trumpet sounding,
> And banners flying:[164]

and the injustices perpetrated in the name of justice — it is 'a shameful thing that acts of parliament should be in a free state'.[165]

In this early work Blake also attacks abstract philosophical systems, which have no relation to human life. His satire is clearly directed against the abstract and 'dead' mechanistic philosophy as typified by Newton and Locke:

> To be, or not to be
> Of great capacity,

Like Sir Isaac Newton,
Or Locke, or Doctor South,
Or Sherlock upon death?
I'd rather be Sutton.[166]

For he did build a house
For aged men & youth,
With walls of brick & stone.
He furnish'd it within
With whatever he could win,
And all his own.

He drew out of the Stocks
His money in a box,
And sent his servant
To Green the Bricklayer
And to the Carpenter:
He was so fervent.

The chimneys were three score,
The windows many more,
And for convenience
He sinks & gutters made,
And all the way he pav'd
To hinder pestilence.

Was not this a good man,
Whose life was but a span,
Whose name was Sutton,—
As Locke, or Doctor South,
Or Sherlock upon Death,
Or Sir Isaac Newton?[167]

Thomas Sutton was a man of creative imagination imbued with a true social conscience. With fervour he gave all he had for others.

When Blake attacks Newton, Locke and Bacon he is, in reality, attacking the social system which used such mechanistic philosophies to justify its ideology. As we have seen on several occasions, it is both the materialistic philosopher and the priesthood of orthodoxy which are targets for Blake's social criticism. The former makes Imagination subservient to visible, transitory nature through deism, natural religion, and the latter imprisons Imagination by preaching belief in a transcendent (remote), invisible, impersonal, abstract God. Instead of drawing attention to the spiritual experience 'within', it is directed to a world of non-experience 'without'.

In *An Island In the Moon* Blake also satirizes the priesthood which after reducing innocent children to poverty by its worldly power and teaching of self-denial, hypocritically offers pity and charity. This satire is expressed most forcibly in the song sung by 'Mr Obtuse Angle'.[168] It is the first draft of the poem 'Holy Thursday' later included in *Songs of Innocence* (see p. 119). Here innocence is sullied and suppressed by False Man, who encourages and supports poverty in others, that is, poverty of soul, not merely material poverty through such evils as the exploitation of labour.

In the poem *Tiriel* (written about 1789), Blake gives us a picture of the perversion and suppression of true innocence, of creative and selfless Imagination, in a passage of striking and horrific imagery:

The child springs from the womb; the father ready stands to form
The infant head, while the mother idle plays with her dog on her couch:
The young bosom is cold for lack of mother's nourishment, & milk
Is cut from the weeping mouth: with difficulty & pain
The little lids are lifted & the little nostrils open'd:
The father forms a whip to rouze the sluggish senses to act
And scourges off all youthful fancies from the new-born man.
Then walks the weak infant in sorrow, compell'd to number footsteps
Upon the sand ...[169]

Once the innocent child's mind is conditioned and limited by the father — by rigid authority — then creative and selfless imagination must inevitably remain undeveloped and passive. Creative imagination and self-lessness, two essential elements in an all-embracing social conscience and the foundation of true innocence, of universal brotherhood, are nipped in the bud, have their wings clipped, by fallen, ignorant and blind reason.[170]

Since the true teachings of Christ are not being put into practice, Blake exhorts his fellow men to join him in 'Mental Fight', in building the prophetic community Jerusalem. This is the message, too, of the prose preface to *Milton*. Blake calls upon 'Young Men of the New Age' to renew the arts, to renew creative and imaginative living in Britain and to combat those who would 'depress Mental & prolong Corporeal War',[171] to combat those who are ignorant and spiritually blind. This idea of the spread of prophetic, imaginative vision to the whole of mankind is the major theme of Blake's epic poem *Jerusalem*:

I will not cease from Mental Fight,
Nor shall my Sword sleep in my hand
Till we have built Jerusalem
In England's green & pleasant land.[172]

This is the antithesis of John Milton's resignation in *Paradise Regained* which is imbued with the moral that we must endure oppression until such time as God sees fit to intervene:

> What wise and valient man would seek to free
> These thus degenerat, by themselves enslav'd,
> Or could of inward slaves make outward free?[173]

Milton's Paradise is a product of his 'limited' and passive remote God, but Blake's God is 'unlimited'. He is ceaselessly creative and active, and moreover, He 'only Acts & Is in existing beings or Men'.[174] Blake, in short, sees it as being the responsibility of men and women and not of a transcendent God to transform evil into good, oppression into freedom. In *Jerusalem*, Blake calls on us to exert our own divine and creative energies to save ourselves, to save Fallen Man. Earlier on in this chapter we saw that in response to the cry:

> O God of Albion, descend! deliver Jerusalem from the Oaken Groves!

Los, the Imagination, answers, in fury,

> Why stand we here trembling around
> Calling on God for help, and not ourselves, in whom God dwells,
> Stretching a hand to save the falling Man?

Milton was of the view that only Divine Providence could change existing systems. Blake is clearly critical of a philosophy of 'Providence'. He repudiates such a philosophy and its assumption that only a super-natural power can change things for the good in human affairs. He sees that it is used to endorse the existing conditions — social, economic, and so forth — by accepting a preordained hierarchical structure. Moreover, and, for Blake, significantly, it obviates the moral need for men to assume a living and progressive responsibility for their less fortunate fellow men. Such a preordained, rigid outlook on human affairs is the product of a static social system and of a limited (Urizenic) and passive education which finds endorsement in Lockian philosophy.

Throughout his life Blake challenges the whole system of thinking and morality which has been created in the 'Abyss of the Spectre',[175] of the five senses. We can hardly reiterate often enough that, to Blake, any knowledge built on limited sense-impressions cannot be true knowledge. It is the 'passive' thinker, or materialist, who has built the 'Looms of Generation'.[176]

The 'Looms of Generation' represent the philosophical and religious systems of those who formulate sociological ideologies and moral laws from their limited outlook:

> Ah weak & wide astray! Ah shut in narrow doleful form,
> Creeping in reptile flesh upon the bosom of the ground!
> The Eye of Man a little narrow orb, clos'd up & dark,
> Scarcely beholding the great light, conversing with the Void,
> The Ear a little shell, in small volutions shutting out
> All melodies & comprehending only Discord and Harmony;
> The Tongue a little moisture fills, a little food it cloys,
> A little sound it utters & its cries are faintly heard,
> Then brings forth Moral Virtue the cruel Virgin Babylon.
> Can such an Eye judge of the stars? & looking thro' its tubes
> Measure the sunny rays that point their spears on Udanadan?
> Can such an Ear, fill'd with the vapours of the yawning pit,
> Judge of the pure melodious harp struck by a hand divine?
> Can such closed Nostrils feel a joy? or tell of autumn fruits
> When grapes & figs burst their covering to the joyful air?
> Can such a Tongue boast of the living waters? or take in
> Ought but the Vegetable Ratio & loathe the faint delight?
> Can such gross Lips perceive? alas, folded within themselves
> They touch not ought, but pallid turn & tremble at every wind.[177]

The answer to all these questions is clearly 'No'. When man is confined within the 'Vegetable Ratio', that is, within a rational system derived from evidence provided by the perceptions of the five senses, then the 'Eye' of Imagination becomes blind. It is blind when man is confined within the 'Ratio' of good and evil, or love of God and love of woman. This was the mental state of John Milton. His God, set against the love of woman, is, to Blake, non-existence or 'Void'. For Blake it is axiomatic that 'Every thing that lives is holy.'[178] In contrast, the negation of living things is 'unholy' and cruel. This cruelty is peculiar to Babylon, Jerusalem's opponent. Closely associated with Babylon is Rahab, who symbolizes the false church of this world, which, therefore, is also the opponent of Jerusalem — and hence the crucifier of Christ.[179] Babylon negates and restrains Imagination, Christ, by its strict and rigid moral laws. Jerusalem is the city where Imagination is free.

Abstract, strict and rigid moral laws — the 'Net' of Urizen's natural religion — are alien to and destructive of human life. Blake notes that all institutions which are dominated by Urizenic/Satanic systems of thought

— such as the Church schools and universities — teach passive obedience to those who decree what human behaviour and effort should be: 'Obedience to the Will of the Monopolist is called Virtue, and the really Industrious, Virtuous & Independent … is driven out.'[180]

Such a state of silent obedience in the face of the Urizenic/Satanic system is the state of 'Single Vision & Newton's sleep'.[181] It is a state of 'fatal Slumber' from which Blake urges us to 'rouze ourselves'.[182]

Blake, addressing Satan through Los, exclaims:

> If you account it Wisdom when you are angry to be silent and
> Not to shew it, I do not account that Wisdom, but Folly.[183]

In *Milton* Blake contends that any discussion about wisdom and knowledge, including religion and philosophy, which does not take conscientious cognizance of the social and human realities of life, is like 'conversing with the Void'.[184] Such a 'lifeless', abstract discussion, an invention of Urizen, denies a 'Conscience in Man'. A society which is based on the 'Single vision' of 'Bacon, Newton, Locke', who 'Deny a Conscience in Man',[185] is a spiritual 'Void outside of Existence'.[186]

Jerusalem, the regenerated human society, is true 'Existence'; it is not merely existence, liberty, in a socio-political sense. Indeed, as has been emphasized already, socio-political liberty is secondary to, or, differently expressed, is an effect of spiritual liberty. The regenerative force in the creation of Jerusalem is the creative imagination. Spiritual liberty, Jerusalem, is unthinkable and unattainable without Imagination, which, again as already stressed, is a catalystic element in the process of giving life to a true social conscience, which embedded in selfless and all-embracing love, in the spirit of Christ, is a prerequisite for the creation of universal brotherhood.

In the creative act, Imagination is the complete liberty of the spirit: 'Imagination is surrounded by the daughters of Inspiration, who in the aggregate are call'd Jerusalem.'[187]

Where selfless love, true social conscience, and brotherhood become a way of life, there Jerusalem exists. In such a society man is fully conscious of the truth that — in contrast to John Milton's heaven-dwelling God, outside human experience: 'All Deities reside in the Human Breast.'[188]

Of Milton's religion Blake writes in *The Marriage of Heaven and Hell*: 'in Milton, the Father is Destiny, the Son a Ratio of the five senses, & the Holy-ghost Vacuum!'[189] The world of rationalism is governed by a fatal and remorseless destiny. The God of natural religion is the God of the world of space and time, it is a world which functions in accordance with strict and rigid calculable laws. In this rationalist world, a world unreal to Blake, there can be no question of creative and free will. Man is no more than an insignificant cog in a vast machine. He is a cog to which a true social conscience is clearly not attributable. For Blake man's 'true destiny is to realize the royalty of his own nature'.[190]

Any 'Ratio of the five senses', that is, any 'rationale', any logical abstraction derived, hypothetically, from what the physical senses observe, and any spiritual 'Vacuum', 'Unbelief', as to the existence of the Holy Ghost, of the divine in man, go hand in hand with man's total reliance on 'the Vegetated Mortal Eye's perverted & single vision'.[191] In such a man the 'Eye of Imagination' is blind and fettered. The power of Poetic Genius, of Imagination, is perverted by abstract reasoning which sees only the 'Ratio', and when Imagination is thus perverted man is divorced from life. He falls.

The struggle between Real Man, the Imagination, and False Man, the Ratio, runs, as a main theme, through *The Four Zoas, Milton*, and *Jerusalem*. There are two paths open to man. He can either help build the path which leads to Jerusalem, to true brotherhood of man, or tread the outworn path trod by those who accept analytical reason as man's supreme faculty — as Milton did, for instance — and the postulation of an inaccessible and impassive God. This is the path which leads to 'Nobodaddy', the false God of this world.

> Why art thou silent & invisible,
> Father of Jealousy?
> Why dost thou hide thyself in clouds
> From every searching Eye?
>
> Why darkness & obscurity
> In all thy words & laws,
> That none dare eat the fruit but from
> The wily serpents jaws?[192]

The resemblance of 'Nobodaddy' to Urizen, the God of this world, is obvious.

The activity of building the path which leads to Jerusalem implies love of humanity and of the world in which man undergoes his spiritual education. John Milton, as an example of the rationalist, attempts to cast out his selfhood by denouncing love of the world and taking refuge in his abstract mental deities. But, for Blake, selfhood is not overcome and transcended by denouncing love of the world and humanity. Indeed, he sees that the 'idiot Reasoner'[193] not only fails to overcome his selfhood but becomes even more enmeshed in it.

To separate oneself from the trials and tribulations of active life in the human world is to create 'Selfhood' which, spiritually, is a state of death.[194] To 'murder the Divine Humanity'[195] in man is to fall into the sleep of Newton's 'single vision'.

Blake, speaking through the redeemed Imagination of John Milton, through the true poet, sees that selfhood, Satan, 'evil', 'the State of Death & not a Human existence',[196] has been imposed on man. Denouncing the moral laws of Church and priesthood as 'Satan's holiness' he says:

> Satan! my Spectre! I know my power thee to annihilate
> And be a greater in thy place & be thy Tabernacle,
> A covering for thee to do thy will, till one greater comes
> And smites me as I smote thee & becomes my covering.
> Such are the laws of thy false Heav'ns; but the Laws of Eternity
> Are not such; know thou, I come to Self Annihilation.
> Such are the Laws of Eternity, that each shall mutually
> Annihilate himself for others' good, as I for thee.
> Thy purpose & the purpose of thy Priests & of thy Churches
> Is to impress on men the fear of death, to teach
> Trembling & fear, terror, constriction, abject selfishness.
> Mine is to teach Men to despise death & to go on
> In fearless majesty annihilating Self, laughing to scorn
> Thy Laws & terrors, shaking down thy Synagogues as webs.
> I come to discover before Heav'n & Hell the Self righteousness
> In all its Hypocritic turpitude, opening to every eye
> These wonders of Satan's holiness, shewing to the Earth
> The Idol Virtues of the Natural Heart, & Satan's Seat,
> Explore in all its Selfish Natural Virtue & put off
> In Self annihilation all that is not of God alone,
> To put off Self & all I have, ever and ever. Amen.[197]

The freed Imagination revolts against, and reveals the true nature of, the systems of thought which teach men 'trembling and fear'. To inculcate fear of death, fear of any kind, is to emasculate man, to deprive him of his creative energy. Such a man is quite incapable of annihilating 'himself for others' good'. He is forced into the dark cavern of the struggle for self-survival. For him a social conscience is meaningless. In him only the 'Natural Heart' can speak. The 'Natural Heart' — a Pauline expression

(1 Cor 15:39–49) — is the heart of man in this material world, out of touch with eternity.[198]

From the viewpoint of Imagination, the Church and State, who teach self-sacrifice and 'negation' of the world, are the real 'selfhood' and negator of human existence. The churches, synagogues of Satan, fail completely in their spiritual duty. The Church and State represent systems of thought which 'impress on men the fear of death'. But Imagination, Poetic Genius, Christ in Man, the Real Man, teaches 'Men to despise death'. The laws of false heaven are not the laws of eternity. That 'each shall mutually/Annihilate himself for others' good' is the religion of universal brotherhood (see pp. 351–2). Moreover, it is the religion of Imagination because it recognizes that death is no more than an episode in Life, a state through which one passes, awakening to a life of continuous spiritual creativity.

Blake opens the first chapter of *Jerusalem* with the lines:

Of the Sleep of Ulro! and of the passage through
Eternal Death! and of the awakening to Eternal Life.

This theme calls me in sleep night after night, & ev'ry morn
Awakes me at sun-rise; then I see the Saviour over me
Spreading his beams of love & dictating the words of this mild song.[199]

Towards the end of *Jerusalem* Blake gives us a more comprehensive vision of the true religion than in the lines from Milton quoted above:

Albion said: 'O Lord, what can I do? My Selfhood cruel
Marches against thee, deceitful, from Sinai & from Edom
Into the Wilderness of Judah, to meet thee in his pride.
I behold the Visions of my deadly Sleep of Six Thousand Years
Dazling around thy skirts like a Serpent of precious stones & gold
I know it is my Self, O my Divine Creator & Redeemer.'

Jesus replied: 'Fear not Albion: unless I die thou canst not live;
But if I die I shall rise again & thou with me.
This is Friendship & Brotherhood: without it Man is Not.'
...
Albion reply'd: 'Cannot Man exist without Mysterious
Offering of Self for Another? is this Friendship & Brotherhood?'
...
Jesus said: 'Wouldst thou love one who never died
For thee, or ever die for one who had not died for thee?
And if God dieth not for Man & giveth not himself
Eternally for Man, Man could not exist; for Man is Love
As God is Love; every kindness to another is a little Death

In the Divine Image, nor can Man exist but by Brotherhood'.[200]

Elsewhere in these pages we discuss the importance Blake attaches to 'Contraries' and noted the distinction he makes between 'Contraries' and 'Negations'.[201] In *Jerusalem* Los states:

> Negations are not Contraries: Contraries mutually Exist;
> But Negations Exist Not. Exceptions & Objections & Unbeliefs
> Exist not, ...
> If thou separate from me, thou art a Negation, a meer [sic.]
> Reasoning & Derogation from me, an Objecting & cruel Spite
> And Malice & Envy ...[202]

The separation of men from each other is caused by the 'Negation', which is the Spectre, the 'Reasoning Power in Man'.[203] The 'Negation' is a

> ... false Body, an Incrustation over my Immortal
> Spirit, a Selfhood which must be put off & annihilated alway.[204]

A Urizenic society is a society of 'Negations'. One limited viewpoint, interest or desire negates the other. There is no spiritual communion between men. The emphasis is on satisfying the needs of the selfhood. In a society of 'Negations' neither baptism nor communion have any real meaning.[205] These two sacraments are reduced to mere repetitious rituals and their original meanings are destroyed (see pp. 347–8). Blake understands them as complementary: the casting away, washing away, of Error and the acceptance of Truth. Communion, the Lord's Supper, symbolizes the brotherhood of man in the body of Christ. Through Imagination we can experience true Communion, we can experience ourselves as one with 'the Divine Humanity':

> The Eternal Body of Man is the Imagination, that is, God himself,
> The Divine Body, Jesus: we are his Members.[206]

In a Urizenic society the Imagination, Christ, the Divine Body, does not exist. To experience the inner meaning of the Last Supper would be tantamount to bringing about the destruction of such a society. Social conscience and universal brotherhood are anathema to a Urizenic society.

In Jerusalem, on the other hand, where 'Contraries mutually exist' and where the selfhood is annihilated and each man exists for the other, there every thought and action is grounded in a loving social conscience and universal brotherhood is alive. In such a brotherhood every man and woman would be able to say, with Paul, 'Not I, but the Christ in me'.

Jerusalem can be manifested only through the selfless love of the individual for the 'All'.

BLAKE'S SYMBOLISM

Our considerations in this chapter have a twofold aim: to characterize — as distinct from define — some of Blake's more important symbols and, through quotations and brief expositions, to acquaint the reader not too familiar with Blake's work with some of his major ideas and themes.[1]

Blake creates his own mythological figures — Los, Urizen, Enitharmon, Orc, and so on — for two main reasons both of which are aimed at rousing us from the lethargy of habit and convention, at making us consciously experience, rather than 'sleepily' nod acquiescence: he either asks us to avoid the associations of traditional mythology and thus clear our minds of preconceived ideas and comprehension, or he asks us to look at an ancient and accepted principle from an entirely new point of view. We shall have occasion to discuss several of Blake's main mythological figures in greater detail in later chapters; here we shall be mainly concerned with a number of his most frequently used symbols.

Blake's symbols, and his use of them, demand constant inner alertness on our part. We find that it is necessary to oust preconceptions and 'cleanse our organs of perception'.

Let us consider a typical example.[2]

When, in the eighteenth century, 'thunder' was mentioned in relation to God's wrath, both the speaker/writer and the listener/reader would instinctively accept the justice of God's wrathful thunder. Such a conception had been drummed into men's minds since their early childhood. If, on the other hand, the speaker did not accept the justice of the Divine Thunder of Wrath, then he would have to explain to the listener why he did not. In the process of doing so, the immediacy — and the point — of the symbolism would be lost. Here, in a nutshell, is Blake's dilemma. For him, too, thunder is a symbol of God's wrath, but it is Urizen who is his god of thunder, and Blake is far from accepting that Urizen's thunder is divinely just, for Urizen summarizes the basic philosophy and attitude of mind with which he, Blake, identifies many of the evils of the Western world. He is the tyrannical, sullen, self-contemplating, avenging deity, the inscriber of the law of stone, the law of the Mosaic 'thou shalt not'. Blake's dilemma is twofold: on the one hand, he cannot cause disruption and disintegration of the living relationships and effects with which he is concerned by interpolating rational propositions and logical arguments in regard to the nature of Urizen's thunder; and, on the other hand, he needs the impact of his symbolism to be immediate. Above all he needs us, the readers, to apprehend what he means by, say, the thunder of Urizen, by an imaginative and creative response. He asks us, in short, to re-create the feeling of outrage, the sense of sorrow, the experience of barrenness and desolation, and so on, which his soul, as the creator, has undergone. He appeals, of course, to our imagination, not to our reason. It is our business, too, to create, not to 'Reason and Compare'.[3]

Blake's dilemma is ours, too. In all likelihood both his mythological figures and his symbolism appear to us at first to be unfathomable — not at all intuitively, immediately, understood. Neither is familiar to us from our conventional upbringing. Nevertheless, if we follow Blake, with an open mind and senses, we do gradually begin to comprehend more and more intuitively the complex content of both. Blake helps us towards such comprehension. By constant repetition, in a variety of contexts, he helps us 'cleanse' our organs of inner perception so that an eventually immediate recognition of, and rapport with, his symbols and mythological figures can emerge. However, we need to be inwardly alert, for his mythological figures may undergo changes from passage to passage, from poem to poem. This should come as no surprise, for Blake does not present us with abstract ideas, concepts, petrified, once and for all, into Urizenic moulds, but with living ideas and principles, either in different phases of growth and inner development — sometimes progressive, sometimes retrogressive, but always changing; or this or that idea, principle, is being considered from a different point of view. Blake also helps us to understand and experience what his major mythological figures mean by substantiating the meaning in his poetic symbolism. Admittedly we need to rely, once again, on our imagination and not our reason, because we cannot, in Urizenic fashion, formulate a definition once and for all and apply it rigidly wherever a symbol occurs. The meaning of a symbol changes according to the slant of the poet's approach. A qualifying phrase or situation may also change its meaning.

With this warning in mind against any attempt to 'rigidify' Blake's symbolism we shall now look at some of his frequently used symbols.[4]

First let us consider some of the symbols commonly associated with matter and, by Blakean analogy, with the unimaginative life.

'Non-entity' is a frequently used term and conception with Blake and means the final stage in the descent to non-existence. He often implies that 'non-entity' and non-existence are synonymous. 'Non-entity' represents an almost complete absence of definite form:

> Jerusalem is scatter'd abroad like a cloud of smoke thro' non-entity.[5]

Other terms which Blake uses frequently to describe this 'cloudy' state — which sometimes approaches non-being — are 'Shadow', 'Spectre', 'form of vegetation' (that is, the world of nature as distinct from that of spirit), 'night of oblivion', and 'negation', the latter being, it would seem, almost synonymous with 'non-entity'. In *Jerusalem* 'negation' is described as being without organization,[6] formless. In the conclusion to *Milton* Blake describes the 'negation' as 'the Spectre, the Reasoning Power in Man';[7] 'Reasoning Power' being understood to be inductive reasoning as distinct from intuitive apprehension.

'Generation' is the comprehensive term most frequently used by Blake to describe the earth, earthly existence, and ideas associated with that existence. 'Generation' signifies the whole of the sense-perceptible, phenomenal world, which is a symbol of the 'incorporeal, invisible' spiritual world (just as time is the symbol of Eternity).

When Blake depicts the fall of Ahania — Urizen's Emanation (see pp. 284-7) — he associates this world of generation with the cave, darkness, and non-entity:

> Into the Caverns of the Grave & places of Human seed
> Where the impressions of Despair & Hope enroot for ever:
> A world of Darkness. Ahania fell far into Non-Entity.[8]

The symbol of the cave is first used in *The French Revolution* (1791), where Blake describes a rosy future when man will 'raise his darken'd limbs out of the caves of night' so that, as a result, 'his eyes and his heart expand'.[9] In the fourth 'Memorable Fancy' of *The Marriage of Heaven and Hell* an angel takes Blake to see his 'eternal lot':

he took me thro' a stable & thro' a church & down into the church vault, at the end of which was a mill: thro' the mill we went, and came to a cave: down the winding cavern we groped our tedious way, till a void boundless as a nether sky appear'd beneath us & we held by the roots of trees and hung over this immensity.[10]

The 'cave', the 'void boundless', that is, the indefiniteness, and the 'roots of trees', all are symbolic of the material world.

In the *Visions of the Daughters of Albion*, Blake speaks of 'religious caves',[11] clearly signifying that the material world has darkened and imprisoned the creative imagination. The cave here is a symbol of man's mental limitations.

Beginning with *The Four Zoas* Blake's symbolic employment of the 'cave' is almost without exception with reference to the material world or the material life. In association with the 'cave' or 'cavern' other material symbols are frequently alluded to or named — 'rock', 'cloud', 'tree', 'ice', and so forth. Indeed, in the three long Prophetic Books, *The Four Zoas, Milton* and *Jerusalem*, Blake often piles up symbolical meanings. A striking example of this is in the First Book of *Jerusalem*. After discussing the 'Mundane Shell' (see pp. 191–4), the 'Vegetative Universe', and the 'abstract Voids between the Stars' — all connoting materiality — Blake continues:

> There is the Cave, the Rock, the Tree, the Lake of Udan Adan,
> The Forest and the Marsh and the Pits of bitumen deadly,
> The Rocks of solid fire, the Ice valleys ...[12]

The most unusual of these symbols is Udan Adan, the Lake of the Indefinite — the 'indefinite' being a marked characteristic of the material world (see pp. 74–5). Earlier in *Jerusalem*, Blake speaks of 'the deadly deeps of indefinite Udan-Adan'.[13]

Blake frequently uses symbols of the material world to describe a psychological state. For instance:

> Instead of Albion's lovely mountains & the curtains of Jerusalem,
> I see a Cave, a Rock, a Tree deadly and poisonous, unimaginative.[14]

Here the 'mountains' and the 'curtains' represent a spiritual or intuitive apprehension of reality, whereas the 'cave', the 'Rock', and the 'Tree', represent varying degrees of the lack of imagination.

One of Blake's many striking passages which portray a psychological state in concrete imagery is his description of Los's search through the bosom of fallen Albion:

Fearing that Albion should turn his back against the Divine Vision,
Los took his globe of fire to search the interiors of Albion's
Bosom, in all the terrors of friendship entering the caves
Of despair & death to search the tempters out, walking among
Albion's rocks & precipices, caves of solitude & dark despair.[15]

Here the material symbols represent the mental state of the degenerated man, Albion, who has fallen away from Vision, from the Divine Imagination. The 'globe of fire' by which Los examines Albion's bosom is a symbol of poetry or the creative imagination.

In *Jerusalem* we learn that the average sensual man, Reuben,

... fled with his head downwards among the Caverns
Of the Mundane Shell which froze on all sides ...[16]

The reference to freezing enhances the picture Blake wishes us to have of man's fall into a blind state of inflexibility, into a state where expansion is nullified. The Fall into generation, into the 'grot & grave beneath the Moon, dim region of death',[17] resulted in the narrowing and contracting of man's senses into patterns of thought incapable of expansion, of creative imagination. Elsewhere Blake describes this state metaphorically as a sleep 'in the Cave of Adam'.[18] The 'Cave of Adam', obviously meaning the skull, is the place where Reuben sleeps while his senses are being limited.[19] Blake also resorts to metaphysical terminology, as, for instance, in the following statement:

If Perceptive Organs vary, Objects of Perception seem to vary:
If the Perceptive Organs close, their Objects seem to close also.[20]

As already intimated, the cave is only one of a number of symbols dealing with the restricted and inflexible state of being. Another, of which mention has already been made, is the 'rock' or 'stone'. In *The Book of Urizen* Blake gives us a picture of Urizen — symbolizing both fallen man and the generated earth — as 'laid in a stony sleep'.[21] Blake makes a striking use of the symbols of the 'rock' and the 'cave' in his description of 'the Eternal Man (who) sleeps in the Earth':

... leaning his faded head
Upon the Oozy rock inwrapped with the weeds of death.
His eyes sink hollow in his head, his flesh cover'd with slime
And shrunk up to the bones; alas, that Man should come to this!
His strong bones beat with snows & hid within the caves of night,
Marrowless, bloodless, falling into dust, driven by the winds.
O how the horrors of Eternal Death take hold of Man!
His faint groans shake the caves & issue forth thro' the desolate rocks.[22]

In *The Book of Ahania* Blake uses the 'rock' to symbolize restrictive morality: Urizen poisons 'the rocks with his blood', then smites Fuzon (the spirit of passion) with one of them. After the 'rock' 'enters his bosom' 'it fell upon the Earth,/Mount Sinai in Arabia'[23] where Moses received the restrictive Commandments.

In *Jerusalem* the 'rock' again symbolizes natural religion and natural morality. There we hear that the Sons of Albion, who are waging war against Christ, the Imagination, and against Jerusalem,

... build a stupendous Building on the Plain of Salisbury, with chains
Of rocks round London Stone, of Reasonings, of unhewn Demonstrations
In labyrinthine arches (Mighty Urizen the Architect) thro' which
The Heavens might revolve & Eternity be bound in their chain.
Labour unparallel'd! a wondrous rocky World of cruel destiny,
Rocks piled on rocks reaching the stars, stretching from pole to pole.
The Building is Natural Religion & it's Altars Natural Morality,
A building of eternal death, whose proportions are eternal despair.[24]

Blake often associates the 'rock' with water — another symbol for matter or the generative life:

The Corse* of [Man *del.*] Albion lay on the Rock; the sea of Time and Space
Beat round the Rock in mighty waves ...[25]

A passage in *Jerusalem* links the three material symbols: clouds, rocks and water. After declaring that Albion's, Fallen Man's, 'Starry Wheels' (of inductive reasoning) turn 'every little particle of light & air' into 'a Rock of difficulty & a Cliff/Of black despair', Blake describes 'the narrow Sea between Albion & the Atlantic Continent':

Its waves of pearl become a boundless Ocean bottomless,
Of grey obscurity, fill'd with clouds & rocks & whirling waters.[26]

The 'boundless Ocean ... of grey obscurity' is the Sea of Time and Space, that is, the materialistic barrier and limitation which separates Albion — Fallen Man or, more specifically, men of England — from the imaginative, unrestricted life, here symbolized by the Atlantic Continent. In a later passage in *Jerusalem* Blake uses similar symbolism to show what this restricted life of limited, 'cavern'd' perception has done to England:

You are now shrunk up to a narrow Rock in the midst of the Sea.[27]

* i.e. corpse.

And in another passage he tells us that the 'Sea of Time and Space' has almost engulfed the tiny, limited, 'Urizenic' world of the:

Frozen Sons of ... Bacon, Newton & Locke.[28]

Throughout the three major prophetic books the 'Sea of Time and Space' is consistently symbolic of material life. Water is one of the most constant symbols in Western literature for matter and the materialistic viewpoint. It is an ideal symbol for Blake's purpose. A central image, to which we have already referred, is that of the fallen Albion lying outstretched, 'shrunk up to a narrow rock in the midst of the Sea'. Towards the end of *Jerusalem*, shortly before the 'Breath Divine' awakens him, we find Albion lying asleep and cold on his Rock:

Howling winds cover him: roaring seas dash furious against him:
In the deep darkness broad lightnings glare, long thunders roll.
The weeds of Death inwrap his hands & feet, blown incessant

And wash'd incessant by the for-ever restless sea-waves foaming abroad
Upon the white Rock. England, a Female Shadow, as deadly damps
Of the Mines of Cornwall & Derbyshire, lays upon his bosom heavy,
Moved by the wind in volumes of thick cloud, returning, folding round
His loins & bosom, unremovable by swelling storms & loud rending
Of enraged thunders ...
And the Body of Albion was closed apart from all Nations.

Over them the famish'd Eagle screams on boney Wings, and around
Them howls the Wolf of famine; deep heaves the Ocean black, thundering
Around the wormy Garments of Albion, then pausing in deathlike silence.[29]

This is an imaginative vision of the island, Albion, as Eternal Man, asleep in the midst of waves of materialism; the seaweed round the shores as 'weeds of death'; and the fog and clouds — often considered characteristic of the island — as the 'Female Shadow', that is, the material world oppressing his spirit. The cold and the rock signify that man's senses are no longer responsive to spiritual values.

Whenever Blake uses such terms as 'water', wat'ry way', 'wat'ry world', 'wat'ry shore' symbolically we can be sure that he is concerned with the erroneous path of materialism man has followed. For instance, to emphasize Noah's materialistic state Blake writes metaphorically that 'Noah shrunk beneath the waters'.[30] A description of Enion, the Emanation of Tharmas, associates 'wat'ry' with other terms indicative of indefiniteness: 'shadow', 'mist' and 'air':

> I went to seek the steps
> Of Enion in the gardens, & the shadows compass'd me
> And clos'd me in a wat'ry world of woe when Enion stood
> Trembling before me like a shadow, like a mist, like air.[31]

These lines give us one of Blake's most familiar uses of the water symbol. It indicates illusoriness and instability.

In his later works, the symbol of water sometimes has such derogatory overtones that it appears to connote not merely the illusory natural world but 'evil'. For instance, in *Jerusalem*, speaking of the deteriorating spiritual condition of England, Blake writes:

> In all the dark Atlantic vale down from the hills of Surrey
> A black water accumulates.[32]

When he wishes to indicate that 'evil' days have befallen the whole world, Blake states that 'all the Earth was in a wat'ry deluge.'[33]

Many more passages could be quoted to illustrate the centrality of the symbol of water in Blake's depiction of the phenomenal world and the materialistic way of life. With few exceptions, for example 'the Two Fountains of the River of Life'[34] and 'the Four Rivers of the Water of Life',[35] these symbolic references to water are derogatory. Neither education nor philosophy, both of which Blake sees as being ensnared in the Urizenic net of empirical, materialistic science, escapes his critical eye:

> I turn my eyes to the Schools & Universities of Europe
> And there behold the Loom of Locke, whose Woof rages dire,
> Wash'd by the Water-wheels of Newton: black the cloth
> In heavy wreathes folds over every nation: cruel works
> Of many Wheels I view, wheel without wheel, with cogs tyrannic
> Moving by compulsion each other, not as those in Eden, which
> Wheel within Wheel, in freedom revolve in harmony & peace.[36]

Here again we meet with Blake's criticism of rationalism. 'Locke rationalized thought and freedom; Newton rationalized stars'.[37] The fifth line in the passage just quoted neatly illustrates Blake's notion of 'wheels', a term which he often uses in a derogatory sense as an image of callousness. Here the Newtonian wheel and the Lockian loom are symbols of a mechanical and rationalistic approach to life, an approach which, in fact, kills life! Incidentally, the association between 'water', 'wheel' and 'loom' is obvious: the great wheel is driven by water, and the loom is driven by the wheel. With Blake we may therefore say: 'the Schools & Universities of Europe' are driven by materialism.

The 'Tree', rooted in the phenomenal world, is central to another group of symbols. Not used in a derogatory sense in Blake's early poetry, the tree, especially the oak, particularly in the prophetic books, becomes one of Blake's constantly used representations of the phenomenal world and the materialistic philosophy. From 1793 onwards, the trees and roots are frequently used symbols of the material world or life. In *Jerusalem*, in particular, Blake associates the oak with Druidism:

> O God of Albion, descend! deliver Jerusalem from the oaken Groves![38]

In the address 'To the Jews', Blake writes:

Your Ancestors derived their origin from Abraham, Heber, Shem and Noah, who were Druids, as the Druid Temples (which are the Patriarchal Pillars & Oak Groves) over the whole Earth witness to this day.[39]

By its association with Druidism, a natural religion, the oak becomes a symbol to Blake of everything which he associates with the deists and the adherents, or promulgators, of an inductive or rationalistic rather than an intuitive or imaginative approach to truth. The devotees of materialistic science and philosophy still worshipped in Albion's Oak Groves:[40]

And there they combine into Three Forms named Bacon & Newton & Locke In the Oak Groves of Albion which overspread all the Earth.[41]

Bacon, Newton & Locke, and their followers, are:

> Strucken [*sic*] with Albion's disease, they become what they behold.[42]

This catastrophe has resulted from the narrowing and shrinking of man's perceptions. Blake sees mankind spiritually asleep 'among the Oaks of Albion'.[43]

For Blake, the Groves of Oak have the most terrible associations, for they were sanctuaries of the satanic Druid religion, which perpetrated:

> ... Human Sacrifices
> For Sin in War & in the Druid Temples of the Accuser of Sin beneath
> The Oak Groves of Albion that cover'd the whole Earth beneath his
> Spectre.[44]

Druidism we may note here symbolizes for Blake the religion of Natural Man, deism. It is the whole system of 'Good' and 'Evil', of the accuser of sin, and human sacrifice. One of Blake's several symbols of nature is the serpent. For instance, in *Europe: A Prophecy* (1794) he describes the imaginary temple at Verulam as 'serpent form'd', with 'oak-surrounded pillars'.[45] Moreover, we may note that it was made of 'massy stones ... plac'd in order of the stars'. It was built when the senses of man had been closed, 'barr'd and petrify'd against the infinite'. Then:

> Thought chang'd the infinite to a serpent, ...
> ... and man fled from its face and hid
> In forests of night: then all the eternal forests were divided
> Into earths rolling in circles of space, that like an ocean rush'd
> And overwhelmed all except the finite wall of flesh.
> Then was the serpent temple form'd, image of infinite
> Shut up in finite revolutions, and man became an Angel,[46]
> Heaven a mighty circle turning, God a tyrant crown'd.[47]

Human sacrifice, for Blake, is the keynote of Druidism. Twice he refers to the 'Wicker Man' (a wicker basket in which the victim would be hung over a burning fire) in which human beings, innocent as well as guilty, were burned alive.[48] We need not concern ourselves here with the historical accuracy of Blake's conception of the Druids. We can understand 'human sacrifice' in a more extended sense. For instance, to subject mankind to rationalism to the exclusion of Imagination, to close the senses, to darken the organs of perception, is to sacrifice man's humanity and dignity. The lines preceding those just quoted describe in fact, the closing of the senses. It was then the Druid temple was built:

> ...when the five senses whelm'd
> In deluge o'er the earth-born man; then turn'd the fluxile eyes
> Into two stationary orbs, concentrating all things:
> The ever-varying spiral ascents to the heavens of heavens
> Were bended downward, and the nostrils' golden gates shut,
> Turn'd outward, barr'd and petrify'd against the infinite.[49]

In the first passage quoted above from *Europe* Man flees from the serpent and hides 'in forests of night'. Earlier in the poem Blake speaks of the 'all devouring fiery kings',

> Devouring & devoured, roaming on dark and desolate mountains,
> In forests of eternal death, shrieking in hollow trees.[50]

The association of the 'forests' with 'night' and with 'hollow trees' gives us a clue to their symbolic significance. They are accumulations of error, where spiritual light is gone and spiritual life is lost. Another clue is the imagery of the 'forests of affliction' growing from one 'root of mystery' under Urizen's heel, which spread until:

> He beheld himself compassed round
> And high roofed over with trees.[51]

We then hear that:

> The Tree still grows over the Void
> Enrooting itself all around,
> An endless labyrinth of woe![52]

This shows us what we might call Blake's 'philosophical' conception and source of the symbol of the forest, but, as several Blakean scholars have pointed out, Blake's symbolism is invariably related to social and worldly reality. In this instance, we recall that in Blake's day there were growing objections to the continuing existence of the extensive royal forests and the heavily wooded estates of the landed gentry and aristocracy. These could well have been cleared and handed over to the less privileged and struggling farmers. In 'The Tyger'[53] we can recognize uninhibited spiritual revolt rising among 'eternal forests' of Urizen, the God of this world, the Satanic Holiness, who is 'Oppos'd to Mercy'.[54]

One of Blake's most bitter criticisms of the priesthood, orthodox theology, was that it affected to explain many biblical stories and concepts as 'Mysteries'. Since, for Blake, the things of the spirit were the most real, 'an open secret' (Goethe), he is clearly highly critical of any approach to knowledge and truth which looked upon them as mysteries. Such a religion of reason, conforming to Lockian philosophy, that is, measuring all knowledge by means of sense perception, Blake describes as the 'Tree of Mystery'. As we have already seen, Blake pictures this Tree springing up under the heel of Urizen,[55] the promulgator of rationalism and materialism. In *The Four Zoas* this event is described as follows:

> ... till underneath his heel a deadly root
> Struck thro' the rock, the root of Mystery accursed shooting up
> Branches into the heaven of Los.[56]

These 'branches' take root again wherever they touch until:

> Urizen ... found himself compass'd round
> And high roofed over with trees.[57]

Here Blake is saying that mankind is deluged by and enrooted in a religion which considers all manifestations of divinity, or religious truth, to be mysterious on the grounds that they are not amenable to demonstrations and proof by inductive science. Ritual and dogma, Blake feels, are nothing other than means of perpetuating this error. In *The Four Zoas*, Blake gives us a striking picture of Urizen, sitting on his rock, brooding 'in the deeps beneath the [tree *del.*] roots of Mystery in darkest night'.[58] He commands a temple to be built. This temple is the priesthood's means of keeping secret and hidden the truths which should be known to all men:

> And in the inner part of the Temple, wondrous workmanship,
> They form'd the Secret place, reversing all the order of delight,
> That whosoever enter'd into the temple might not behold
> The hidden wonders, allegoric of the Generations
> Of secret lust, when hid in chambers dark the nightly harlot
> Plays in Disguise in whisper'd hymn & mumbling prayer. The priests
> He ordain'd & Priestesses, cloth'd in disguises beastial,
> Inspiring secrecy; & lamps they bore; intoxicating fumes
> Roll round the Temple; ...[59]

This passage gives us a good idea of Blake's abhorrence, not only of what ritual had done to religion, but also of what 'secrecy' and a restrictive moral code had done to man's attitude towards sexual chastity.[60]

Earlier on it was stated that the symbol of the tree is not used in a derogatory sense in Blake's early poetry. Indeed, Blake's use of the tree symbol (Tree of Mystery, Oak, forests, grove, etc.) affords us a good occasion to emphasize the point made at the beginning of this chapter, namely, that we should not seek to define a symbol precisely and apply that definition wherever the symbol occurs; that, in other words, we should not fall into the trap of binding Blake's symbols into 'petrify'd' conditions, for to do so would be to apply Urizen's mistaken ideal of 'One Law'.[61] We need to remember that the identities of Blake's mythological figures and the significance of his symbols undergo change and development.

So, for instance, the meaning of the tree in 'Love and harmony combine',[62] in *Poetical Sketches* (1769–1778), could hardly be further from Urizen's 'Tree of Mystery'. Indeed, the oak first appears in Blake as the protector of innocence. In 'The Echoing Green':

> Old John, with white hair,
> Does laugh away care,
> Sitting under the oak.[63]

And in 'To Summer'[64] the trees of the forest (here oak trees) are depicted as offering protection against the fiery sun 'beneath our thickest shades'. In both these early poems the joy implicit in the symbol of the tree is obvious. Other examples are found in 'The Couch of Death',[65] 'The Blossom',[66] and 'The Little Black Boy'[67] — in the latter, incidentally, there is a reference to the 'cloud' without the unfavourable symbolic overtones characteristic of Blake's later use of the term.

Even Urizen, lamenting the 'climes of bliss',[68] still remembers, with a pathetic glance back across the intervening years, when:

> ... joy sang in the trees & pleasure sported on the rivers,
> And laughter sat beneath the Oaks, & innocence sported round
> Upon the green plains, & sweet friendship met in palaces.[69]

In 'The Little Black Boy' and in 'Night' happiness and rejoicing are associated with the 'grove', which later, as we have already seen, is one of Blake's symbols associated with Druidism:

> For when our souls have learn'd the heat to bear,
> The cloud will vanish; we shall hear his* voice,
> Saying: 'Come out from the grove, my love & care,
> And round my golden tent like lambs rejoice.'[70]

And:

> Farewell, green fields and happy groves,
> Where flocks have took delight.
> Where lambs have nibbled, silent moves
> The feet of angels bright ...'[71]

In *America, a Prophecy* (1793), however, we have already progressed towards the Druidic Oak Groves of Albion. Here we find the Urizenic, Royalist oppressors, confronted by the freedom fighters — the 'terrible men', Washington, Franklin, Paine, Warren, and others:

> Crouch howling before their caverns deep, like skins dry'd in the wind.
> They cannot smite the wheat, nor quench the fatness of the earth;
> They cannot smite with sorrows, nor subdue the plow and spade;
> They cannot wall the city, nor moat round the castle of princes;
> They cannot bring the stubbed oak to overgrow the hills.[72]

In the last line, the hills of freedom are threatened by 'the secret forests'.[73] These few lines illustrate admirably how integrated Blake's symbolism

*Christ's.

is. For instance, 'caverns' are characteristic shelters for those who are subservient to Urizen; they are spiritually desiccated, 'like skins dry'd in the wind'. And it is Urizenic oppression which brings about blight, famine, grief and barrenness, and builds barriers of alienation, walls of exclusion and fortifications.

As the idea of the single tree progressively occupies Blake's imagination, we find it more and more frequently carrying unfavourable overtones, so that already in *Tiriel* (c. 1789) the tree has become a symbol of degeneration. In *The Marriage of Heaven and Hell* (etched about 1790–1793) the implications are even more obvious. There the Angel of the fourth 'Memorable Fancy' sits 'in the twisted root of an oak',[74] propounding his theory of the afterlife. The 'Angel' here is, satirically, the 'good' person of orthodox religion, which, of course, Blake strongly criticizes for its hypocritical and 'cruel' rationalism and materialism.

The one tree which Blake never speaks of in a derogatory sense is the apple tree; it receives his constant approbation. The reason for this is to be seen, perhaps, in Blake's approval of almost anything, any activity, which bears nourishment, for man's sustenance and well-being.

Another symbol which Blake uses to denote the rational as opposed to the intuitive apprehension of reality is the 'star'. The stars symbolize the partial truth man may gain by means of the five senses and a philosophy (Lockian) 'rooted' in those senses.

A passage in *The Four Zoas* shows that Blake associates the stars with mathematics:

Thus were the stars of heaven created like a golden chain
To bind the Body of Man to heaven from falling into the Abyss.
Each took his station & his course began with sorrow & care.

In sevens & tens & fifties, hundreds, thousands, number'd all
According to their various powers, subordinate to Urizen
And to his sons in their degrees & his beauteous daughters,
Travelling in silent majesty along their order'd ways
In right lined paths outmeasur'd by proportions of [weight & measure *del.*]
    number, weight
And measure, mathematic motion wondrous along the deep,
In fiery pyramid, or Cube, or unornamented pillar square
...
Others triangular, right angled course maintain. Others obtuse,
Acute [& Oblong *del.*], Scalene, in simple paths; but others move
In intricate ways, biquadrate, Trapeziums, Rhombs, Rhomboids,

Paralellograms triple & quadruple, polygonic
In their amazing hard subdu'd course in the vast deep.[75]

To emphasize the derogatory implications of such a mathematically
designed starry world, Blake draws our attention to its subordination to
abstract reason, Urizen. His criticism of the use of mathematics as a
means of arriving at truth comes to succinct expressions in his annota-
tions to Sir Joshua Reynold's 'Discourses' (c. 1808): 'God forbid that
Truth should be Confined to Mathematical Demonstration.'[76]

Blake also associates the mathematical symbol of the star with the
wheel, a symbol of industrial commerce. The 'Starry Wheels' symbolize
rationalistic, inductive science and the effect it has had on Albion or
society in general. In *Jerusalem* the friends of fallen Albion stand pale

> ... around the House of Death,
> In the midst of temptation & despair, among the rooted Oaks,
> Among reared Rocks of Albion's Sons; at length they rose
> With one accord in love sublime, &, as on Cherub's wings,
> They Albion surround with kindest violence to bear him back
> Against his Will thro' Los's gate to Eden. Four-fold, loud,
> Their Wings waving over the bottomless Immense, to bear
> Their awful charge back to his native home; but Albion dark,
> Repugnant, roll'd his Wheels backward into Non-Entity.
> Loud roll the Starry Wheels of Albion into the World of Death,
> And all the Gates of Los, clouded with clouds redounding from
> Albion's dread Wheels, stretching out spaces immense between,
> That every little particle of light & air became Opake,
> Black & immense, a Rock of difficulty & a Cliff
> Of black despair, that the Immortal Wings labour'd against
> Cliff after cliff & over Valleys of despair & death.[77]

It is hardly necessary to comment at any length on this passage. The
central meaning is clear and most of the imagery and symbolism will be
familiar from our discussion hitherto in this chapter.[78]

As we have come to expect, the 'infernal trio', Bacon, Newton and
Locke, are held responsible for the 'black despair' of those who suffer
under the domination and confinement of 'Mathematical Demonstra-
tion'. In *Jerusalem*, Blake gives us an insight into his 'awful Vision'[79] of
the effect the cruel philosophy of 'starry' materialism has had on
humanity:

I see the Four-fold Man, The Humanity in deadly sleep
... O Divine Spirit, sustain me on thy wings,
That I may wake Albion from his long & cold repose;
For Bacon & Newton, sheath'd in dismal steel, their terrors hang
Like iron scourges over Albion: Reasonings like vast Serpents
Infold around my limbs ...[80]

In common with most of his symbols that of the 'star' also reveals various 'faces'. For instance, in an early poem, 'To the Evening Star', the star is greeted as the 'fair-hair'd angel of the evening',[81] and in *A Vision of the Last Judgement* (1810) the 'church Universal' appears as the woman crowned with stars, with the moon beneath her feet.[82] We may note there that the 'Church Universal'[83] is the only church Blake recognizes. Its doctrine is the everlasting Gospel — the Gospel of Love and Forgiveness, and its congregation the brotherhood of man.

But, in general, Blake's 'stars' are associated with Urizenic oppression in one guise or another. In *America, a Prophecy*, we learn that when Urizen 'call'd the stars around his feet', the whole universe became disorganized and took on its present frigid form:

In that dread night when Urizen call'd the stars round his feet;
Then burst the center from its orb, and found a place beneath;
And Earth conglob'd, in narrow room, roll'd round its sulphur Sun.[84]

And in *The Four Zoas* Urizen recalls how he disobeyed the Divine Vision rather than guide man, who was wandering on the ocean:

I well remember, for I heard the mild & holy voice
Saying, 'O light, spring up & shine,' & I sprang up from the deep.
He gave to me a silver scepter, & crown'd me with a golden crown,
[Saying *del.*] & said, 'Go forth & guide my Son who wanders on the ocean'
I went not forth: I hid myself in black clouds of wrath;
I call'd the stars around my feet in the night of councils dark;
The stars threw down their spears & fled naked away.[85]

Allegorically, we can interpret these lines somewhat as follows. Thought has failed to act as man's guide, preferring to rule to the exclusion of, above all, Imagination and love. The imagery of 'naked' stars seems to suggest their spirituality as distinct from materiality. In other words, the spirits of the stars were horrified at Urizen's deed and rejected him, leaving behind the dead, spiritless star of materialism.

Later in *The Four Zoas* we find that even Urizen wishes to break out of the prison he himself has brought into being:

> Can I not leave this world of Cumbrous Wheels,
> Circle o'er Circle ...[86]

When 'the Sciences were fix'd' by Urizen,

> ... every human soul terrified
> At the turning wheels of heaven shrunk away inward, with'ring away.[87]

and we see him:

> Gaining a New dominion over all his Sons & Daughters, & over the
> Sons & Daughters of Luvah in the horrible Abyss.[88]

Materialistic thought and the conception of a mechanical Newtonian universe, the 'starry wheels', now completely dominate the minds and hearts of men. They are truly in the deadly sleep of the spirit. Blake would have us understand here that those who reject vision and imagination, and seek to oust love from its rightful centre in the heart, are in Ulro, in the 'Abyss', in the state of total error. In *Jerusalem* Ulro is described as 'the space of the terrible starry wheels of Albion's sons'.[89]

These 'starry wheels' also constitute the system of natural religion. In *Jerusalem*, Blake twice associates them with Druidism. Orthodox religion is also likened to a fiery wheel:

> I stood among my valleys of the south
> And saw a flame of fire, even as a Wheel,
> Of fire surrounding all the heavens: it went
> From west to east, against the current of
> Creation, and devour'd all things in its loud
> Fury & thundering course round heaven & earth.[90]
> By it the Sun was roll'd into an orb,
> By it the Moon faded into a globe
> Travelling thro' the night; for, from its dire
> And restless fury, Man himself shrunk up
> Into a little root a fathom long.
> And I asked a Watcher & a Holy-One
> Its Name; he answered: 'It is the Wheel of Religion'
> I wept & said: 'Is this the law of Jesus,
> This terrible devouring sword turning every way?'[91]
> He answered: 'Jesus died because he strove
> Against the current of this Wheel; its Name
> Is Caiaphas, the dark Preacher of Death,
> Of sin, of sorrow & of punishment:
> Opposing Nature! It is Natural Religion;

But Jesus is the bright Preacher of Life
Creating Nature from this fiery Law
By self-denial & forgiveness of Sin'.[92]

Here again we may note the complexity of Blake's symbolism. The motion of a wheel, cyclical motion, in Blake's cosmos is not in itself bad, for Eternity itself, Christ Himself, is here seen operating on benign cyclical principles. But whereas the one cyclical motion is that of an abstract system founded in a material creation and producing a rotational system which moves everything by compulsion — Commandment and Law — the other, Christ's motion, leaves man free to answer Jerusalem's call:

> England! awake! awake! awake!
> Jerusalem thy Sister calls!
> Why wilt thou sleep the sleep of death
> And close her from thy ancient walls?[93]

Related to, if not identical with, the 'Starry Wheels'[94] are the wheels of the dark Satanic Mills, the 'Mills of resistless wheels',[95] 'the hidden wheels'[96] of Satan.

Another aspect of the symbol of the star can be seen in, for example, the 'Introduction' to the *Songs of Experience*. The relevant lines are:

> Turn away no more;
> Why wilt thou turn away?

This question is addressed to the 'lapsed soul' of Man who persists in turning away from Christ, the 'Holy Word'. The statement is then made:

> The starry floor,
> The wat'ry shore,
> Is given thee till the break of day.[97]

Now, to arrive at a closer understanding of the significance of the last three lines, we need to digress a little.

There are two ways of looking at the 'fallen world'. We can look at it either as 'fallen', or as a protection against a far worse place of existence. Man might have fallen further: into total chaos, or non-existence.[98] Mercifully, 'the starry floor' and 'the wat'ry shore' were given to man as protection against total disintegration, as a limit beyond which man cannot fall. We have an analogous conception in Christ's (or Los's) act of mercy[99] in fixing the limits of opacity and contraction. These 'limits' on the Fall are set so that man may still be regenerated.

Our phenomenal, natural world, is pervaded by forces we call natural laws, which, however devoid of individual spirit, however mindless and automatic, do nevertheless lend a solid foundation for life on which the Imagination (Los) may create and build. The role of natural law — 'Bowlahoola' — as the foundation upon which the imaginative creativity can build is what is implied in Blake's conception that the creation of the natural, phenomenal world of space and time is 'an act of Mercy'. Without this act of mercy we would not find that 'In Bowlahoola Los's Anvils stand & his Furnaces rage...'[100] Were it not for Bowlahoola there would be:

> No human form but only a fibrous Vegetation,
> A Polypus[101] of soft affections without Thought or Vision.[102]

In short, the motive power of Bowlahoola is none other than the creative imagination.

Now let us return to the last three lines from the 'Introduction' to the *Songs of Experience* quoted above.

It should be clear from the above that the warning given earlier against attempting to define Blake's symbols too closely, needs to be heeded. We could, for instance, interpret both the 'starry floor' and the 'wat'ry shore' quite simply as having associations with Satanic/Urizenic materialism in what for Blake is its purely 'evil' aspect, and leave it at that. But these symbols also have positive connotations in Blake's mind: they are used here to denote the Mercy of Divine Providence. By extension we may, in fact, justifiably assert here that Blake is quite prepared to accept Newtonian science — which we can see here as the 'starry floor', that is to say, the automatic, lifeless accuracy of the movements of the heavenly bodies (including the earth); he is quite prepared to accept the validity of such mechanistic science, providing it is confined to dealing with the purely physical, the 'floor', of experience, and does not indulge in perverted reductionist explanations of psychic and spiritual experience.

Let us now proceed to a consideration of another 'group' of symbols in which the 'garment' and the 'loom' play a major role.

We have previously seen that Blake associates the 'wheel' with the 'loom'.[103] He uses both as symbols of a rationalistic — non-intuitive — apprehension of reality. Newton's mechanistic universe and the mechanistic psychology of Locke fit perfectly together — as inevitably as the 'chain' of cause and effect in a mechanistic, lifeless and spiritless, universe. A striking example of Blake's conception of the Urizenic cruelty of the loom can be seen, in its association with mills, prisons and workhouses, in *Jerusalem*. Here Los, Imagination, is viewing the disastrous effects of these Urizenic inventions on humanity:

> The Looms & Mills & Prisons & Work-houses of Og & Anak,
> The Amalekite, the Canaanite, the Moabite, the Egyptian.[104]

They are the inventions of the enemies of Imagination and spiritual freedom and are all associated with material repression and spiritual oppression. The nations named were all enemies of the Israelites and, therefore, of Jerusalem, of spiritual liberty, which is the very foundation and sustenance of universal brotherhood. Og symbolizes the system of justice, which is a direct, logical consequence of the false religion based on the error of the promulgation of the Ten Commandments, which, in turn, subjects individuals to general law and restricts their creative imagination and energies. Og is depicted by Blake as 'scaled with iron scales from head to feet, precipitating himself into the Abyss with the Sword & Balances'.[105] Og and Anak, with Satan and Sihon, constitute an infernal, 'evil' quaternary, whose function it is to oppose man's progress towards eternity, towards the realization of his own spiritual essence and being.[106]

An illuminating insight into Blake's use of the symbol of the loom can be gained by considering it in conjunction with the activity of weaving and the products created: clothing, garments, and their symbolic associations (Blake, it is worth reminding ourselves, had a good practical knowledge of the looms and weaving, for both his father and his brother, James, were hosiers).

Let us first consider the symbolism of the 'garment'. It is an ambiguous symbol. It can, of course, be 'put on' or 'taken off'; but, more significantly, perhaps, it can become confused with one's real self. There is always the danger of becoming a dunce, like Satan, who does 'not know the Garment from the Man',[107] of mistaking the true being, the essence, of a man, his individuality, for the condition, the state, in which he may be at any one moment in his life, or through which he may be passing at any one phase in his development.

The 'garment' may be potentially redemptive, or it may be imprisoning and therefore destructive. In his three long prophetic books Blake gives us many examples of both possibilities.

The potentially redemptive aspect is brought out in Los's response to the urging by Urthona's Spectre that he, Los, and his Emanation, Enitharmon, should create counterparts for the 'Spectres of the Dead':

> Stern desire
> I feel to fabricate embodied semblances in which the dead
> May live before us in our palaces & in our gardens of labour.[108]

Then Enitharmon erected looms:

> And call'd the Looms Cathedron; in these Looms she wove the Spectres
> Bodies of Vegetation, singing lulling Cadences to drive away
> Despair from the poor wandering Spectres ...[109]

Although the 'Spectres of the dead' are unreal, that is, devoid of true humanity, of spirit, being under the abstracting influence of Urizenic abstract reason, when they descend through the 'Gate of Pity'[110] (Enitharmon's broken heart) they begin to take on new forms. In the process of the creation of 'garments', of 'clothes' of human flesh, Enitharmon plays two roles: as Los's inspiration she 'sighs' the spectres forth upon the wind and Los receives them into his creative hands; and, as physical mother, she clothes the spectres with human flesh.[111]

The process of the redemptive creation of 'garments' for the incarnating soul is described again in the lines:

> In Golgonooza Los's anvils stand & his Furnaces rage,

He and his sons:

> ... labour at the forges Creating Continually
> ...
> In periods of Pulsative furor, beating into [bars del.] wedges & bars,
> Then drawing into wires the terrific Passions & Affections
> Of Spectrous dead. Thence to the Looms of Cathedron convey'd,
> The Daughters of Enitharmon weave the ovarium & the integument
> In soft silk ...
> With songs of sweetest cadence to the turning spindle & reel,
> Lulling the weeping spectres of the dead, Clothing their limbs
> With gifts & gold of Eden. Astonish'd, stupefied with delight,
> The terrors put on their sweet clothing ...[112]

The spectres, abstractions, become concrete, take on the 'garments' of physical reality with delight. Here Blake shows us a way of thinking about the human flesh, the human body, not now to be seen solely as a necessary lower limit of contraction, but as the creation of a loving creator, Los/Christ, in which delight can be taken.

In parenthesis we could say here that the process of creation we have just witnessed also gives us a picture, an organic conception, of art itself; spectres, abstract ideas, are conceived in 'heartburst',[113] shaped with pain and difficulty and, finally, given form, made flesh, able then to sustain life independent of the creator. Through the process of birth, of assuming a physical 'garment', the Spectres now have the possibility, the path open to them, to find their way back to Eternity through the world of generation. In *Jerusalem* Blake makes the further point that, as the Incarnation of Christ makes clear, generation is an image of regeneration.[114]

Another beautiful expression of the redemptive aspect of the garment, the activity of weaving, and the loom itself appears in *Milton*:

> ... every Generated Body in its inward form
> Is a garden of delight & a building of magnificence,
> Built by the Sons of Los ...
> And the herbs & flowers & furniture & beds & chambers
> Continually woven in the Looms of Enitharmon's Daughters,
> In bright Cathedron's golden Dome with care & love & tears.[115]

Blake does not, however, let us lose sight of the 'higher' point of view: that of the eternal, spiritual world of which this 'vegetable earth' is but a Shadow,[116] an image, and, hence, a delusion. From this point of view the Looms are agencies of death:

> Arise, O Sons, give all your strength against Eternal Death
> Lest we are vegetated, for Cathedron's Looms weave only Death,
> A Web of Death ...[117]

In opposition to the redemptive creative activity of Los and his Emanation, Enitharmon, Satan and his assistants:

Build Mills of resistless wheels to unwind the soft threads & reveal
Naked of their clothing the poor spectres before the accusing heavens,
While Rahab & Tirza far different mantles prepare: webs of torture,
Mantles of despair, girdles of bitter compunction, shoes of indolence,
Veils of ignorance covering from head to feet with a cold web,
We look down into Ulro ...
The Mills of Satan and Beelzeboul* stand round the roots of Urizen's tree.[118]

The Urizenic mills employed to unwind the threads woven on Enitharmon's looms produce the 'nakedness' that is shame, guilt and self-contempt inculcated into the soul of man by orthodox religion, the

*Greek for 'Baalzebub'.

religion of sin, chastity, accusation and punishment; all the garments which cover 'from head to feet' are symptoms of false shame; they are 'clothings' which restrict the human spirit.

But, Blake consistently insists, there is a greater power than the might of the Urizenic God: the power of Christ, of love and forgiveness, self-sacrifice and brotherhood. Round Christ, too, is woven the 'Body of Death' (seen from the viewpoint of Eternity), in the 'Female Tabernacle' (i.e. Mary), on the looms of Enitharmon and her daughters in Cathedron (i.e. the body of Woman, particularly the womb); He, the 'Universal Humanity', also receives 'the integuments woven'. And then, in a Urizenic attempt to shame Him, He is clothed in the false garment, the scarlet robe of mock royalty. So, 'the Mills of Satan',

... unweave the soft threads, then they weave anew in the forms
Of dark death & despair, & none from Eternity could Escape
But thou, O Universal Humanity — who is One Man, blessed for Ever —

Receivest the Integuments woven.[119]

This 'One Man, blessed for Ever', through his selfless love and willing self-annihilation, is the one Power who, setting the example for the whole of humanity, can strip off the garment of false religion and thus re-establish the nakedness of innocence:

He puts off the clothing of blood, he redeems the spectres from their bonds.
He awakes sleepers in Ulro ...[120]

The example set by Christ is followed, in the end, even by Urizen who casts off his false religion and philosophy and is spiritually regenerated:

... renew'd, he shook his aged mantles off
Into the fires. Then, glorious bright, Exulting in his joy,
He sounding rose into the heavens in naked majesty,
In radiant Youth; ...[121]

The opposite of this redemptive assumption of 'garments' is seen in Urizen's attempt to assume the attributes of the God of the Old Testament (Psalms 104:2; Proverbs 30:4):

'Am I not God?' said Urizen, 'Who is Equal to me?'
'Do I not stretch the heavens abroad, or fold them up like a garment?'[122]

In his selfhood, self-centredness, Urizen clearly cannot understand the selfless act of 'putting on' of garments by which selfhood is annihilated.

Whereas the Imagination can perceive the 'woven' body as a merciful limit, as a merciful 'garment', a gift of the Creative World, Christ, reason can do no other than see it as a material prison. True spiritual existence is, of course, obtained by 'putting off' the garment of the body.

We see then that Blake's conception of the symbolic 'garment', 'Loom', and the activity of 'weaving', is ambiguous. Once alerted, the reader frequently finds the same image viewed from different perspectives in Blake's three great epic poems. On occasion, two opposing perspectives converge in one passage — as, for instance, in the passage in *The Four Zoas* quoted (in two parts) above.[123]

Hitherto, in our discussion of these symbols, our illustrative examples have been taken, with two exceptions, from *The Four Zoas*. Many more could be cited, particularly from the three great prophetic books, but, to keep this chapter to a reasonable length, we shall confine ourselves to a few further examples from *Milton* and *Jerusalem*.

In *Milton*, too, we hear Enitharmon's looms vibrating:

> ... with soft affections, weaving the Web of Life
> Out from the ashes of the Dead ...[124]

This 'Web of Life', in contrast to Urizen's 'Web of Religion',[125] his 'Net of Religion',[126] does not carry 'direful', 'twisted', and 'knotted', connotations, but is to be seen as an enspirited necessity in the process towards regeneration.

We saw earlier that Los warns against becoming 'vegetated', 'for Cathedron's Looms weave only Death/ A Web of Death'... However, Los's view here is — as we previously noted — from the perspective of Eternity, according to which 'life' in the world of generation constitutes spiritual 'death'; whereas from the perspective of our own world the weaving of the looms of Cathedron is a life-endowing, beauty-bestowing, benevolent activity without which we would never see:

> ... the gorgeous clothed Flies that dance & sport in summer
> Upon the sunny brooks & meadows; every one the dance
> Knows its intricate mazes of delight artful to weave:
> Each one to sound his instruments of music in the dance,
> To touch each other & recede, to cross & change & return:
> These are the Children of Los ...
> ... These are the Sons of Los: These the Visions of Eternity,
> But we see only as it were the hem of their garments
> When with our vegetable eyes we view these wondrous Visions.[127]

All the phenomena of the world about us — including gorgeously 'clothed Flies' — are visions of Eternity if seen with the Imagination. The spiritual cause, the creative Sons of Los, Christ Himself, can only be seen after we realize that our 'cavern'd' sense organs only perceive a small portion, the 'hem', of the totality of existence, which is mainly spiritual and, as Blake insists, always spiritually caused.

In *Milton*, Milton's own garment is a most important image in the poem's symbolism. His first action is to take 'off the robe of the promise' and ungird 'himself from the oath of God'.[128] It is the step he takes prior to his re-descent to this world, for, choosing of his own free will to undertake a pilgrimage of inner transformation, he does not need to be 'clothed' with a merciful garment of flesh as do wailing spectres. He is descending in order to redeem the nations of the world — and himself — from the Urizenic fetters which had previously inhibited his creative imagination.[129] Addressing Satan/Urizen, his Spectre, Milton declares: 'Know thou, I come to Self Annihilation'.[130] This is the John Milton who descended into Blake's Cottage Garden, 'clothed in black'.[131] These garments signify:

> … a false Body, an Incrustation over my Immortal
> Spirit, a Selfhood which must be put off & annihilate alway.[132]

Continuing in the same spirit as in his address to Satan, Milton says to his Emanation,[133] Ololon, that he has come:

> To cast off Rational Demonstration by Faith in the Saviour,
> To cast off the rotten rags of Memory by Inspiration,
> To cast off Bacon, Locke & Newton from Albion's covering,
> To cast off his filthy garments & clothe him with Imagination.[134]

These 'rotten rags' and 'filthy garments' are cast off as a prelude to the moment when Milton assumes the clothes of redemption and returns 'from flames of fire tried & pure & white'.[135]

The ambiguity of the significance of the 'garment' is brought into focus in *Milton* when, for instance, Blake distinguishes between the 'Clothing' of 'Cruelty' and the 'Garment of Pity & Compassion like the Garment of God', and again when he draws a contrast between souls descending to the body and being delivered from it.[136] We find a similar ambiguity in the symbol of the garment in *The Four Zoas*, where Blake distinguishes between the 'mantles of life & death',[137] the latter being the 'death clothes' he associates with the Web of Urizen.

In Milton's address to his Emanation, Ololon, he also speaks of the alternative, negative aspects of the garment symbol. The Urizenic philosopher, priest and scientist — 'the idiot Questioner':[138]

> These are the destroyers of Jerusalem, these are the murderers
> Of Jesus, who deny the Faith & mock at Eternal Life,
> Who pretend to Poetry that they may destroy Imagination
> By imitation of Nature's Images drawn from Remembrance.
> These are the Sexual Garments, the Abominations of Desolation,
> Hiding the Human Lineaments as with an Ark & Curtains
> Which Jesus rent & now shall wholly purge away with Fire
> Till Generation is swallow'd up in Regeneration.[139]

Another striking example, in *Milton*, of the two meanings of the 'garment' symbol is given in the shadowy Female's threat to put on a false garment, a garment of cruelty, and Orc's plea to her to 'put on' a Female Form 'with a garment of Pity & Compassion like the garment of God' and not 'create & Weave this Satan for a covering', that is, for a selfhood.[140]

In *Jerusalem* we find much of what we have seen in both *The Four Zoas* and in *Milton*: two types of weaving and alternative garments. For example:

> Why should Punishment Weave the Veil with Iron Wheels of War
> When Forgiveness might it Weave with Wings of Cherubim.[141]

There is, in short, merciful weaving:

> ... his Emanation
> Joy'd in the many weaving threads in bright Cathedron's Dome,
> Weaving the Web of Life for Jerusalem;[142a]

and destructive weaving.[142b]

The 'garment', in its beneficial, positive sense, is associated with the Divine Vision:

> In Great Eternity, every particular Form gives forth or Emanates
> Its own peculiar Light, & the Form is the Divine Vision
> And the Light is his Garment. This is Jerusalem in every Man,
> A Tent & Tabernacle of Mutual Forgiveness, Male & Female Clothings.
> And Jerusalem is called Liberty among the Children of Albion.[143]

And, in contrast, we find the 'fallen garment', which Albion puts on when he begins to worship Vala, the seductive Goddess of Nature (regenerated Albion 'worships' Jerusalem, of course):

> O how I tremble! how my members pour down milky fear!
> A dewy garment covers me all over, all manhood is gone!
> At thy word & at thy look, death enrobes me about
> From head to feet, a garment of death & eternal fear.[144]

In several examples quoted to illustrate Blake's dynamic and symbolic use of looms and woven garments we have found him associating them with the Mill. Let us now look briefly at some of its symbolic meanings.

In general terms we may say that the Mill is a perfect image of the mind of the rational deist who strives to reduce the world of living form and beauty to a sandstorm of atoms.[145] A 'dark Satanic Mill' symbolizes any form of unimaginative mechanism: the logical method of Aristotle, the basis of dogmatism; the industrial machinery which enslaves men, women and children; the Newtonian astronomical universe; the mechanical ability to churn out uninspired art, and so on. Earlier on in this chapter we saw that Blake considers schools and universities to be devoid of imaginative power and the growing generation therefore subjected to the crushing, cruel mills of analysis, in which the loom of Locke is washed by the water-wheel of Newton to create a black cloth of reason. In *Jerusalem*, Jerusalem herself is described as being a slave in the mills of analysis.[146] In *Milton*, the entire astronomical universe is described as a mill:

> O Satan ... art thou not Prince of the Starry Hosts
> And of the Wheels of Heaven, to turn the Mills day & night?
> Art thou not Newton's Pantocrator, weaving the Woof of Locke?
> To Mortals thy Mills seem every thing, ...
> Thy Work is Eternal Death with Mills & Ovens & Cauldrons.[147]

To those who see only what rationalism dictates, the 'Mills seem every thing'.

These lines come very shortly after those beginning 'And did those feet in ancient time'.[148] The 'dark Satanic Mills' signify the materialistic philosophy under which England was suffering in Blake's day — as it still is — rather than the actual enormous mills of industrial Britain. Satan here is 'Newton's Pantocrator', weaving the 'Woof of Locke', and is shortly to be revealed as Urizen, the 'Miller of Eternity', the 'Prince of the Starry Wheels'.[149] Urizen, in his mills of reductive reason, attempts to grind down creation and to destroy the 'minute particulars' which constitute the individuality of each human being.

As repeatedly stated in these pages, in Blake's view orthodox religion, the religion of Urizen, is destrucive of the creative and imaginative impulses in man. It is not surprising then to find the Satanic Mill being symbolic of such religion:

And the Mills of Satan were separated into a moony Space
Among the rocks of Albion's Temples, and Satan's Druid sons
Offer the Human Victims throughout all the Earth, and Albion's
Dread Tomb, immortal on his Rock, overshadow'd the whole Earth,
Where Satan, making to himself Laws from his own identity,
Compell'd others to serve him in moral gratitude & submission,
Being call'd God, setting himself above all that is called God
And all the Spectres of the Dead, calling themselves Sons of God,
In his Synagogues worship Satan under the Unutterable Name.[150]

Satan/Urizen's mills are certainly destructive,[151] but they nevertheless also have a positive function to perform in Los's world. Satan/Urizen's mills are as much associated with the Spiritual Harvest as Los's winepress and the iron tools — the plough, harrow and roller[152] — which Los forges as essential 'instruments/ Of Harvest'.[153] It is in Satan/Urizen's mills where the husks of the harvest are ground away. The destroyer, therefore, has a vital function to perform in the process of spiritual birth, growth and maturation, even though he does not understand it.

In *The Four Zoas*, where the Mill is 'Dark Urthona's', but the flail is in the hands of Urizen, we learn that 'all Nations were threshed out, & the stars thresh'd from their husks'.[54] Like chaff the nations were tossed into the seas.[155] It is clear that the 'husks' or the nations are symbolic of Urizenic dominion — in the form of division and self-centredness — by means of which all true human brotherhood has been rendered impossible. It is Urizen's assistants, Rahab and Tirzah, who support him in his divisive labours, weaving men into nations.[156] They have also helped to weave man's natural body, as opposed to the spiritual body,[157] and together they create the oppressors, 'all the Kings & Nobles of the Earth.'[150]

When people separated into nations and turned hostile to one another, they each shrunk into 'Selfhoods'. It is primarily Urizenic fear which causes this 'Shrinking' process, this consolidation into a fortified, barriered state of selfhood. The isolated selfhood — be it in a single man or woman, or in a nation — is opposed to any formation of a larger group. Conflict, aggression, war, are the inevitable result of self-centredness. Urizenic, isolated individuals and nations, erect barriers around themselves, barriers which inhibit any experience of a higher, universal identity to be found in universal brotherhood. Indeed, the selfhood, the shrunken, false self, lives in doubt and fear of others, or, as Reuben, the average sensual man, expresses it: 'Doubt is my food day & night.'[159] When people separated into nations and turned hostile to one another, they became the 'Negation' of the brotherhood of man. The primal fault is that of Urizen,

> ... whose labours vast
> Order the nations, separating family by family.[160]

However, Urizenic conflict and war can also be seen as a preparation of a New Age. In *Milton*, for instance, we see warfare as 'the Great Harvest & Vintage of the Nations'.[161] Urizen's 'Plow' passes 'over the Nations'. Significantly, although Urizen is the 'Plowman',[162] reason cannot originate anything and it is the Imagination, Los and his sons, who provide the ideas for the New Age. Hence, in *Milton*, the 'Plow' to pass over the nations is Los's,[163] and is forged by all four of Los's eldest sons.[164]

Now, we should do Blake an injustice if we were to understand him as condemning the coming into being of nations. In themselves they are good; they are manifestations of the infinite variety of mankind. But in the process of separation under the aegis of Urizen, each nation — and this applies equally to each one of us who is born into a natural body — loses consciousness of the totality, of universal brotherhood, of true spiritual liberty.

In the distant past, mankind flourished under liberty; there were no divisions between peoples. The universal brotherhood will one day come again when Jerusalem returns and can 'overspread all the Nations'.[165] Then we shall be able to say to Urizen and his 'assistants':

> O Mystery ... Behold thy end is come!
> Art thou she that made the nations drunk with the cup of Religion?
> Go down, ye Kings & Councellors & Giant Warriors,
> ...
> Lo, how the Pomp of Mystery goes down ...[166]

We have to realize that it is not the 'old', 'degenerate' Urizen who is the 'Plowman' and plays a vital role in 'the great Harvest & Vintage of the Nations'.[167] The Urizen whose flail is instrumental in the process in which 'all Nations were threshed out, & the stars thresh'd from their husks', is the 'regenerate' Urizen, who works in harmony with the other three Zoas, Los/Urthona, Tharmas and Luvah. He has, in short, 'annihilated' his selfhood, circumcised his 'excrementitious/ Husk and Covering', and revealed his true 'lineaments'.[168] His mill is destructive, but in a positive sense. Let us look at this process of 'destruction' from a wider perspective.

Elsewhere we have recognized that implicit in fallen Urizen's empirical philosophy is the inference that spirit is an illusion, is unreal, and that matter, all that which can be perceived by the physical eye (or its extensions: microscope and telescope), weighed and measured, is the only reality. According to such a philosophy even thought is caused by matter and its vibrations!

Such a philosophy — and its offspring, natural religion — is an obstruction to the intuitive insight, the true spiritual vision, of the spiritual essence. The 'excrementitious Husk and Covering', that is, the natural body, 'is an Obstruction to the Soul or Spiritual Body'.[169]

The spiritual essence is hidden from those who are seduced by natural religion and the philosophy of materialism, that is, by fallen Urizen, Rahab and Tirzah. It is this illusion that matter is the only reality which, forming an 'excrementitious Husk and Covering', treasured and defended by the Urizenic selfhood, must be cast out, ground down and winnowed away. The illusions of corporality, and 'the Idol Virtues of the Natural Heart ... Selfish Natural Virtue',[170] obscure the spiritual form of truth and must be 'circumcised', annihilated, if selfless love and universal brotherhood are to be realized.

Self-annihilation always implies the rejection of Error. It involves the subjugation of the selfhood, the Spectre, the Urizenic reasoning power, of the divided man, for,

> This is a false body, an Incrustation over my Immortal
> Spirit ...[171]

It is a 'husk' which must be cast out.

The sense of selfhood, of false self, often reprehended in *Milton* and *Jerusalem*, opposes the principle of spiritual, creative liberty, Jerusalem. It is self-centred individuality which denies individual genius, the Christ, in other men. Blake would have us recognize that, subject to the sovereignty of the principle of brotherhood, the individual genius, the wisdom peculiar to each one of us, [172] needs to, indeed, must achieve its full development without imposing itself and its conditions on the genius of any other person.

Only when the 'husk' in which fallen Urizen has imprisoned mankind — as well as himself — has been cast off can the enspirited, enlightened view of reality be attained. Or, differently expressed: the vision of the spiritual unity and divine nature of discrete individualities can only be attained by a realization of brotherhood and universal love in everyday life, in morality, social and political life, and so on:

> He who would see the Divinity must see him in his Children,
> One first, in friendship & love, then a Divine Family, & in the midst
> Jesus will appear; so he who wishes to see a Vision, a perfect Whole
> Must see it in its Minute Particulars, ...[173]

When the 'husks' have been cast out, then we shall not fail to perceive unity of discrete individualities nor shall we ignore equality of 'value'. Indeed:

> Superior, none we know: inferior, none: all equal share
> Divine Benevolence & joy; for the Eternal Man
> Walketh among us, calling us his Brothers & his Friends.[174]

The 'false' individualist is the tyrant, is fallen Urizen/Satan. He makes 'to himself Laws from his own identity'.[175] He projects himself onto others, instead of granting liberty to all identities.[176] The apotheosis of the self (Satan/Urizen/Spectre) is the outcome of a denial of the union of the All in the One, or, as Blake also expresses it, it is a denial of the 'concentering vision'.[177] The genuine spiritual individualist, that is, he who has cast out his 'excrementitious husk & covering', looks to others, not to self. This is real liberty, not a 'pretence of Liberty/ To Destroy Liberty'.[178] With Blake we ask:

> What is Liberty without Universal Toleration?[179]

To requote:

> In Great Eternity every particular Form gives forth or Emanates
> Its own particular light, & the Form is the Divine Vision
> And the Light is his Garment. This is Jerusalem in every Man.[180]

Once the 'husk' has been cast out, the 'Peculiar Light' can radiate out and 'co-mingle' with all other Peculiar Lights in brotherhood and love.

The delusion that man is nothing more than natural, mortal, or, as Blake says in *The Four Zoas*, a 'Worm of sixty winters',[181] that the spiritual world is non-existent, is associated with a morality which causes man to seek 'the caves of sleep'.

> Forsaking Brotherhood & Universal Love, in selfish clay
> Folding the pure wings of his mind, seeking the places dark
> Abstracted from the roots of [Nature *del.*] Science ...[182]

Three further symbols, closely associated with each other, Blake variously uses to denote a similar force and attitude of mind in regard to reality are the net, the web, and the veil — in particular, the Veil of Vala.

In *The Book of Urizen*, Urizen, as we shall see in the next chapter, explores his 'dens':

> A cold shadow follow'd behind him
> Like a spider's web, moist, cold & dim,
> ...
> Till a Web, dark & cold, throughout all
> The tormented element stretch'd
> From the sorrows of Urizen's soul.
> ...
> None could break the Web, no wings of fire,
> So twisted the cords, & so knotted
> The meshes, twisted like to the human brain.
>
> And all call'd it The Net of Religion.[183]

This 'Web', or 'Net', is evidently a product of perverted, 'Twisted', fallen reason. It is obvious from what we have seen hitherto of Blake's conception of Christ that he does not object to any inspiration of true religion; what he objects to here is the ecclesiastical control of Man's beliefs and, as a consequence, of his life. Caught in the net, the web, of religion, man's spiritual senses shrink:

> The Senses inward rush'd, shrinking
> Beneath the dark net of infection;
>
> Till the shrunken eyes, clouded over,
> Discern'd not the woven hipocrisy [sic].[184]

Becoming what he beholds, man, limited to physical sense-perception, not only does not perceive the 'woven hipocrisy', but, in the reductive process, becomes animal-like, crawling upon the earth, a minion of Satan. It is relevant to remember here that worldly religion is also likened to a 'Wheel of fire' against which Christ strove.

Consequent upon the Fall of Satan/Urizen all spiritual 'seeds' fall into the womb, either of Mother Earth or of a mothering creature. In Blakean terms, we may visualize Mother Earth, as a vast net or 'gin'[185] in which the seed is ensnared. Those human embryos which develop sufficient Imagination recognize this net as a mysterious veil separating them from spiritual reality.[186] The rending of the Veil of the Temple by Christ symbolizes the power of the Imagination to see into the world of spiritual reality and thus, also, through the falseness imposed upon man by Urizen.[187]

Blake is not only a man of the future, but he was also very definitely aware of the ills of his own time, keenly aware of social, political and religious injustice. A good example of his indignation is expressed in the following lines from *Visions of the Daughters of Albion*:

> With what sense does the parson claim the labour of the farmer?
> What are his nets & gins & traps; how does he surround him
> With cold floods of abstraction, and with forests of solitude,
> To build him castles and high spires, where kings & priests may dwell.[188]

Here Blake is concerned with the unjustifiable custom of tithing. He attacks the parson for deceiving the people with vague abstract pious hopes. The religion and law of oppression are based on such deception.

Illusions and dreams are consolations encouraged under Urizen's 'net of religion', 'the dark net of infection'. The laws of oppression built

> ... the Churches, Hospitals, Castles, Palaces,
> Like nets & gins & traps to catch the joys of Eternity,
> And all the rest a desert;
> Till, like a dream, Eternity was obliterated & erased.[189]

The Establishment, the privileged few, seeks, in 'good' works, to salve its conscience over the poverty and disease for which they, the oppressors, are largely responsible. It builds hospitals, i.e. places of 'charity', for the destitute and aged (the inmates often being both despised and exploited).

Seen in a larger context we may say that man, under the direful Net or Web of Urizen has lost all vision of Eternity, of spiritual reality.

In *The Four Zoas*, Nights vii and viii, and in *Jerusalem*, Vala is the contrary to Jerusalem (being her shadow, 'Babylon'). She represents both rejection of vision, and the evil that results from such rejection in the sphere of morality. She is therefore another of Blake's symbols of the illusion that man knows as the phenomenal world, the physical universe. She is 'Nature, Mother of all', the 'Mother of the Body of Death'[190] and at the same time she represents the principle of 'evil' which causes man to accept the illusion. She therefore also personifies 'Natural Religion', 'Natural Morality' or 'Mystery'.

The Building* is Natural Religion & its Altars Natural Morality,
A building of eternal death, whose proportions are eternal despair.
Here Vala stood turning the iron Spindle of destruction.[191]

She is also the source of these errors.[192]

From this characterization of Vala it is not difficult to comprehend that
her veil can be seen to represent: the human body of flesh;[193] the Mundane
Shell, i.e. the crust of matter which encloses us;[194] the code of moral law[195]
— i.e. the reasonings of those who are blind to spiritual reality;[196] and,
clearly, the Veil in the Temple which conceals the divinity,[197] and which
Christ rends at the Crucifixion.[198]

The close association between the veil of Vala and the web (or net) of
Urizen is self-evident:[199]

> This is the Net & Veil of Vala among the Souls of the Dead.[200]
> And the Veil of Vala is composed of the Spectres of the Dead.[201]

The 'Spectres' of the dead are those spirits who are without 'a con-
centering vision'[202] which would supply them with 'the food of life'.[203]
Vala's veil is the 'Veil of Moral Virtue woven for Cruel Laws'[204] — the
laws of natural religion. It proceeds from limited reason and sense-
perception — blind to spiritual reality; and, as it hides the Divine
Humanity, God, from the sight of man, in the sphere of morality the veil
signifies opposition to visionary brotherhood and love.

It is clear to the reader by now that, for Blake, 'Matter' is a delusion,
or, rather, in our present context, a thin coating of reality. It is, in other
words, the Veil of Vala, mistaken for reality by those whose vision is
single, Newtonian, that is, limited to mere physical sense-perception.

A symbol closely associated with the Veil of Vala is the 'Mundane
Shell':

> ... the Veil of Vala, which Albion cast into the Atlantic Deep
> To catch the Souls of the Dead, began to Vegetate & petrify
> Around the Earth of Albion among the Roots of his Tree.
> This Los formed into the Gates & mighty Wall between the Oak
> Of Weeping & the Palm of Suffering beneath Albion's Tomb.
> Thus in process of time it became the beautiful Mundane Shell,
> The Habitation of the Spectres of the Dead, & the Place
> Of Redemption & of awaking again into Eternity.[205]

---

*i.e. the Druid Temple at Stonehenge.

Here the Veil of Vala is used in two ways: by Vala to trap and enclose the world of generation; by Los to keep the 'evil' influences of the fallacious attribution of reality to the images of single, 'Natural', Newtonian vision, out of generation as far as possible.

In *The Four Zoas*, we find the Mundane Shell described as the world created by the agents of Urizen:

Petrifying all the Human Imagination into rock & sand.[206]
... within its walls & cielings [sic.]
The heavens were clos'd, and spirits mourn'd their bondage night & day,
...
Thus was the Mundane Shell builded by Urizen's strong Power.[207]

Here the Mundane Shell, Urizen's creation, signifies the total of the errors created through relying solely on the five physical senses for the attainment of knowledge.

Urizen thinks he is formulating a merciful limit beyond which reality cannot shrink. But he is deceiving himself; and, in fact, he masterminds the building of Ulro, the reductive state of abstract brooding on the self which petrifies the human imagination 'into the rock & sand' of the material, natural world.

In *Milton*, the Mundane Shell is represented as a shadow of the ideal world. It is

... a vast Concave Earth,* an immense
Harden'd shadow of all things upon our Vegetated Earth.[208]

We have previously seen that Blake is convinced that 'every Natural Effect has a Spiritual Cause'.[209] In *Jerusalem* there is a passage which endorses this view and has particular relevance to man's conception of the universe — in this instance, the Mundane Shell — and the power it has to determine and regulate his percepts. The 'Spiritual Causes' here are the Daughters of Albion, who, prior to the apocalypse, that is, before Albion 'threw himself into the Furnaces of affliction',[210] are unable to wake from spiritual sleep themselves. Symbolically, they may be seen as spiritual forces which mislead man, as forces which control human, natural or 'Vegetative powers',[211] that is, cause dependence on the senses, not on intuition. In the passage in question they are seen sitting:

---

*i.e. a universe like the inside of an egg.

> ... within the Mundane Shell
> Forming the fluctuating Globe* according to their will:
> According as they weave the little embryon nerves & veins,
> The Eye, the little Nostrils & the delicate Tongue, & Ears
> Of labyrinthine intricacy, so shall they fold the World,
> That whatever is seen upon the Mundane Shell, the same
> Be seen upon the Fluctuating Earth woven by the Sisters.[212]

Perception is here attributed — like all natural and mental functions — to the activities of spiritual beings. In this instance, the Daughters of Albion cause man to perceive as he conceives, that is, materialistically. In other words, an error is insinuated into man's mind and immediately he finds it manifested objectively.

In *Milton* and *Jerusalem* the symbol of the Mundane Shell often refers derogatively to the religion of mankind:

... the Druids rear'd their Rocky Circles to make permanent Remembrance Of Sin, & the Tree of Good & Evil sprang from the Rocky Circle & Snake Of the Druid, ...
And framed the Mundane Shell Cavernous in Length, Bredth & Highth.[213]

In its moral significance, therefore, the Mundane Shell is another term for what Blake calls 'Natural Religion':

> Self-righteousness conglomerating against the Divine Vision:
> A Concave Earth wondrous, Chasmal, Abyssal, Incoherent,
> Forming the Mundane Shell ...[214]

Now, as we have seen earlier on, the act of the creation of the 'World of Generation' can be regarded to be either an 'evil', demonic act in that it encloses man in the 'Mundane Shell', in a world governed by space and time, which shuts him off from Eternity, and petrifies the creative imagination, or it can be seen to be an act of mercy in that it prevents man from falling endlessly into the 'Indefinite'. Like most of Blake's symbols, the symbol of the 'Mundane Shell' operates differently in different contexts. So, for instance, we find the twofold aspects of the creation and significance of the 'natural' environment quite clearly expressed in relation to the symbol of the 'Mundane Shell'. In so far as the mortal, natural world is illusory and delusive its creation is attributed to Urizen, the Daughters of Albion, or to the Druids; however, as mortality also

---

*i.e. an indefinite form.

makes possible the reawakening of the spirit in man, the building of the
'Mundane Shell' is attributed also to 'an act of Mercy',[215] to the mercy of
Eternity acting either directly,[216] or through Los, whose creations:

> ... became the beautiful Mundane Shell,
> The Habitation of the Spectres of the Dead, & the Place
> Of Redemption & of awaking again into Eternity.[217]

In all instances, the Shell is a symbol of fallenness and division, but in one
context it is the Newtonian obstacle which excludes Imagination and
must be penetrated by it — as in Blake's illustration of 'Milton's Track'
entering the Mundane Shell from outside;[218] in another context the Mun-
dane Shell is the structure which Los creates as a defence against Chaos,
Ulro, that is, against the state of the deadly sleep of the spirit, the mode of
life which rejects vision and relies solely on fallen reason — and therefore
lives in the errors of materialism and restrictive, Urizenic morality.
Using the term Chaos instead of Ulro, Blake writes of Urizen that:

> ... he lay, clos'd, unknown,
> Brooding shut in the deep ...
> ... petrific abominable chaos.[219]

The chaos is the confused, brooding, doubting and despairing mind of
the man without Vision. It is man's 'Rational Power', his Spectre, the
'Great Selfhood, Satan', who preaches materialism and proclaims himself
God.[220] This deist God is remote and inaccessible. He dwells in physical
space beyond the 'blue Mundane Shell', beyond the Newtonian starry
sky, but Blake insists that only Chaos exists beyond the stars.[221] In Blake's
world of Vision, Christ, Imagination, exists actively in our own
bosoms,[222] whereas in Urizen's world, man is shut off from the creative
power within the universe, within his fellow men, and within himself.
He shrinks 'up from existence'.[223] Spiritually he is 'dead', for Imagina-
tion is existence.[224] We are not only members of Christ, but, in Christ, in
the Imagination, we are members of each other.[225] In the Imagination, in
Christ, we form and create the brotherhood of man. Within the Mun-
dane Shell, in the world in which we live and move and have our being,
we can either submit to the iron fetters of Urizenic rationalism, or expand
'in the Bosom of God, the Human Imagination'.[226] We can either remain
in the spiritual darkness of ceaseless corporeal strife and all which that
entails, or, recognizing the Divine Essence within our fellow men and
being constantly refreshed and regenerated through 'Mental Fight',[227]

ever 'expand' into universal brotherhood. Either the spiritual sun can shine within and endow man with constant new life, or the material sun can scorch down from without and dessicate all true humanity. Man can, in short, turn 'his back to the Divine Vision' and accept no more than 'a round disk of fire somewhat like a Guinea' as the only reality, or he can see 'an Innumerable company of the Heavenly host crying "Holy, Holy is the Lord Almighty" '.[228]

The spiritual sun is 'within' the man of imaginative vision; the corporeal sun, the sun of reason, is an alien, destructive force 'without', which must, in the Great Vintage and Harvest, be raised up, transformed and redeemed. This process of transformation and redemption occurs when man learns to 'see thro' & not with the eye', when his organs of perception are spiritual, not physical.

Since ancient times, the sun has been a symbol of the higher spiritual essence in the universe and man. In Blake, Los, which, it is reasonable to suppose, is an anagram of *sol* (Latin: the sun), represents many of the symbolic values which tradition attributes to the sun. Blake frequently conceives of divinity in the perfect form of the shining circle in the heavens:

> Then the Divine Vision like a silent Sun appear'd above
> Albion's dark rocks ...
> ... and in the Sun a Human Form appear'd,
> And thus the Voice Divine went forth upon the rock of Albion.[229]

Another passage in *Jerusalem* clearly associates the sun with Christ:

> This theme calls me in sleep night after night, & ev'ry morn
> Awakes me at sun-rise; then I see the Saviour over me
> Spreading his beams of love & dictating the words of this mild song.[230]

Los, the guardian of spiritual vision, the 'Spirit of Prophecy',[231] the poet and spiritual revolutionary, directly inspires Blake himself:

> ... Los descended to me:
> And Los behind me stood, a terrible flaming sun, just close
> Behind my back ...
> ... he kissed me and wish'd me health,
> And I became One Man with him arising in my strength.[232]

Blake frequently equates, with varying degrees of directness, the sun with poetry or the creative imagination. Another example is given in a letter to Thomas Butts (22 Nov. 1802):

> Then Los appear'd in all his power:
> In the Sun he appear'd, descending before
> My face in fierce flames; in my double sight
> 'Twas outward a Sun: inward Los in his might.[233]

In a conversation with Henry Crabb Robinson Blake tells him that he has had a vision of the spiritual sun: 'You never saw the spiritual Sun. I have. I saw him on Primrose Hill.'[234]

He also said: 'Do you take me for the Greek Apollo?' In answer to Robinson's 'No!' Blake continued: 'That (pointing to the sun in the sky) that is the Greek Apollo. He is Satan!'[235] The spiritual sun Blake identifies with Christ, the Imagination, the material sun, with reason (materialism): 'The dead Sun is only a phantasy of evil Man.'[236]

On several occasions, Blake speaks of the material sun as being the 'sulphur sun' — the powerful mephitic odour which sulphur, when burning, emits is traditionally associated with hell-fire:

> And many said: 'We see no Visions in the darksome air.
> Measure the course of that sulphur orb that lights the darksome day;
> Set stations on this breeding Earth & let us buy & sell'.
> Others arose & schools erected, forming Instruments
> To measure out the course of heaven. Stern Urizen beheld
> In woe his brethren & his sons ...[237]

The 'many' and the 'others' were seduced to adopt Urizen's, Satan's viewpoint. They defy Imagination and see only the material world.[238] Instead of seeing the sun as a source and haven of spiritual life and energy, the materialistic rationalist measures out the course of the stars, draws mathematical lines across the heavens and, ultimately, enmeshes himself in a spider's web of mathematical analysis.

As we have already seen, the material stars are in Urizen's sphere of influence. The 'Spectre of Albion' — Satan or Urizen — inhabits

> ... the Newtonian Voids between the Substances of Creation.
>
> For the Chaotic Voids outside the Stars are measured by
> The Stars, which are the boundaries of Kingdoms, Provinces
> And Empires of Chaos invisible to Vegetable Man.
> ...
> From Star to Star, Mountains & Valleys, terrible dimension
> Stretch'd out, compose the Mundane Shell, a mighty Incrustation ...[239]

The material sun (forged by Los — see K260 BOL: 27–45) is the principal 'star' and Urizen has been appointed, by the Eternal One, 'leader of his hosts', that is, Urizen is the charioteer of the material sun.[240]

Blake sees a parallel between the 'inner', psychological division in man and the way in which he, in his rational, mathematical thinking, divides the forces in the universe into distinct phenomena. Just as, in the Fall, the unified individual disintegrates into 'Spectre' and 'Emanation', so also the materialist disintegrates the totality into conflicting elements — for example, into the dead spherical body, the 'spectrous' sun, which provides a focus for Newtonian laws of gravitation, and the 'emanation'[241] of life-giving light and warmth which, mysteriously, is produced by the apparently lifeless, 'spectrous' body. If men see the sun as a 'divided' image, it is not to be wondered at that they should 'become what they behold', that is, conform to the same image. The materialist becomes the centre of his mechanically structured little universe. He becomes a microcosm of an abstract, dead macrocosm, and he discounts as meaningless and fanciful the creative imagination within him except in rare moments when, for the sake of his sanity, he needs to opt out of the oppressive, Urizenic rat race characteristic of a subhuman life devoted to material gain and accumulation. Blake would have us know that if we were to see the sun, our fellow men, nature, as he sees them, then we would see our own humanity in the same living light. Then the 'Spectre' and the 'Emanation' would disappear. Their functions would be integrated back into a human nature which no longer acted as a 'darksome' lifeless mechanism, but as a living, expressive unity of vision, creative energy and desire, seeing everything that lives as holy and harmoniously working together in brotherly love.[242]

The natural world is largely dependent for its life on the daily cycle of the rising and setting sun. The sun can, therefore, readily be accepted as a central symbol of the natural cycle. Seen from the sense-experiential viewpoint it signifies nothing but an indefinitely repetitive cycle in time of dullness and sameness, 'unable to do other than repeat the same dull round over again';[213] but, seen from an imaginative viewpoint, the sun's daily reappearance and renewal suggests resurrection into Eternity. Hence the symbol of the sun has two forms: one form being the form of its eternal, spiritual life, which is experienced by the Imagination, the other the form of its physical death, with which the selfhood has rapport. The sun of spiritual life is God Himself (Rev 21:23); the sun of death is the swastika, or, as Blake expresses it, the 'Scythed Chariot' of the Druid Britons.[243a]

In Eternity, we must remember, Urizen/Lucifer, the 'Prince of Light', is representative of the true sun, of Christ/God, the essence of spiritual enlightenment; but, in his pride to 'be like the most High', he is 'brought down to Hell, to the sides of the pit'![244] Lucifer/Satan/Urizen, the representative of the spiritual sun, falls into spiritual darkness, into the world of generation. The Fall of the Prince of Light is the macrocosmic counterpart of the fall of the spiritual essence of man into an imprisoning microcosmic physical body. This 'body' is, like the physical fallen sun, a 'shadow' of the spiritual sun, seen as the only reality by the 'cavern'd' man, the man of fallen reason, of fallen Urizenic enlightenment.

Throughout his life Blake seeks spiritual enlightenment. Indeed, he himself uses the word 'enlightenment' to describe the experience he had following his visit to the Truchsessian Gallery.[245] All we need to note here in connection with this visit is that he found renewed strength of reliance upon inward vision for his inspiration. He found himself restored to the 'light of Art'.[246] The enlightenment to which he found himself restored was that of creative imagination, of Los/Christ, which stands in contrast to Urizenic enlightenment, to the Urizenic/Satanic form of rational enlightenment consolidated in the world of generation by such men as Francis Bacon, Thomas Hobbes, René Descartes, Isaac Newton, John Locke, Rousseau and Voltaire.

The so-called 'real' sun as ordinarily perceived 'is Satan', the dead matter of Newtonian physics. The 'Spiritual Sun' — which Blake beheld on Primrose Hill and, we may safely assume, could see anywhere — is the physically perceived sun illuminated by, endowed with, spiritual light. It is 'nature' transfigured by vision. The false, 'evil Man',[247] is the spiritually blind rationalist, materialist, who sees 'with' the eye; the 'true Man'[248] is the visionary who sees 'thro' ' the eye. He is the visionary who is able to transcend materialistic explanations.

At the very beginning of the nineteenth century Blake writes:

> To find the Western path
> Right thro' the Gates of Wrath
> I urge my way;
> Sweet Mercy leads me on:
> With soft repentant moan
> I seek the break of day.
>
> The war of swords & spears
> Melted by dewy tears

> Exhales on high;
> The Sun is freed from fears
> And with soft grateful tears
> Ascends the sky.[249]

To comment in any detail on this poem is not relevant to our present context, but, in passing we may note that the West (the direction of America) is synonymous with freedom; Wrath is revolution; Mercy is Christ Himself; the 'repentant moan' is that of selfishness surrendering to imagination; and, finally, that corporeal war gives way to the rising spiritual sun, which is poetry and art freed from Urizenic corruption and spiritual darkness, or, we could also say, is in an extended sense, the 'Mental Fight' which is of the very essence in the creation of the New Jerusalem, universal brotherhood and selfless love.[250]

Annotating his sixth illustration to Milton's *L'Allegro* Blake writes: 'The youthful Poet, sleeping on a bank by the Haunted Stream of Sun Set, sees in his dream the more bright Sun of Imagination.'[251] Here Blake depicts the two suns, the 'natural sun', which is death, and the 'Spiritual Sun', which is life.[252] In the illustration the sun of this physical world, a tiny, orange-red sphere which hovers just above the horizon, is dwarfed by the Great Globe of Vision. Blake's juxtaposition of the two suns explicitly points to the superiority of the 'Sun of Imagination' over the sun of this world, and hence of the Imaginative over 'natural' vision, of Imagination over rationalism, of Christ over Lucifer/Satan/Urizen.

We have spoken of Satan/Urizen as being the 'sun-god' of the Enlightenment. By this we do not mean, however, that he is literally the god of the physical sun. In terms of the basic symbolism of the Four Zoas, to which we shall return in more detail in Chapters 7–9, none of the four can literally be the god of any external form or force, for each represents primarily an aspect of the human psyche. Indeed, Los himself says on one occasion to his Emanation, Enitharmon: 'in the Brain of Man we live & in his circling Nerves, ... this bright world of all our joy is in the Human Brain'.[253]

The fallen external sun is, as it appears to our organs of perception, created by the human imagination, by Urthona/Los. It may appear — according to how well 'cleans'd' our organs of perception are — as a ball of fire, a golden guinea, or a chorus of angels:

> The Sun's Light when he unfolds it
> Depends on the Organ that beholds it.[254]

However, although Urthona/Los is the 'creator', it is Urizen — in his eternal aspect — who is more closely associated with the sun than any of the other three Zoas. Urizen's place in Eternity is the South, that is, the place of the sun. But in *The Four Zoas* we learn that he covets and usurps the North, the sphere of Urthona, the Imagination, which he Urizen, Reason, desires to rule. In Night v we hear that imbalance and confusion reign in the cosmos — and hence also in the human soul. Urizen fails to obey the Word, the 'mild & holy voice' of Christ, the Divine Vision, to 'go forth & guide' man who 'wanders on the ocean', that is, in the world of generation. When thought assumes the role of ruler rather than that of guide, then both spiritual love, Luvah, and Imagination, Urthona, are weakened, if not destroyed.[255] As already stated, Urizen's place in Eternity is in the South. His seizure of the North from Urthona is a part of the cause of the Fall of Man.

Luvah, too, is a usurper. He conspires with Urizen to establish empire over man. They are both described as being activated by 'foul ambition'.[256] Whereas Urizen would rule over man's imagination, Luvah, emotions, would dominate man's reason. Rather than co-operate with Urizen, Luvah seizes Urizen's 'Chariot of Day' drawn by the 'Horses of Light'. Then:

How rag'd the golden horses of Urizen, bound to the chariot of Love.[257]

Here, of course, love is no longer selfless, it is no longer manifesting itself in its highest spiritual form. Luvah and Urizen 'contend in war around the holy tent' of Albion.[258] Each contends that he is superior to the other. The ideal unity, totality, is 'fragmented'. 'Am I not God?', asks Urizen. 'Who is equal to me?'.[259] And Luvah makes a similar claim: 'am not I/ The Prince of all the hosts of Men, nor equal know in Heaven?'[260] When, contributing to the process of the Fall of Man, Luvah 'seize'd' [sic] the Horses of Light, & rose into the Chariot of Day', he has his turn in the South, the place of the sun. In *Milton*, Luvah's bulls are described as dragging 'the sulphur Sun out of the Deep'.[261]

Before looking more closely at Luvah in relation to the sun, let us just note that, after he usurps the North, Urizen is 'enclosed' in cold darkness, for he is shrouded in 'the Direful Web of Religion'[262] and all light is intercepted by 'the Tree of Mystery'. In other words, when reason dominates over the other soul faculties, man, instead of being spiritually enlightened, is spiritually 'endarkened'. Nevertheless, Urizen is still conventionally addressed as 'Prince of Light',[263] and he still worships in 'the temple of the Sun'. But now the temple is no longer that of Christ, of the Spiritual Sun, but of Satan/Urizen, fallen reason. Urizenic Man worships the physical, Newtonian sun.

It is worth quoting here, at length, a passage from Night viii of *The Four Zoas* to give some impression of Blake's view of the spiritual powerlessness of man when confusion reigns in his soul:

> ... Urizen gave life & sense by his immortal power
> To all his Engines of deceit: that linked chains might run
> Thro' ranks of war spontaneous: & that hooks & boring screws
> Might act according to their forms by innate cruelty.
> He formed also harsh instruments of sound
> To grate the soul into destruction, or to inflame with fury
> The spirits of life, to pervert all the faculties of sense
> Into their own destruction, if perhaps he might avert
> His own despair even at the cost of every thing that breathes.
>
> Thus in the temple of the Sun his books of iron & brass
> And silver & gold he consecrated, reading incessantly
> To myriads of perturbed spirits; thro' the universe
> They propagated the deadly words, the Shadowy Female absorbing
> The enormous Sciences of Urizen, ages after ages exploring
> The fell destruction.[264]

Here Blake gives us a picture of fallen Urizen who would appear to be a power of enormous strength. But it is appearance, Newtonian, only. Urizen, the warring priest, seen from the viewpoint of Eternity, the Totality, is ineffectual both as tyrant and as preacher. The only apparent listener is the Shadowy Female, Luvah's fallen Emanation, Vala, who ensnares Urizen till he:

> Sitting within his temple furious, felt the num(m)ing stupor,
> Himself entangled in his own net, in sorrow, lust, repentance.[265]

It is only when Urizen abandons his efforts to repress man's passion, instinct, and imagination, that is, Luvah, Tharmas, and Urthona/Los, that he can shake the 'snows from off his shoulders':

> ... renew'd, he shook his aged mantle off
> Into the fires. Then, glorious bright, Exulting in his joy,
> He sounding rose into the heavens in naked majesty,
> In radiant youth ...[266]

Now, each Zoa is in some way responsible for the Fall, but in *The Four Zoas* the ultimate responsibility is assigned, not to Urizen, but to Luvah,

who 'siez'd the Horses of Light & rose into the Chariot of Day'.[267]
Passion usurps the place of Reason, taking over its function of 'guiding'
the will of man, or, rather, of dominating the will. When Reason fails
to guide, fails to function as a power of discrimination, then Luvah,
Passion, the usurper, does not selflessly 'guide', but selfishly
dominates. This situation is emphasized when we hear that the
'Dark'ning Man', walking with Vala 'in dreams of soft deluding slum-
ber',[268] is no longer able to exercise conscious discrimination and judge-
ment, for the 'Splendor' of Urizen, the Prince of Light, is faded,[269] and
he, man, is mentally 'Slumberous'.[270] A consequence of this spiritual
'slumber' is that man worships Luvah as the god of the natural world.
Now the Fall is consolidated and 'the dark Body of [Man del.] Albion' is
'Cover'd with boils from head to foot, the terrible smitings of Luvah'.[271]

With regard to 'the terrible smitings of Luvah', we need to remind
ourselves here of our earlier discussion regarding the selfhood. Blake
speaks of Satan as being the selfhood, the empirical 'encapsulated' human
ego. Now, Satan can attack us on different psychic frontiers, as it were.
Satan/Urizen, fallen reason, closes man's senses to the spiritual world and
is the cause of the externalization of the phenomenal world. In contrast to
the selfless, brotherly love (Agape) of prelapsarian Luvah, the sexual love
(Eros) of fallen Luvah attacks fallen man with inner conflicts of guilt,
sexual guilt. Fallen Luvah, selfish lust, is an aspect of 'Satan the Selfhood'
— that Satan who smites Job with sore boils. Satan's/Urizen's natural
morality,[272] his 'Selfish Virtue of the Natural Heart',[273] recoils on itself; it
inculcates condemnation of others and rebounds in self-condemnation.[274]

When Urizen, Reason, falls, then erotic love, selfish lust, assumes
control and when this happens Albion, man, exclaims:

> O cruel pity! O dark deceit! can love seek for
> dominion?
> And Luvah strove to gain dominion over Albion ...[275]

Satan the Tempter appears first in Blake not as Urizen, but as Luvah:

> ... when Luvah in Orc became a Serpent, he descended into
> That State called Satan.[276]

In *Milton* Urizen is Satan, but earlier, in *The Four Zoas*, Satan is Orc,
the fallen form of Luvah. In fact, Los/Urthona is the only one of the four
Zoas who does not descend into the state of Satan, for he it is who keeps
'the Divine Vision in time of trouble'.[277]

We have digressed a while from our present theme of the symbol of the sun to show not only how, but also why, when Albion, man, loses 'the Divine Vision', then 'true Man'[278] collapses into False Man. It is False Man who no longer perceives the spiritual sun, the 'humanized', Christ-filled sun. All he can perceive is the 'disk' of the lifeless corporeal sun; He is then in a 'state nam'd Satan' which comes into being, as we have endeavoured to show, not only when Urizen/Reason falls, but also when Luvah/Love degenerates into selfish, erotic love. In both cases the spiritual sun is hidden from man's experience. The spiritual, 'humanized' sun, may be seen as a symbol of eternal brotherhood. Fallen man, in a moment of realization of his fallen state, cries out:

> ... futurity is before me
> Like a dark lamp. Eternal death haunts all my expectation.
> Rent from Eternal Brotherhood we die & are no more.[279]

This would be true, if it were not for Los, the creative imagination, who keeps 'the Divine Vision in time of trouble', who builds the City of Imagination, Golgonooza, and hence the foundation of Jerusalem, and who, through his selfless labours, becomes one with the Divine Vision, Christ, the very essence of Agape, brotherly love.

It is clear from what has been said so far about prelapsarian Luvah that there is a close relationship between him and Christ, on the one hand, and with the Serpent, on the other. In his fallen form, Orc, Luvah became a serpent:

> But when Luvah in Orc became a Serpent he descended into
> That State call'd Satan.[280]

We see, therefore, that there is a close association between Christ and the Serpent.

Now, we need to remind ourselves here that the ancient symbol of the Serpent is not representative of 'evil' exclusively, but is itself ambiguous. Essentially, of course, the Serpent is the Tempter in the Garden of Eden, but, in Blake, it is a more complex symbol. For instance, it is synonymous with the fallen body of man (Laocoon, entwined by serpents, can be seen as man 'cavern'd' in fallen nature). However, since the Serpent sheds its skin it is also symbolic of immortality. This idea in itself has two aspects: it is negative if it means interminable natural cycles of death-in-life; it is positive if it suggests spiritual immortality. The Serpent, Luvah in Orc, is suggestive of both natural generation and spiritual regeneration. Christ

himself had to enter the world of natural generation, the cycle of physical
birth and death in order to bring about the regeneration, the spiritual
renewal, of the fallen world of Generated Man in which Satan/Urizen
reigns. That the reign of love, of universal brotherhood, on earth will be
brought about by regeneration through the Imagination, through
Christ, is what Blake constantly calls on us to recognize and inwardly
experience. As we shall see in Chapter 8, the meaning of such a vision is
quite incomprehensible to Urizenic Man.

Blake brings the association between Christ and Luvah in Orc, the
Serpent, to our attention in several ways. For instance, in his illustration
to *Paradise Lost*, entitled 'Michael foretelling the Crucifixion', the head of
the Serpent is transfixed by the same nail which pierces Christ's feet. The
body of the Serpent twines round the Cross itself. A serpent wound
round a cross is, in fact, a traditional symbol for Christ crucified.[281]
Another telling example is given in *The Four Zoas*. In Night viib we read:

> They vote the death of Luvah & they nail'd him to the tree,
> They pierc'd him with a spear & laid him in a sepulcher.[282]

And in Night viii:

> Thus was the Lamb of God condemn'd to Death.
> They nail'd him upon the tree of Mystery...[283]

Los, Imagination, the guardian of the Divine Vision, is the first who
recognizes that Christ replaces 'Serpent Orc'[284] as the operative form of
Luvah when he says to his Emanation, Enitharmon:

> ... look! behold! take comfort!
> Turn inwardly thine Eyes & there behold the Lamb of God
> Clothed in Luvah's robes of blood descending to redeem.[285]

We can understand this replacing of Orc (as the operative form of Luvah)
by Christ as being spiritual revolutionary energy, which brings Christian
brotherhood into being, replacing the political revolutionary energy
(Orc) which fought and failed to achieve fraternity. Christ puts on
Luvah's robes of blood so that the vision of brotherhood will not be lost
with the failure of Orc, or, in Blake's own words:

> Lest the state call'd Luvah should cease.[286]

Here we cannot go into any great detail as to the nature of Orc, but, in
a few words, we could say that he represents, in man, an imprisoned
Promethean energy which struggles to burst free; he represents a power

which spasmodically erupts in revolutions (in history we could mention the French and American Revolutions, for instance). He is the power which struggles to overcome restrictions and limitations, to overcome the oppressive power of Urizen — both in individual man and in society. Such a power is regarded as evil by conventional morality, by the Establishment. In Blake the coming of Christ is the appearance of Orc in a completely transformed form. Whereas Orc is the driving force of the world of generation, Christ/Los — Orc's creator — is the power of spiritual regeneration. As we shall see in Chapter 10, the close association between Los and Christ, the creative imaginative power in man, and *the* Creative Power, Imagination, is recognized by Albion, who, having acknowledged the cruelty of his selfhood, is growing in spiritual awareness and vision to the point where he is prepared to go through the process of self-annihilation. Just before throwing 'himself into the Furnaces of affliction'[287] he says to Christ:

> I see thee in the likeness & similitude of Los my friend.[288]

Moreover, Albion now recognizes Christ as his 'Divine Creator & Redeemer'.[289]

In *Jerusalem* the affinity between Los and Christ is clearly shown when we hear that Los joins the 'Divine Body, following merciful'[290] fallen Albion, who, having turned his back on the Divine Vision, has turned from 'Universal Love':[291]

> ... but mild, the Saviour follow'd him,
> Displaying the Eternal Vision, the Divine Similitude,
> In loves and tears of brothers, sisters, sons, fathers and friends,
> Which if Man ceases to behold, he ceases to exist.[292]

It is Los, the shaper and creator, the friend of Albion, of man, who is the 'hero' of all Blake's later poems. He is the spiritual or imaginative impulse and energy in life. Labouring at his anvil and giving 'bitter death' to evil, or Satan, he gives to the Spectre visions of beauty and truth by 'embodying' him, by building the Spiritual City of Golgonooza for him, and by destroying (transforming) those systems of restrictive morality and philosophy which harden both the senses and the emotions of Man. 'All Quarrels', says Los:

> ... arise from Reasoning: the secret Murder and
> The violent Man-slaughter, these are the Spectre's double Cave,
> The Sexual Death living on accusation of Sin & Judgment,

To freeze Love & Innocence into the gold & silver of the Merchant.
Without Forgiveness & Sin, Love is Itself Eternal Death.[293]

One of the most frequently used groups of images in Blake's three great prophetic books is that of Los's furnaces and forges, hammer and anvil. We have already seen that the iron-forging activity, characteristic of the blacksmith, Los, often appears in association with the weaving activity of his Emanation, Enitharmon. Los's furnaces of Bowlahoola and Enitharmon's Looms of Cathedron are the fundamental elements of the new industrial age.

Blake clearly believed that industrialization could benefit all mankind, that it could provide the physical basis for a utopian existence. He saw, however, that the industrialists, the capitalists, were under the domination of the prevailing philosophy of Urizenic materialism and that, as a consequence, they would exercise ever greater tyranny in their oppression of the multitudinous poor.

Under the domination of Urizen iron symbolizes the rigidity and cruelty which sanction the exploitation of downtrodden humanity in the factories and the destruction of men in war. It is iron-forging (in an extended sense) which provides both the factory machinery and the weapons of war.[294] In *Jerusalem* Blake draws a parallel between modern industrial Britain and the civilization of ancient Egypt which flourished under slave labour. Fallen Albion's sons are cast in the same mould as these ancient tyrants; they construct an abstract philosophy; declare war against Christ,[295] the philosophy of love (Erin),[296] Los's furnaces and Golgonooza[297] and Jerusalem.[298] In short, 'Albion's Druid sons' practise slavery, human sacrifice, in an industrial society.[299]

However, as already intimated, Blake also sees the benefits which can accrue to the whole of mankind when the creative imagination, Los, assumes an active role in the new 'Iron Age'. In Blake's prophetic books, furnaces, forges, pulleys, chains, hammers and anvils are everywhere in London, a major centre of the industrial world:

> Loud sounds the Hammer of Los & loud his Bellows is heard
> Before London to Hampstead's breadths & Highgate's heights,
> To Stratford & old Bow & across to the Gardens of Kensington
> On Tyburn's Brook: loud groans Thames beneath the iron Forge
> Of Rhintrah & Palamabron, of Theotorm & Bromion,* to forge
>   the instruments

*The four faithful sons of Los.

Of Harvest, the Plow & Harrow to pass over the Nations.[300]

The Harvest ushers in the millennium, when imaginatively inspired government, and hence happiness and prosperity for everyone, will prevail. Political oppression, symbolized by the reference to Tyburn, the site of the famous gallows in London,[301] and Urizenic institutions, represented by the alms-houses at Stratford, will then give way to the creative efforts of Los and his sons, symbolized by their labours at the furnace and anvil to transform an unjust and tyrannical system into an imaginative foundation for universal brotherhood, in which every man and woman will be free to realize the full potential of his or her true humanity.

We see, then, that iron, iron-forging, is a symbol with two contrasting meanings.

As mentioned above, Blake sees the new Iron Age, the industrial age, as being founded on human sacrifice. One instance of explicit sacrifice occurs in *The Four Zoas* (repeated in *Jerusalem*):

> Luvah was cast into the Furnaces of affliction & sealed,
> And Vala fed in cruel delight the furnaces with fire.
> Stern Urizen beheld, urg'd by necessity to keep
> The evil day afar, & if perchance with iron power
> He might avert his own despair; in woe & fear he saw
> Vala incircle round the furnaces where Luvah was clos'd.[302]

The furnaces of affliction in which Luvah is sacrificed here symbolize both the contemporary industrial furnace[303] to which ordinary men and women are subjected through unjust and inhuman Urizenic oppression, and the suppression of the forward-looking spiritual revolutionary, the imaginative man of creative energy. Luvah can be interpreted here as representing revolutionary France.[304] Vala, antagonistic to spiritual perception,[305] feeds the Urizenic furnaces of affliction. Urizen, watching as Luvah is sacrificed, represents the 'iron-hearted tyrant'[306] of the Establishment (in Britain) witnessing the events taking place across the Channel in France. His self-interest and desire to retain the status quo reinforce his determination to fend off the 'evil day' of social reform in Britain. Indeed, to avert such reform through 'iron power' — which we may interpret quite literally as being the power he holds through the weaponry manufactured in his foundries and factories where, as the 'great Work master',[307] he rules with a rod of iron over his workers. The 'voice of Luvah',[308] representing the afflicted — the oppressed and under-privileged — in both England and France, cries out from 'the furnaces of Urizen':[309]

> They have surounded me with walls of iron & brass. O lamb
> Of God clothed in Luvah's garments![310]

Here Blake identifies the Lamb of God, the victim of materialism and rationalism, natural religion and natural morality, with all suffering men, women and children in the industrial Iron Age.

Brass is also associated with Urizen's rigid tyranny. For instance, Urizen writes with 'his iron pen'[311] in 'books of iron and brass'.[312] However, as already stated, iron is a symbol with two contrasting faces — and the same may be said of brass. It is not only Urizen, fallen Reason, but also creative imagination, Los, who is associated with iron — and with brass.

Los, the 'labourer of ages',[313] 'the Lord of the Furnaces',[314] 'builds the City of Art, Golgonooza, with these two metals'.[315] Though imperfect, for it is 'in the Shadowy Generation',[316] Golgonooza, the City of Imagination, opens 'new heavens & a new Earth beneath & within',[317] and is a necessary prelude to the coming into being of the New Jerusalem. Golgonooza can be understood to be a foreshadowing of the New Jerusalem. Like the New Jerusalem, the City of Golgonooza is also four-square.[318]

Just as the ancient Iron Age had its positive aspect in that more efficient and labour-saving agricultural tools could be made, so also the New Iron Age, which in Urizen's hands oppresses and enslaves man, possesses the potential — in Blake's view — to bless man. In Los's workshop the iron furnace is representative of free creative activity, not, as in Urizen's sweatshops, of the elimination of such activity. What is needed in order that man's industrial power should be 'free' to build the New Jerusalem is the spiritual formative and imaginative vision of brotherhood.[319] Industrialism and rationalism must enhance the dignity of man, not degrade it. For this to happen, cold, abstract and 'iron-hearted' Urizen must freely gain the insight to be 'converted' to the persuasion of golden Los,[320] who is described in *Jerusalem* as:

> Putting on his golden sandals to walk from mountain to mountain,
> He takes his way, girding himself with gold & in his hand
> Holding his iron mace.[321]

The New Iron Age — our age — must be transformed into a New Golden Age.[322]

Urizen, the tyrannical individual fallen Reason, must work harmoniously with Los, the creative imagination. He must be united with Los, with Christ, then mankind will be united in brotherhood. Thus at the end of *Jerusalem* when the 'excrementious/Husk & Covering'[323] has been cast off,

> ... bright beaming Urizen
> Lay'd his hand on the South & took a breathing Bow of carved Gold:

and:

> Urthona Northward in thick storms a Bow of Iron ...[324]

Once man, Albion, has recognized that he 'cannot exist but by Brotherhood'[325] and overcomes his selfhood, offers his 'Self for Another' in 'Friendship & Brotherhood',[326] then 'The Furnaces of affliction' are transformed into 'Fountains of Living Waters flowing from the Humanity Divine'.[327]

Blake sees the New Iron Age, guided by Imagination in harmonious harness with Reason, creatively labouring to emerge, through the 'Furnaces of affliction', into the New Golden Age of Love and Brotherhood. Then Jerusalem's Spirits of Love, Seraphim, and Spirits of Wisdom, Cherubim, will rejoice together among her 'little ones',[328] and it will be true that 'Man is love/As God is Love'.[329]

* * * * *

The purpose of this chapter has been to shed light on some of the fundamental meanings of Blake's symbols. There are many others we have not touched upon at all; to attempt to do so would take us well beyond the limits of the present work. Nonetheless, it is hoped that the reader will now be able to gain a better understanding not only of the chapters which follow, but of Blake's great work as a whole.

It will, no doubt, now be clear that to interpret Blake's symbols, to experience their archetypal meanings, to make them our own, is far from being an easy process. It is true, of course, that to experience fully the inner meaning of the work of any great thinker, poet, painter or composer, is a lifelong process. It is so to a very marked degree in the case of Blake. He 'asks' that we suspend all previously held convictions, that, in short, we 'annihilate' our selfhood and 'cleanse our organs of perception'. To remain in Urizenic self-contemplation and detachment is to set up impenetrable barriers to any understanding of Blake. In his own words:

If the Spectator could enter into these Images in his Imagination, approaching them on the Fiery Chariot of his Contemplative Thought, ... or could make a Friend & Companion of one of these Images of wonder, which always intreats him to leave mortal things (as he must know), then would he arise from his Grave, then would he meet the Lord in the Air & then he would be happy.[330]

Blake felt it to be his divinely appointed task to uproot the 'forests of affliction'[331] which restrain the creative imagination. Symbolically, we recall, forests are traditional places where the way is lost and the light obscured. Under Urizen's autocracy man hides in 'forests of night'[332] which are composed of dead trees. There he is enmeshed in rooted errors of the dogmatic, unimaginative, life-destroying and abstract rationalizing mind.

Blake exhorts us to affiliate ourselves with him in his task:

The Nature of my Work is Visionary or Imaginative; it is an Endeavour to Restore what the Ancients call'd the Golden Age.[333]

6

THE CREATION MYTH

Blake, in common with all profound thinkers of a religious nature, was fascinated by man's archetypal myths, in particular by those concerned with the eternal questions of the creation of the world and of man, and of man's relation to the world and to himself.

Very soon after writing such clearly political poems as *The French Revolution* (1791) and *America, a Prophecy* (1793), Blake gives us his first attempt at cosmogonic myth* — *The First Book of Urizen* (1794).[1]

Now, for reasons which will become apparent during the course of this chapter, Blake's questioning mind could not rest satisfied with the simple Old Testament myth of creation.[2] But, as will also become apparent, he would have largely accepted the following account from the Gnostic tradition:

Out of the mist of the beginnings of our era there looms a pageant of mythical figures whose vast, superhuman contours might people the walls and ceilings of another Sistine Chapel. Their countenance and gestures, the roles in which they are cast, the drama which they enact, would yield images different from the biblical ones on which the imagination of the beholder was reared, yet strangely familiar to him and disturbingly moving. The stage would be the same, the theme as transcending; the creation of the world, the destiny of man, fall and redemption, the first and last things ... Almost all the action would be in the heights, in the divine or angelic or deimonic realm, a drama of pre-cosmic persons in the supernatural world, of which the drama of man in the natural world is but a distant echo ... God's erring Wisdom, Sophia, falling prey to her folly, wandering in the void and darkness of her own making, labouring her passion into matter, her yearning into soul; a blind and arrogant Creator, believing himself

---

*Cosmogony is concerned with the questions of 'how' and 'why' the universe and man came to be as we find them; 'how' and 'why' evil came into being; 'how' and 'why' man may be redeemed from that evil, and so forth.

the Most High and lording over the creation, the product, like himself, of fault and ignorance; the Soul, trapped and lost in the labyrinth of the world ... seeking to escape and frightened back by the gatekeepers of the cosmic prison, the terrible archons; a Saviour from the Light beyond venturing into the nether world, illuming the darkness, opening a path, healing the divine breach; a tale of light and darkness, of knowledge and ignorance, of serenity and passion, of conceit and pity, on the scale not of man but of eternal beings that are not exempt from suffering and error.[3]

This lengthy passage has not been quoted because it necessarily reflects Blake's own vision of the Creation and the role of the Saviour (though it will become apparent as we proceed through this and the following chapters that in many respects it does), but because, if he had been able to read it, he would have recognized a myth far more congenial to his own intuitive experience than that of the Old Testament. For instance, the Bible's failure to give any motive for the Creation does not satisfy Blake; and the concept of a Creation which is *itself* the Fall seems to him both more philosophically profound and psychologically probable than that of a Creation which takes place *before* the Fall. Furthermore, the Old Testament myth did not satisfactorily explain the presence of suffering and evil in the phenomenal world, the world of mankind.

Genesis presents creation as God's benevolent act. The evils of later life arise from primeval man's disobedience to God's commands. In Blake's vision, however, evil lies, not in man's disobedience, but in the despotic command of an Eternal, a god, Urizen. Hence, for Blake, creation cannot be the act of a benevolent God. In *The Book of Urizen* Blake traces Urizen's despotism to his primeval selfishness and self-withdrawal, to his selfhood. We can understand this as being the macrocosmic origin of microcosmic, human self-centredness and selfishness. This act of withdrawal, separation, is the beginning of Blake's myth.

The theme of the divisive life is stated in the 'Preludium' to *The Book of Urizen*:

> Of the primeval Priest's assum'd power,
> When Eternals spurn'd back his religion
> And gave him a place in the north,
> Obscure, shadowy, void, solitary.[4]

The 'primeval Priest' is the original despot, Urizen (Reason). This 'shadowy' and 'solitary' Being is described succinctly in the following lines:

> Lo, a shadow of horror is risen
> In Eternity! Unknown, unprolific,
> Self-clos'd, all-repelling: what Demon
> Hath form'd this abominable void,
> This soul-shudd'ring vacuum? Some said
> 'It is Urizen'. But unknown, abstracted,
> Brooding, secret, the dark power hid.[5]

Blake's description here is a clear statement of the character of Urizen (Reason; 'you reason'; 'your reason'). Abstracted from the harmonious interweaving and interacting of the Whole, reason is uncreative. It no longer sees infinity but 'self' alone. It repels all that is not of 'self'.

Urizen (Reason), divided from the other Eternals when he attempts to usurp their power, loses his knowledge of Eternity and Infinity, of the spiritual world. He attains his separate consciousness, self-consciousness, only after he has lost the all-embracing spiritual perception of the Whole. He is now a 'Self-contemplative Shadow',[6] for, as Blake says in the tractate 'All Religions are One' (2nd series), 'He who sees the Ratio only, sees himself only'.[7] This — in so far as it exists for Blake at all — is original sin. Original sin, for him, is the self-centred act of a portion of a whole; such an act disrupts and destroys any whole — individual, social or cosmic — because it is the agent of 'abstracted, brooding, secret,' isolation.

It is worth noting that the adjectives and nouns Blake uses in the seven lines just quoted graphically indicate the kind of 'evil' Urizen represents.[8] It would be difficult to find a better characterization of the self-centred, egocentric human being. He, too, is unknown, unprolific, self-enclosed, all-repelling, abstracted, brooding, secret and dark. He, too, is a 'shadow of horror' living in an 'abominable void' and 'shuddering vacuum' — separated, as he is, from his fellow men. Here Urizen can be recognized as the arch-enemy of human brotherhood. Moreover, Blake is saying that the seeds of animosity, disharmony and destruction were sown before the appearance of man. Blake expands this theme to show that from this self-centred separation of souls emerge all other 'evils' — such as Los's jealousy.

Yet the attempt to dominate others is Urizen's well-intentioned error, for he sincerely believes that through his laws he can improve life: 'I have sought for a joy without pain'.[9]

> Laws of peace, of love, of unity,
> Of pity, compassion, forgiveness;

> Let each chuse [sic] one habitation,
> His ancient infinite mansion,
> One command, one joy, one desire,
> One curse, one weight, one measure,
> One King, one God, one Law.[10]

In the lines preceding this passage, Urizen speaks of his activity:

> Here alone I, in books form'd of metals,
> Have written the secrets of wisdom,
> The secrets of dark contemplation,
> By fighting and conflicts dire
> With terrible monsters Sin-bred
> Which the bosoms of all inhabit,
>
> Seven deadly Sins of the soul.
> Lo! I unfold my darkness, and on
> This rock place with strong hand the Book
> Of eternal Brass, written in my solitude.[11]

In *The Book of Ahania* (1795) we find a similar utterance:

> ... when Urizen shrunk away
> From Eternals, he sat on a rock
> Barren: a rock which himself
> From redounding fancies had petrified.
> ... he wrote
> In silence his book of iron.[12]

Urizen is both God the law-giver and Moses the law-declaimer. The rigid and unyielding — unimaginative — laws are inscribed on equally rigid and inflexible material. Urizen has written down his wisdom as a result of his conflicts with the seven deadly sins of the soul. 'The Book of eternal brass' is the book of false ethics which, because it ignores the precept that 'One law for the Lion & Ox is Oppression',[13] not only impoverishes man, but, as we shall see, gives rise to hypocritical pity. Within the limitations of his restricted vision, Urizen has good intentions. But the limitations are catastrophic, for he cannot see that by asserting one right pattern of conduct he is himself creating the 'Seven deadly Sins of the soul'. In the place of spiritual freedom is restraint, 'limitation', and, above all, the dogma of right and wrong, of good and evil. At first sight Urizen's regime appears to be both justified and even attractive — and seen from the point of view of reason it is. But the disquiet of the Imagination, roused by the word 'laws', is reinforced by the repetition of the word 'one'. It is here that the flaw in Reason, the flaw in Urizen's world, becomes apparent. Everything that is valued by the Imagination, everything valued in Eternity — such as love, forgiveness, compassion, peace and unity — is to be dealt with by one inflexible law, by a single yardstick. In short, in his effort, well-intentioned but misguided, to establish the values of Eternity permanently, Urizen ignores one great principle of Eternity and of the Imagination, namely, that everything should be understood, esteemed and judged, in the light of its own separate identity.

We see, then, that Blake achieves the remarkable feat of explaining how 'evil' could have its origin in Eternity without, at the same time, denying the original good intentions of the Creator. Indeed, it is the usurper's, Urizen's, good intention itself which leads him into Error. This Error is intensified by his belief that through his laws he can improve life and by his wish to create a world where joy is permanent and pain non-existent:

> I have sought for a joy without pain,
> For a solid without fluctuation.[14]

Here is sown the cosmic seed for that which manifests itself in the world of mankind as spiritual torpidity. True, creative humanity lives by continuous formation and transformation, but Urizen yearns for 'a solid without fluctuation', for permanence without change. He yearns for the unity of submissive obedience to the One Law, which would then guarantee permanence. Imagination, on the other hand, strives for intuitive insight into the 'inner' law of each individual which is in constant process of metamorphosis. The rational would petrify, the imaginative vivify.

Urizen's tragedy is that, having separated himself from the One, having instigated the fragmentation of the Whole, he seeks oneness, longs for unity. His error lies in his failure to recognize that, without the interplay and counteraction of contraries, such as joy and pain, a living, dynamic unity is not possible. Joy could not be experienced unless pain also existed. An invariable, unfluctuating permanence would be lifeless. Permanence obviates creativity and imagination and thus dulls consciousness. All the 'evils' of the fallen world, of experience, feed upon the dogma of absolute reaction to change. Permanance, changelessness, is the cradle of Newtonian sleep! Indeed, the greater the fluctuation, the greater the contrast between the contraries, the more intense and expansive does consciousness grow.

Urizen seeks for 'joy without pain' and a 'solid without fluctuation' in what he calls

> The eternal abode of my holiness,
> Hidden, set apart ...[15]

Here it should be remembered that 'holiness' is a word which Blake often uses in a pejorative sense; as, for instance, the virtue of the Pharisees, the state of the 'Fiends of Righteousness', who are 'in Holiness/Opposed to Mercy'[16] and who enact and execute cruel laws.

For anyone to set himself apart from others and to assume a 'garment' of 'holiness' — implying that others are unholy — is anathema to Blake. For him, 'everything that *lives* is holy [my italics]' and no true and creative individuality can be more holy than another. Urizen (the Pharisee), with his reductive vision, is opposed to Mercy, to Christ, who, for him, is a delusion.[17]

Urizen, then, cannot see that in a living world all things are constantly renewed and that permanence, paradoxically, is the one condition that kills. This blindness is emphasized in his exclamatory question to the Eternals:

> Why will you die, O Eternals?
> Why live in unquenchable burnings?[18]

The fiery excitement of a life of continually active and renewed creative and imaginative impulse appears to the rigid Urizenic mind to be like burning in Hell. Indeed, Urizen says that he 'fought with the fire'.[19] He cannot live with and in 'the fire of life'. For Blake, Christ is not only the 'Lord *of Love*' but also the 'God *of Fire*'.[20] Urizen's error is complete. He sees the flames of the creative 'Mental Fight' with the reductive, single vision of the materialist, as nothing other than 'unquenchable burnings'; he views them, with the moral vision of orthodoxy, as evil or death. To him the passions of the life of Eternity are so many separate deaths. He cannot possibly see them as being of the essence of the creative imagination. From his isolated viewpoint of 'holiness', he sees the duality within every breast as the irreconcilable duality of good and evil, and he devises a code of law to enforce rigid conformity to the 'good'. He has, as we have already remarked, failed to see that contraries are an essential and vivifying ingredient of human life.

Urizen's proclamation of the 'One Law' incites 'rage, fury, intense indignation'[21] in the other Eternals, in the 'enormous forms of energy'.[22] They are horrified observers of Urizen's aberrant thought and yet do not desire an irreversible separation from him — for their salvation, like his, lies in the ultimate reunification of Urizen and themselves. They respond to counteract his error. But, separated as they are from him, they themselves are no longer in harmonious equilibrium,[23] and their response is not one of benevolent omnipotence. Indeed, as we have already seen, it is catastrophic:

> Sund'ring, dark'ning, thund'ring,
> Rent away with a terrible crash,
> Eternity roll'd wide apart,
> Wide asunder rolling;
> Mountainous all around
> Departing, departing, departing,
> Leaving ruinous fragments of life
> Hanging, frowning cliffs, &, all between,
> An ocean of voidness unfathomable.[24]

In the action of 'sund'ring' and of 'departing' lies the great catastrophe (seen from the higher viewpoint of Eternity). In Infinite Life there is, of course, no division, only multiplicity, diversity, in unity. Hereafter, complete, harmonious and creative unity is impossible until such time as Albion, Fallen Man, is reunited with his Emanation, Jerusalem, and stands before the love and mercy of Christ.[25] However, we are anticipating. All that the Eternals can do at this stage is to limit the disaster as much as possible.

But error breeds error. Here we see that, in their reaction to Urizen's self-righteousness, the other Eternals give way to the temptation of moral outrage and indigation, and, in doing so, they, rather than Urizen, are responsible for the succeeding stage of the Fall, that is, the creation of the universe, in that they separate Urizen's world from Eternity, directing 'flames of eternal fury' at him'.[26] But there is

> ... no light from the fires: all was darkness
> Into the flames of Eternal fury.[27]

The pretensions of the intolerant and restrictive morality of reason are answered by the unforgiving and uncontrollable wrath of the human faculties of emotion, instinct — and imagination.

In more general terms what we see here is this: reason, separated from

Imagination and love, and thus self-centred, self-restrictive — 'a self-contemplating shadow'[28] — cannot be wisdom; though, of course, Urizenic Man thinks himself to be wise. Imagination and love, separated from reason and thus uncontrolled, similarly cannot themselves be other than distortions, excesses of themselves.

In his headlong flight to hide from the black flames, in

> ... quenchless flames
> To the desarts and rocks he ran raging
> To hide; but he could not: combining,
> He dug mountains & hills in vast strength,
> He piled them in incessant labour,
> In howling & pangs & fierce madness,
> Long periods in burning fires labouring
> Till hoary, and age-broke, and aged,
> In despair and the shadows of death.[29]

Thus Urizen falls amid 'fragments of life' and, in the chaos of creation, he digs a cave for himself in earth and rock and creeps into it. This is his world. Like God in Newton's *Opticks*, Urizen 'formed matter in solid, massy, hard, impenetrable, moveable particles'. From the very expression 'Till hoary, and age-broke, and aged' we can see how closed off from Eternity Urizen now is, for age does not exist in Eternity.

Finally, then, Urizen constructs a vast cavern:

> ... a roof vast petrific around
> On all sides he fram'd, like a womb,[30]

in the shape of a globe, thus obstructing his vision of Eternity. Here, then, we see Urizen toiling in anguish to give more form to his world of error and death so that it may be better separated from Eternity and its life 'in unquenchable burnings'. In spite of this tremendous effort, however, his world still remains a relative chaos, 'unorganized'.[31] Sundered from Eternity, from reality, Urizen becomes indefinite and sinks in a 'stony sleep'.

Up to now we have seen Urizen as the creator, the counterpart to Plato's demiurge, but at this stage he also seems to be the creation itself, for Los

> ... round the dark globe of Urizen
> Kept watch for Eternals to confine
> The obscure separation alone.[32]

In short, Urizen himself represents the result of the process of degeneration as well as being closely involved as a cause of that process. According to Blake's cosmic paradox, Urizen clearly is both at one and the same time. In his 'obscure separation', and 'unorganized' as he is, Urizen symbolizes one vital stage in the process of emanation, or descent, which ultimately leads to the creation of the earth. When, indeed, the Eternals ask,

> 'What is this?', and give themselves the answer:
> ... Death.
> Urizen is a clod of clay.[33]

— there is an obvious implication that he is the microcosm man or the earth itself. He is, in fact, described a little later as 'cold, featureless, flesh or clay'.[34] He is both demiurge and creation.

Now, by closing himself off from Eternity Urizen has also effected a separation from the being to whom he is closest, who, paradoxically, is the imaginative creator of form himself, Los. The Urizenic, analytical mind cannot go beserk — it may be permitted to describe Urizen's recent actions in such a manner — without, at the same time, distorting the imagination. The suffering and anguish of Los is a bitter refrain throughout the rest of the poem, as we shall see.

If the analytical mind 'petrifies' and collapses into a perpetual state of deathlike icy winter, it cannot but have a deleterious effect on the imaginative, creative vision too. If one faculty 'falls', all other faculties are harmed.

Los, the eternal prophet, watchman and guardian of Eternity, the imaginative creator of forms, confronted by the formlessness of Urizen, from whose side, in the act of separation, he has been rent, rouses his fires, hoping to reshape Urizen into some semblance of his former, uncorrupted, external existence. Being the great creator of forms, Los waits for the moment 'to confine/ The obscure separation alone',[35] to give it form. At present, Urizen is 'unorganiz'd, rent from Eternity'[36] and Los is therefore also in agony. His separation from Urizen means that he himself is also 'divided'. Without Urizen he has only

> ... a fathomless void for his feet,
> And intense fires for his dwelling.[37]

Though Urizen now lies 'dead', he is not so eternally, for eternal death is impossible in Blake's conception of existence.[38] The spirit, the inner essence, knows nothing of death. It does not exist. However, Urizen is now at the extreme 'limit' of being, bordering on non-entity and therefore threatening to destroy existence altogether. Los, 'affrighted/At the formless, unmeasurable death',[39] that is, seized by a cosmic fear for existence itself, sets to work to fix, to confine the 'limits' of Urizen's fall and thus preserve both Urizen and his world from complete annihilation. But first Los must himself become part of Urizen's world, however incompletely:

> Los howl'd in a dismal stupor,
> Groaning, gnashing, groaning,
> Till the wrenching apart was healed.[40]

Los clearly hopes that the separation between himself and Urizen will only be temporary, that is, until the 'perturbed Immortal, mad raging'[41] recovers his senses. But this Urizen on his own cannot do. He cannot be 'cured' without Los's creative aid.

However, Los cannot completely unite with Urizen — 'the wrenching of Urizen heal'd not'.[42] If it had healed, then the process of 'downward' emanation (descent) would have ceased, and the next stage, that of the creation of man, would not have taken place.

Until Los acts, Urizen 'exists' only as an obscure and unstable identity:

> Cold, featureless, flesh or clay,
> Rifted with direful changes
> He lay in a dreamless night.[43]

Urizen for all his aspirations to inculcate permanence, has not only no form, but is also a 'victim' of continual meaningless change.[44] Eventually Los sets to work to give him form. It is a constant theme in Blake that error can be destroyed only after it has taken form. In Blake's view, it is the function of art to express the faults of man as well as to reform them. It is the creative artist, Los, creative imagination, who gives

> ... a body to Falsehood that it may be cast off for ever.[45]

Los is appalled at the enormity of his task and howls in fright and rage at 'the formless, unmeasurable death'[46] to which his creative genius has to give form. Yet error must reach its most 'condensed' state before regeneration can begin, and Los, weakened though he is by his separation and fall, knows that he must labour on 'the changes of Urizen'.[47] To fulfil this task Los moves from the spiritual sun into the smithy:

> The Eternal Prophet heav'd the dark bellows,
> And turn'd restless the tongs, and the hammer.[48]

Thus it is Los, not Urizen, who, impelled by cosmic fear, completes the creation of the phenomenal world. He 'rouz'd his fires'[49] and begins to fix and give form to the chaotic and formless changes of Urizen's monstrous creation, of Urizen himself. Los watches

> ... in shudd'ring fear
> The dark changes, & bound every change
> With rivets of iron & brass.[50]

As fast as Urizen changes, Proteus-like, in meaningless transformation which would never end, Los takes every new fleeting form as it appears and gives it permanence. Gradually, as we shall soon see, a total body is created. But first Los divides eternity into time, 'the horrible night into watches'.[51] At this point in the process of creation, Urizen, 'his prolific delight obscur'd more & more',[52] fades into the background for a while and Los assumes the role of the demiurge, the creator. He creates chronological time,

> ... forging his chains new & new
> Numb'ring with links hours, days & years.[53]

Seen from the spiritual viewpoint of the Eternal, Los is as much at fault in creating a barrier between the world of Eternity, the spiritual world, and the phenomenal world of time and space[54] as the solipsistic Urizen had been.

Urizen's changes, like the Days of Creation in Genesis, are seven in number. Los forges mankind out of these changes, motivated, as we have seen, not by the desire to create, but in fear of death. The changes of Urizen, shortly to be described, are symbolic of the forming of man's natural body: the shrinking up of flexible senses into the confinement of a 'cavern'. When the process is complete Urizen

> ... threw his right Arm to the north,
> His left Arm to the south,[55]

That is, the fallen Urizen faces west.[56]

Now, in declaring that Urizen was rent from Los's side, Blake is making concrete the concept that time and the universe began the 'descent' from Eternity together. We need to remember, therefore, that at this stage in the process of emanation our phenomenal world as we know it is not yet included in the universe. Our Earth, together with the other planets, was created after time had been generated.

In the stanzas describing Los's work on Urizen we learn that, first, the 'Eternal Mind' (Urizen)

> ... bounded, began to roll
> Eddies of wrath ceaseless round & round,
> And the sulphureous foam, surging thick,
> Settled, a lake, bright & shining clear,
> White as the snow on the mountains cold.
> Forgetfulness, dumbness, necessity,
> In chains of the mind locked up,
> Like fetters of ice shrinking together,
> Disorganiz'd, rent from Eternity.[57]

Urizen has forgotten Eternity. He is divided from his kind and can no longer converse with them. He is bound by the chains of inevitable cause and effect.

Los's work on Urizen's mind continues until it, reason, is bound and encumbered:

> Restless turn'd the Immortal inchain'd,
> Heaving dolorous, anguish'd unbearable;
> Till a roof, shaggy wild, inclos'd
> In an orb his fountain of thought.[58]

Los creates a skull (a head with its hair). He creates the 'cavern' in which, in darkness and floating in fluid, rests the brain, the tool of human, fallen reason separated from the Divine Intelligence, from Divine Reason.

Then, during seven ages 'of dismal woe' (repeated seven times), Los gives a contracted and fallen physical form to Urizen himself, restricting, at the same time, his sense perception. A body of a kind that the 'modern' brain can perceive, is now created.

In the first age the spine is formed:

> In a horrible, dreamful slumber,
> Like the linked infernal chain,
> A vast Spine writh'd in torment
> Upon the winds, shooting pain'd
> Ribs, like a bending cavern;
> And bones of solidness Froze
> Over all his nerves of joy.[59]

Three times, in quick succession, Blake has used the symbol of the chain.
We can understand it as being symbolic of a being who has forgotten
timeless Eternity where

> Earth was not, nor globes of attraction.
> The will of the Immortal expanded
> Or contracted his all flexible senses.
> Death was not, but eternal sprung,[60]

and has fallen into the chain of inevitable cause and effect, into the
necessity of the linear sequence of time.

In the second age, the seat of the passions, the heart, and then the blood
vessels are created:

> From the caverns of his jointed Spine
> Down sunk with fright a red
> Round Globe,* hot burning, deep,
> Deep down into the Abyss;
> Panting, Conglobing, Trembling,
> Shooting out ten thousand branches†
> Around his solid bones.[61]

In the next age Los forms the corporeal eyes, the

> ... nervous brain shot branches‡
> Round the branches of his heart
> On high into two little orbs,
> And fixed in two little caves.[62]

In the fourth age the two corporeal ears

> ... in close volutions
> From beneath his orbs of vision
> Shot spiring out and petrified
> As they grew.[63]

Then:

> Hanging upon the wind,
> Two Nostrils bent down to the deep.

* The heart.
† The blood vessels.
‡ The nervous system.
§ The spirals of the inner ear.

> And a fifth Age passed over,
> And a state of dismal woe.[64]

Following on this, in order to appease a

> ... ghastly torment sick,
> Within his ribs bloated round,
> A craving Hungry Cavern;
> ... like a red flame, a Tongue
> Of thirst & of hunger appear'd.[65]

Finally,

> ... a seventh Age passed over,
> And a state of dismal woe,[66]

and we see fallen Urizen, with arms outstretched, facing west.

Blake has here described the development of the four senses: sight, hearing, smell and taste; but there is as yet no mention of the fifth, touch,[67] which he identifies with sex, for the two sexes have not yet been created.

Let us pause here and look once again at Blake's use of symbols. In his version of Genesis he consistently uses symbols which stress the continuing processes of emanation, forms verging 'downwards' to spiritual non-entity, to matter itself. So, for example, in the seven stanzas describing Urizen's sevenfold 'state of dismal woe' we find some of the terms associated with matter and the unimaginative life. For instance, the word 'cavern' occurs three times and 'cave' once; three times 'branches' are mentioned, symbolic of continuing separation from unity.[68] The imagery of the 'orb' is also used three times, and is further emphasized by the use of the term 'globe', and the activity of 'englobing', and the description of the 'hungry cavern' being 'within his ribs bloated round'. The formation of a 'globe', or an 'orb', always involves an act of separation from the totality. As we shall see shortly, a 'globe of blood' separates from Los, when, after the binding of Urizen, he begins to feel pity, for 'pity divides the soul'.[69] The downward direction, the moving away from the cosmic, from the all-embracing spiritual Eternity, to a point of finite solidification, is emphasized by the repeated use of such terms and imagery as:

> ... down sunk with fright a red
> Round Globe, hot burning, deep

Deep down into the Abyss; ...[70]
Hiding carefully from the wind,
His eyes beheld the deep ...[71]
Two Nostrils bent down to the deep; ...[72]
He threw his right Arm to the north,
His left Arm to the south
Shooting out in anguish deep,
And his feet stamp'd the nether Abyss.[73]

We also see Blake using such obvious images associated with matter and the process of solidification and rigidification (Urizenic characteristics) as: 'bones of solidness froze'; 'solid bones'; 'roof ... enclosed' (skull). The eyes, we learn, are 'fixed' and the ears 'petrified as they grew'. Such images as those of 'the Immortal' being 'inchain'd' and of the 'linked infernal chain' serve to emphasize further the Fall into the physical world's law of cause and effect, which is a law 'invented' by the rational mind of materialism.[74]

The sevenfold repetition of the phrase 'And a state of dismal woe', which 'passed over' each of the seven ages, further underlines Urizen's descent into error. Here the point needs to be made that Urizen is not bad, evil — as, for instance, Satan is in Milton's *Paradise Lost* and in Dante's *Divine Comedy*. He is in error — in an error which originated in his initial separation from the other Eternals.

We left Urizen facing west, lying 'in a deadly sleep'.[75] Horrified at his failure in arresting Urizen's continuing fall, Los's own creative urge slackens. 'His great hammer fell from his hand.'[76] One by one the closed senses have been beaten out on his anvil. The narrow channels of perception, from which — according to Locke — reason learns, have been formed:

All the myriads of Eternity
All the wisdom & joy of life
Roll like the sea around him,
Except what his little orbs
Of sight by degrees unfold.

And now his eternal life
Like a dream was obliterated.[77]

But Los himself, who has had to do this work, has not been unaffected. On the contrary, until he can re-energize himself, as it were, he suffers a similar fate. He becomes what he beholds —

> The bellows & hammer are silent now;
> A nerveless silence his prophetic voice
> Siez'd; a cold solitude & dark void
> The Eternal Prophet & Urizen clos'd.[78]

The inspiration of Los is frozen into deformity. He falls and is absorbed into Urizen, whose influence becomes universal. It was Los who 'bound every change/ With rivets of iron & brass'[79] — two metals upon which Urizen inscribes his laws. Now, Los too has to endure the limitations to which he has given petrified form. Becoming what he beholds he unites with Urizen; he becomes 'one' with what he has created. Los falls.

> Ages on ages roll'd over them,
> Cut off from life & light, frozen
> Into horrible forms of deformity.
> Los suffer'd his fires to decay;
> Then he look'd back with anxious desire,
> But the space, undivided by existence,
> Struck horror into his soul.[80]

In giving form to both Urizen and himself, Los has destroyed the freedom they had previously enjoyed. He remains motionless for 'ages on ages'. He 'looks back' with regret. This period, empty of creative activity, grows into a 'void' between him and the eternal, spiritual world.[81] Urizen has reduced the immortal vision to a nervous fear and despair. We can understand this as follows: The actual embodiment — we could also say 'naturalization' — of a system of thought, of a code of conduct and of law, causes the creative shaping spirit of Imagination to despair and then to unite itself with the 'embodied' idea, that is, with the body of nature. Or, differently expressed, through Los's activity cosmic wisdom has been 'incarnate', confined in a philosophical system; but it is a philosophical system which has come into being through separation from Imagination — and Love — and is, therefore, rooted in reason and not imbued with wisdom. When, as has now happened, Imagination is assimilated into that system, it really loses its power, it loses its fiery vivyfying creativity and its ability to incite active, original thought. We are reminded here of Blake's exclamation:

> I will not Reason & Compare: my business is to Create[82]

However, Los is not 'imprisoned' in Urizen's 'dark void'. Though 'sleeping', he is not 'bound in a deadly sleep'[83] as Urizen is. Impelled by the desire and energy which are never altogether absent from the creative principle, Los awakens, he looks 'back with an anxious desire'. The 'space' he sees strikes horror in his soul because not only have 'Ages on ages' rolled over him and Urizen, ages which were frozen into lifeless and dark forms of deformity, ages which were unfilled by activity, but also because Urizen's universe is inert, is, indeed, 'a solid without fluctuation'.[84] Los sees that the universe which has been formed is void, without life. 'Space undivided by existence' is not true space, since space, conceived as a 'receptacle', is void until it contains spatial objects.

We now enter the next stage in the Fall. Just as the creation of Urizen's world comes about through Los's divisive fear, so its animation comes into being through a further process of division which has its source in pity. Now, pity is not an unequivocal virtue for Blake. There is both Divine Pity imbued with love and mercy, such as that of which Blake speaks in the poem 'The Divine Image',[85] and there is false pity, hypocritical pity. False pity

> ... would be no more
> If we did not make somebody Poor.[86]

When we profess sorrow for those whom we 'enclose', imprison, dominate, and weep for them, then, for Blake, the tears shed are hypocritical. Such are the tears we shall now see Los shedding and, later, those which Urizen sheds for his victims — 'he wept & called it Pity'.[87]

It was Los, we remember, who

> ... bound every change
> With rivets of iron & brass.[88]

and enchained Urizen. He now experiences dismay at the disaster suffered by the solipsistic fallen reason and he contemplates with pity — that is, 'false' pity — the lonely, deathlike state of Urizen. Seeing what has happened he is divided by pity and sheds false tears:

> Los wept, obscur'd with mourning,
> His bosom earthquak'd with sighs;
> He saw Urizen deadly black
> In his chains bound, & Pity began,
> In anguish dividing & dividing,
> For pity divides the soul.[89]

Los becomes the image of the death he pities.[90]

> Thus the Eternal Prophet was divided
> Before the death image of Urizen.[91]

Los, then, is divided by pity and, following his eternal, essential nature, sets to work to give form to his pity. A 'globe of life blood' is separated from him and is gradually given female form.

Just as error breeds error, so separation, a cardinal sin in Blake's view, breeds separation. The human divides into male and female, into the sexual. The Fall from Eternity, the spiritual world, continues:

> The globe of life blood trembled
> Branching out into roots,
> Fibrous, writhing upon the winds,
> Fibres of blood, milk and tears,
> In pangs, eternity on eternity.
> At length in tears & cries imbodied,
> A female form, trembling and pale,
> Waves before his deathly face.
>
> All Eternity shudder'd at sight
> Of the first female now separate,
> Pale as a cloud of snow
> Waving before the face of Los ...
>
> At the first female form now separate
> They call'd her Pity, and fled.[92]

Here we can supplement our earlier comment on 'false pity'.

Pity, devoid of selfless love and wise compassion, is a judgemental, that is, a rational act. It divides man's soul, because 'to pity' then really implies that one places oneself above the person 'pitied'; it means to judge, to reason. In one way or another, the person pitying enjoys a position of superiority (social background, education, wealth, etc.). For Blake such 'pity' implies tyranny, since he who pities dominates, rules over, the person who is being 'pitied'. Blake illustrates the rational element in such 'false pity' in a full-page illustration (plate 17), which shows Enitharmon, Los's Emanation (feminine counterpart), 'a globe of life blood', being formed from the head of Los. Pity, false pity, in other words, is a formation, a creation of the brain, of reason. It does not flow freely and selflessly from the heart. Blake's description of this 'globe of life blood' as branching out into fibrous roots like nerves issuing from the brain, further underlines this point.

On plate 19 we are shown Los's female counterpart, Enitharmon, emerging from him. We can understand this to mean, amongst other things that creativity (art) is now separated from its true source in divine inspiration. This is the last stage of the Fall. Los is now not only enclosed in the limited, restricted world, but also divided. So, from the formerly androgynous immortal, the separated feminine principle, Enitharmon, the first Emanation, is born, bringing into being both sexes and the process of natural generation. Now there is no such thing as sexual generation in Eternity, in the spiritual world. At the appearance of Enitharmon the Eternals are confronted with a being which is completely alien to them, hence they shudder at the sight of 'the first female now separate'. It is not at the female principle they shudder — this already existed in the androgyne Los, but at the dualism which has come into existence by the fact that the female is 'divided' from the male principle.

There is one further step to be taken in this last stage of the Fall. The world of generation, as we know it, does not begin until the first child of nature is born. We shall return to this first 'natural' birth after we have looked at the reaction of the Eternals in more detail.

We have just seen that the sight of a separate female form gives rise to horror/ in the 'unfallen' Eternals. The immediate consequence of their horror is their command that 'curtains of darkness',[93] a 'Tent', be woven around Los and Enitharmon to bind them in a void and shut them off from the sight of Eternity:

> With infinite labour the Eternals
> A woof wove, and called it Science.[94]

Here Blake uses the term 'science' to denote the kind of learning and knowledge which, derived through our restricted physical senses (symbolized here by the 'curtains of darkness') acts as a barrier, rather than an opening, to true wisdom and understanding.[95] In other words, at the sight of the division into nature, the Eternals impulsively react by rejecting Los just as they had repudiated Urizen earlier. Now, the powers of the unfallen Los, that is, Urthona,[96] are those of imaginative and freely creative perception, and those of unfallen Urizen may be described as being the guiding 'reins' of cosmic conceptualization, but in *The Book of Urizen* we see that the falling Urizen is shrinking to the limited mental process of abstraction, and that the 'rent' Los dwindled to a fixed perception of the temporal even as his Emanation, Enitharmon, 'hardens' into a materialized perception of space.[97] Such are their states in *The Book of Urizen*. In later chapters, particularly those dealing with *The Four Zoas*, we shall follow both Los's and Enitharmon's struggle to regain the spiritual freedom and unity they have lost in the Fall and Urizen's regaining of his true role as guiding Intellect as distinct from domineering, restrictive reason. It is, then, the uncomprehending and impulsive reaction of the surviving Eternals which brings about the complete fall of man, his separation from Eternity, for they both reject the self-restrictive faculty of reason and the self-divided power of perception. The actions of the Eternals, first of weaving the woof they call science, and then erecting and closing it down — in the form of a 'tent', so that spiritual vision is lost by man, are the actions of Powers who are in a weakened condition. They are weakened because their Co-Eternal, Urizen, Divine Intellect, has fallen away from them. Such actions may, indeed, be seen as archetypes of the tyrannical, judgemental and shut mind, which, according to Blake, inevitably erects 'curtains of darkness', shuts out 'Spiritual Perception',[98] and restricts man to a 'cavern'd' existence dominated by the five physical senses. It is true that, no longer able to perceive the eternal and infinite with their spiritual senses, Los and Enitharmon give substance to the fallen ideas of the temporal and the spatial,[99] but it is the unfallen, but weakened, Eternals who are the initial spiritual cause of the spiritual actions attributed to Los and Enitharmon. Although it was not their intention, it is the Eternals who bring into being a finalized and objective — completely separate — order of fallen nature. They 'shut out' that for which they themselves are responsible. As we have already recognized, the paradox lies in this: the isolation of any one part of a whole militates against the life of the whole. We are back again to the First Cause, the ultimate error, the 'original sin': Urizen's separation from his Co-Eternals.

It is within this newly created and confined world that the process of animation continues. It progresses through three phases. The first, as we have seen, through pity — Los pities Urizen who is lying 'deadly black', bound in the chains Los himself has forged. This hypocritical pity causes a further division to take place. Los causes himself to divide into a fallen, yet active form of himself and into his tearful Emanation, Enitharmon, who is, of course, also a divided self. She has been separated from the eternal, yet fallen, Los; therefore she is, in part, a woman of the world of nature. Los, even though divided, is still the active, creative principle. He is the creative, male principle, but now divided from the receptive inspiring principle without which creativity is virtually powerless. Enitharmon, 'the first female form', is both the inspiring empathy which a fallen condition of life offers as the Imagination's inspiration, and the female principle.

Now the stage is set for all the conflicts and errors ('sins') of inhar-
monious sexuality to begin. Again false pity manifests itself. Los pities his
divided self and embraces Enitharmon:

> ... Los saw the Female & pitied;
> He embrac'd her; she wept, she refus'd;
> In perverse and cruel delight
> She fled from his arms, yet he follow'd.[100]

Cruel coyness, false modesty and hypocritical restraint — attitudes of
soul induced, as we shall see, by the influential power of Urizen — do
not, however, prevent the process of generation, for Los begets Orc 'on
his divided image'. Los and Enitharmon are now in the world of genera-
tion, a world where the divided pair can only give birth to an endless
succession of repeated divided self-images.

> Eternity shudder'd when they saw
> Man begetting his own likeness
> On his own divided image.[101]

The greater the degree of division, the more intense the shudderings of
Eternity, until, at the birth of Orc, they appear paralysed. When
Enitharmon produces 'a man Child to the light'[102]

> A shriek ran thro' Eternity,
> And a paralytic stroke,
> At the birth of the Human shadow.[103]

It is now, when generation takes place and the child Orc is born, that
the Eternals finalize the process of the separation of time-space from
Eternity-Infinity by closing the 'tent' of 'science' so that 'No more Los
beheld Eternity'.[104] Los's God-like stature is now diminished to that of a
mortal. This diminution is further emphasized when Orc's coming into
existence is described as 'the birth of the Human shadow', for here we
have the first being who has been formed entirely in a fallen world, the
'vegetable earth' which 'is but a Shadow' of the eternal Spiritual
World.[105]

Incomprehension has given rise to fear among the Eternals, fear for
their own security, fear of what the future could hold in store for them.
Their fear and their act of restricting mankind in the tent of science reveal
that they have become Urizenic. As above, so below.

With the beginning of the third phase of animation, the birth of Orc, a
new situation arises: that of father, mother and son. As Orc grows, Los,

now in his fallen state, succumbs to jealousy, which is further evidence of division, symbolized here by a series of girdles around his bosom. These eventually form the chain with which Los binds Orc to the top of a mountain. Jealousy enchains them both:

> O sorrow & pain!
> A tight'ning girdle grew
> Around his bosom.* In sobbings
> He burst the girdle in twain;
> But still another girdle
> Oppress'd his bosom. In sobbings
> Again he burst it. Again
> Another girdle succeeds.
> The girdle was form'd by day,
> By night was burst in twain.
>
> These falling down on the rock
> Into an iron Chain
> In each other link by link lock'd.
> They took Orc to the top of the mountain.
> ...
> They chain'd his young limbs to the rock
> With the Chain of Jealousy
> Beneath Urizen's deathful shadow.[106]

Here Los, divided in his soul[107] and his vision limited, makes an error. He can no longer see the totality of events and conditions. He places Orc 'Beneath Urizen's deathful shadow', that is, he offers up Orc's life to the death-shadow of a limited moral intellect. But the very opposite to that which he intends occurs, for the life-forces in Orc are more powerful than Los realized. They have a powerful voice and his cries rouse Urizen from his death-like repose:

> The dead heard the voice of the child
> And began to awake from sleep;
> All things heard the voice of the child
> And began to awake to life.[108]

The creation of the natural world is now complete. It is instinct with life.

Upon this life Urizen is now free to impose his will, for Orc is in chains on 'the rock' and Los is weakened:

---

*i.e. Los experiences heart-constricting jealousy.

And Urizen, craving with hunger,
Stung with the odours of Nature,
Explor'd his dens around.[109]

The result of Los's action, performed without true vision, gives rise to Urizen's exploration of his dens.[110] That is, it gives impetus to just the kind of materialistic science and one-sided rationalistic enquiry which are anathema to the man of creative imagination. Man, uninspired and without true vision, is his own worst enemy!

With the exception of one short episode concerning Los and Enitharmon — which we shall consider in some detail shortly — the concluding stanzas of *The Book of Urizen* give witness to the rank dissemination of Urizen's influence over the world of generation.

As Urizen wanders through his universe:

He form'd a line & a plummet
To divide the Abyss beneath;
He form'd a dividing rule;

He formed scales to weigh;
He formed massy weights;
He formed a brazen quadrant;
He formed golden compasses,
And began to explore the Abyss;
And he planted a garden of fruits.[111]

Urizen's world is not an ensouled, living organism, but a visionless, lifeless, Newtonian world, divided, weighed and measured by the instruments of empirical science. The garden he sets out will grow plants of death; in the centre will stand, not the Tree of Life, but the Tree of Death, the Tree of Mystery (see pp. 46–7), described by Blake, for the first time, in 'The Human Abstract'. There Urizen is shown 'knitting' a 'snare' and then watering the ground with his hypocritical tears:

Then Humility takes its root
Underneath his foot.

Soon spreads the dismal shade
Of Mystery over his head;
...
And it bears the fruit of Deceit,[112]

and here the Raven of death makes its nest.

Urizen is unimpeded by Los, the imaginative, life-filled creative forces, for the inspiration of Los is inhibited:

> But Los encircled Enitharmon
> With fires of Prophecy
> From the sight of Urizen & Orc.[113]

The 'fires', the creative actions of Los, ought to be prophetic in their function, but here they appear to be only jealously possessive. But are they? A closer examination shows that matters are more complex than at first appears on the surface. At one level we can certainly concede that Los is hiding Enitharmon from Orc because he is jealous of their son. But at another, higher, level, he hides her for quite a different reason. However, before considering this 'higher' reason for his action, let us first discuss how it can come about that Los, who later is praised for his guardianship of the Divine Vision in times of trouble, could fall prey to such an aberration of the soul as jealousy?

To give an answer to this question we need to retrace our steps. We remember that it was the birth of Orc which caused the Eternals to close the 'tent'. Because of them, Los, at this stage of his own development, could no longer behold Eternity. As a consequence of his reduced power of spiritual vision (which we see him gradually regaining in Blake's great epic poems), and of the growing fragmentation of his vision of totality, further divisions within his soul are inevitable. Jealousy is one such significant 'division'. Division breeds division, or, as we have previously noted, separation breeds separation. This 'inner' division gives rise to the 'outer' division, to the 'encircling of Enitharmon' from the sight of Orc. Los, as creative imagination, is here depicted at a nadir, at a weak point in his own creative urge. It is this weakness in spiritual perception of the Whole which 'allows' such a deleterious quality of soul as jealousy to take root, and which is also the immediate cause of Los committing the error of placing Orc beneath 'Urizen's deathful shadow'. The ultimate cause is, of course, spiritual, namely, the closing of the 'tent' by the Eternals so that Los loses awareness of the Whole, the Spiritual reality.

However, this loss is not total. Though fallen, Los still retains some creative, imaginative power, which is active in harmony with the spiritual totality. Realizing this, we can now find an answer to our next question: Why does Los hide Enitharmon from Urizen too? It is here that Los is functioning at a 'higher' level, not now with the 'fires' of jealousy, but with the 'fires' of prophecy he is still able to arouse.[114]

Now, to gain some insight into the significance of separating Enitharmon from Urizen, from fallen reason, we need to know a little more about Enitharmon's nature and role than is apparent from *The Book*

of Urizen. It is true that we hear nothing very significant about Enithar-
mon, Los's Emanation, in this poem, yet not only her role but also her
qualities and significance must have been 'present' in Blake's creative
mind, even if no more than in embryo, when he wrote it in 1794 (only a
year later he was working on *The Four Zoas*). A more rounded and living
picture of Enitharmon will gradually emerge in later chapters. For our
present purposes it is sufficient to mention that she symbolizes the spiri-
tual power of inspiration of creative man, of the creative imagination,
Los, and that, as his Emanation, she is the feminine 'part' of his being.
We have seen that she, though still a 'part' of Los, has been separated
from him; that the whole of eternal Los has himself, in the Fall, divided
into two 'parts' — a 'lesser' Los and an Emanation. Enitharmon, there-
fore, has qualities characteristic of Los, but, being divided from him, in a
weaker potency, as it were. The quality that she represents here is poetic
vision, or, rather, she represents what is left of vision in the phenoenal
world after the Fall.

Now, Urizen's exploration of his 'dens' with the analytical science of
'a line and a plummet' is a strong threat to this weakened faculty of
vision. Urizen could destroy such visionary power altogether and
thereby destroy the very means by which man may be regenerated, for it
is only through the cultivation of Imagination and spiritual vision that
man can once again be reunited with the Divine Family, with Christ, the
Source of all things.[115] Hence, Los, the 'Eternal Prophet' must hide, must
protect Enitharmon from the destructive power of Urizen, Fallen
Reason. Moreover, as the prophetic spirit — as distinct from the jealous
father — Los sees that he must also hide Enitharmon from the raw
revolutionary energy of Orc. So, even the act of hiding his Emanation
from Orc was not motivated solely by jealousy. To subject 'weakened'
vision to ruthless, revolutionary energy is tantamount to destroying it.

When the action of Los is not prophetic, but possessive, jealous, in
function, then the act of 'encircling' necessarily 'naturalizes', mor-
talizes, and thus the 'enormous race'[116] of descendants to which Enithar-
mon gives birth have to assume a form of life which ensnares them within
natural, mortal limitations.

Meanwhile, Urizen continues to explore his visionless — materialistic
— world. He sickens at what he sees:

> ... his world teem'd vast enormities,
> Fright'ning, faithless, fawning
> Portions of life, similitudes.[117]

The word 'similitudes' here implies the notion that this phenomenal world is a poor imitation of an ideal world, of Heaven. For instance, Urizen's (Rational Man's) eyes see the world unimaginatively and simply cannot perceive the sun as being anything other than a round disc in shape like a guinea; he certainly cannot see a heavenly host![118] He sickens most of all at the sight of his eternal creations now appearing as his corporeal sons and daughters: emerging mankind, the animal and vegetable kingdoms, and, especially, the four separated elementals, his sons, Thiriel (ether, air), Utha (water), Grodna (earth) and Fuzon (fire). They are elemental forms of fallen existence:

> Most Urizen sicken'd to see
> His eternal creations appear,
> Sons & daughters of sorrow on mountains
> Weeping, wailing. First Thiriel appear'd,
> Astonish'd at his own existence,
> Like a man from a cloud born; & Utha,
> From the waters emerging, laments:
> Grodna rent the deep earth, howling
> Amaz'd; his heavens immense cracks
> Like the ground parch'd with heat, then Fuzon
> Flam'd out, first begotten, last born.[119]

Fuzon is described as 'first begotten, last born' because fiery energy is at the heart of creation, but such is also its destructive force that it will only appear again, in its pure form, that is, as the spiritual fire which consumes nothing but errors, at the Last Judgement.[120]

As Urizen wanders on he sees his race enclosed in darkness and begins to grow aware of his error:

> He in darkness clos'd view'd all his race,
> And his soul sicken'd! he curs'd[121]
> Both sons & daughters; for he saw
> That no flesh nor spirit could keep
> His iron laws one moment.[122]

The realization that the law of iron he had promulgated cannot be kept is Urizen's tragedy, since it is he who has proclaimed his laws as the ideal of life. Urizen's world is self-contradictory and based on self-deception and self-destruction, for not only is it animated by forces which destructively oppose each other, but it is also, in principle, a divided existence in which one half of life lives upon the death of the other half. He sees that, under his legal provisions,

... life liv'd upon death;
The Ox in the slaughter house moans,
The Dog at the wintry door.[123]

In a fallen world everything lives on something else: the ox is nourishment for man; and what one takes for himself, another lacks — the dog hungers. One rigid law, he recognizes now, is impossible in the world he has created.

Confronted with the cold starkness of a world in which only the physical material is accepted as reality,

... he wept & he called it Pity
And his tears flowed down on the winds.[124]

Urizen sheds the hypocritical tears of abstract pity as he contemplates his creation. His pity is hypocritical because it is self-pity; it is a lament at himself, at his own creation. Such pity further strengthens the condition of division in the world of men. Appearance shows him all-powerful, but appearance is illusion; in reality Urizen is impotent. Paradoxically, it is through this 'pity', through these sorrows at his own failure, that Urizen achieves some degree of direful success, for he now resorts to a further device: if reason, logic, cannot support and enforce his law, superstition may. Out of the sorrowful experience of Urizen's, of Rational Man's, imperfections, a further imperfection comes into being: the false religion of the Tree of Mystery:[125]

Cold he wander'd on high, over their cities
In weeping & pain & woe;
And where ever he wander'd, in sorrows
Upon the aged heavens,
A cold shadow follow'd behind him
Like a spider's web, moist, cold & dim,
Drawing out from his sorrowing soul,
The dungeon-like heaven dividing,
Where ever the footsteps of Urizen
Walked over the cities in sorrow;
Till a Web, dark & cold, throughout all
The tormented element stretch'd
From the sorrows of Urizen's soul.
And the Web is a Female in embrio.
None could break the Web, no wings of fire,

> So twisted the cords, & so knotted
> The meshes, twisted like to the human brain,
>
> And all call'd it The Net of Religion.[126]

The 'Net of Religion' is a further restriction imposed upon mankind from 'without'; it can be seen as the complementary twin of the 'tent' of Newtonian science. The Web, called the 'Net of Religion' has meshes 'twisted like to the human brain', which not even the most inspired poet can break; it is evidently the product of fallen Reason mingled with abstract pity. Seen from the limited viewpoint of reason this rational religion, natural religion, brings to man the 'reasonable' knowledge of good and evil, it imposes on him a system of moral virtue. The religion of morality, devised by the cold, 'twisted' brain, is the religion of the deists, of Satan, the 'god of this world'.[127] It is the religion of the Tree of Mystery on which Christ, who transgressed against the Urizenic laws of the Pharisees, was crucified.[128]

The 'Web', the 'Net of Religion', imposes further limits on Urizen's children. It causes them to follow, to a greater or lesser degree, restrictive and oppressive laws of uniformity (conformity) by further limiting their powers of perception and individual creative energy.* It is formed from Urizen's sorrow at his failure to enforce his laws of logic. So, in spite of his impotence, some degree of success has been achieved.

As we have seen, Urizen's 'sons & daughters' are all cursed by him when he realizes that it is impossible for them to comply with his 'iron' laws. This curse, now strengthened by the 'Net of Religion', causes a further narrowing of man's perceptions. Man recapitulates the archetypal constriction and shrinking of Urizen's divine senses.[129] Clearly, this shrinking of the senses closes man off from the spiritual world and hence from the experience of Eternity. Such exclusion from direct experience of the world of the spirit brings with it such concepts and beliefs as, for instance, death and sin, both of which are erroneous manifestations of spiritual disease.[130] Any element, portion, which no longer experiences itself as an integral part of an Eternal Whole is in a condition of soul-spiritual disease, of disharmony:

> Then the Inhabitants of those Cities †
> Felt their Nerves change into Marrow,

---

*The one follows from the other.
†i.e. the cities of Egypt.

> And hardening Bones began
> In swift diseases and torments,
> In throbbings & shootings & grindings
> Thro' all the coasts; till weaken'd
> The Senses inward rush'd, shrinking
> Beneath the dark net of infection.[131]

When the 'Net of Religion', like a veil, is imposed on the inhabitants of the cities, then, as mentioned already, the shrinking of the senses cuts them off from any knowledge of Eternity. Blake now draws our attention to a further consequence of the narrowing and shrinking of the senses: man has no knowledge of what it is that has cut him off:

> ... the shrunken eyes, clouded over,
> Discern'd not the woven hipocrisy;
> But the streaky slime in their heavens,
> Brought together by narrowing perceptions,
> Appear'd transparent air; for their eyes
> Grew small like the eyes of a man ...[132]

The 'woven hipocrisy', the 'streaky slime', is, of course, the Net of Religion. It is to be understood as an 'original error' in the foundations of Urizen's universe, not as a mere temporary and erroneous human system of thought.

With the final restriction of the senses, the creation of Urizen's world is complete. Human history begins.

The climax of the shrinking process is expressed by Blake in an ironic parody of Genesis (6:4). Urizen's sons and daughters continue to shrink:

> Six days they shrunk up from existence,
> And on the seventh day they rested,
> And they bless'd the seventh day, in sick hope,
> And forgot their eternal life.[133]

The diseases of the soul of the universe, symbolized in the generation of the microcosmic earth and of man, are summed up in these few lines.

Shrunk from his infinite into finite form, man sees only the Newtonian universe. Indeed, for him only that universe exists. Divided and 'roofed' within cities — a microcosmic recapitulation of the macrocosmic 'closing' of the 'tent' by the Eternals — people forget 'their eternal life', their spiritual origin.

> And their thirty cities divided
> In form of a human heart.[134]
> No more could they rise at will
> In the infinite void, but bound down
> To earth by their narrowing perceptions
> They lived a period of years;
> They left a noisom body
> To the jaws of devouring darkness.[135]

Urizen's, Fallen Reason's, explorations have resulted in the 'invention' of death and in man's acceptance of death as the end of existence — an obvious consequence of being in bondage to 'earth by narrowing perceptions'. The concept of 'death' can only invade man's mind when he has lost sight of Eternity. A further consequence of being 'bound down to earth' is that man now proliferates Urizen's own error and proclaims him God:

> And their children wept, & built
> Tombs in the desolate places,
> And form'd laws of prudence, and call'd them
> The eternal laws of God.[136]

Governed by the fallen reason, man cannot consider the risks involved in imaginative living. That takes a courage rational man does not possess. By forming 'laws of prudence' precautions are taken against the unknown. The children of Urizen fear futurity.

The world of man has become a universe of death. Such a universe is allegorically named Egypt in the Bible. In Blake it is identified with the 'englobed' chaos of the 'salt Ocean',[137] a product of Urizen's hypocritical weeping:*

> And the thirty cities remain'd
> Surrounded by salt floods, now call'd
> Africa: its name was then Egypt.[138]

Division and 'enslavement' to Urizen's tyranny are complete; the brotherhood of man is lost. The cities of Urizen's creation are enclosed in materialism, in the Sea of Time and Space, and the inhabitants live in perpetual separation from brotherhood:

> ... their eyes could not discern
> Their brethren of other cities.[139]

*In Blake, Egypt symbolizes slavery because of the bondage of Israel.

One of Urizen's sons, Fuzon, is not prepared to accept the bondage imposed on his fellow men and on himself. He is the apocalyptic element, fire, or passion, whose powers are closely associated with those of the triad Urthona-Los-Orc, and who, in *The Book of Ahania*, is associated with Christ.[140]

The Book of Urizen ends with the departure of those who are not inhabitants of Urizenic cities, that is, those 'sons and daughters' who still retain some desire for an imaginative and creative life:

> So Fuzon call'd all together
> The remaining children of Urizen,
> And they left the pendulous earth.
> They call'd it Egypt, and left it.[141]

We have just stated that Fuzon and Orc are closely associated. Now, although Orc, who had enlivened Urizen and Nature, has been given no further mention in *The Book of Urizen* since we left him chained on the top of a mountain, he has nevertheless continued to exert an enlivening power. It is this power that infuses Fuzon, the quality of fire, to gather together such children of Urizen as are not altogether 'wither'd & deafen'd & cold',[142] that is, completely in the power of Urizen, and to lead an exodus from an 'earth' which has become subject to Urizen's dictatorship. Fuzon, in fact, is the first member of humanity to attempt to overcome a Nature which has shrunk into finiteness. Right at the end of *The Book of Urizen* we are given a hint of possible salvation from the enslavement to narrowed perception, from Urizen's, Reason's, tyranny.

*****

From Blake's *Book of Urizen* we can gain a strong sense of the internal threat embodied in the domineering power of analytical (fallen) reason, in the 'fallen angel' of thought. Blake brings powerfully to our awareness — for some of us for the first time, perhaps — that cold, abstract, and self-centred Urizen is active in each one of us.

In this poem — and in *The Book of Los* — Blake begins to expound a triple doctrine (developed in greater detail in his three great epic poems, *The Four Zoas, Milton* and *Jerusalem*), cosmogonical, historical and psychological, in a single symbolism.

From our study of *The Book of Urizen* we have seen that Blake puts before us a picture of the separation of the Eternals, their loss of unity, and the subsequent creation of the earth and of primeval man, Adam and Eve.

Blake also tells us about the shattering of the individual's innocent and unconscious being-at-one with the Whole and the ensuing confusion of spirit. Man has fallen victim to the error of externalization, to the 'without', and has lost the experience of his 'inner' essence, of the 'within'. He has lost the knowledge that the One, the Whole or macrocosm, is inherent in man, the microcosm. As the ancient Chinese expressed it, 'The ten thousand things are there complete, inside us.'[143] Through his faculty of discursive thought, developed at the expense of his faculty of creative imagination, Man has isolated himself from and can no longer, by imaginative extension of his individual self, perceive, know, the Whole. Moreover, his God — if he admits to the existence of one at all — is some external power or other which has its being in an inconceivable 'somewhere-out-there'. More immediately, individual man has isolated himself from nature and from his fellow men. He lives, in spiritual darkness and poverty, in and through his Spectre, his 'Rational Power'.

The man of creative imagination and energy, on the other hand, manifests, in varying degrees according to his individual power of selfless and intuitive vision, a potentially limitless and expanding spiritual enrichment through his relation to the innumerable other parts-of-a-Whole which make up the enspirited and ensouled totality. Whereas Urizen loses himself in dark self-contemplation and perceives a dead world around him and death within himself, Los, creative imagination — as we shall see in later chapters — labours ceaselessly as guardian of the Divine Vision and perceives eternal spiritual life. He experiences, through his own imagination, that he is within the Whole and the Whole within him.[144] He experiences that

> The Eternal Body of Man is the Imagination, that is, God himself,
> The Divine Body, Jesus: we are his Members.[145]

The creative imagination is that faculty in man through which he expands himself and enables him to be, to experience himself to be, a microcosm of the Whole, and, conversely, the creative imagination can enrich man to such an extent that the Whole is immanent, is experienced to be immanent, in his individual soul and spirit.[146]

It was just stated that the Whole can be experienced as being immanent in the 'part', in the individual mind. Another way of expressing this would be to say that the macrocosm is, or is in, the microcosm.[147] Blake 'uses' his intuitive and imaginative experience of the macrocosm to explore the microcosm. This is nowhere more evident than in his 'use' of the Fall in *The Book of Urizen*.

The Fall is the act whereby man leaves his state of innocence, in which he dwells effortlessly in cosmic consciousness, and moves into the limited self-consciousness of experience. In the world of experience, man finds himself in a state in which he is aware of the separate impulses and inter-acting conflicts of his soul-faculties. He experiences, or, at any rate, is given the opportunity to experience, that he is in a state of disintegration. Now, when he realizes that it is through the exercise of one faculty in particular, the intuitive and creative imagination, that he can regain his 'Spiritual Perception'[148] of the Whole, the process of reintegration can begin. This process involves a transcendence of experience and the con-comitant achievement of an expanded and higher consciousness which is without the strife man normally goes through in the Urizenic world of experience. But because he has experienced such strife, this new con-sciousness is of a greater breadth and clarity than that he had enjoyed in his original unfallen state.

In this process of 'fall' and 'ascent' we can now comprehend that Urizen's role is of the utmost importance. Seen from the viewpoint of the Eternal his acts are disastrous; but, seen from the viewpoint of the individual incarnated soul, they are ultimately beneficial. The efforts involved in transforming the divisions between men and women into universal brotherhood, of breaking through the 'Web of Religion' and offering oneself, in self-annihilation, to the 'Religion of Jesus', the religion of mutual forgiveness and selfless love, and, in so doing, also banishing such abberations of soul as jealousy and cruelty, doubt and despair, the efforts involved in imaginatively living through the universe created by Urizen give birth to a richness and translucence of soul and spirit which man otherwise would not be able to achieve.

True self-knowledge — not, of course, to be confused with Urizenic self-centredness — is the starting point from which 'cavern'd' and expanded vision can be brought into fruitful and harmonious interplay.[149] During the spiritual journey through 'fall' and 'ascent', Urizen's solipsism, which allows of no living communion, no spiritual, real communication between the peoples of the earth, is gradually 'worked through', regenerated, so that finally men may be seen to converse 'together in visionary forms dramatic' and walk together 'as One Man'.[150]

The seed sown in *The Book of Urizen* goes through metamorphoses of 'being' and, as we shall see, blossoms forth and bears fruit in *The Four Zoas* and in *Jerusalem*.

7

THE FOUR ZOAS: THE TRIUMPH OF IMAGINATIVE LIFE

In the last chapter, we were concerned to enter into Blake's vision of the Fall. There we saw something of the nature of the 'cold', restrictive, power of Urizen and of the creative power of Los. Both the Fall and the roles of Urizen and Los are taken up again in *The Four Zoas* in an expanded form.

We hear Urizen again proclaiming that he is God:

I am God from Eternity to Eternity.[1]

He usurps a place in the divine hierarchy which rightly belongs to Christ, the Imagination. As we have previously seen, Urizenic Man attributes to natural phenomena a reality which belongs to the eternal forms. But, in reality, natural phenomena are only shadows, for:

There Exist in that Eternal World the Permanent Realities of Every Thing which we see reflected in this Vegetable Glass of Nature.[2]

Urizen makes his positivist position very clear when, to Los, he says:

Art thou a visionary of Jesus, the soft delusion of Eternity?
Lo I am God, the terrible destroyer, & not the Saviour.
...
The Spectre is the Man. The rest is only delusion and Fancy.[3]

The Book of Urizen gives us Blake's imaginative apprehension of man's 'fall into the Generation of decay & death', his 'fall into Division', that is, man's subjection to the restrictive faculty of discursive, analytical reason — represented in Blake by, above all, Urizen's faithful servants Newton, Locke and Bacon.

The Four Zoas gives us a more expanded version of Blake's vision of the Fall and the role that Urizen plays in it. But it does not stop there. The theme is threefold: man's loss of spiritual, universal brotherhood, or, we could say, 'the loss of the identity of divine and human natures',[4] which was the cause of the Fall and brought about the creation of the natural, physical world (separated from the spiritual world); his 'struggle to regain this identity in the fallen world'[5] — a struggle which was led by Los, the Imagination, and completed by Christ, the Imagination; and, thirdly, the Apocalypse.

This threefold theme in regard to man's evolution is introduced by Blake in the lines:

> His fall into Division & his Resurrection to Unity:
> His fall into the Generation of decay & death, & his
> Regeneration by the Resurrection from the dead.[6]

In this and the following two chapters on *The Four Zoas* we shall be concerned with the process of 'Regeneration', with man's struggle to regain the identity of his divine and human nature — a struggle in which the guardian of the Divine Vision, Los, plays the vital role; and with man's resurrection and regaining of universal brotherhood in which, finally, Urizen too can, and must, actively participate. As we shall see, Urizen is able to 'repent', to reject error and embrace truth, he is able to experience consciously what Blake calls a Last Judgement:

Urizen said: 'I have Erred, & my Error remains with me.
What Chain encompasses? in what Lock is the river of light confin'd
That issues forth in the morning by measure & in the evening by carefulness?
Where shall we take our stand to view the infinite & unbounded?
Or where are human feet? for Lo, our eyes are in the heavens'.[7]

When Urizen relinquishes his 'clouding' (obscuring) and constricting hold upon the creative power of imagination he, too, is able to share the soul's unbounded vision.

Before proceeding with our discussion of our threefold theme, which, with the exception of a few passing comments on passages in earlier Nights, will be based on the last three of the nine 'Nights',[8] a few introductory words should be said about the principal characters in *The Four Zoas*.

The characters we shall be meeting most frequently are: Albion, the four Zoas, and their Emanations.

Albion personifies the whole human being and, at the same time, the whole of mankind. In *The Four Zoas* we meet him as Fallen Humanity. His Emanation, or 'wife', in the spirit, is Jerusalem. She represents the pure spiritual nature, the perfect freedom, which man enjoyed before he lost his vision of Eternity (Eden) and which he, by conscious effort, can regain. On earth she cannot remain with Albion as his 'wife', though she continues to inspire him. She is united with him again at the resurrection of his spiritual body. In the unfallen state — which we have to regain consciously through the casting out of error in the fallen state — man is in harmony with himself and with the 'world'.

The fallen state is a condition in which each of the four primal powers, or faculties, the Zoas — Tharmas, Urthona, Luvah and Urizen — betrays its own true nature and presumes to dominate others. Any faculty which seeks to usurp the place of another, assumes a characteristic not rightly his. He disturbs the order of the totality — be it in nature, the human psyche (with which we shall be largely concerned), or society (from which stance we could equally well have chosen to read Blake's poem).

Urizen is the Zoa who, in his unfallen state is Intellect. In his fallen state he represents discursive, analytical reason and is opposed to Imagination, the intuitive, spiritual nature of man. In his worst state of 'fallenness' be becomes Satan. In Eternity he is the Prince of Light.

Luvah is Passion, Love. In his unfallen state his identity blends with that of Christ. He is the Prince of Love. Fallen, Luvah becomes Orc and in that guise represents violent lustful and revolutionary forces.

Urthona is Imagination and is in constant opposition to discursive, analytical reason. In the fallen world he is named Los, the imagination or creative faculty in man.

Los is the keeper of the Divine Vision in the phenomenal world of time and space. He also represents time. He is the only Zoa who can mediate the restoration of man to full awareness of Eternity (Eden).

Tharmas is Instinct, the innocent sense of wholeness which makes the individual, or mankind, a harmonious unity.

Each of the four Zoas, portrayed as male, has a feminine counterpart, an Emanation. In imaginative states, in Eternity, the Emanations are united, with, at one with, their male counterparts. In the fallen state, in the world of time and space, they are separate from the male and conceived as being 'outside'. 'The word "emanation" in Blake means the object-world: creatures in Eden, female in Beulah, object or nature in Generation, abstraction in Ulro'[9] An Emanation represents the distinctive activity, external manifestation, or product of the Zoa who is her counterpart. In the world of generation we could say that the Emanation represents the form of all things a man creates and loves.

Ahania is Urizen's Emanation. She is Pleasure. The division of the two is caused by the fact that the abstract philosopher, Urizen, has yet to learn 'that Enjoyment & not Abstinence is the food of Intellect'.[10]

Vala is Luvah's Emanation. She has a twofold role: as the outward manifestation of emotion, passion; and as the natural world. In *Jerusalem* she is spoken of as the goddess of Nature.'[11] In her lowest state of fallenness she becomes Rahab and Tirzah.

Enitharmon is the Emanation of Los/Urthona. She is Spiritual Beauty. Her outstanding emotion is pity.

The Emanation of Tharmas is Enion. Whereas Tharmas represents the body, she represents the generative instinct.[12]

Unlike the Emanations of the other three Zoas, Enitharmon is not an 'evanescent shade', for in the world of time and space she is:

> ... a vegetated mortal wife of Los,
> His Emanation, yet his Wife till the sleep of Death is past.[13]

Whereas Los represents time, Enitharmon represents space. In Chapter 5 we saw Los and Enitharmon working harmoniously together. This working together to redeem Urizen, Orc and others, to regenerate Fallen Man, begins, in *The Four Zoas*, at the end of Night vii.

In this world, the Emanation, wife, is, ideally, her counterpart's 'concentering vision', his comforter and co-worker, but her separate will produces all the torments of love and jealousy. In her self-centred pride she seeks dominion over her counterpart. She is jealous of all activities which take his attention away from her, and seeks to prevent him pursuing the tasks before him. She is, in short, 'lost' to him. This loss leaves the 'male' a selfish and ravening spectre. His rational power, unchecked by his counterpart, dominates him, so that, for instance, he condemns all pleasures as sin. In order to be able to co-operate harmoniously and constructively, the Emanation must renounce her desire for dominion and sacrifice her selfishness, just as her counterpart must also annihilate his selfhood and sacrifice himself. Only then can both, as one, become members of the Brotherhood of Man, which is Christ Himself.

It should be stressed that the characterization of the Zoas and their Emanations given in the above few lines are of a very general nature. They are, of course, as complex in themselves and in their interrelationships as, for instance, the multifarious aspects of the human psyche itself. However, it is hoped that the reader who is not yet familiar with Blake's four Zoas and their Emanations will glean sufficient clues in these and the following pages to form a fair idea of their complex natures. It is not irrelevant to note, incidentally, that Blake himself writes:

Four Mighty Ones are in every Man; a Perfect Unity
Cannot Exist but from the Universal Brotherhood of Eden,
The Universal Man, to Whom be Glory Evermore. Amen.
What are the Natures of those Living Creatures the Heavenly Father only
Knoweth. No Individual [Man *del.*] knoweth not can know in all Eternity.[14]

* * * * *

In the first Night of *The Four Zoas* we learn of the crippling of Tharmas and Los, of Instinct and Imagination — signs rather than causes of human fragmentation.

Tharmas, we have just noted, is the innocent sense of wholeness, 'instinct'. He is also the 'body', that is, the body as a young child knows it, unselfconsciously. In Night i he is also described as being the 'Parent pow'r'.[15] He is the parent in the sense that the child is father of the man. Just as small children are often subconsciously aware of 'atmospheres' long before either reason or emotion (Urizen or Luvah) can identify them, so Tharmas, and his Emanation, Enion, show throughout an instinctive awareness not only of the Fall, but also of the possibility of regeneration. The process of fragmentation of wholeness and, conversely, of reintegration, is sensed by Tharmas before any of the other Zoas. What Tharmas senses in regard to the Fall is twofold; on a universal level he senses the Fall of humanity from a dreamlike state of innocence to an awakened, conscious knowledge of the world of experience; and, on an individual level, the transition from a dreamlike state of self-awareness to a wakened state of self-consciousness, to an awareness of separateness from others, and, we should add, to an awareness of inner division and separateness from the Unfallen Reality.

It is first in Night ii that Blake emphasizes the ultimate cause of the Fall, namely, the conflict between emotion and reason, Luvah and Urizen.

The process of regeneration, reintegration, sensed by Tharmas, is a possibility which is always open to man. In *The Four Zoas* it is anticipated in various degrees from Night i onwards — with, as we shall see, particular emphasis in Night vii. In the first Night Blake focuses our attention on this possibility in no uncertain terms when he asks the Daughter of

Beulah — the daughter of direct inspiration — to sing not merely of man's Fall but of 'his Resurrection to Unity'.[16]

Here we should consider the following two points:

Blake often shows himself to be understanding the Gospels literally. However, he is not a fundamentalist who simply accepts that man's salvation took place in the past, nearly 2,000 years ago in historical time, and that all we need to do today is to recognize Christ's deed of loving self-sacrifice after the fact, and imitate it (on a smaller scale, of course, and within the limitations of human nature). Blake certainly accepts the reality and historicity of the Crucifixion on Golgotha nearly 2,000 years ago. It was the archetypal Christian self-sacrifice for the salvation of the whole of humanity (Christians and non-Christians alike). But if this deed were merely to be related to historical time, to be an event which belonged solely to the past, then it would be little more than nourishment for the memory. Man would be able to 'imitate', 'reproduce' it (on a smaller scale), but he would not be able to 'produce' it, experience it imaginatively within his own soul. A sacrifice — any deed — which remains solely in the past, in the memory, is an abstraction. It remains outside of imaginative experience, outside of real life, of the eternal present. Memory, we shall learn in Night vii, is to be identified with the Spectre which man perceives when he turns his back on the Divine Vision.[17] For Blake the 'Spirit of Jesus' is active here and now.[18] When in *Jerusalem* Albion asks:

> Cannot Man exist without Mysterious
> Offering of Self for Another? is this Friendship & Brotherhood?

Christ gives the answer quoted several times in these pages:

> Wouldest thou love one who never died
> For thee, or ever die for one who had not died for thee?
> And if God dieth not for Man & giveth not himself
> Eternally for Man, Man could not exist; for Man is love
> As God is Love; every kindness to another is a little Death
> In the Divine Image, nor can Man exist but by Brotherhood.[19]

Here Blake is speaking of the Crucifixion as a necessary continuous process which every man and woman must experience imaginatively and spiritually if his thoughts and deeds are to proclaim him ready to participate in the founding of the City of Freedom and Peace, Jerusalem, and the creation of universal brotherhood.

The second point to be made is this: Blake is not of the persuasion of those Eastern mystics who regard life on earth, in the world of time and space, to be of little if any real significance. It is true that, for Blake, the world of generation is but a symbol of the spiritual world,[20] and a world of 'decay & death'. Nevertheless, it is an essential world. In Blake's view it is essential to the process of regeneration, for without it the Incarnation of Christ, the Imagination, could not have taken place and man would be condemned to a spiritually dead existence in an eternal void.

If we now look at Blake's conception of redemption with the two points just made in mind, we can recognize that what he attempts to do in *The Four Zoas* is to bring together historical time, memories of the past, with the imaginative experience of timelessness, of the eternal present. Historical time and physical space are clearly not to be ignored. Brought together with, and seen in the light of, the imaginative experience of the eternal present, both can take on a new significance. Thus the moments of hope of, say, Resurrection, the reminders of the ever-present possibility of redemption — which occur in the darker Nights — serve a vital function. They lift us out of the temporal and spatial by prompting us to realize that we are free, at any moment in our lives, to reject 'mind-forg'd manacles', that we are free to reject the Urizenic doctrine that such fetters are inevitable, that we are free to reject the philosophy which proclaims irrevocable limitations within the 'Circle of Destiny'.[21]

In such moments of freedom we can glimpse the truth, namely, that such fetters, written down in Urizen's dark 'Book of brass',[22] are 'mind-forg'd', 'invented' by rational discursive thought. They are created in the Urizenic minds both of the oppressor and of the afflicted, the repressed, who accept the manacles.

For the spiritually free, imaginative mind, measured time is insignificant, an illusion, in comparison with the creative moment in which eternity is experienced.[23]

However, Blake would also have us realize that we are equally free — at all stages of our lives — to accept the temporal and spatial. Every moment and every place are presented to us as 'material' for imaginative transformation by us — not merely for ourselves, but for our fellow men. Indeed, the time–space environment can be imaginatively enriching and stimulating when, with Los, we cleanse our organs of perception. In this realization Blake differs fundamentally from those mystics who have contempt for this world of error. For such mystics the highest reaches of spiritual development are attained by adopting what is tantamount to a contemptuous attitude to earth-existence. They believe that it is only by divorcing the soul from the body (by assuming the cloak of chastity and freeing themselves from earthly matters) that their apotheosis can be achieved. Blake is not of this conviction. He makes this quite plain in, for instance, his poem *Milton*. In Blake's view, it is precisely because John Milton was contemptuous of this world that he isolated himself, for most of his life, not only from his three wives and three daughters, but also from the City of Jerusalem, from the divine vision of universal brotherhood. Blake sees such an attitude to life on earth as a gross error and so, fittingly, in the poem *Milton*, John Milton is seen undertaking a voluntary descent into this world, not a flight from it. John Milton's new life on earth begins with his re-entering a physical body and it culminates in his union with his Emanation, Ololon.

It is pertinent to remind ourselves here that it is to a daughter of Beulah that Blake appeals to sing of Man's 'Resurrection to Unity'. Now, the Daughters of Beulah are, amongst other things, personifications of Faith and Hope and, in *The Four Zoas*, we learn that they are also creators of 'Spaces':

> The daughters of Beulah follow sleepers in all their Dreams,
> Creating spaces, lest they fall into Eternal Death.[24]

Imaginatively experienced, then, time and space are seen as 'the mercy of Eternity'.[25] However limiting the 'Mundane Shell' of time and space[26] may be at its worst, the absence of such a world would bring with it the total loss of our identity as human beings. It is preferable to live in a Urizenic (constricted) world in which active opposition to spiritual intuition prevails than in a world in which all possibility of self-development is extinguished. The Nirvana of the Buddhist, that is, the extinction of the individual spirit and absorption into the Supreme Spirit is not the world Blakean man seeks — in such a world the realization of universal brotherhood in freedom and love is not possible.

In so far as the Mundane Shell, the environment of mortal man, is illusory and delusive its creation is attributable to Urizen and his agents. In *The Four Zoas* we hear that they are engaged in

> Petrifying all the Human Imagination into rock & sand ...[27]

and creating a world for man in which

> ... immovable, within its walls & cielings
> The heavens were clos'd, and spirits mourn'd their bondage night & day[28]

Seen in the light of its Urizenic nature (Urizen we remember represents active opposition to spiritual intuition, to spiritual freedom and individual creativity and initiative) the Mundane Shell symbolizes the totality of errors due to one-sided reliance on the five senses and constrictive, abstract reason.

But mortality, the natural world, is also the environment in which the spirit can awaken, and in this sense the Mundane Shell is attributable to the 'mercy of Eternity', to Christ the creator,[29] or, through Los, to the Imagination:

> God is in the lowest effects as well as in the highest causes;
> for he is become a worm that he may nourish the weak. For let it
> be remember'd that creation is God descending according to the
> weakness of man, for our Lord is the word of God & every thing
> on earth is the word of God & in its essence is God.[30]

An example of the creative Word acting through Los is given in *Jerusalem*:

> ... the Veil of Vala, which Albion cast into the Atlantic Deep
> To catch the Souls of the Dead, began to Vegetate & Petrify
> Around the Earth of Albion among the Roots of his Tree.
> This[31] Los formed into the Gates & mighty Wall between the Oak
> Of Weeping & the Palm of Suffering beneath Albion's Tomb.
> Thus in process of time it became the beautiful Mundane Shell,
> The Habitation of the Spectres of the Dead, & the Place
> Of Redemption & of awakening again into Eternity.[32]

In Night vii Urizen reads to his daughters from his Book of Brass[33] and propounds his inhuman and Antichristian[34] recipe for the conduct of human affairs:

Listen, O Daughters, to my voice. Listen to the Words of Wisdom,
So shall you govern over all; let Moral Duty tune your tongue.
But be your hearts harder than the nether millstone.
To bring the Shadow of Enitharmon beneath our wondrous tree,
That Los may Evaporate like smoke & be no more,
Draw down Enitharmon to the Spectre of Urthona,
And let him have dominion over Los, the terrible shade.
Compell the poor to live upon a Crust of bread, by soft mild arts.
Smile when they frown, frown when they smile; & when a man looks pale
With labour & abstinence, say he looks healthy & happy;

And when his children sicken, let them die; there are enough
Born, even too many, & our Earth will be overrun
Without these arts. If you would make the poor live with temper,[35]
With pomp give every crust of bread you give; with gracious cunning
Magnify small gifts; reduce the man to want a gift, & then give with pomp.
Say he smiles if you hear him sigh. If pale, say he is ruddy.
Preach temperance; say he is overgorg'd & drowns his wit
In strong drink, tho' you know that bread & water are all
He can afford. Flatter his wife, pity his children, till we can
Reduce all to our will, as Spaniels are taught the art.[36]

These 'Words of Wisdom' constitute one of Blake's most potent expressions of a divided humanity and of man's inhumanity to man. Quite clearly, for Urizenic man universal brotherhood is inconceivable. Fill a man's mind with the spirit of capitalism so that he thinks of his state of poverty as having been caused by some fault of his own; then deaden his individual spirit with hypocritical and condescending kindness! Such satanic counsel furnishes us with a good example of the way Blake frequently broadens the sphere of his observation to extend beyond the personal to the social.[37] Moreoever, what he says can as frequently be understood in psychological terms. In this instance, reason is sowing self-contempt, doubt, and a sense of guilt, all of which paralyse honest indignation, individual creativity and initiative.

Now, the immediate purpose of Urizen's lesson in satanic sociology is to try to intimidate Orc. But Orc is still defiant in his revolutionary energy and curses Urizen's 'cold hypocrisy' as he begins to divide into two beings — into a weak worm 'unbound from wrath', symbolizing Urizen's image of a revolt against authority which has been rendered harmless, and into a chained man, symbolizing Orc's image of himself as a victim of Urizenic oppression:

Then Orc cried: 'Curse thy Cold hypocrisy! already round thy Tree
In scales that shine with gold & rubies, thou beginnest to weaken
My divided Spirit. Like a worm I rise in peace, unbound
From wrath. Now when I rage, my fetters bind me more.
O torment! O torment! A Worm compell'd! Am I a worm?
Is it in strong deceit that man is born? ...
... King of furious hail storms,
Art thou the cold attractive power that holds me in this chain?

I well remember how I stole thy light & it became fire
Consuming. Thou Knowest me now, O Urizen, Prince of Light,
And I know thee ...[38]

At this stage Urizen would appear to have conquered Orc, revolutionary and creative energy. But in reality he is terrified at Orc's claim that he is Luvah reborn into time and space. The words 'I stole thy Light' refer back to Luvah's seizure of Urizen's 'Horses of Light'.[39] Here we are told how this stolen light became a fire for consuming, not for growth. Instead of bringing warmth to, say, government and law, the spirit of compassion and love, Luvah, in his form as Orc, is described as a consuming fire which threatens revolutionary warfare:

And Orc began to organize a Serpent body
Despising Urizen's light & turning it into flaming fire,
...
And turning [wisdom del.] affection into fury, & thought into abstraction,
A Self consuming dark devourer rising into the heavens.[40]

Creative, imaginative thinking turns ever more cold, abstract and inhuman.

Not only is Urizen terrified at Orc's claim that he is Luvah, but he is envious that Orc can:

Flame high in pride & laugh to scorn the source of his deceit.[41]

Moreover, Urizen deceives himself when he contends that 'weakness stretches out in breadth & length',[42] that is, he deceives himself when he thinks that Orc, in his form as a weak worm, is innocuous, for soon this worm 'organizes' itself a serpent body and climbs the Tree of Mystery — the forbidden Tree whose fatal fruit brings spiritual death. Under the spellbinding power of reason's hypocrisy, Orc, in order to express himself at all, becomes a hypocrite. In a corrupt world, all impulses are corrupted, and Orc's honest rage now takes the form of conspiracy and cunning in the materialistic serpent:

Sneaking submission can always live.[43]

When Orc rages honestly, that is, when he is true to his real energies, which are those of art, of the creative impulse — he is, we must remember, the son of Los — then he is held down by Urizenic chains.

Orc, as the 'serpent', is symbolic of the erroneous identification, by orthodox religion, of energy with evil. Orc, as the 'worm' who creeps in silence, is the 'Antichrist, Creeping Jesus'.[44] The true Christ, for Blake, is a Being of infinite creative energy:

> For he acts with honest, triumphant Pride,
> And this is the cause that Jesus died.[45]

He did not:

> Give any Proofs of Humility ...[46]

The serpent is given a number of overlapping and related meanings by Blake. Hypocrisy ranks high in the list. Urizen himself, as we have seen elsewhere, sheds tears of hypocritical pity. The 'ancient Elf',[47] Urizen, induces hypocrisy in others by external pressure. The object of oppression is thus corrupted. We have just seen this happening to Orc. His revolutionary spirit degenerates:[48]

> No more remain'd of Orc but the Serpent round the tree of Mystery.[49]

He then loses all semblance of his original humanity, for when:

> ... Luvah in Orc became a Serpent, he descended into
> That State call'd Satan.[50]

It would appear that Urizen has mastered Orc, for to become a serpent implies that one adopts the belief that the phenomenal world is the only reality and that no validity can be given to spiritual intuitions. Orc, originally the avowed opponent of natural religion,[51] becomes what he beholds, he becomes his own opposite. However, as already mentioned, Urizen deceives himself, for Orc, although weakened, has not been completely subverted. His spirit retains a strength which, ultimately, destroys the Tree of Mystery.[52] In Blake's view, the effect of 'morality', what Urizen in his lecture to his daughters calls 'Moral Duty', is to inculcate in the suppressed individual — and in society as a whole, dominated by Urizenic authoritarianism — a psychology of guilt and punishment which, in turn, gives rise to a timid piety. Such piety is, in his view, an insult to human dignity and is accompanied by exacerbated indignation against the oppressor and his repressive code. A consequence of the debasement of human emotion can lead to the arousal of strengthened antagonism towards the oppressor. Urizen does not understand this, for he, like Albion, who has handed over his 'Scepter'[53] to Urizen, has lost the 'Divine Vision'[54] of Christ and His doctrine of the forgiveness of sins which forms the very essence of the brotherhood of man.

Eventually Urizen, too, will be able to say, with Albion:

> O Human Imagination! O Divine Body! I have Crucified,
> I have turned my back upon thee into the Wastes of Moral Law.[55]

We have seen that, immediately following on Urizen's reading from his Book of Law proclaiming his Satanic social policy, Orc recalls his original actions as Luvah. Urizen fears that the threat to his divinity comes from Luvah, who is so closely associated with Jesus Christ, the Prince of Love.

Now, Urizen is not aware of the significant ambiguity of the image of the serpent wound round the Tree of Mystery, of Good and Evil. He has 'suffer'd' Orc, in 'serpent form compell'd'

> ... to climb that he might draw all human forms
> Into submission to his will, nor knew the dread result.[56]

The very triumph of error is prophetic of its defeat. The real solution is Christ, whose garments are Luvah's robes of blood. When Urizen sees 'Orc a serpent form' and Jesus simultaneously, all his great reasoning power cannot reconcile the Prince of Love and Peace with the King of War.[57] Here Blake is partially working with the Christian typological tradition which has always recognized the relationship between the Serpent and Christ. For instance, the raising of the brazen serpent in the wilderness (Numbers 21:6–9) is considered to be a foreshadowing of the crucifixion of Christ: 'And as Moses lifted up the serpent in the wilderness, even so must the Son of man be lifted up: that whosoever believeth in him should not perish, but have eternal life.' (John 3:14–15). The typological tradition affirms both the doctrine that Christ reversed the process of descent upon which man embarked at the foot of the Tree of Knowledge of Good and Evil, and the mythical recognition that He and the serpent are parallel counter-archetypes. Blake, in the two lines just quoted from Night vii, echoes the words: 'And I, if I be lifted up from the earth, will draw all men unto me' (John 12:32). Recognizing Orc as Luvah, Urizen has to nail Orc to the Tree when he assumes 'a Serpent body',[58] thus foreshadowing the crucifixion of Christ:

> Thus was the Lamb of God condemn'd to Death.
> They nail'd him upon the Tree of Mystery, ...[59]

Error itself is prophetic of truth.

A few words regarding Blake's conception of the meaning of the Crucifixion are appropriate here. Generally, the term Crucifixion is used by Blake in criticism of the Urizenic practice of moral judgement. The historic event of Christ's crucifixion on Golgotha is understood by Blake to be the ultimate manifestation of the Urizenic moral law.[60] Interpreting the Crucifixion as a symbol, Blake sees in every instance of restriction, or inhibition, of creative imagination, perpetrated by the will of Urizen, or Satan, a renewed crucifixion of the Lamb, of the Christ in man, on the 'Tree of Mystery', the symbol of man's spiritual enslavement by the moral law. The Crucifixion is a perpetually recurring event in the life of every true Christian.[61] It is a perpetual exhortation to brotherhood and self-sacrifice. Christ Himself nailed the 'Serpent Bulk of Nature's Dross ... to the Cross',[62] and in doing so freed Fallen Man from enslavement to self-contempt and a sense of guilt which the artificial Urizenic code of morality impressed upon him. Fallen Man frees himself by Christlike self-annihilation from all forms of submission to manifestations of the Urizenic accusations of sin. Instead of redeeming sin in the sense of ortho-doxy, instead of 'purchasing' freedom of Fallen Man from sin, 'Christ ... put it off on the Cross'[63] and sacrificed himself voluntarily so that, as Paul expresses it, 'through death he might destroy him that had the power of death, that is, the devil; and deliver them who through fear of death were all their life subject to bondage' (Hebrews 2: 14–15). This liberation of Fallen Man from the sense of guilt and the fear of death — both of which have risen in man through the machinations of one-sided, discursive reason, fallen Urizen — is performed by Christ, as Luvah, in Night viii. Urizen, as we have seen, is uneasy; he is terrified at Orc's claim that he is Luvah. Moreover, he is ignorant of the 'dread result' of Orc's transform-ation into a serpent form winding up the Tree of Mystery. His dis-ease is prophetic, for the deed of liberation performed by Christ as Luvah will be 'dread' for the satanic form of Urizen. Ultimately it will be an occasion for rejoicing for the whole human being, including what is best in Urizen himself.

With Orc's transformation complete, Night vii starts a new movement in which Los for the first time in *The Four Zoas* assumes a semblance of the heroic role he will play so fully in *Jerusalem*. He has been a witness to the scene between Urizen and the young rebel, Orc. He has shared the pains of Urizen[64] and 'felt the Envy in his limbs like to a blighted tree' as Urizen 'fixed in Envy sat brooding' over Orc. Urizen's Tree of Mystery, repressive morality, has branched 'into the heaven of Los'.[65] After Orc's ascent of the Tree of Mystery, of Evil and Good, Los sits 'in showers of Urizen watching cold Enitharmon', while Enitharmon's Shadow is 'drawn down, Down to the roots' of the tree to weep over Orc.[66] The first part of Urizen's strategy has succeeded: 'To bring the Shadow of Enitharmon beneath our wondrous tree'.[67] It remains to be seen whether the second part of the Urizenic scheme will be realized: 'That Los may Evaporate like smoke & be no more' and that the Spectre of Urthona may 'have dominion over Los'.[68]

Blake now takes up the theme again which he treated in *The Book of Urizen*: jealousy and the torments of love. The lament of Los over his Emanation, Enitharmon, makes the point that she is 'beaming summer loveliness' and 'delectable' in his absence, but 'cold pale in sorrow' and forbidding in his presence. He laments his fading creative powers and the necessity of struggling with 'great monsters of the animating worlds' instead of singing of 'the joys of love', as he had done in his unfallen form.[69] To Los, Enitharmon is unresponsive, for she has entered upon the final phase of her fall. As the Shadow of Enitharmon, that is, as inspiration repressed, she descends the Tree of Mystery and embraces a diminished Los, 'The Spectre of Urthona', that is, the selfhood of fallen man, a shadow of the imaginative power man once possessed.

At this stage, Los has yet to mature into the artist and prophet, the creative and positive imagination he is to become.[70] In the embrace between the Spectre of Urthona and the Shadow of Enitharmon we have 'the meeting of a decayed imaginative will, the day-to-day life of even a poet like Blake, with the decayed joy of imagination that any poet's beloved is likely to become.'[71]

Enitharmon has yet to learn to love Los in his essential role as artist-prophet. The meeting between the Shadow and the Spectre can be seen as depicting the human soul in which the imagination is not yet healthily inspired as a creative power in harmony with itself. Just as Los will only be liberated and therefore freely creative when he has recognized and accepted the Spectre within himself, that is, the aspect of himself which is in touch with the darker realities of the human soul,[72] so, too, Enitharmon has to learn to love the darker side of Los before she can love him for what he is at his creative best. In order to take this step in recognition she must first go through the experience of confronting that which is 'worst' in herself.[73] She has to confront her own Shadow. Now, we could easily think that to bring about this confrontation and self-recognition, an initial step in the process of regeneration, Blake here providentially introduces a new character, a *deus ex machina* — Enitharmon's Shadow. This, however, is not the case, for the Shadow represents that aspect of Enitharmon which we find in the Lambeth Books[74] and earlier Nights of *The Four Zoas*, where she symbolizes the non-visionary conception of space which results from the philosophy of the five senses and all that that implies in man's conception of morality, personal relationships, and so on.

In Night vii the Shadow of Enitharmon is seen by the Spectre of Urthona 'Beneath the Tree of Mystery' and 'among the leaves & fruit' of that tree.[75] In Night i we hear that she:

> Refus'd to open the bright gates; she clos'd and barr'd them fast
> Lest Los should enter into Beulah thro' her beautiful gates.[76]

The 'gates', according to whether they are represented as 'open' or 'closed', symbolize the acceptance or rejection of the visionary communion with the Divine Humanity, with Christ. In Night v these 'gates' are momentarily 'open', that is to say, Enitharmon's imaginative powers are momentarily awoken,[77] but after that momentary experience they remain 'barr'd' until, as we shall shortly see, the crisis in Enitharmon's process of regeneration is reached and they burst open. When that moment arrives Enitharmon, together with Urthona's Spectre and Los, can assume her regenerative labours on behalf of humanity.

Another passage, in Night i, may help us to envisage the nature of the Shadow of Enitharmon (we should note here that, in nearly every case in Blake, the shadow-activities are represented as female. This implies that the reference is primarily to matters of 'perception', not of reasoning, which is 'spectrous', or masculine). In Night i Enitharmon represents error in the regions of both thought based entirely on erroneous, spiritually blind perception, and of a morality with its roots in natural religion. She exults in a 'Song of Death' over fallen man.[78] Enitharmon's power subdues Los, the 'fierce prophetic boy'[79] and 'visionary',[80] and, together, they appear as powers of this world, nourished by 'fleshly bread' and 'nervous wine'.[81]

When the visionary spirit in Los asserts itself and he smites Enitharmon 'upon the Earth',[82] she calls on Urizen for aid.[83] Urizen descends and the spiritual subjection of Los is completed in an alliance with Urizen and a reconciliation with Enitharmon.

Here, of course, Enitharmon is not acting in accordance with her spiritual reality; when she does, then she works in harmony with the creative imagination, with Los, as an inspiring force, in the process of the regeneration, the reintegration, of man. The Enitharmon we have just been considering is not the true Enitharmon, but the Shadow of Enitharmon.

Returning now to Night vii we see the Spectre of Urthona (that is, the dark double of the creative imaginative power, the 'decayed imaginative will') and the Shadow of Enitharmon (the 'decayed joy of imagination') re-enacting the story of Eden under the Urizenic Tree of Mystery. Each gives an account of the Fall of Man 'among the intoxication fumes of Mystery'.[84] We need not discuss these two accounts in any detail but note that there is a parallel between the Shadow's envy of and fascination with Vala, 'the Mother of Harlots',[85] and Spectre's sexual rivalry with 'that demon Los'.[86]

These two accounts of the Fall, in which exist sexual strife and frustration, and the sexual re-enactment of the Fall as described in Genesis, are explicitly portrayed, are immediate preambles to the consolidation of error which finds expression in the copulation of the most deeply fallen aspects of both Urthona and Enitharmon, an act which results in the birth of 'a wonder horrible',[87] a 'Shadowy Female', whose appearance releases the full horror and threat of antagonism to imaginative vision:

> ... a Cloud; she grew & grew
> Till many of the Dead burst forth from the bottom of their tombs
> In male forms without female counterparts, or Emanations,
> Cruel and ravening with Enmity & Hatred & War,
> In dreams of Ulro, dark delusive, drawn by the lovely shadow.[88]

The engendering of the Shadowy Female, a fallen form of Vala, constitutes the nadir in the process of fragmentation, of the Fall. Once reached, the lowest point can either result in complete stagnation and spiritual death, or it can harbour the seed for an 'upward' turn, a reversal of the 'downward' process. Progress in the 'upward' process may be either fast or slow, but the actual turning point happens in a flash, outside, 'yardstick space' and 'clock time'.[89] It is a moment that Satan cannot touch.[90] This turning point, from fall and fragmentation, division, to ascent and unity, is indicated by Blake in the laconic words 'But then' in the following passage which follows on immediately after the lines just quoted:

> The Spectre terrified gave her Charge over the howling Orc.
> Then took the tree of Mystery root in the World of Los,
> Its topmost boughs shooting a fibre beneath Enitharmon's couch,
> The double rooted Labyrinth soon wav'd around their heads.[91]
> *But then** the Spectre enter'd Los's bosom. Every sigh & groan
> Of Enitharmon bore Urthona's Spectre on its wings.
> Obdurate Los felt Pity. Enitharmon told the tale
> Of Urthona. Los embraced the Spectre, first as a brother,
> Then as another Self, astonish'd, humanizing & in tears,
> In Self abasement giving up his Domineering lust.[92]

In this moment of inspiration Los embraces the hitherto dominating and 'devouring',[93] rationalizing Spectre. Fallen Man's imaginative will and his imagination are joined again and the humanizing process of regeneration can at last begin. The Imagination, as creator, unites, combines with its own power of abstraction, with its own rational power. In divided man the abstracting, rationalizing power falls into the delusion of Ulro, of mistaking mental fabrications (such as time and space) for Absolutes. Hence the Spectre's description of himself as:

> … wand'ring
> The deeps of Los, the slave of that Creation I created.[94]

In order to regain the unity of 'Strong Urthona', of whom Los is the embodied, the 'Vehicular form',[95] Los must first combine with his Spectre. He does, through pity, which here is not divisive but reunifying. The next step towards the unity of Urthona is now before Los: he must reunite in harmony with his Emanation, Enitharmon. At this point in the process of reintegration the Spectre utters fundamental truths to Los:

> Thou never canst embrace sweet Enitharmon, terrible Demon, Till
> Thou art united with thy Spectre, Consummating by pains & labours
> That mortal body, & by Self annihilation back returning
> To life Eternal; be assured I am thy real self,
> Tho' thus divided from thee & the slave of Every passion

*My italics.

Of thy fierce Soul. Unbar the Gates of Memory; look upon me
Not as another, but as thy real Self ...[96]

Although his earlier boast to Enitharmon that he is superior to Los is
not justified,[97] the Spectre's memories of the unity and harmony of
Eternity are true, and he can therefore see the necessity for the reunion of
himself, as Urthona, with his Emanation. He now shows Los that he,
Los, stands before the possibility of the manifestation of two utterly
different worlds:

If we unite in one, another better world will be
Open'd within your heart & loins & wondrous brain,
Threefold, as it was in Eternity, & this, the fourth Universe,
Will be Renew'd by the three & consummated in Mental fires;
But if thou dost refuse, Another body will be prepared
For me, & thou, annihilate, evaporate & be no more.
For thou art but a form & organ of life, & of thyself
Art nothing, being Created Continually by Mercy & Love divine.[98]

By this revelation Los learns the necessity of 'Self annihilation'. The
Spectre here reveals that he, Los, has the faculty by means of which man
can 'go out' of himself and 'enter into' other human beings; he reveals
that regeneration does, indeed, can only come about through the agency
of creative imagination.

Los recognizes the truth of the Spectre's statement:

... Spectre horrible, thy words astound my Ear
With irresistible conviction. I feel I am not one of those
Who when convinc'd can still persist: tho' furious, controllable
By Reason's power. Even I already feel a World within
Opening its gates, & in it all the real substances
Of which these in the outward World are shadows which pass away.
Come then into my Bosom, & in thy shadowy arms bring with thee
My lovely Enitharmon. I will quell my fury & teach
Peace to the soul of dark revenge & repentance to Cruelty.[99]

Los chooses the way of self-annihilation, but, as we shall soon see, he
has a fair way to go yet before he is finally regenerated, for Enitharmon is
not yet ready to hear the message of 'Peace to the soul' and to assist Los in
his labours. Nevertheless, Los has regained part of the lost unity of Eter-
nity and is now free, for a while, as Imagination, to act in a way which
approximates to the 'mental war' of Eternity (as distinct from 'corporeal
war' on earth). He is free to begin to create the City of Art:

```
... mingling together with his Spectre,
... Los perform'd
Wonders of labour —
They Builded Golgonooza, Los labouring builded pillars high
And Domes terrific in the nether heavens, for beneath
Was open'd new heavens & a new Earth beneath & within,
Threefold, within the brain, within the heart, within the loins:
A Threefold Atmosphere Sublime, continuous from Urthona's world.[100]
```

The task of Los here, in building Golgonooza, is to give forms to all uncreated things (see Appendix 3) particularly threefold man. Though 'continuous' with the unfallen world, which is fourfold, the world here created is 'Threefold', not fourfold, for, as we have already seen, Los has not yet been able to unite with his Emanation, his female counterpart.[101] Union with the divine is not possible without the presence of the Emanation (see p. 344).

Expressed in the lines just quoted from *The Four Zoas* is Blake's conviction that all causation is spiritual, that the Imagination is the prenatal power which forms the human body.

Los, as we have seen, has learnt the necessity of 'Self annihilation'. Yet salvation is not achieved easily, for, as already mentioned, Enitharmon flees from the embrace of Los and the Spectre and hid beneath Urizen's tree, and Los is therefore not yet strong enough to prevail in his new realization of truth. Though he knows better, he, like Adam, joins his beloved in eating of the fruit of Urizen's Tree of Mystery. Enitharmon herself is in despair:

```
When In the Deeps beneath I gather'd of this ruddy fruit,
It was by that I knew that I had Sinn'd, & then I knew
That without a ransom[102] I could not be sav'd from Eternal death:
... thenceforth in despair
I spend my glowing time; but thou art strong & mighty
To bear Self conviction; take then, Eat thou also of
The fruit & give me proof of life Eternal or I die.[103]
```

Enitharmon's despair leads her to think she is doomed to eternal death and needs Los to prove his possession of 'life Eternal' by also eating the 'ruddy fruit'. Los plucks the fruit, eats, and sits down in despair:

```
And must have given himself to death Eternal, But
Urthona's spectre in part mingling with him, comforted him.[104]
```

Time, 'clock-time', begins to serve both as consoler and redeemer for the dejected imagination:

> Being a medium between him & Enitharmon.[105]

But their reunion:

> Was not to be Effected without Cares & Sorrows & Troubles
> Of six thousand years* of self denial and of bitter Contrition.[106]

These two lines give us a very clear statement of Blake's mature point of view that existence in the 'mundane' world is desirable because it is the providentially appointed means through which man can gain reunion with the Divine.

Here, then, beneath the boughs of the serpent-encircled Tree — with its false Urizenic identification of energy with evil — Los is overshadowed. He, too, falls victim to the Urizenic moral system. Is, then, the second part of Urizen's satanic scheme now about to be realized: 'That Los may Evaporate like smoke & be no more'? For Urizen's purpose the moment of Los's despair is too late, for the Spectre of Urthona is not exerting 'dominion over Los',[107] but is acting in a consoling and redemptive role. Moreover, the very dominance of the Tree over passion and imagination, the very poignancy of the sense of sin and guilt, no matter how falsely defined by Urizen, awakens the inner desire for liberation, regeneration. Indeed, the experience of despair over sin and guilt can prove to be spiritually stimulating, that is, it can arouse an incisive and deeply felt need for an entirely new mode of being. The seed for such a need was sown when the 'topmost boughs' of the Tree of Mystery sprouted to form roots 'in the world of Los'.[108] The insinuating and hidden influence of evil and 'mystery' now reveals itself to the creative human imagination, for it has made itself manifest in the upper, conscious world of Los's being. A leap forward, an imaginative leap, is now called for; a break from Urizenic entrapment. Both Los and Enitharmon have the 'inner substance', the spiritual resources, to make such a regenerating step. They have both gone through such depths of suffering — and been aware of the cause and meaning of it — to be able to perceive the possibilities of the 'turning point' of which we spoke earlier. Through their suffering they have not only become different in themselves, but through their grief and sorrow they have discovered

---

*Six thousand years is a traditional figure.

within themselves a depth of humanity which is capable of both reconciliation and, above all, forgiveness. The inner 'act' of reversal, of regeneration, is, as already indicated, precipitated by the eating of the 'ruddy fruit', that is, through being 'filled with doubts in self accusation'.[109] It is activated through a despair that would lead to 'death eternal', if it were not for 'Urthona's spectre in part mingling with' Los[110] and acting, as Time, as a comforter. And it is given an inner power to progress through Los's free embrace of the Spectre and Enitharmon, through, we may say, his imaginative act of forgiveness. In the remaining part of Night vii, and in the two final Nights, Blake focuses our attention on the renewal of creative life which has its fountainhead in that moment of 'Grace'.

We have heard the Spectre claiming that he is Los's 'true self'. This is patently not true. If it were, then Urizen's insistence in Night i that:

The Spectre is the Man. The rest is only delusion & fancy[111]

would be true, and Los, Real Man, would 'evaporate like smoke & be no more'. Nevertheless, the Spectre's claim is instrumental in inducing Los to 'listen' to and recognize the dark and sinister aspects of himself — uncontrollable passion, hatred,[112] pleasure at the sight of others' torment,[113] possessiveness, and so on. Once Los has acknowledged his errors, given them form (see Appendix 3), the ground is prepared on which he can overcome them.

We know already that Los began building Golgonooza around Enitharmon after the birth of Orc in Night v,[114] but his motive for doing so was chiefly jealousy.[115] Nevertheless, the prospect of Orcian revolt had a positive side, for it fired poetic intuition into creative activity. Now, however, in Night vii, Los is motivated by genuine concern for others and it is the Spectre who proposes the new motive for creative activity. We now witness one of Blake's most moving myths emerging out of the cooperation between Los and his brotherly Spectre:

The Spectre of Urthona wept before Los, saying, 'I am the cause
That this dire state commences. I began the dreadful state
Of Separation, & on my dark head the curse & punishment
Must fall unless a way be found to Ransom & Redeem'.

What he here says is true, for he can be equated with that aspect of Urthona which caused the divine blacksmith to drop his hammer, to lose his creative will.[116]

The Spectre continues:

> But I have thee my Counterpart, miraculous,
> These spectres have no Counterparts, therefore they ravin
> Without the food of life. Let us Create them Counterparts,
> For without a Created body the Spectre is Eternal Death.[117]

Urthona's Spectre knows himself to be 'the Spectre of the Living',[118] he can 'comingle' with Los, the 'vehicular form' of Urthona, the creative imagination of man. Los is his 'Counterpart'. He knows that he is not one of the 'Spectres of the Dead',[119] and that the only way to save such spectres from eternal death is to create 'Counterparts' for them. Counterparts must be created for all the spectres of human existence, for all the wandering fragments of spirit, 'the terrific Passions & Affections',[120] which have not yet been given form. To be saved they must be given form, they must incarnate and thus be freed from an unreal world, from 'a land of Abstraction'.[121] It is with the knowledge of his 'terrific Passions & Affections' and the consciousness of being at one with Los, the Imagination, that the Spectre of Urthona can propose a new motive and redemptive direction for Los's creative energy and imagination: namely, to create forms for man's fears, desires, frustrations, dark impulses and shadowy hopes, negative and destructive thoughts. We may understand this as meaning that, without such 'forms', the world of man is spectral, spiritually 'dead'. In such a world there is no poetry, no music, no art. Without such nourishment for his soul, man remains 'insane, brutish, Deformed'.[122] Poetry, music, art — beauty in all its forms — transforms that which is 'ugly', 'deformed' and 'brutish'; brings into the light of day that which otherwise would fester in the darkness of the soul. The Spectre of Urthona urges Los to save a world which is devoid of imagination by merging imagination with it; to make imaginative counterparts for the mass of men. Los's acceptance of the Spectre means that the Spectre finds his place as an integral and necessary part of mature creative, imaginative consciousness — a part which is made up of such elements as an intimate knowledge of passion, guilt and sin; dark visions of inner emptiness and unfulfilled longing — with all the frustration which that entails; the experience of 'weeping & trembling, Filled with doubts in self-accusation';[123] and so on. The acceptance of the Spectre — the admission of susceptibility to doubt, for instance — gives the creative imagination, Los, added energy and strength, for he can now address himself to both the convictions (the faith) and the doubts of his fellowmen. He can stir the human soul in all its facets. Through accepting the Spectre the creative activity of the human imagination is enhanced. Both the 'light' and the 'dark' truths of life are recognized in the totality of the imagination.

Los now sees a way to salvation. He answers his Spectre by urging upon him — and Enitharmon — an inward vision of Christ, the archetypal 'Counterpart':

> ... Now I feel the weight of stern repentance
> Tremble not so, my Enitharmon, at the awful gates
> Of thy poor Broken Heart. I see thee like a shadow withering
> As on the outside of Existence; but look! behold! take comfort!
> Turn inwardly thine Eyes & there behold the Lamb of God
> Clothed in Luvah's robes of blood descending to redeem.
> O Spectre of Urthona, take comfort! O Enitharmon!
> Could'st thou but cease from terror & trembling & affright.
> When I appear before thee in forgiveness of ancient injuries,
> Why should'st thou remember & be afraid? I surely have died in pain
> Often enough to convince thy jealousy & fear & terror.
> Come hither; be patient; let us converse together, because
> I also tremble at myself & at all my former life.[124]

The Lamb of God, of Love, is the counterpart of revolution, of Orc, who is wrathful.

The Spectre responds to this vision, but Enitharmon does not yet do so. She replies that she sees the Lamb of God descending but fears:

> ... that he
> Will give us to Eternal Death, fit punishment for such
> Hideous offenders: Uttermost extinction in eternal pain:
> An ever dying life of stifling & obstruction: shut out
> Of existence to be a sign & terror to all who behold,
> Lest any should in futurity do as we have done in heaven.[125]

Enitharmon does not yet understand the principle of regeneration. She is still filled with the sense of guilt and sin of Urizen's world. Los, on the other hand, under the sway of his vision of love and still warmed by the experience of brotherhood which he has with his Spectre, by whom he has been stirred with the idea of forming counterparts for the spectres of the dead, speaks to Enitharmon of his imaginative desire:

> ... to fabricate embodied semblances in which the dead
> May live.[126]

Salvation is Los's and Enitharmon's function. He and she must serve as sacrificial victims on whose life the 'piteous victims of battle'[127] may feed:

> To form a world of sacrifice of brothers & sons & daughters
> To comfort Orc in his dire sufferings ...[128]

Whereas Enitharmon still sees the Lamb of God as a condemning judge, Los sees Christ as the archetype of self-giving Humanity, which man should strive to emulate.

In his resolve to 'give himself', Los recaptures the fire of Urthona; he is imbued with the creative strength of Eternal Man:

> ... look, my fires enlume afresh
> Before my face ascending with delight as in ancient times![129]

Los feels his old creative powers. Through the experience of Christ's selfless love, Los has found his way back to creative imagination. He has released the inner divine essence from the restraints of the selfhood.

Moved by this regeneration of Los's creative imagination, Enitharmon at last encourages him in his labour. She urges him to give forms to the piteous spectres and agrees to help him 'to fabricate embodied semblances':

> Enitharmon spread her beamy locks upon the wind & said,
> 'O Lovely terrible Los, wonder of Eternity, O Los, my defence & guide,
> Thy works are all my joy & in thy fires my soul delights;
> If mild they burn in just proportion, & in secret night
> And silence build their day in shadow of soft clouds & dews,
> Then I can sigh forth on the winds of Golgonooza piteous forms
> That vanish again into my bosom; but if thou, my Los,
> Wilt in sweet moderated fury fabricate forms *sublime*,
> Such as the piteous spectres may assimilate themselves into,
> They shall be ransoms for our Souls that we may live'.[130]

Enitharmon will assist Los as long as he abstains from wrath. Symbolically, Enitharmon is the artist's inspiration; here she is shown, dramatically, as being his helpmeet and refining influence. Heeding her plea for 'sweet moderated fury', Los,

> ... his hands divine inspir'd, began
> ...
> To modulate his fires; studious the loud roaring flames
> He vanquish'd with the strength of Art, ...[131]

He subordinates his fiery prophetic powers to his creative artistic function.[132]

Now Los and Enitharmon together begin their work of creation:

> And first he drew a line upon the walls of shining heaven,
> And Enitharmon tinctur'd it with beams of blushing love.
> It remain'd permanent, a lovely form, inspir'd, divinely human.[133]

It is noteworthy that Los draws the 'line', that is, the 'lovely form', on the 'walls of shining heaven'. This 'line' is the form created for the unformed 'Passions and Desires'.[134] Now, in some respects the 'shining heaven', the sky, is one of the most indefinite objects of perception conceivable. What Blake does here is to show us imagination giving the indefinite and inhuman, the spectral, a definite and humanized form. Definiteness, in Blake, is constantly connoted of the higher life of the spirit, whereas indefiniteness is associated by him with the false rules prevailing in Urizenic (rationalistic, materialistic) philosophy, religion and art.[135] Forms are clearly defined when clearly imagined. To give the indefinite a definite and humanized form is a task undertaken by the creative imagination. Without imagination chaos rules supreme.[136]

Before looking at the last few lines of Night vii let us retrace our steps a little.

We have seen that, troubled by the sense of guilt and sin, Los, the Spectre of Urthona, and Enitharmon, have all three felt the need for redemption and have planned to use their artistic creations as sacrificial victims, as 'ransoms' for their sins.[137] Now, here we need to recollect that in an earlier passage in Night vii Blake has introduced a theme close to his heart, 'the Forgiveness of Sins', without which brotherhood cannot prevail, we cannot exist as true men.[138]

In the earlier passage referred to and quoted above Los urges Enitharmon to accept the spirit of self-sacrifice and mutual forgiveness, for 'Such are the Gates of Paradise'.[139] In his appearance before Enitharmon, 'in forgiveness of ancient injuries', Los may be identified with Christ.[140] In having 'died in pain/Often enough to convince' Enitharmon's 'jealousy & fear & terror' Los has repeatedly enacted the selfless, loving deed of Christ's self-annihilation on the Cross from which He asked that man be forgiven for his spiritual blindness.

If Los and Enitharmon were to imbibe fully Christ's spirit, if they could forgive each other, they would be self-redeemers, redeem themselves and each other from 'within'. No redeemer in the orthodox sense would be needed: nor would they need to sacrifice their creations, their 'children', to an accuser,[141] to the moral law established by a Urizenic God.

Los's vision of Christ is given no further mention in Night vii, but when the moment of sacrifice arrives:

> Los Loved them & refus'd to Sacrifice their infant limbs,
> And Enitharmon's smiles & tears prevail'd over self protection.
> They rather chose to meet Eternal Death than to destroy
> The offspring of their Care & Pity.[142]

The imaginative deed of creating forms, giving of their very essence, and of embodying abstractions (negative ideas), brings spiritual enlightenment to both Los and Enitharmon. They have learnt how to sacrifice themselves, not their 'offspring'. In the 'embodied semblance', created by Los, order is brought to the warring Zoas. All conflicting Spirits[143] are drawn:

> From out the ranks of Urizen's war & from the fiery lake
> Of Orc ...[144]

into the warfare of ideas, into 'Mental fight', into spiritual brotherhood.

In this succinct statement is contained one of Blake's major contentions: all inhuman, 'corporeal' warfare and conflict springs from the central failure in man to use and develop his powers of creative, artistic imagination.

First to be drawn out are Rintrah and Palambron, Wrath and Pity. With their transformation, Orc is also transformed:

> First Rintrah & then Palambron, drawn from out the ranks of war,
> In infant innocence repos'd on Enitharmon's bosom.
> Orc was comforted in the deeps; his soul reviv'd in them:
> As the Eldest brother is the father's image, So Orc became
> As Los, a father to his brethren, & he joy'd in the dark lake
> Tho' bound with chains of Jealousy & in scales of iron & brass.[145]

In earlier works, Rintrah and Palambron, as the fallen sons of the Spirit of Prophecy, transmit Urizen's laws to men.[146] For instance, in *The Song of Los*, Rintrah 'gave abstract Philosophy to Brama in the East'[147] and:

> To Trismegistus, Palambron gave an abstract Law:
> To Pythagoras, Socrates & Plato.[148]

But from now[149] on they are regenerated and act as assistants to their parents, Los and Enitharmon, in the work of regeneration. They can now be recognized as the regenerated sons of regenerated creative imagination, for, as we have remarked earlier, Los's fiery prophetic powers are now subordinated to his creative function.

What we see happening here is law beginning to give way to love; Urizenic oppression, legalism and dogmatism, giving way to brotherhood.

The transformation of those who have acted as Urizen's agents also has its effect on Orc, anarchy, revolution — Urizen's extreme opponent. For although Los and Enitharmon had many sons (and daughters),[150] they are all aspects of Orc. For instance, Rintrah (just Wrath) and Palamabron (Pity), to mention but two, are the beginnings of revolution.[151] Under the influence of Los's experience of Christ's teaching of the forgiveness of sins, the inner transformation is beginning to take place in Orc too, so that, eventually, 'corporeal' revolution is subordinated to spiritual revolution.[152]

Tharmas, fallen into formlessness, also rejoices in the new forms Los and Enitharmon are creating, for, among them, he hopes to find and reunite with his lost Emanation, Enion,[153] who, when united with him, supplies his inspiration.[154] We shall return to Tharmas's refinding of 'form' and reunion with Enion in a later chapter, but a few words regarding him are relevant at this point.

Tharmas's special sense is the tongue, called the 'Parent Sense'.[155] As such it symbolizes communication of many kinds — verbal, perceptual and sexual. Tharmas is, as already stated, the 'Parent pow'r'[156] because 'communication', intercourse, is the beginning of generation. In his unfallen form we could say that Tharmas represents spiritual communication, spiritual fellowship, brotherhood, in which the individual experiences himself at one with the totality, with the Divine. The Fall brings with it divisions: in the psyche, into two sexes, and so forth. This fall from perfect unity makes communication, intercourse, as we know it in the world of generation, necessary. In Blake's account of the Fall in *The Four Zoas* it is the fall of Tharmas (speech) which precipitates the fall of man from 'Universal Brotherhood' into the age of iron, where he is a slave to the repressive, rigid and loveless laws of Urizen (discursive reason).

Even Urizen is drawn into Los's influence. The creative part in him is reborn in Rintrah. But Urizen's 'Spectrous form', that which is antagonistic to imaginative vision, will not allow itself to be 'drawn away'.[157] Urizen is partially enlightened, but the next Night sees 'his Spectrous form' appear as Satan-Urizen. Early in Night viii we find Urizen beneath the Tree of Mystery, where he plans the final stage in his campaign to assume complete control of the universe.[158]

Night vii ends with Los being astonished to find that he loves what can be saved in Urizen:

> Startled was Los; he found his Enemy Urizen now
> In his hands; he wonder'd that he felt love & not hate.
> His whole soul loved him; he beheld him an infant
> Lovely.[159]

True creative imagination is selfless and forgiving. It is imbued with the Spirit of Christ. This is what Blake meant when he says that:

> Jesus & his Apostles & Disciples were all Artists,[160]

whose works were destroyed by the Churches.

Blake is of the view that all life can be permeated by true Imagination, by Christ Himself.

When true Imagination informs man's thoughts, feelings and actions, then universal brotherhood is a reality.

8

THE FOUR ZOAS:
THE CULMINATION
OF ERRORS

In Night viii the Fall reaches its nadir on the limit of contraction.[1] As we have previously remarked, reaching the lower limit also marks the beginning of the process of regeneration — indicated here by Albion beginning to wake, sneezing seven times.[2] The stirring of Albion 'in the arms of tender mercy & loving kindness' awakens love in his children. This is the 'Promise Divine'[3] discovered by Los when 'he felt love & not hate' for 'his enemy Urizen'.[4] Los now beholds:

> ... the Divine Vision thro' the broken Gates
> Of [Enitharmon's *del.*] thy poor broken heart, astonish'd,
> melted into Compassion & Love.[5]

The 'natural' heart now begins to be permeated by imaginative promptings and a wonderful transformation takes place in Enitharmon, who, hitherto, has symbolized the dominating female will.[6] She sees 'the Lamb of God upon Mount Zion'[7] and then reveals herself as the creative self-giving partner of Los in 'sweet labours of Love', in the task of imaginative regeneration:

> Los could enter into Enitharmon's bosom & explore
> Its intricate Labyrinths now the Obdurate heart was broken
> ... Then Enitharmon erected Looms ...
> And ... in these Looms she wove the Spectres
> Bodies of vegetation, singing lulling Cadences to drive away
> Despair from the poor wandering spectres; and Los loved them
> With a parental love, for the Divine hand was upon him
> And upon Enitharmon, & the Divine Countenance shone
> In Golgonooza. Looking down, the daughters of Beluah saw
> With joy the bright Light, & in it a Human form,
> And he knew he was the Saviour, even Jesus: & they worshipped.[8]

Christ, the Human Form Divine, the archetypal herald of self-realization through self-annihilation, enters and illumines the human heart. Los and Enitharmon:

> Wondering with love & Awe they felt the divine hand upon them.[9]

Los now represents the redeeming power of time and Enitharmon the providence of space. Although the form given to the Spectres is an inferior, 'vegetated' form, it is far better than non-entity. Without it they would vanish for ever and be unredeemable. Once the movement towards Apocalypse has been set in motion, death is changed into 'sleep' and the 'sleeping' forms of time and space can be transformed into the human forms of art. The human form thus finally realized by the imagination is the Human Form Divine of Christ Himself.

We have arrived at a threshold, as it were. At this threshold the powers of damnation seem to be as strong as those of salvation. The extremes of error and truth, of despair and hope, of death and life, appear almost simultaneously.

The wars of Urizen still rage. He himself is baffled to discover now that Christ and Luvah and Orc are different forms of the same power. Being above all an advocate of rigid orderliness and demarcation Urizen cannot comprehend that love and 'revolt' are both functions of passion,[10] and that they are complementary — the former being eternal, the latter, in its serpent form, temporal:

> When Urizen saw the Lamb of God clothed in Luvah's robes,
> Perplex'd & terrifi'd he stood, tho' well he knew that Orc
> Was Luvah. But now he beheld a new Luvah, Or One
> Who assum'd Luvah's form & stood before him opposite.[11]

Earlier we saw that Urizen's spiritual enlightenment was only partial and momentary. We now see him still beneath the Tree of Mystery where, as was mentioned at the end of the previous chapter, he is planning the final stages of his campaign to take total control of the universe:

> Communing with the Serpent of Orc in dark dissimulation.[12]

Though enemies, Urizen and Orc are nevertheless spiritually allied in the state called Satan:

> And with the Synagogue of Satan in dark Sanhedrim,
> To undermine the World of Los & tear bright Enitharmon

To the four winds, hopeless of future. All futurity
Seems teeming with endless destruction never to be repell'd.[13]

On seeing the 'new Luvah', Urizen, in desperation, 'warlike preparations fabricated'[14] to destroy Enitharmon and 'the World of Los'. But the tyrannous ambition of spectral Urizen and fiery Orc merges into the most extreme form of selfhood and the battle takes a direction Urizen had not intended:

Terrified & astonish'd, Urizen beheld the battle take a form
Which he intended not: a Shadowy [male del.] hermaphrodite black & opake;
The soldiers nam'd it Satan, but he was yet unform'd & vast.
Hermaphroditic it at length became, hiding the Male
Within as in a Tabernacle, Abominable, Deadly.[15]

Meanwhile, Los, keeping his love alive and continuing to believe in brotherhood, contemplated 'Enormous Works':

... inspir'd by the holy Spirit.-
Los builds the Walls of Golgonooza against the stirring battle
That only thro' the Gates of Death they* can enter to Enitharmon.
Raging they take the human visage & the human form,
Feeling the hand of Los in Golgonooza & the force
Attractive of his hammer's beating & the silver looms
Of Enitharmon singing lulling cadences on the wind;
They humanize in the fierce battle, ...[16]

Los, 'inspired by the Holy Spirit', forces the 'terrors' who wish to destroy Enitharmon, to 'humanize' — the first step towards redemption. As we already noted, to wage war is, for Blake, to misdirect psychic energy. It is the task of Los and Enitharmon here to attract such misdirected energy to their world of beauty and brotherhood. Out of non-human, unreal, deathly formlessness, Los and Enitharmon labour continually to 'embody', bring into full being, whatever is potentially human, real and alive. Before evil (error and death — a Urizenic invention) can be seen clearly as a non-entity which must be cast off, all that is real under its domination must be continually re-created. What is left over after this creative process disappears, since it is only delusion, and will be consumed in 'Mental flames'.[17]

Urizen is now joined by Vala, the Shadowy Female, who pronounces the descending Saviour to be:

*i.e. the 'terrors'.

... the murderer of my Luvah, cloth'd in robes of blood.[18]

Vala, the Goddess of Nature, is, we remember, the Emanation of Luvah, passion and generative love. She sees in Christ the destroyer of the god of the generative world, the vegetative god of natural religion, and calls to Satan/Urizen for revenge against this new revelation. But before we witness the confrontation between infinite 'Translucence'[19], Christ, and the Limit of Opacity, Satan, that is to say, between ultimate truth and ultimate error, we hear 'sons of Eden' sing 'round the Lamb of God':

Glory, Glory, Glory to the holy Lamb of God
Who now beginneth to put off the dark Satanic body.
Now we behold redemption. Now we know that life Eternal
Depends alone upon the Universal hand, & not in us
Is aught but death in Individual weakness, sorrow & pain.
...
He puts off the clothing of blood, he redeems the spectres from their bonds.
He awakes sleepers in Ulro; the Daughters of Beulah praise him;
They anoint his feet with ointment, they wipe them with the hair
                                                    of their head.
... we now behold
Where death Eternal is put off Eternally.
Assume the dark Satanic Body in the Virgin's womb,
O Lamb Divine! it cannot thee annoy. O pitying one,
Thy pity is from the foundation of the World, & thy Redemption
Begun Already in Eternity. Come then, O Lamb of God,
Come, Lord Jesus, come quickly.[20]

Meanwhile 'war roar'd round Jerusalem's Gates' and we see the 'Shadowy hermaphrodite black & opake', previously 'unform'd', take 'a hideous form':

Seen in the aggregate, a Vast Hermaphroditic form
Heav'd like an Earthquake lab'ring with convulsive groans
Intolerable; at length an awful wonder burst
From the Hermaphroditic bosom, Satan he was nam'd,
Sons of Perdition, terrible his form, dishumaniz'd, monstrous,
A male without a female counterpart, a howling fiend
Forlorn of Eden & repugnant to the forms of life.

And Satan is described as being:

Abhorr'd, accursed, ever dying an Eternal death,
Being multitudes of tyrant Men in union blasphemous
Against the Divine image, Congregated assemblies of wicked men.[21]

Urizen now summons the Synagogue of Satan[22] in the midst of which:

> ... beamed
> A False Feminine Counterpart, of Lovely Delusive Beauty
> Dividing & Uniting at will in the Cruelties of Holiness.
> Vala, drawn down into a Vegetated body, now triumphant.
> The Synagogue of Satan Clothed with her Scarlet robes & Gems,
> And on her forehead was her name written in blood, 'Mystery'.[23]

The 'true' female counterpart, or Emanation, is the capacity for vision (or sometimes the vision itself). The 'False Feminine Counterpart' can here be interpreted as being the body of falsified perceptions, the sum of moral and perceptual error. This 'body' summarizes all the evils embodied in the 'sisters' Rahab and Tirzah before they themselves had been touched by the process of regeneration (see Chapter 7). The 'Cruelties of Holiness' refer to the tyranny of the moral law fabricated by Urizen. Vala here has become Rahab, the Scarlet Woman of Revelation (17: 3–5). She is 'Mystery, Babylon the Great, the Mother of Harlots'.[24] 'Mystery', 'mystery's woven mantle',[25] the 'Robes of Luvah',[26] and the 'Vegetated Body',[27] all symbolize the moral and metaphysical errors of 'mundane' life, of the conception of life created by the agents of Satan/Urizen, in contrast to the truth of Eternity, the 'Spiritual body'.[28]

Whilst Vala's revenge against the 'Lamb of God' is being prepared, Los and Enitharmon are busy re-creating Jerusalem, the lost spiritual liberty of mankind and the true Emanation of Albion:

> Enitharmon wove in tears, singing songs of Lamentations
> And pitying comfort as she sigh'd forth on the wind the spectres
> And wove them bodies, calling them her belov'd sons and daughters,
> Employing the daughters in her looms, & Los employ'd the sons
> In Golgonooza's Furnaces among the Anvils of time & space,
> Thus forming a vast family, wondrous in beauty & love,
> And there appear'd a Universal female form created
> From those who were dead in Ulro, from the spectres of the dead.
> And Enitharmon named the Female, Jerusalem the holy.
> Wond'ring, she saw the Lamb of God within Jerusalem's Veil;
> The Divine Vision seen within the inmost deep recess
> Of fair Jerusalem's bosom in a gently beaming fire.[29]

In opposition to this new spiritual liberty, celebrated in the Edenic song to which reference was made a little earlier on, are now set the forces of tyrannical and oppressive hatred:

... Satan, Og & Sihon[30]
Build Mills of resistless wheels to unwind the soft threads & reveal
Naked of their clothing the poor spectres before the accusing heavens,
While Rahab and Tirzah far different mantles prepare: webs of torture,
Mantles of despair, girdles of bitter compunction, shoes of indolence,
Veils of ignorance covering from head to feet with a cold web.
We look down into Ulro; we behold the Wonders of the Grave.[31]
Eastward of Golgonooza stands the Lake of Udan Adan, In
Entuthon Benithon, a Lake not of Waters but of Spaces,
Perturb'd, black & deadly; on its Islands & its Margins
The Mills of Satan and Beelzeboul stand around the roots of Urizen's tree;
For this Lake is form'd from the tears & sighs & death sweat of the Victims
Of Urizen's laws, to irrigate the roots of the tree of Mystery.[32]

Udan-Adan is the condition of formlessness, of the indefinite,[33] Chaos.
Los, the creator of form, therefore builds Golgonooza on its verge.[34] Both
Entuthon Benithon and Udan-Adan represent a state of non-visionary life
and are therefore closely linked with the symbolic meanings of Spectre,
Urizen, Tirzah and Rahab (prior to their 'regeneration'). The
regenerative labours of the Imagination, Los, aim at the destruction, or,
rather, the transformation, of the state of error. Accordingly, the sym-
bolic centre of his activities, Golgonooza, is placed close to the lake of
'tears & sighs & death' in Entuthon. It is in the Lake of Udan-Adan:

> Where souls incessant wail, being piteous Passions & Desires
> With neither lineament nor form ...[35]

In complete contrast to the 'black & deadly' Lake of Udan-Adan is the
Furnace of Los, the 'Lake of Los',[36] where all errors, cruelties and
falsehoods are cast (that is, states, not individuals). There the crude 'ore'
is smelted, the 'slag' consumed, and the 'molten iron' cast into new
forms.

All seems lost when Satan and his agents 'unweave the soft threads' the
Daughters of Enitharmon have woven and:

> ... weave them anew in the forms
> Of dark death & despair,[37]

thus entangling man evermore securely in Urizenic abstractions.

But, at this nadir point, the Lamb, the 'Universal Humanity', receives
'the Integuments woven' and puts off the 'clothing of blood', Luvah's
robes.

When Christ casts off the clothing of falsehood and delusion, tyranny and natural religion — represented in Night vii and viii by the conjunction of Orc, the Urizenic Tree of Mystery, and the Shadowy Female (Vala/Rahab), 'he redeems the spectres from their bonds' and 'awakes sleepers in Ulro'.[38]

As yet only those in Eden and Beulah and those like Los and Enitharmon who have inwardly enacted their own self-sacrificial love are able to recognize Christ's suffering as redemptive. Although both Urizen and Vala see that something new and 'revolutionary' is happening, they are unable to conceive of any other sufferer than the old Luvah. Urizen, as we have seen, is 'perplex'd & terrifi'd'. He knows that 'the Lamb of God clothed in Luvah's robes'[39] is a new Luvah, but he cannot reconcile this knowledge with Luvah's 'Serpent form' as Orc. Vala herself has no perception of the Lamb and what he represents. She sees only her spouse's, Luvah's, murderer. She is antagonistic to spiritual perceptions and, hence, to the Human Form Divine.[40] She is a prime representative of materialism[41] and for her the imagination of Los, who sees Christ —

> Give his vegetated body
> ...
> To be cut off & separated, that the Spiritual body may be Reveal'd[42]

— has no reality and no meaning. She does not have the imaginative vision to see what is happening. For a long time she has lamented Luvah's absence. But she has never known that is he actually always present or very near.[43] Now he is right beside her in two forms: in his desbasement he is Orc on the Tree of Mystery; in his transfiguration he is the crucified Christ.

Vala/Rahab now appears by Satan's side — he has taken over from Urizen — when he calls together 'twelve rocky unshap'd forms'.[44] They constitute the Synagogue of Sanhedrin who find the Lamb guilty of transgressing against Urizenic Law:

> Thus was the Lamb of God condemn'd to Death.
> They nail'd him upon the Tree of Mystery, weeping over him
> And then mocking & then worshipping, calling him Lord & King.[45]

The crucifixion is followed by an epiphany of Rahab:

> But when Rahab had cut off the mantle of Luvah from
> The Lamb of God it roll'd apart, revealing to all in heaven
> And all on Earth, the Temple & the Synagogue of Satan, & Mystery

Even Rahab in all her turpitude. Rahab divided herself;
She stood before Los in her Pride among the Furnaces,*
Dividing & uniting in Delusive feminine pomp, questioning him.[46]

Now Los, who has been in despair since Christ's Crucifxion, who is, in fact, guilty of error in despairing, has learnt a great deal about the nature of human error and how to face up to it and transform it and he is, therefore, able to respond to anger and petulance 'with tenderness & love not uninspired':[47]

I am that shadowy Prophet who six thousands years ago
Fell from my station in the Eternal bosom. I divided
To multitude & my multitudes are children of Care & Labour.
O Rahab, I behold thee. I was once like thee, a Son
Of Pride, and I have also pierc'd the Lamb of God in pride & wrath.[48]

'O Rahab, I behold thee': Just as the Veil of the Temple, which hid the Holy of Holies from the eyes of the people, was rent at Christ's death on the Cross (Matt 27:51), so here a mystery is revealed — the true nature of Rahab. Here Los also reveals the depth of his insight when he identifies himself with Rahab as one who has also 'pierc'd the Lamb of God in pride'.

Los then goes on to give an account of his descendants, which include Rahab (just as the lineage of Jesus in Matthew includes Rahab — as well as other questionable women, such as Uriah's wife, Bathsheba), and then voices Blake's crucial distinction between 'States & Individuals':

There is a State nam'd Satan; learn distinct to know, O Rahab!
The difference between States & Individuals of those States.
The State nam'd Satan never can be redeem'd in all Eternity.[49]

Blake here develops the conception that although a state — such as tyranny (Satan) — may be eternal, no individual need occupy that state in a new universe. Although 'the state nam'd Satan' is unredeemable, individuals are redeemable if they 'put off Satan Eternally'[50] and in 'offering of Self for Another'[51] accept the reality of universal brotherhood.

Los ends the dialogue with Rahab by exhorting her to set Jerusalem free.

Los's tender words are a moving expression of the true Christian

*i.e. of creation.

maxim that one should hate the sin but love the sinner. They illustrate beautifully that the imaginative creative principle in man is inextricably bound up with compassion and love.

However, Rahab, who, we may note here, is herself a form of Christianity in its most perverse guise of inquisitor and accuser, does not heed Los's exhortation, and

> ... burning with pride & revenge, departed from Los.
> Los drop'd a tear at her departure, but he wip'd it away in hope.
> She went to Urizen in pride; the Prince of Light beheld
> Reveal'd before the face of heaven his secret holiness
> Darkness & sorrow cover'd all flesh. Eternity was darkened.[52]

Although Rahab appears to be unmoved by Los's speech, Los does wipe away a tear 'in hope', suggesting that salvation is still possible. As we shall soon see, her actions henceforth do, in fact, promote the process of her own disintegration in her present mood and form, and also set in train a new development in Urizen and Satan.

First Rahab appears to Urizen who still sits 'in his web of deceitful religion'.[53] Whereas his earlier terror at the appearance of Satan did not bring any sign on Urizen's part that he recognized the Satanic within himself, now, when Rahab appears before him,

> ... the Prince of Light beheld
> Reveal'd before the face of heaven his secret holiness.

Self-recognition is precipitated by his encounter with Rahab. In Blakean terms we may say that error, by taking a visible and, therefore, vulnerable form, precipitates the victory of truth. The triumph of Satan and Rahab over Christ and Jerusalem is such a vulnerable form, for it is no more than temporary.

The result of Rahab's appearance is that Urizen 'divides' within himself.[54] The separated part becomes a dragon:

> ... scales his neck & bosom
> Cover'd & scales his hands & feet.[55]

That which is most characteristic of Urizen, iron-hard rigidity, remains:

> A form of Senseless Stone.[56]

Urizen, in his dragon form, regrets his loss of human form and envies the humanity of Los and Tharmas.

The deep division within Urizen has already been manifested in the disintegration of his autocratic rulership over the human soul and the phenomenal world. Satan's and his feminine equivalent's, Rahab's, activities independent of him are clear indications of the crumbling of his hegemony. Through this division, however, Urizen achieves a certain degree of self-understanding. But as yet this self-recognition is too dim to lead to self-healing. The knowledge of what is both hideous and erroneous in himself has yet to be brought home to him. As yet it is only his 'dragon' form which contemplates his petrified humanity.[57] His brain-bound ego-centredness, that which is so characteristic of him, has not yet faced up to this error in himself. Knowledge of what is erroneous and hideous in himself must be realized by Urizen in his most characteristic form, that is, not merely in his 'dragon' form or some other separated form. Only then can Urizen heal himself. Only then can the ills in human society caused by tyrannical Urizenic power be remedied. Nevertheless, in his debasing new shape Urizen is able to recognize:

> That not of his own power he bore the human form erect
> Nor of his own will gave his Laws in times Everlasting.[58]

He recognizes that he is not the totality, that he is but a finite part within a much larger humanity, only a portion of the human psyche. In so doing, he moves closer to the vision of the sons of Eden who, contemplating the Lamb of God, sang:

> Glory, Glory, Glory to the holy Lamb of God
> Who now beginneth to put off the dark Satanic body.
> Now we behold redemption. Now we know that life Eternal
> Depends alone upon the Universal hand, & not in us
> Is aught but death In individual weakness, sorrow & pain.[59]

The process of disintegration which, if inwardly perceived and recognized, can form the prelude to that of re-integration, regeneration, finds expression again in the lines:

> ... his human form a Stone,
> A form of Senseless Stone remain'd in terrors on the rock,
> Abominable to the eyes of mortals who explore his books.
> His wisdom still remain'd, & all his memory stor'd in woe.[60]

But, over and against his 'stony form', his 'scaly form'

> ... forgets his wisdom in the abyss,
> In forms of priesthood, in the dark delusions of repentance

Repining in his heart & spirit that Orc reign'd over all,
And that his wisdom serv'd but to augment the indefinite lust.[61]

Urizen, Reason, sees Orc, belligerent Wrath (a lower form of Luvah; repressed love turned to war) — whose consort is the Shadowy Female, Rahab, whom Urizen, overcome by a 'dull & numming stupor ... pitying he began to embrace'[62] — Urizen sees Orc has now gained in power and, risen furiously into the heavens, 'reign'd over all'. The struggle between Urizen and Orc has yet to be resolved. Balance/brotherhood between them has yet to be achieved. At the moment, passion has the upper hand and the narrow-minded, self-satisfied, unimaginative and repressive rationality has been undermined and its exclusiveness destroyed.

Here we need to remind ourselves that it was the two primal powers or faculties, Urizen and Luvah, who, together, had been agents of man's Fall because they set themselves up as gods and, conspiring against each other for dominion over man, allowed the conflicts between themselves (between reason and passion, emotion) to obscure the truth that the sole reality is the Divine Spirit in man and that this spirit is at one with Christ, the Imagination.[63] Once the Zoas in man begin the process of individual self-assertion then division occurs and man 'falls' from the Divine Unity. Insistence on 'Selfhood' is the cause of the infraction of the Ideal Unity, of Spiritual Brotherhood; it is the cause of the 'fall into generation & decay'.[64] Both Urizen and Luvah, cognizant of their dragon and serpent forms, respectively, are now beginning to realize that, as they exist at present, they are no more than subhuman:

Attempting to be more than Man We become less ...[65]

Elsewhere Blake writes that these

eternal principles or characters of human life ... when separated from man or humanity, who is Jesus the Saviour, the vine of eternity, they are thieves and rebels, they are destroyers.[66]

Now, we have just seen that the self-contentedness of repressive and exclusive rationality has been destroyed and that passion, in its lowest form, is gaining the upper hand. Urizen himself has taken on a dehumanized form. Paradoxically, in so doing, he also takes a decisive step towards his own salvation, for, as Los has demonstrated in his dialogue with Rahab, man's perfection does not lie in the enhancement

of one's encapsulated self, but in the recognition of kinship with all
aspects of life, including one's 'enemies', or, differently expressed, with
all the hitherto despised portions of one's self.[67] The righteous must
acknowledge their affinity with the harlot, for all are one in the Divine
Humanity.

Accompanying Urizen's first steps towards true self-knowledge is the
reappearance of Urthona and Tharmas. They, too, 'felt the stony stupor'
felt by Urzien 'rise/ Into their limbs'.[68] But these two faculties, soul
forces, imagination and the instinctive sense of universality, consolidate
what remains to them of creative energy by giving it to, uniting it with,
Los:

> And Tharmas gave his Power to Los, Urthona gave his Strength
> Into the youthful Prophet for the Love of Enitharmon
> And of the nameless shadowy female in the nether deep,
> And for the dread of the dark terrors of Orc & Urizen.[69]

As Urizen 'forgets his wisdom in the abyss',[70] Tharmas and Urthona
give their power to Los for the approaching contest. But now the dele-
gation of power to Los is quite different from the irresponsible renuncia-
tions and 'diseased' usurpations in earlier Nights which brought about
the distintegration of the soul's faculties. Los can now be trusted not to
act as a tyrannical autocrat. All those human faculties which are now
capable of loving and awakening humanity and, hence, of resisting error,
work together in harmony and brotherhood. The lost universal brother-
hood of man is now, it would seem, within reach. However, as we shall
see in the final stages of Night viii, the consolidation and refortification of
the powers of imagination and prophecy are met by a strengthening of
the power of Error, of Satan and Rahab. But before the further divisions
and re-formations of Satan and Rahab take place which bring Night viii
to a close, the voices of the Emanations of Urizen and Tharmas, Ahania
and Enion rise again. Their songs recapitulate and emphasize the major
contrasts that have developed during this Night[71] — the contrast between
natural and spiritual, rational and visionary.

In the exchange between Ahania and Enion we hear the voices of the
banished portions of reason and instinct. They have been silent since
Night iii. They have both fallen into a 'void',[72] into a spiritually
deadening depression. Ahania is quite incapable of summoning up the
faintest glimmer of mental pleasure; Enion is similarly unable to evince an
inkling of instinctual life. Ahania's intellectual pleasure has not been

missed — especially not by 'abstracted' and desiccated Urizen. The only sign that Enion's instinctual sense of wholeness ever functions has been Tharmas's wistful hope that she will appear again.

The voices of the outcasts, Ahania and Enion, presage apocalypse.

The chant of Ahania is sheer despair. Her view of the human condition is that of someone who is unimaginative, uninspired but reasonable, for she

> Saw not as yet the Divine Vision; her eyes are toward Urizen.[73]

In her 'voice incessant' calling 'on all the children of Men'[74] Ahania perceives life only as it is conditioned and dominated by death. For her, man has no higher plane of existence than that of other, lower forms of life:

> Listen to her whose eyes behold the dark body of corruptible death
> Looking for Urizen in vain; in vain I seek for morning.
> The Eternal Man sleeps in the Earth, nor feels the vig'rous sun
> Nor silent moon, nor all the hosts of heaven move in his body.
> His fiery halls are dark, & round his limbs the Serpent Orc
> Fold without fold encompasses him, And his corrupting members
> Vomit out the scaly monsters of the restless deep.
> They come up in rivers & annoy the nether parts
> Of Man who lays upon the shores, leaning his faded head
> Upon the Oozy rock inwrapped with the weeds of death.
> His eyes sink hollow in his head, his flesh cover'd with slime
> And shrunk up to the bones; alas, that Man should come to this!
> His strong bones beat with snows & hid within the caves of night,
> Marrowless, bloodless, falling into dust, driven by the winds.
> O how the horrors of Eternal Death take hold on Man!
> His faint groans shake the caves & issue thro' the desolate rocks,
> And the strong Eagle, now with numming cold blighted of feathers,
> Once like the pride of the sun, now flagging in cold night,
> Hovers with blasted wings aloft, watching with Eager Eye
> Till Man shall leave a corruptible body; he, famish'd, hears him groan,
> And now he fixes his strong talons in the pointed rock,
> And now he beats the heavy air with his enormous wings.
> Beside him lies the Lion dead, & in his belly worms
> Feast on his death till universal death devours all.
> And the pale horse seeks for the pool to lie him down & die,
> But finds the pools filled with serpents devouring one another.
> He droops his head & trembling stands, & his bright eyes decay.
> These are the Visions of My Eyes, the Visions of Ahania.[75]

Ahania sees the world as deathly. However, in the desolation of man's fallen state, in this world of corruption and death, there is also the seed of a new life. The reference to 'the dark body of corruptible death' can be seen to be a reminder to us of the 'dark Stanic body' which Christ 'puts off',[76] and the 'morning' which Ahania seeks may be interpreted as being the Morning of the Resurrection of Christ.

In response to Ahania's vision of hideous decay and death, Enion, Tharmas's Emanation, sings a song of new hope and new life. She has now the task of inspiriting Ahania. This is particularly relevant and appropriate for it was Enion's powerful death instinct which drew Ahania down 'to the margin of Non-Entity' — instinct's 'wails from the dark deep'[77] over animal and human suffering[78] had ruined the joy of the mind. Now Enion manifests a wiser instinct, for she has developed through suffering and 'death' and instinctively feels the stirrings of new life, which she wishes to make felt in the gentler and softer areas of the mind, in Ahania:

> Fear not, O poor forsaken one! ...
> Once I wail'd desolate like thee; my fallow fields in fear
> Cried to the Churchyards & the Earthworm came in dismal state.
> I found him in my bosom, & I said the time of love
> Appears upon the rocks & hills in silent shades; but soon
> A voice came in the night, a midnight cry upon the mountains:
> 'Awake! the bridegroom cometh!'[79] I awoke to sleep no more;
> But an Eternal consummation is dark Enion,
> The wat'ry Grave. O thou corn field! O thou vegetater happy!
> More happy is the dark consumer; hope drowns all my torment,
> For I am now surrounded by a shadowy vortex drawing
> The spectre quite away from Enion, that I die a death
> Of better hope, altho' I consume in these raging waters.
> ...
> Listen, I will tell thee what is done in the caverns of the grave.
> The Lamb of God has rent the Veil of Mystery, soon to return
> In Clouds & Fires around the rock & the Mysterious tree.[80]

Enion, having experienced 'death' in an awakened, conscious state ('I awoke to sleep no more'), describes it from 'within' the 'watr'y Grave'. Through the very process of 'death', her deathly spectre, her temporal selfhood, is drawn away from her true humanity, from her living, eternal self. It is the former which is 'lost' in the grave. When man wakens from spiritual sleep then the spectre can be cast out:

> Each Man is in his spectre's power
> Untill the arrival of that Hour
> When his Humanity awake
> And cast his Spectre into the Lake.[81]

Ahania, Urizen's 'Shadowy Feminine Semblance'[82] has remained 'outside' the grave; she has hitherto been an onlooker, not a participator, in the 'death' process through which Enion has gone. As the image of Urizen's false religion,[83] she is blind, asleep, to the truth that the spectre, the selfhood, must be 'cast away'. Ahania can only see death as being the end of life, for she sees the world as deathly. Enion, on the other hand, has become cognizant of the reality that, to the regenerate man, the condition of death will be 'a thing Forgotten':

> The furrow'd field replies to the grave. I hear her reply to me:
> 'Behold the time approaches fast that thou shalt be as a thing
> Forgotten; when one speaks of thee he will not be believ'd.
> When the man gently fades away in his immortality,
> When the mortal disappears in improved knowledge, cast away
> The former things, so shall the Mortal gently fade away
> And so become invisible to those who still remain'.[84]

Mortality will be an illusion which has been overcome.[85]

Ahania's song, or chant, is fundamentally a lament. Her very anguish suggests that man, even in his all-pervasive, one-sided rationality, is dimly aware that he is in need of more than a naturalistic vision of life.

Ahania's dilemma is this: her visions cannot take man out of a fallen world for the 'eye' of the materialist's mind is confined within the limited circumference the uninspired mind has rigidly established. Sense-perceptible facts of the world of limiting reason present a barrier past and through which Ahania's 'felt' needs cannot penetrate. In order that she should be able to pass such a barrier she must hearken to and follow the voice of the instinctual feeling of wholeness and the experience of 'life' in 'death' which issues forth from Enion, from the Enionian element which is embedded in her (that is, in everyone's) soul.

Enion has the faith of 'organized' innocence, of wise innocence, which has been achieved through the suffering she has gone through. Suffering, even unto 'death', is an essential aspect of experience. Enion's new state is not one of ignorance, but it is one of joy. It is a state of innocence which dwells with knowledge, a state in which the bitterness of experience has been met, assimilated, and transmuted, transcended. Wise innocence, 'organized' innocence, does not reject experience, but transcends it in imaginative vision. The faith of 'organized' innocence, the inner certainty as to the reality of unity (of the total 'organism'), the wisdom born of divisive experience, is expressed by Enion in the following way:

> Listen. I will tell thee what is done in the caverns of the grave.
> The Lamb of God has rent the Veil of Mystery, soon to return
> In Clouds & Fire around the rock & the Mysterious Tree.
> As the seed waits Eagerly watching for its flower & fruit,
> Anxious its little soul looks out into the clear expanse
> To see if hungry winds are abroad with the invisible army,
> So Man looks out in tree & herb & fish & bird & beast
> Collecting up the scatter'd portions of his immortal body
> Into the Elemental forms of every thing that grows.
> ...
> ... wherever a grass grows
> Or a leaf buds, The Eternal Man is seen, is heard, is felt,
> And all his sorrows, till he reassumes his ancient bliss.[86]

Here Blake, through Enion, gives us, in imaginative vision, a picture of the union of individual man's spirit with all other human spirits and with the spiritual entities which make up the total organism, the universe inhabited by men. Ideally, it is a unity in conscious spiritual being. It is a perfect spiritual homogeneity. Though this unity can only be known through intuitive vision, glimpses and indications of it are perceptible to the enlightened mind behind the veil of the phenomenal world.

Representative of a mode of spiritual enlightenment, Enion's voice pierces beyond desolation and despair, for the 'lost' delight of instinctual unity still knows its own potential power.

Blake, we should note, is not suggesting in these lines that the continually renewed impulse of nature in springtime towards rebirth — which is just as ceaselessly thwarted every winter — should be regarded as an argument for resurrection (as, for instance, the devotees of natural religion would do). Such an impulse in nature towards rebirth is not the cause of Albion's, Man's, regeneration. Enion, speaking here for the deepest emotion in each one of us, sees 'natural' renewal, not as evidence, but as an inspiration, an incentive to man to strive for spiritual rebirth. Blake, with Paul, knows that resurrection is of the spiritual not the natural body.[87]

Enion represents something which cannot be touched by death, which, despite the apparent finality of the grave, is deathless. Despite long suffering in the Caverns of the Grave, deprived of light, the 'instinct' of wholeness, Enion, is imbued with hope and wills life instead of death. In her fallen state, Enion represents the generative instinct in the natural world, the world of generation, that is, the instinct to regenerate natural life. In her spiritual state she represents the faith, the hope, in spiritual regeneration. In both her aspects she is imbued with the will to live and love of life. She knows, intuitively, that death is the key to a new life. Tharmas, Enion's counterpart, knows, too, that without her, 'Love & Hope are ended!'[88] In Night iv he cries out:

> ... All my hope is gone! [Enion *del.*] for ever fled![89]

The active force in the process of renewal, or spiritual regeneration, is, in Blake's vision, the active human will imbued with hope and faith and nourished by love, the ultimate source of which is the Imagination, Christ, who Himself has been in the Caverns of a Grave and risen in the spiritual body. True, Real Man, is Imagination and Love.

The delicate seeds of new life are, as Enion's chant shows us, small acts of kindness struggling to grow. Every sowing of a new seed, indeed:

> ... every kindness to another is a little Death
> In the Divine Image, nor can Man exist but by Brotherhood.[90]

Every delicate seed, every 'kindness', 'sown' with hope and love, flourishes in the hope and promise of immortality, of the resurrection in the spiritual body; it flourishes in defiance of the illusory limits imposed by the Urizenic conception of physical death.

Regeneration, as we learn from Enion, may be a long and laborious process, fraught with difficulties, disappointments and apparent failures, so that man may have to embark on the process more than once. In the lines:

> That Man should Labour & sorrow, & learn & forget, & return
> To the dark valley whence he came, to begin his labours anew.[91]

And in such a passage as:

> Jerusalem, pitying them, wove them mantles of life & death,
> Times after times ...[92]

Blake makes it clear that he believes in the reincarnation of human souls, in repeated lives on earth, until such time as men and women have worked out their ultimate regeneration, resurrection.[93]

Man is the recipient of Christ's mercy, pity and love, and if he fails, no matter how many times, he is always given another opportunity to start all over again and to bring with him, from the spiritual world, the fruits of his previous strivings. In short, Blake says that opportunities for regeneration are continually being presented to us. Enion's song reveals that Albion, Eternal Man, empathizes with all the activities of nature. Through the power of Imagination, the images of nature are 'remembered' as images in the creative human mind. The spiritual awakening of Albion is expressed in Enion's song through his reconciliation with 'eternal' nature. Alienated nature is embraced:

> ... his voice
> Is heard throughout the Universe; wherever a grass grows
> Or a leaf buds, The Eternal Man is seen, is heard, is felt,
> And all his sorrows, till he reassumes his ancient bliss.[94]

The process of reunificiation has begun. Blake's 'concentering vision'[95] speaks through Enion here. It synthesizes a multiplicity of entities into a unity. Earlier it was pointed out that Enion is the first Emanation to respond to the Fall into Division; here we find her to be the first to sense the possibility of complete recovery, regeneration.

However, the 'Mental Fight' is not yet won. Even as these signs of regeneration manifest themselves, Rahab secures a partial triumph. Indeed, at first she appears to triumph over all:

> ... she took Jerusalem
> Captive, a Willing Captive, by delusive arts impell'd
> To worship Urizen's Dragon form, to offer her own Children
> Upon the bloody Altar.[96]

Paradoxically, she it is — not Los or Enitharmon — who responds to Enion's vision. Los and Enitharmon, in spite of the fact that events in Night viii are redemptive, still despair — just as the disciples despaired in the days leading up to Christ's crucifixion. They seem to respond only to Ahania and proceed 'despairing of Life Eternal'[97] to bury the body of Christ:

And Los & Enitharmon took the Body of the Lamb
Down from the Cross & plac'd it in a sepulcher which Los had hewn
For himself in the Rock of Eternity, trembling & in [fear *del.*] despair.[98]

Now it is true that Rahab has taken Jerusalem a willing captive (freedom has become the slave of reason and self-righteousness), but, at the peak of her apparent triumph, Rahab recognizes that hers is but a hollow victory, for:

> ... when she saw the form of Ahania weeping on the Void,
> And heard Enion's voice sound from the caverns of the Grave,
> No more spirit remain'd in her. She secretly left the Synagogue of Satan,
> She commun'd with Orc in secret. She hid him with the flax
> That Enitharmon had number'd, away from the Heavens,
> She gather'd it together to consume her Harlot Robes
> In bitterest contrition; sometimes Self condemning, repentant,
> And sometimes kissing her Robes & Jewels & weeping over them;
> Sometimes returning to the Synagogue of Satan in Pride,
> And sometimes weeping before Orc in humility & trembling.[99]

The process of self-division is here reflected quite forcibly within Rahab. She vacillates between pride-filled allegiance to the Synagogue of Satan and humble 'weeping before Orc'; between the retention and the abandonment of the body of falsehood, of her 'Robes & Jewels', her 'Harlot Robes'. In her moments of contrition we can see her response to Enion's chant. Enion, the first Emanation to sense regeneration, comes, as we have seen, to Ahania's aid. Here we see her coming to Rahab's aid too, in the sense that the effect she has is to rekindle conscience in Rahab, who, we remember, symbolizes the false Church, the opponent of Jerusalem, and the crucifier of Christ.[100]

Her triumph is no more than partial. We recollect that when she dominated the Synagogue of Satan (another image of fallen Urizen) she was also apparently triumphant over Christ at the Crucifixion. But, as Los tells her at the end of the long speech in which he reveals himself to her,[101] her triumph is short-lived, for, by causing the death of Christ, she has allowed life to enter into her world of death.

Throughout Night viii the processes of reintegration are met with strong forces of division. At the end of this Night the forces of good and evil (to use these terms in an orthodox, non-Blakean, sense) are equipoise, though the scales appear to fall in favour of Satan, for the final words are:

> The Synagogue of Satan therefore, uniting against Mystery,
> Satan divided against Satan, resolv'd in open Sanhedrim
> To burn Mystery with fire & form another from her ashes,
> ...
> The Ashes of Mystery began to animate; they call'd it Deism
> And Natural Religion; as of old, so now new began
> Babylon again in Infancy, call'd Natural Religion.[102]

In these closing lines of Night viii, just before the Apocalypse begins in the next Night, Blake gives us the depressing view of human life as an unending series of cycles in which everything happens as it has and will always happen. He allegorizes the replacing of an older false religion, with its emphasis on mysterious revelation, by the new false religion of deism, of 'rationalized' religion. Deism, as we have already remarked, was to Blake not merely a religion without revelation, but the epitome of all forms of rationalized religion. The animated 'Ashes of Mystery' replace supernatural revelation by natural reason. Spectral reasoning forms another Rahab from her own ashes. Blake, the man of creative imagination, could no more accept the Urizenic god of the Church than he could accept the Urizenic universe of Newton. A religion of reason, to Blake, is error incarnate; *the* negation of truth. It is Satan.[103]

Such a nadir point, as reached at the end of Night viii, must, in Blake's view, form the seed for a vision of the Last Judgement:

> When Imagination, Art & Science & all Intellectual Gifts,
> all the gifts of the Holy Gost, are [despis'd *del;*] look'd upon
> as of no use & only Contention remains to Man, then the Last
> Judgement begins, & its Vision is seen by the Imaginative Eye
> of Every one according to the situation he holds.[104]

The effect of the apparent triumph of the Synagogue of Satan is to highlight Error and to prepare the cleansing 'water' in which inhuman incrustrations can be washed away, or, as Blake expresses it in *Jerusalem*, from which 'the excrementitious Husk & Covering' evaporates 'into Vacuum'

> ... revealing the lineamants of Man,
> Driving outward the Body of Death in an Eternal Death & Resurrection,
> Awaking it to life ... rejoicing in Unity.[105]

The enlightened view of reality, the vision of the spiritual unity, is only to be attained by a realization of brotherhood and universal love.

THE FOUR ZOAS:
THE LAST JUDGEMENT

Blake's most exuberant and inventive poetry, probably the most energetic and awesome in the language, is to be found in Night ix of *The Four Zoas*.[1]

There is nothing like the colossal explosion of creative power in the ninth Night of *The Four Zoas* anywhere else in English poetry. There are great visions of Hell, of the Creation, of the Fall, of the unfallen state, even of the resurrection; but English poets have been inclined to fight shy of the *Dies Irae*. The City of God has often enough appeared in the distance to the earth-bound visionary; it has often been described, and even reached at the end of a personal pilgrimage; but as an eternal form remote from the world of time, not as a phoenix arising in the human mind from the ashes of the burned mysterious universe.[2]

Night ix begins with the despair of Los and Enitharmon who labour at building the City for regenerated human community. But they are labouring in despair because their mortal, physical eyes appear to see Luvah/Christ still in his sepulchre. They are both misled by physical appearances, for both believe that Christ is dead:

> And Los & Enitharmon builded Jerusalem weeping
> Over the Sepulcher & over the Crucified body
> Which, to their Phantom Eyes, appear'd still in the Sepulcher.[3]

Although Los and Enitharmon began the redemptive process in Night vii, they are not as aware of its results in the same way as Enion is at the end of Night viii. She senses that death has already begun to give birth to new life, that Christ:

> ... stood beside them in the spirit, separating
> Their spirit from their body ...[4]

Enion and her counterpart, Tharmas, representative of the instinctive faculty of the human soul, sense and herald the apocalypse. Tharmas, indeed, trumpets forth:

> A mighty sound articulate: 'Awake, ye dead, & come
> To Judgement from the four winds! Awake & come away!'[5]

Los, however, is not a herald, he is an agent of events. For instance, in rending the universe, he re-enacts Christ's rending of the Veil and thereby initiates the Apocalypse:

> Terrifed at Non Existence,
> For such they deem'd the death of the body, Los his vegetable hands
> Outstretch'd; his right hand, branching out in fibrous strength,
> Siez'd the Sun; his left hand, like dark roots, cover'd the Moon,
> And tore them down, cracking the heavens across from immense to
> immense.[6]

Although his 'Phantom Eyes' are limited to perceiving only the crucified body, his spirit, on the other hand, responds to the influence of Christ's presence. Enion and Tharmas instinctively sense that 'Non Existence' is overcome through the physical death of Christ. Los and Enitharmon are still in terror of 'Non Existence'. Although, as we have seen in Nights vii and viii, Los has progressed further than the other three Zoas towards a recognition of the meaning of Christ's archetypal sacrifice on the Cross, he has not yet reached conscious comprehension of the meaning of the Resurrection. Unable, then, to believe in the resurrection of the body, Los and Enitharmon begin the apocalyptic process by Los's uncomprehending but imaginatively relevant attack upon nature as conceived by the Urizenic mind. It is with this imaginative thrust at the deadness of the Urizenic cosmos that the Last Judgement begins:

> Then fell the fires of Eternity with loud & shrill
> Sound of Loud Trumpet thundering along from heaven to heaven
> A mighty sound articulate: 'Awake, ye dead, & come
> To Judgement from the four winds! Awake & Come away!'[7]
> Folding like scrolls of the Enormous volume of Heaven & Earth,
> With thunderous noise & dreadful shaking, rocking to & fro,
> The heavens are shaken & the Earth removed from its place,
> The foundations of the Eternal hills discover'd:[8]
> The thrones of Kings are shaken, they have lost their robes & crowns,
> The poor smite their oppressors, they awake up to the harvest,
> The naked warriors rush together down to the sea shore
> Trembling before the multitudes of slaves now set at liberty:
> They are become like wintry flocks, like forests strip'd of leaves:
> The oppressed pursue like the wind; there is no room for escape.[9]

At the Last Judgement 'the world will be consumed in fire',[10] that is, the physical world, including our five physical senses, will be 'consumed', transmuted, by the influx of spirituality.[11] Then, 'the whole creation will ... appear infinite and holy, whereas it now appears finite & corrupt'.[12] In other words, at the Last Judgement 'the doors of perception' will be 'cleansed' and 'everything would appear to man as it is, infinite'.[13]

Los, Imagination, both experiences and causes the destruction of the world of illusion, the false Urizenic world in which most men and women participate and which they consider to be the only reality. We can contrast the activity of Los here with that of Urizen in Night ii in which a false order is constructed which, because of its inherent spiritual weaknesses, soon disintegrates.

Los, fortified now by the power and strength of Tharmas and Urthona,[14] destroys what is left of the disorganized Zoas. In the realistic scenes depicted in the last six lines of the passage quoted above,[15] there are clear historical and political references. The stress on vengence, even more vividly depicted later in the Night,[16] recalls the mood of earlier poems — such as *America, a Prophecy* (1793) — which suggests the acceptance of physical violence as necessary to achieve social reform in the 'fallen' world. This is clearly out of tune with the conviction held by Blake in later years that it is spiritual regeneration, founded on forgiveness rather than retribution and accusation, which is man's true task and goal. But we need to remind ourselves that the oppressors, the 'tyrants', who here receive their punishments are also the 'tyrants' within our own souls; they are the 'tyrants' within us which hinder the development of true humanity. Blake is here reiterating that they must be cast out through 'revolutionary' acts of imaginative vision. Inhibitions of one or other faculty of the soul, often leading to psychic disorders, are often treated by those who have recovered from them as though they were 'external' forces of a detrimental and disintegrating nature, whereas, in reality, they are often, if not always, 'internal' and self-generated.

As important as the political vision of freedom may be, it is nevertheless of far less significance than Blake's more profound themes of spiritual regeneration and freedom. Political freedom follows as a matter of course if spiritual freedom has been achieved. The latter is the source and foundation of the former. But to claim that political freedom ensures spiritual freedom is not justifiable — such a claim is a purely Urizenic conception.

The cracking apart of the heavens lets loose the 'Spectre of Enitharmon',[17] 'on the troubled deep',[18] for she has reigned over Newtonian (materialistic) space. The Spectre of Urthona, who has controlled the measured (clock) time of nature, receives her in a faint embrace:

> ... their bodies lost, they stood
> Trembling & weak, a faint embrace, a fiery desire, as when
> Two shadows mingle on a wall; they wail & shadowy tears
> Fell down, & shadowy forms of joy mix'd with despair & grief —
> Their bodies buried in the ruins of the Universe —
> Mingled with the confusion. Who shall call them from the Grave?[19]

Space and time — as we know them on earth — have become two shadows, and even they are 'lost' when the wall of the natural world falls in ruins. No longer perceived as substantial the shadowy Spectres of Enitharmon and Urthona vanish. Then:

> Rahab & Tirzah wail aloud in the wild flames; they give up themselves to Consummation.[20]

Orc, too, soon functionless in his serpentine form, is consumed in his other form of 'fierce raving fire'.[21] The forces of physical revolution, Orc, wrapped round the Urizenic tree of good and evil, have to give way to the spiritual forces of revolution, Christ; and, in the process, the religion of retribution and accusation, the Tree of Mystery, of Error, is also consumed so that, in due course, 'the religion of Jesus, the everlasting Gospel',[22] forgiveness and universal brotherhood, can flourish. Consumed, then, are also the rigid laws of Urizen:

> The books of Urizen unroll with dreadful noise ...[23]

And all the while Tharmas is sounding his trumpet:

> ... from the clotted gore & from the hollow den
> Start forth the trembling millions into flames of mental fire,
> Bathing their limbs in the bright visions of Eternity.[24]

This, of course, is Blake's vision of the day to be striven for when everyone on earth will be able to see 'through' a visionary eye.

Meanwhile, Nature, as fallen reason sees it, is now reduced to chaos:

> Trembling & strucken by the Universal stroke, the trees unroot,
> The rocks groan horrible & run about; the mountains &
> Their rivers cry with a dismal cry; the cattle gather together,

Lowing they kneel before the heavens; the wild beasts of the forests
Tremble; the Lion shuddering asks the Leopard; 'Feelest thou
The dread I feel, unknown before? My voice refuses to roar,
And in weak moans I speak to thee.[25]

Next we hear that:

In the fierce flames the limbs of Mystery lay consuming with howling
And deep despair. Rattling go up the flames around the Synagogue
Of Satan ...
... The tree of Mystery went up in folding flames.[26]

Finally:

Mystery's tryants are cut off & not one of them left on Earth.[27]

Los's act of 'cracking the heavens'[28] of the Urizenic world brings about
the revelation of truth in a convulsive moment of destruction. The
various disparate 'personalities', which were essential to Blake's earlier
configuration of error, collapse — ultimately to reform themselves into a
unified humanity. If we consider the process from a psychological
viewpoint we could say that the intricate rationalizations, which have
maintained the generally held illusion of material reality and 'created' a
world of disparate and conflicting 'details', undergo a precipitate and
drastic process of simplification — leading to a reunified humanity — by
being opened up to the 'mental fire', to the influx of spirituality, which
so far has been excluded from human life. The 'cracking' of the heavens
destroys the barriers which have sealed off the physical world from the
'fires of eternity'. When humanity is open to the process of purification
by 'flames of mental fire':

Then, like the doves from pillars of Smoke, the trembling families
Of women & children throughout every nation under heaven
Cling round the men in bands of twenties & of fifties ...[29]

The image of the family presented here is indicative of the kind of
family characteristic of a regenerated humanity and forms a striking
contrast to the family of the fallen Urizenic world. The image of the
family can either suggest the Family of Man (an image of universal unity);
or it can imply the very opposite: an enclosed unit which, if not always on
the defensive against others, does regard others as 'outsiders'. Such a
family is of course, self-centred. The kind of love it manifests is criticized
by Blake, who calls it 'soft Family-Love':

> Is this thy soft Family-Love,
> Thy cruel Patriarchal pride,
> Planting thy Family alone,
> Destroying all the World beside?[30]

Now, one of the primal messages which Blake imparts to us in Night ix is that it is imperative to annihilate self-centredness and to educate ourselves to a realization of universal brotherhood. The spiritual Eden is the dwelling place, or state of mind, of the Divine Family, that is, of those who have achieved the Brotherhood of Man. In the last passage quoted from *The Four Zoas* we see families gathering not in exclusive units of three or four, but in groups of 'twenties & of fifties'. The forming of such extended families has regenerative effects on society, mankind, as a whole and we find it paralleled by the joyful and selfless reconciliations of the Zoas and Emanations which manifest themselves later in Night ix.

Already at this early phase of the apocalypse we can recognize that all the episodes we have looked at are events in an internal and external transformation which individual man and mankind as a whole experience as terrifying and devastating, on the one hand, and exhilarating and enlivening, on the other. We experience the collapse of accepted and timeworn rules and customs, the cataclysmic disintegration of the natural, physical world as we have perceived it under the limiting and suppressive power of fallen reason (materialism). But we also experience the inner joy of liberation from both physical and, above all, psychic enslavement. Instead of the solid and dark Urizenic universe, instead of the limiting yet, for the spiritually timid, reassuring horizons of 'stony' earth and Mundane Shell, there emerges what seems, at first, to be a chaotic co-mingling of 'clotted gore' and 'fierce raving fire'. But then we see, when the 'black deluge'[31] has completed its ravaging and all forms of tyranny are obliterated, the cleansing

> ... flames rolling intense thro' the wide Universe
> Began to enter the Holy City. Ent'ring, the dismal clouds
> In furrow'd lightnings break their way, the wild flames liking up
> The Bloody Deluge: living flames winged with intellect
> And Reason, round the Earth they marched in order, flame by flame.[32]

In this striking imagery of an orderly march of 'living flames with intellect and Reason' we perceive the beginning of a process of reconciliation between the ancient enemies Orc and Urizen. This process is accompanied by 'the bright visions of Eternity'[33] which begin to penetrate the sleep of Eternal Man, of Albion. The spiritual voice of man cries out — as yet weakly — from 'Beyond this Universal Confusion'.[34] From

> A Horrible rock far in the South;... forsaken when
> Urizen gave the horses of Light into the hands of Luvah.[35]
> Albion cries with heavenly voice:
> Bowing his head over the consuming Universe, he cried:
> 'O Weakness & O weariness! O war within my members!
> My sons, exiled from my breast, pass to & fro before me.
> My birds are silent on my hills, flocks die beneath my branches.
> ...
> Where once I sat, I weary walk in misery & pain.
> For from within my wither'd breast grown narrow with my woes
> The Corn is turned to thistles & the apples into poison,
> The birds of song to murderous crows, My joys to bitter groans,
> The voices of children in my tents to cries of helpless infants,
> And all exiled from the face of light & shine of morning
> In this dark world, a narrow house, I wander up & down.
> I hear Mystery howling in these flames of Consummation.[36]

Albion's, Man's, lament, as he awakens from a horrendous nightmare, echoes those of Ahania and Enion: everything that was beautiful and good has been perverted and becomes its opposite. No longer is there abundant and energetic youthful life and happiness, only sterile misery, suffering and death. However, as weak and weary as Albion is, consciousness of his spiritual illness is dawning. He struggles to awaken:

> When shall the Man of future times become as in days of old?
> O weary life! why sit I here & give up all my powers
> To indolence, to the night of death, when indolence & mourning
> Sit hovering over my dark threshold? tho' I arise, look out
> And scorn the war within my members, yet my heart is weak
> And my head faint. Yet will I look into the morning.[37]

He is aware of his weakness. Nevertheless, his will is strong. Man, individually and collectively, realizes that the war is *within* himself and that it is within his power to end it.

Raising himself from his 'rocky' slumbers, Albion now begins the process of human integration; he begins to reassume his rightful role. The first step he takes in this process is to issue a stern challenge to Urizen:

O Prince of Light, where art thou? I behold thee not as once
In those Eternal fields, in clouds of morning stepping forth
With harps & songs where bright Ahania sang before thy face
And all thy sons & daughters gather'ed round my ample table.
See you not all this wracking furious confusion?

Then, in words which recall Christ's call to Lazarus in the tomb,[38] Albion
cries:

Come forth from slumbers of thy cold abstraction! Come forth,
Arise to Eternal birth! Shake off thy cold repose,[39]
Schoolmaster of souls, great opposer of change, arise!
That the Eternal worlds may see thy face in peace & joy.[40]

Urizen must awake from his 'slumbers of abstraction'[41] so that, as Albion
says to him:

... thou, dread form of Certainty, maist sit in town & villlage
While little children play around thy feet in gentle awe,
Fearing thy frown, loving thy smile, O Urizen, Prince of Light.[42]

Here we must note that Albion is not opposed to 'Certainty', for
Urizen, in his unfallen form, 'was Faith & Certainty'.[43] Certainty is,
indeed, an essential attribute of unfallen Reason. It is the descriptive
word 'dread' which bears the weight of recrimination. Urizenic 'cer-
tainty', in the sense of rigid dogma and law — devised by 'cold abstrac-
tion' in 'cold repose' — must be 'warmed', softened and, above all,
humanized, so that once again little children may play around Urizen's
feet in gentle awe and he, like 'Old John, with white hair', may 'laugh
away care'.[44]

But Urizen — a 'stony form of death', a 'dragon of the Deeps'[45] —
remains silent. Albion, gaining in strength, grows angry at the lack of
response and, in wrath, demands that these fallen forms of Urizen yield
up their power:

... again he cried
Arise, O stony form of death! O dragon of the Deeps!
Lie down before my feet, O Dragon! let Urizen arise.[46]

These deformations should give way and let the true Urizen arise in his
'beautiful proportions':

O how couldst thou deform those beautiful proportions
Of life & person; for as the Person, so is his life proportion'd.
Let Luvah rage in the dark deep, even to Consummation,
For if thou feedest not his rage, it will subside in peace.[47]

Should Urizen fail to respond to Albion's command then he, Albion, will take back the 'crown & scepter' and cast Urizen:

> ... out into the indefinite
> Where nothing lives, there to wander; if thou returnest weary,
> Weeping at the threshold of Existence, I will steel my heart
> Against thee to Eternity, and never recieve thee more.
> Thy self-destroying, beast form'd Science shall be thy eternal lot.[48]

Albion, in denouncing Urizen, shows that not only does he admit his mistake in allowing fallen reason to rule over his faculties, but also that, as fully awakened humanity, he understands basic psychological and spiritual principles. If, he is saying here, Urizen allows Luvah-Orc to rage, or, differently expressed, if he, Urizen, refrains from nurturing and augmenting that rage by setting up rigid opposition to it, then, eventually, it will subside.

Albion now gives Urizen his first opportunity to make progress in self-recognition, for he, Urizen, learns that the cruel Orcian energy of which he is so terrified is, in fact, a product of his own attributes. He hears that Albion's anger against him:

> ... is greater than against this Luvah,[49]
> For war is [cruel del.] energy enslav'd, but thy religion,
> The first author of this war & the distracting of honest minds
> Into confused perturbations & strife & honour & pride,
> Is a deciet so detestable that I will cast thee out
> If thou repentest not, & leave thee as a rotten branch to be burn'd
> With Mystery the Harlot & with Satan for Ever & Ever.[50]

The waging of war is a perversion of energy, an enslavement of organic energy, but Luvah-Orc — who is that energy — is less guilty than Urizen, the enslaver. Luvah-Orc's war is the inevitable expression of energies which Urizen has repressed. It was Urizen's idea of self-centred holiness which engendered the conflict within Albion's members, which, in short, initiated the eternal strife of the psyche, the human soul.

A further liberating insight Urizen now gains is that even Rahab can be redeemed 'from Error's power', but that Error itself is unredeemable and must be rejected:

> Error can never be redeemed in all Eternity,
> But Sin, Even Rahab, is redeem'd in blood & fury & jealousy —

That line of blood that stretched across the windows of the morning[51] —
Redeem'd from Error's power. Wake, thou dragon of the deeps![52]

Albion is here repudiating the major errors, perpetrated by tyrannical
rationalism and Urizenic moral virtue responsible for mankind's long
spiritual illness.

Now, at last, Urizen responds:

... anxious his scaly form
To reassume the human; & he wept in the dark deep,
Saying: 'O that I had never drunk the wine nor eat the bread
Of dark morality, or cast my view into futurity, nor turn'd
My back, dark'ning the present, clouding with a cloud,
And building arches high, & cities, turrets & towers & domes
Whose smoke destroyed the pleasant gardens, and whose running kennels[53]
Chok'd the bright rivers; burd'ning with my Ships the angry deep;
Thro' Chaos seeking for delight, & in spaces remote
Seeking the Eternal which is always present to the wise;
Seeking for pleasure which unsought falls round the infant's path
And on the fleeces of mild flocks who neither care nor labour;
But I, the labourer of ages, whose unwearied hands
Are thus deform'd with hardness, with the sword & with the spear
And with the chisel & the mallet, I, whose labours vast
Order the nations, separating family by family,
Alone enjoy not.[54]

Urizen regrets that he ever took the antisacramental wine and bread of
'dark morality', that, in other words, he was actively involved in bring-
ing about the transubstantiation of the divine into the merely natural. He
repents his anxious concern with futurity instead of manifesting loving
concern for the present. He at last understands that the joys of Eternity
are in the present moment, that the power of Infinity can be held in the
palm of one's hand. He recognizes that his emphasis on the building of
cities and forming of trade routes which 'Chok'd the bright rivers' in the
interest of commerce and a privileged few has brought unhappiness to
mankind; he sees that an overindustrialized and urbanized society —
rooted in selfish profit motives — is of a predatory nature, feeding on the
weak and defenceless; and he admits that such a society is a direct
consequence of the grasping, self-centred fallen reason, cold and
heartless, of which he is the ultimate source and instigator. He also
recognizes his error in dividing nations from each other, 'separating
family by family'. He it is who has counteracted every striving towards
the realization of universal brotherhood.

In this conscious act of repentance, Urizen renounces all the principles he has obstinately and blindly held hitherto. He casts out his fears of futurity, for 'futurity is in this moment',[55] and cries out:

> Let Orc consume, let Tharmas rage, let dark Urthona give
> All strength to Los & Enitharmon, & let Los self-curs'd
> Rend down this fabric, as a wall ruin'd & family extinct.
> Rage, Orc! Rage Tharmas! Urizen will no longer curb your rage.[56]

In renouncing his hold on the other Zoas he is liberated from the selfhood. He shakes off the snow from his shoulders and casts his 'aged mantles into the fires', and

> ... glorious bright, Exulting in his joy,
> He sounding rose into the heavens in naked majesty,
> In radiant Youth ...[57]

Renunciation of repressive power is equivalent to casting off Error. Urizen's own pure energy immediately emerges from the state of Satan, and he is regenerate.

The nature of sin, of error, for Blake, is that it is a state of separation from others, of being 'self-enclosed'. The casting-out of sin by Urizen prepares him for reunion with his emanation, Ahania. Her reappearance — essential at some point during the process of general renewal and reunificaton — is particularly appropriate at this moment, for Urizen has just acted in accordance with her exhortation in Night iii.[58] Ahania, Pleasure, rising in joy, is restored to her consort. But at the moment of reunion she dies. Urizen's recovery meets with a heartbreaking setback. Precipitately Urizen wishes to embrace Ahania; that is, the mind wishes to take pleasure, enjoyment in its own powers.[59] Such pleasure, however, must wait upon the soul's reintegration with the human faculties of affection, instinct and imagination, with Luvah, Tharmas and Urthona.

Albion, once again calling him 'Prince of Light', reassures Urizen that Ahania will live again when Jerusalem, 'a City, yet a Woman',[60] descends from heaven, like the Bride of the Lamb of God, Who:

> ... tho' slain before her Gates, he self-renew'd remains
> Eternal, & I thro' him awake from death's dark vale.
> The times revolve; the time is coming when all these delights
> Shall be renew'd, & all these Elements that now consume
> Shall reflourish. Then bright Ahania shall awake from death,
> A glorious Vision to thine Eyes, a Self-renewing Vision:

The spring, the summer, to be thine; then sleep the wintry days
In silken garments spun by her own hands against her funeral.
The winter thou shalt plow & lay thy stores into thy barns
Expecting to recieve Ahania in the spring with joy.
Immortal thou, Regenerate She, & all the lovely Sex
From her shall learn obedience & prepare for a wintry grave,
That spring may see them rise in tenfold joy & sweet delight.
Thus shall the male & female live the life of Eternity,
Because the Lamb of God Creates himself a bride & wife
That we his Children evermore may live in Jerusalem
Which now descendeth out of heaven, a City, yet a Woman,
Mother of myriads redeem'd & born in her spiritual palaces,
By a New Spiritual birth Regenerated from Death.[61]

Here we need to pause and look more closely at an aspect of the four
Zoas to which little heed has been paid so far. We have understood the
four Zoas to be functions, faculties, of the human body and soul. Now,
Blake always strives to 'humanize', to give human form, to everything
that man experiences and perceives. Otherwise there is a temptation to
float in a cloud of shadowy, indeterminate existence. The four Zoas are no
exception. He gives them 'solid flesh & blood' by making each the rep-
resentative of a form of human activity. For Luvah Blake chooses the
occupation of winegrower. Wine, by its association with human blood,
on the one hand, and with sexual energy, on the other, is an obvious
symbol for the ambiguity of the energies of love. Urizen, with his 'horses
of Reason', is the Ploughman of Eternity, and he is therefore quite
naturally associated with the sowing of seeds, the harvest, and the baking
of bread, or, in a word, with Bread. Tharmas, symbol of pastoral inno-
cence, is quite naturally the Shepherd. Urthona, whose representative,
Los, is a worker in metals, is the Smith (the lame smith of traditional
myth — Hephaestus, for instance).

Now, the Emanation of the sower is the sown. The Emanation of
Urizen is Ahania. In Night viii, we recollect, Ahania is called 'thou corn
field! the vegetater happy!'[62] She is the 'furrow'd field',[63] the fruitful
mother earth. Ahania, in this context, is the living earth, in which the
seed, sown in her fields, should be the harvest of eternity,[64] Ahania, then,
as the counterpart of Urizen, is always in generation. She represents the
fruitfulness of earth as the Bride of Heaven. But Urizen, in his fallen form
as 'cold abstraction', 'clos'd' in 'cold solitude',[65] separated from creative
imagination, is impotent, has no use for Ahania — for a man's

Imagination is his life. We have seen that Ahania is seen by Urizen as being 'Sin'[66] and 'become like Vala',[67] and that he therefore casts her 'into non-Entity', the place and state of matter. She is banished from the ensouled and enspirited worlds. Both *The Book of Ahania* and the passages in *The Four Zoas* relating to Urizen's casting-out of Ahania, describe the outcast condition of Earth, of Mother Nature, by a Urizenic morality which regards the body as evil. Such a conception, Blake says, is a consequence of all those 'bibles and sacred codes' which teach that Evil 'is alone from the Body'.[68]

At first sight it seems strange that at the very moment Ahania returns to the repentant Urizen she should fall at his feet, dead with the excess of joy, and then be buried in a 'cave':

> ... she fell down dead at the feet of Urizen
> Outstretch'd a smiling corse: they buried her in a silent grave.[69]

But the descent into the 'cave' is the beginning of the process of sowing and harvesting in which Urizen resumes his vocation as Earth's husband and farmer.[70] But we are anticipating events in the apocalyptic process and must return to Albion's reassuring speech, addressed to Urizen, in which he states that 'all the lovely Sex ... shall learn obedience' from Ahania. Now, it is true that, although in much of this poem and elsewhere Blake treats men and woman more or less as equals, there is no denying the fact that he does consider the masculine principle of active creativity as being of greater significance than the feminine principle of receptivity and comforting tenderness. In some respects Blake envisages women as being subservient to men. For instance, in his annotations to Lavater's *Aphorisms on Man* (written about 1788) he remarks: 'Let the men do their duty & the women will be such wonders; the female life lives from the light of the male: see a man's female dependants, you know the man.'[71] For many men and women of the late twentieth century such an attitude may seem far from laudable. However, in our present context Blake means something quite other and more far-reaching. Here, in Night ix, Blake gives us a glimpse of his vision of redeemed humanity. For redeemed humanity 'obedience' does not have the same meaning as it does for 'fallen' men and women, for Natural Man. Both women and men, all regenerated, reborn persons, are to 'live in Jerusalem' and, therefore, have the same relationship as she, the Bride, does to the Lamb. This is made quite clear a little later in the poem when Albion says:

Luvah & Vala, henceforth you are Servants; obey & live.[72]

In Eternity — in the spirit — obedience means loving and selfless allegiance to the Higher Self, to the Christ within us.

Now, though Urizen's redemption is assured, we have seen that his desire to embrace his Emanation, Ahania, was precipitate. Feeling that his recovery has begun, he tries, unwisely but like many a sick person in ordinary life, to rush the process of regaining full health. He is conscious of his error, however, and regrets that it is still with him:

... I have Erred, & my Error remains with me.
What Chain encompasses? in what Lock[73] is the river of light confin'd
That issues forth in the morning by measure & the evening by carefulness?
Where shall we take our stand to view the infinite & unbounded?
Or where are human feet? for Lo, our eyes are in the heavens.[74]

At the revelation of a new birth, of a new spring, and of the Bride as Jerusalem — not merely a woman, but a city within which all may live in harmony — Urizen sheds the last vestiges of his error by accepting the fact that it consisted of trying to impose bonds ('Chain' and 'Lock') on those forces of eternity which, by their nature, are illimitable. He has at last recognized that whereas human eyes are incapable of perceiving the infinite, conceived spatially, true human Vision knows the infinite as part of its own nature. Reminded by Albion, Eternal Man, of his lost glory,[75] Urizen is finally able to recognize the nature of his error — his fear of death and the enslavement to clock-time which resulted from that fear, 'producing in its wake all the evils of a technologically orientated society'.[76]

As Enion had foreseen, the convulsions of human beings involved in the processes of rebirth are felt throughout the universe. Here Urizen's new insight is so apocalyptic that the whole universe explodes:

... riv'n link from link, the bursting Universe explodes.
All things revers'd flew from their centers: rattling bones
To bones Join:[77] shaking convuls'd, the shivering clay breathes:
Each speck of dust to the Earth's center nestles round & round
In pangs of an Eternal Birth ...[78]

The destruction which now ensures is also a new birth in which all existing things retain their 'lineaments', though not yet in their purified form; the victims of oppression still have the marks of their suffering, the tyrants those of the oppressor:

And all the marks remain of the slave's scourge & tyrant's Crown,
And of the Priest's o'ergorged Abdomen, & of the merchant's thin
Sinewy deception, & of the warrior's outbraving & thoughtlessness
In lineaments too extended & in bones too strait & long.[79]

Abasing himself before the unforgiving prisoner whom he, as temporal judge, had unjustly punished, Urizen is now confronted with the Son of Man,[80] Christ, Who appears with his retinue of 'twenty-four venerable patriarchs' and the 'four Wonders of the Almighty', the four Zoas in their unfallen state.[81] Beholding the Vision of Christ, Fallen Man, Albion, and Urizen rise and try to meet the Lord coming to Judgement. But neither Albion nor Urizen is yet able to endure the flames or enter the consummation which they offer.

The progress of regeneration is not a steady one. Just as the recovery from a physical or mental sickness has its advances and occasional slight setbacks or periods of non-activity, so also the process of regeneration has its peaks and troughs. Any form of 'salvation' demands effort, but phases of rest, even slight retrogressions, demanding even greater effort towards recovery, are often essential. At this stage in the process of regeneration we find that more must happen before Urizen has the necessary strength to 'Enter into Consummation'.[82]

It is not only Urizen but Albion too, who cannot 'Enter the Consummation':

The Eternal Man also sat down upon the Couches of Beulah
Sorrowful that he could not put off his new risen body
In mental flames; the flames refus'd, they drove him back to Beulah.
His body was redeem'd to be permanent thro' Divine Mercy.[83]

But whereas for Urizen the rejection signifies that he has to begin the work of the universal harvest and vintage, for Albion a precipitate consummation would mean that his redemption would not be complete — the 'Four Mighty Ones', the Four Zoas, are not yet all harmoniously acting as a 'Perfect Unity'.[84] As an act of Mercy, Albion is therefore given sojourn for a while 'upon the Couches of Beulah'[85] until such time as he may be fully redeemed.

The next step in the process of regeneration is initiated by the sons of Urizen:

Then siez'd the sons of Urizen the Plow; they polish'd it
From rust of ages ...

They beat the iron engines of destruction into wedges:
They give them to Urthona's sons ...
                              ... The Eternal horses
Harness'd, They call'd to Urizen; the heavens moved at their call.
The limbs of Urizen shone with ardor. He laid his hand on the plow.[86]

Urizen takes charge again of his steeds, which had been taken over by
Luvah, and puts them to their proper use — a productive use. Then

        ... Urizen commanded & they brought the Seed of Men.[87]

He sows the seeds of men, of souls, who will be resurrected 'in the harvest
springing up'.[88] Now Ahania comes forth again, casting off her death-
clothes and appearing as the harvest moon.[89] Urizen, having exercised his
selfless creative powers in an activity which unites heaven and earth, is
now reunited with his Emanation, Ahania:

        ... bright Ahania took her seat by Urizen in songs & joy.[90]

   Meanwhile, as the fires of nature have continued to burn, the
serpentine Orc of Satan/Urizen's natural religion, the degenerate form of
Luvah, has:

        ... quite consumed himself in Mental flames,
        Expending all his energy against the fuel of fire.

And Albion 'Regenerate Man', now into his 'holy hands reciev'd the
flaming Demon & Demoness of smoke'.[91]
   Orc and fallen nature, the Shadowy Female, have — in being
consumed in 'Mental flames' — worked towards the restoration of
harmony, which, when it comes, involves their own regeneration into
their pure forms of Luvah and Vala. To them Urizen, now no longer
acting in a domineering way but as the selflessly 'ordering' Intellect, says,
in words which summarize the central themes of the whole poem:

Luvah & Vala, henceforth you are Servants; obey & live.
You shall forget your former state; return, & Love in peace,
Into your place, the place of seed, not in the brain or heart,
If Gods combine against Man, setting their dominion above
The Human form Divine, Thrown down from their high station
In the Eternal heavens of Human [Thought del.] Imagination buried
                                                        beneath
In dark Oblivion, with incessant pangs, ages on ages,
In enmity & war first weaken'd, then in stern repentance

They must renew their brightness, & their disorganiz'd functions
Again reorganize, till they resume the image of the human,
Co-operating in the bliss of Man, obeying his Will,
Servants to the infinite & Eternal of the Human form.[92]

Luvah and Vala now

... entered the Gates of Dark Urthona,
And walk'd from the hands of Urizen in the shadows of Vala's Garden.[93]

The beauties of that Garden are deluding and limited, but they provide
a place of rest and renewal for Luvah and Vala, and later for Tharmas and
Enion.[94] Here they:

... heard not, saw not, felt not all the terrible confusion,
For in their orbed senses, within clos'd up, they wandered at will.[95]

Vala's world is temporary, a limited world where she and Luvah are to
'reorganize'.[96] Only shadows can live in this Garden. It is not the world
of living reality, but a dream-world. But just as dreams have their effect
on man in everyday life, so Luvah and Vala, and later Tharmas and
Enion,[97] are all changed by what happens to them in Vala's Garden. For
instance, Tharmas says to Vala:

O Vala, I am sick, & all this garden of Pleasure
Swims like a dream before my eyes; but the sweet-smelling fruit
Revives me to new deaths. I fade even like a water lilly
In the sun's heat, till in the night on the couch of Enion
I drink new life ...[98]

The return of Luvah and Vala into the 'place of seed'[99] re-establishes
Urizen's rightful place in the 'brain', and prepares the heart for the
reception of a 'reorganized' Tharmas. Here in Vala's Garden, Luvah and
his Emanation, Vala, no longer assailed by the 'terrible confusion of the
wracking universe',[100] renew 'their ancient golden age'.[101] They have
recovered their innocence in the state of reverie, Beulah, the Garden of
Innocence. Blake's imagery of 'organized' innocence, is expressed most
beautifully in the following lines:

Rise up, O Sun, most glorious minister & light of day,
Flow on, ye gentle airs, & bear the voice of my rejoicing.
Wave freshly, clear waters flowing around the tender grass;
And thou, sweet smelling ground, put forth thy life in fruits & flowers.
Follow me, O my flocks, & hear me sing my rapturous song.

I will cause my voice to be heard on the clouds that glitter in the sun.
I will call; & who shall answer me? I will sing; who shall reply?
For from my pleasant hills behold the living, living springs,
Running among my green pastures, delighting among my trees.
I am not here alone: my flocks, you are my brethren:
And you birds that sing & adorn the sky, you are my sisters.
I sing, & you reply to my song; I rejoice, & you are glad.
Follow me, O my flocks; we will now descend into the valley.
...

So spoke the sinless soul, & laid her head on the downy fleece
Of a curl'd Ram who stretched himself in sleep beside his mistress,
And soft sleep fell upon her eyelids in the silent noon of day.[102]

In this hymn of joy to the sun Blake's pastoral vision is triumphant. However, we should not regard this pastoral interlude, the narrative of the renewal of Luvah and Vala, Tharmas and Enion, which continues throughout the summertime whilst Urizen's crop is growing and maturing, as mere escapism. It describes an essential development in man's psychic growth. It has two purposes. One is to show the redeemed view of nature, of physical nature, which, of course, is personified by Vala, the other is to show the psychic redemption of passion as innocence.

In regard to the first purpose, let us retrace our steps a little. Before Vala attains the stage of being a 'sinless soul' she goes through a vital experience on the path to renewal. At first she worships the natural sun. She sees it as the source of her happiness, of her very existence. She has yet to learn that the deification of nature is just as serious an error as the Urizenic one of regarding Newtonian, physical laws as ultimate reality. Luvah, newly enlightened, therapeutically encourages Vala's delusion, telling her that she is no more than grass:

... O thou fair one, sit thee down, for thou art as the grass,
Thou risest in the dew of the morning & at night art folded up.[103]

Like a discerning tutor, Luvah opens Vala's 'eyes' to the recognition of the direful consequences of her fallacious view. A recognition which is preceded by health-engendering despair:

Alas! am I but as a flower? then will I sit me down,
Then will I weep, then I'll complain & sigh for immortality,
And chide my maker, thee O Sun, that raisedst me to fall.
...

O be thou blotted out, thou Sun! that raisedst me to trouble,

That gavest me a heart to crave, & raisedst me, thy phantom,
To feel thy heat & see thy light & wander here alone,
Hopeless, if I am like the grass & so shall pass away.[104]

Like Thel,[105] Vala laments the brevity of such an existence and weeps that she has been brought to life at all. In such a state of despair, however, she is open to Luvah's reassurance that she will survive:

Rise, sluggish Soul, why sit'st thou here? why dost thou sit & weep?
Yon Sun shall wax old & decay, but thou shalt ever flourish.
The fruit shall ripen & fall down, & the flower consume away,
But thou shalt still survive; arise, O dry thy dewy tears.[106]

The rhythm of nature, of the physical sun, is not the be all and end all of human life. Man is more than a being of nature. In him resides an eternal spiritual essence which never dies. Vala, brought to this stage in her own soul-development can now say:

O sun! thou art nothing now to me.
Go on thy course rejoicing, & let us both rejoice together.[107]

Vala has now learnt to give the physical sun and the material world their true value. She can now enjoy the sun and no longer be upset that she will, in course of time, be parted from it, for it is only a limited vision. In her new state of wiser joy, of regained innocence, she sees the natural sun as a mere shadow of the spiritual, the true sun, imaginatively perceived. In her 'bosom a new song arises to my Lord'.[108] She is now in the land of 'organized Innocence', that world of threefold vision which reconciles the energies of lesser levels of vision, and, as we have already seen, she lays 'her head on the downy fleece/Of a curl'd Ram', with its harmless horn.[109]

Vala's song is of a nature now made innocent; of Nature perceived as revealing the glory of Christ, the Giver of Eternal Life. Vala, in her sleep sees Luvah 'Like a spirit stand in the bright air'. She now knows Luvah, who, we recall, is closely associated with Christ.[110] The revival of innocence, which we have just experienced in Vala's transformed view of Nature, instigates the resurrection of the primal spirits, the parents of innocence, Tharmas, the Shepherd, and his Emanation, Enion.

The close interweaving of the faculties of the human soul are beautifully portrayed for us by Blake. First, we see that passion has now grown so closely identified with instinctual innocence that Vala has now become a shepherdess. In Eternity Tharmas is a shepherd. And secondly, we shall see Tharmas and Enion reappear, no longer as bitterly quarrelling adults as in Night i, but as a boy and girl whose innocent squabbles are easily settled by Vala.

Blake introduces the theme of the reunion of Tharmas and Enion and their redemption with consummate skill.

Vala, the 'sinless soul', the innocent child, has grown from childhood to 'motherhood'. She leads her flocks to the riverbank and there sees a vision which is the redeeming contrary to her earlier form of narcissism:

She stood in the river & view'd herself within the wat'ry glass,
And her bright hair was wet with the waters: she rose up from the river,
And as she rose her eyes were open'd to the world of waters:
She saw Tharmas sitting upon the rocks beside the wavy sea.
He strok'd the water from his beard & mourn'd faint thro' the summer vales.
And Vala stood on the rocks of Tharmas & heard his mournful voice:
'O Enion, my weary head is in the bed of death,
For weeds of death have wrap'd around my limbs in the hoary deeps.
I sit in the place of shells & mourn, & thou art clos'd in clouds.
When will the time of Clouds be passed, & the dismal night of Tharmas?
Arise, O Enion! Arise & smile upon my head.
...
Arise, O Enion, arise, for lo, I have calm'd my seas.'[111]

We need to go back to Night i to gain some understanding of what is happening here.

Tharmas, we have mentioned earlier on, is the 'Parent pow'r'. He can be variously described as innocence, instinct, the binding force of the human personality (i.e. the instinctive feeling for totality and unity), and the body — in the sense in which a child knows it, unselfconsciously. He is, in short, the innocent's instinctive trust, his instinctive sense of wholeness.

Not surprisingly, then, Tharmas and his Emanation, Enion, are the first to sense the disintegration of wholeness, just as they are also the first to sense the possibility of reintegration.[112] It is significant, incidentally, that Tharmas quickly — and willingly — gives up his claim to dominance over the other three Zoas and is the first to recognize the primacy of true humanity:

Is this to be A God? far rather would I be a Man,
To know sweet Science, & to do with simple companions.[113]

This insight and the recognition of 'Sweet Science' anticipates the apocalyptic change in consciousness that we see emerging in Night ix until 'sweet Science reigns' (see pp. 331–7).

What Tharmas senses, in Night i, is the Fall of Man, both in the sense of humanity as a whole awakening to its unique gifts for good and its unique capacity for evil, and in the sense of the individual experiencing division within and against himself and from others. The original 'Parent pow'r' of innocence, instinctive trust, and sense of wholeness, is brought into a state of confusion. On an individual level this breaking down of 'innocence' expresses itself, as it did for Adam and Eve, in a sudden awareness of nakedness — in Blake this means 'emotional' nakedness — and a sense of loneliness, both of which form a natural seedbed for such torments of the soul as sexual love and jealousy, and paranoid self-consciousness. Once the human instinctual powers have been thrown into confusion, feelings of sinfulness and victimization arise in the human soul and Man is afflicted by a sense of guilt. Urizenic moral law here finds a ready stage on which to play its devastating role.

Tharmas can also be understood as the 'Parent pow'r' of the other faculties of the human soul: intellect, imagination and emotion, that is, Urizen, Urthona and Luvah. Tharmas is the instinctual faculty (energy) of wholeness, unity, which can comprehend and hold together the other faculties (energies) in harmonious cooperation. With his fall the other faculties must also fall, and thus argument, rivalry, chaos and dis-harmony, reign instead of conversation, cooperation, order and harmony. Instead of cosmic order, cosmic chaos reigns. With the fall of Tharmas, the Cosmic Body slips into chaos.[114]

In Night i we witness the fall of Tharmas and, therewith, the 'falling' away from universal brotherhood. He is separated from his Emanation, Enion. Torments of love and jealousy prey on them both and, not surprisingly, we find them in the middle of a violent quarrel. We need not go into further detail here, but simply record that Enion, his form of prolific delight, conceals herself from him so that he grows 'indefinite' and he is compelled to sink into chaos:

> Tharmas groan'd among his Clouds[115]
> Weeping; then bending from his Clouds, he stoop'd his innocent head,
> And stretching out his holy hand in the vast deep sublime,
> Turn'd round the circle of Destiny with tears & bitter sighs
> And said: 'Return, O wanderer, when the day of Clouds is o'er'
> So saying, he sunk down into the sea, a pale white corse.[116]

The 'circle of Destiny' is the fallen world. The failure of Tharmas and Enion has trapped them in the ceaselessly turning cycle of life and death; they are ensnared in the revolving world of matter with its Urizenic system of cause and effect, natural and moral law.

Now let us return to the scene where Vala hears Tharmas saying:

> When will the time of Clouds be past, & the dismal night of Tharmas?
> Arise, O Enion! Arise & smile upon my head
> As thou dost smile upon the barren mountains and they rejoice.
> When wilt thou smile on Tharmas. O thou bringer of golden day?
> Arise, O Enion, arise, for Lo, I have calm'd my seas.[117]

She hears the voice of a chaos willingly offering to surrender itself. But the power of the Urizenic moral law has still to be broken.

As Tharmas lays his head 'Upon the Oozy rock'[118] Vala calls to Enion. Although there is no response from Enion, Vala's cry has its effect: reviving innocence begins to break the power of Urizen's moral law, and the first signs of the reappearance of cosmic order in place of cosmic chaos, or, we could equally well say, of order and harmony in the human psyche reasserting themselves over chaos and confusion, begin to manifest themselves.

This transformation is delicately indicated by Blake. When Vala goes back into her house and garden — created for her by Luvah[119] — she finds Enion and Tharmas playing there as a girl and a boy:

> The children clung around her knees, she embrac'd them & wept over them.
> Thou, little Boy, art Tharmas, & thou, bright Girl, Enion,
> How are ye thus renew'd & brought into the Gardens of Vala?[120]

These apocalyptic children are reborn into the world of Innocence. Once they reigned in this world, but now must learn afresh what their tasks are.

In contrast to all of the parent–child conflicts earlier in the poem,[121] we here see Vala assuming the nurturing and responsible role of mother vis-à-vis the original 'Parent pow'r' Tharmas, and his Emanation, Enion, who is intimately associated with Nature, Mother Earth. Now, at last, in this pastoral mood of innocence, the childlike primal parents, the 'mighty children'[122] — who have been confused and distressed by the Fall — are cared for. Instinct is now embraced not, as previously, rejected as being an unacceptable 'parent'. Blake is here making the point that 'instinct' has to relearn to trust itself; that man must regain the original certainty that impulse, instinct, does not necessarily lead man to wickedness — as fallen, Urizenic man, filled with doubt, assumes and preaches. Regenerated 'instinct' will, of course, work in harmony with regenerated Urizen, who then will have regained 'Faith & Certainty'.[123]

The point Blake is making here is beautifully portrayed in the lines:

He* went with timid steps, & Enion, like the ruddy morn
When infant spring appears in swelling buds & opening flowers,
Behind her Veil withdraws; so Enion turn'd her modest head.

But Tharmas spoke: 'Vala seeks thee, sweet Enion, in the shades.
Follow the steps of Tharmas, O thou brightness of the gardens.'
He took her hand reluctant; she followed in infant doubts.
Thus in Eternal Childhood, straying among Vala's flocks
In infant sorrow & joy alternate, Enion & Tharmas play'd.[124]

They begin to learn through 'infant' play, sorrow and joy alternating.

These glimpses of Enion and Tharmas, growing into human form in the same measure as the power of Urizen weakens, give us some idea of morality in Blake's visionary universe. When the sense of shame, guilt and separation, created by consciousness of the Urizenic law, have faded away, man is left as a babe in the cradle, and has to undergo his moral education all over again. In 'Auguries of Innocence' Blake writes:

Man was made for Joy & Woe;
And when this we rightly know
Thro' the World we safely go.
Joy & Woe are woven fine,
A Clothing for the Soul divine;
Under every grief & pine
Runs a joy with silken twine.[125]

This, according to Blake, is the lesson all men have to learn when they liberate themselves from the Urizenic law. We have to learn to live with and 'within' the interplay (the dialectic) between joy and woe. We then gradually discover the full potentialities and implications of our own human nature and its relationship with others.

The regaining of the original certainty as to the goodness and rightness of impulse, instinct — which includes the ideal sexual life — is, as Blake is well aware, fraught with difficulties. For, if instinct looks at itself in the light of 'morning', that is, becomes self-conscious, then it ceases to be instinct. Instinct and clarity of awareness are antithetical. Hence we hear

*i.e. Tharmas.

Tharmas saying to Vala:

> ... O Vala, I am sick, & all this Garden of Pleasure
> Swims like a dream before my eyes;
> ... I fade, even like a water lilly
> In the sun's heat, till in the night on the couch of Enion
> I drink new life ...
> But in the morning she arises to avoid my Eyes.[126]

This antithesis can only be resolved through the process of self-annihilation — in the sense in which we discuss it elsewhere in these pages. Through the process of self-annihilation existence in the shadowy, dream-world of Vala's Garden can be transcended. So far we have seen that both Tharmas and Enion have been renewed, 'reborn', with Vala, in 'lower Paradise'.[127] in Beulah, which state, although it implies condemnation of Urizenic, restrictive morality, is lower than the supreme spiritual condition, Eden. They both semi-consciously, as if in a dream, experience the inner conflict between the subconscious life of instinct and the clarity of self-consciousness. They are now ready — through self-annihilation — for the real world, the spiritual world of Eternity; they are now prepared to take the final step in the process of redemption, for truly humanizing reunification in the spirit.

Before Blake gives us a majestic picture of Tharmas 'humanizing', he reminds us that during the pastoral interlude the human harvest has finally come to fruition and regenerated Urizen has arisen as a mighty Harvester to gather in the sheaves.[128] When they are all gathered into:

> ... wide barns with loud rejoicings & triumph
> Of flute & harp & drum & trumpet, horn & clarion.
>
> The feast was spread in the bright South, & the Regenerate Man
> Sat at the feast rejoicing, & the wine of Eternity
> Was serv'd round by the flames of Luvah all day & all the Night.[129]

Here the tiller of the soil, Urizen, and the winegrower, Luvah, work in harmony with one another. A new relationship clearly now prevails between Reason and Passion, Urizen and Luvah, who, in their fallen state, were antagonistic protagonists. The celebration is interrupted by the appearance of Enion. The process of reintegration of the cosmic body and soul is yet to be completed:

> And when Morning began to dawn upon the distant hills,
> [Then del.] a whirlwind rose up in the Center, & in the whirlwind a shriek,

And in the shriek a rattling of bones & in the rattling of bones
A dolorous groan, & from the dolorous groan in tears[130]
Rose Enion like a gentle light; & Enion spoke, saying:
...
'The clouds fall off from my wet brow, the dust from my cold limbs
... Soon renew'd, a Golden Moth,
I shall cast off my death cloths & Embrace Tharmas again.'[131]

Enion, now no longer a shadow in Vala's world,[132] resumes her true
form and is reunited with Tharmas, who, in striking contrast to his
Spectre's brutal sexuality in Night i,[133] mild 'Embrac'd her whom he
sought'.[134]

A powerful picture is now given to us of the joy attending 'the Furious
forms of Tharmas humanizing';[135] nourished by Enion's life-giving and
joy-giving milk.

The roots shoot thick thro' the solid rocks, bursting their way
They cry out in joys of existence; the broad stems
Rear on the mountains stem after stem; the scaly newt creeps
From the stone, & the armed fly springs from rocky crevice,
The spider, The bat burst from the harden'd slime, crying
To one another: 'What are we, & whence is our joy & delight?
Lo, the little moss begins to spring, & the tender weed
Creeps round our secret nest.' Flocks brighten the Mountains,
Herds throng up the valley, wild beasts fill the forests.

Joy thrill'd thro' all the Furious forms of Tharmas humanizing.
Mild he embrac'd her whom he sought; he rais'd her thro' the heavens,
Sounding his trumpet to awake the dead, on high he soar'd
Over the ruin'd worlds, the smoking tomb of the Eternal Prophet.[136]

After the awakening of Nature, Albion, the 'Eternal Man', welcomes
Tharmas and Enion to the Harvest Feast, a communion in which the
bread and the wine are body and blood of a revived, resurrected Nature, a
'Nature' become Man invested with a new and higher spiritual nature.

But then, as in *The Book of Urizen*, on seeing Enion, the assembled
Eternals shudder at the sight of a female form separated from man, for in
Eternity such a separation, division, does not exist. One of the Eternals
discourses on the results of this separation. He begins by stating that man
is a worm, having lost the vision which should illuminate and fire his
body. As a result he has shut himself in selfishness, culminating in
abstract science instead of brotherhood:

> Man is a Worm; wearied with joy, he seeks the caves of sleep
> Among the Flowers of Beulah, in his selfish cold repose
> Forsaking Brotherhood & Univesal love, in selfish clay
> Folding the pure wings of his mind, seeking the places dark
> Abstracted from the roots of [Nature *del.*] Science ...[137]

The Eternals remedy this state of selfishness by casting the 'selfish terror' into earth existence and reopening his vision of 'Brotherhood & Universal love' by giving him life in a family. Here Blake shows us the very opposite of 'soft Family-Love'. Here men and women, through their very division into sexes and into families, can learn the ideal which Tharmas and Enion have achieved. The Eternals themselves, in fact, learn from the human experience:

> ... divided all
> In families we see our shadows born, & then we know
> That Man subsists by Brotherhood & Universal Love.
> We fall on one another's necks, more closely we embrace.
> Not for ourselves, but for the Eternal family we live.
> Man liveth not by Self alone, but in his brother's face
> Each shall behold the Eternal Father & love & joy abound.[138]

The vision presented here reveals Blake's conviction that Christ lives whenever Brotherhood exists. 'Wherever two or three are gathered together in my name there am I in the midst of them' (Matt 28:20). There is true brotherhood. The Human Form Divine, Divine Humanity, Christ in Man, is made visible when men and women 'look' at one another with imaginative vision.

After the Harvest Feast, Urizen rises with his flail, Tharmas with his winnowing fan, and the threshing and winnowing begins, symbolizing the ultimate transformation of reality:[139]

> The morning dawn'd, Urizen rose, & in his hand his Flail,
> Sounds on the Floor, heard terrible by all beneath the heavens.
> Dismal loud redounding, the nether floor shakes with the sound,
> And all Nations were threshed out, & the stars thresh'd from their husks.

> Then Tharmas took the Winnowing fan; the winnowing wind furious
> Above, veer'd round by the violent whirlwind, driven west & south,
> Tossed the Nations like chaff into the seas of Tharmas.[140]

In the newly humanized world we now learn, without being unduly surprised, of the destruction of Mystery. But what does come as a surprise is the way in which Tharmas, whom we have just left, regenerated, gives expression to vengeful joy at Mystery's plight. We have been conducted right up to the very threshold of the redemption of the whole of humanity, of the whole universe, and we can hardly be blamed if we now expect a smooth journey from now on, ending in a triumphant and joyful outcome.[141] However, in Blake's view, we would be guilty of a gross misunderstanding of the meaning of salvation. Let us look at what salvation involves, for Blake, and at the same time consider, in brief, his method of argument. Tharmas' attitude towards the demise of Mystery should then show itself to be integral element in the whole process of redemption as Blake sees it.

For Blake, salvation is not a state which can be won once and for all — either in the universe as a whole or in the individual human psyche. Salvation, in Blakean terms, involves 'intellectual War'.[142] Even those who have an imaginative vision of life lapse into periods of Urizenic doubt, into the despair of cynicism, even into single vision, the Newtonian sleep of rationalism. But, in the striving, creatively living human being, such lapses are nodal points in inner development and are the seedbeds of possible future experience and realization of the 'Divine Humanity',[143] of Christ, the Imagination, continually active within and working through us. We have seen how important the sojourn in the land of Beulah was for the development of Enion and Tharmas.[144] Eternity is a 'place' of continuous activity and now and again even the most active and creative person needs to relax when the energy of Eternity becomes too strong for him or her. Periods of doubt, despair and cynicism can hardly be equated with an experience of repose, but they are, nevertheless, periods in which imaginative creativity can take a rest, as it were. They have, in short, as already suggested, a positive and constructive value.

Underlying 'Mental Warfare' are what Blake calls 'the two Contrary States of the Human Soul'.[145] Now, Blake's poetic argument is frequently, if not always, organized in accordance with his principle of contraries: a progression through a conflict of opposites which, in their contrariness, affirm one another. We see this principle very clearly at work in *The Four Zoas*. For instance, from the moment that Urizen and his sons woke from their dream until very nearly the end of Night ix,[146] the poem alternates between contrasting moods of grief and joy, darkness and light, tension and release. These contrasts, dissonances, are all resolved, leading to affirmation — confirming Blake's maxim that 'Opposition is true Friendship'.[147] For instance, we have seen that the

Harvest Festival is interrupted by the rising of Enion in a whirlwind and a rattling of bones. She addresses the Eternals in the imagery of a rotting corpse, which is soon transmuted into that of the emergence of the Golden Moth from its deathlike wintry cocoon. In a further image of new life we hear that Enion's milk nourishes 'the thirsty sand'. Finally, Enion rejoins her counterpart, Tharmas, as a guest at the Feast. Almost immediately after this moment of harmony and release, tension sets in, a moment of discord, when the Eternal Men shudder at the sight of the 'female form now separate'. This dissonant reaction is compounded by one of the Eternals indicting man as a worm indulging in self-centred escapism. But the discord is resolved in the vision that 'Man liveth not by Self alone, but in his brother's face'. The resolution of contrast leads to a new, affirmatory experience. We are still involved in the Fall, but we have taken steps nearer to redemption and resurrection.

Almost immediately after we have come through this crisis, we are faced with another: Tharmas's vengeful joy at Mystery's destruction, to which we have already alluded, with, at the time, some disconcertment. However, in the light of what has just been outlined, we can understand better why Blake introduces such a discordant and 'dark' tone here: he is laying the foundation, as it were, for the contrast, the 'bright', 'light-filled' step in the regenerative process to be taken. Let us quote the speech Tharmas gives in his vision of a newly humanized world in which Mystery is destroyed while men and women, once 'enslaved' by religious dogma and 'enchained' by Urizenic interests, are liberated. The 'purpose' of the discordant note then becomes apparent; the new-found 'light' shines all the brighter; the 'darkness' is redeemed by the 'brightness' of liberated life:

'O Mystery,' Fierce Tharmas cries, 'Behold thy end is come!
Art thou she that made the nations drunk with the cup of Religion?[148]
Go down, ye Kings & Councillors & Giant Warriors.
Go down into the depths, go down & hide yourselves beneath,
Go down with horse & Chariots & Trumpets of hoarse war.

Lo, how the Pomp of Mystery goes down into the Caves!
Her great men howl & throw the dust, & rend their hoary hair.
Her delicate women & children shriek upon the bitter wind,
Spoil'd of their beauty, their hair rent & their skin shrivel'd up.

Lo, darkness covers the long pomp of banners on the wind,
And black horses & armed men & miserable bound captives.

Where shall the graves recieve them all, & where shall be their place?
And who shall mourn for Mystery who never loos'd her Captives?'[149]

And now the contrast:

Let the slave, grinding at the mill, run out into the field;
Let him look up into the heavens & laugh in the bright air.
Let the inchained soul, shut up in darkness & in sighing,
Whose face has never seen a smile in thirty years,
Rise & look out; his chains are loose, his dungeon doors are open;
And let his wife & children return from the opressor's scourge.

They look behind at every step & believe it is a dream.
Are these the slaves that groan'd along the streets of Mystery?[150]
Where are your bonds & task masters? are these the prisoners?
Where are your chains? where are your tears? why do you look around?
If you are thirsty, there is the river: go, bathe your parched limbs,
The good of all the Land is before you, for Mystery is no more.'[151]

The Tree and River of Life are now triumphant. The Tree of Mystery,
of Good and Evil, of Death, is no more.

This motif is repeated in a moving 'New Song',[152] composed by an
'African Black,'[153] in which he sees himself as he was in his boyhood in his
father's house, surrounded by his brethren and their children. Here Blake
reinforces, in a context of universal brotherhood, the family metaphor he
uses repeatedly in Night ix.[154]

We now come to a scene of even more strident contrasts than we have
seen hitherto. Earlier we saw that Urizen finally responded, with a new
clarity of awareness, to Albion's appeal and that he made a conscious
confession of his misdeeds. This, of course, is what one would expect of
the reasoning faculty. Luvah, on the other hand, representative of
emotional consciousness, needs longer to come to such clarity. We saw,
indeed, that he and his Emanation, Vala, did not consciously respond to
Albion's appeal, but:

> ... entered the Gates of dark Urthona.
> And walk'd from the hands of Urizen in the shadows of Vala's Garden.[155]

They entered the subconscious in which is the world of dreams. At this
stage, however, as though strengthened by Tharmas's vision and having
learnt the lesson of loving obedience,[156] Luvah not only willingly
cooperates with Urizen, who had been his arch-enemy, but
simultaneously, being now harmoniously 'twinned' with regenerated

Urizen, responds consciously to the lesson which he had previously responded to as though in a dream, for he says:

> Attempting to become more than Man We become less.[157]

He realizes, as do the other Zoas in turn, that if any one part of a whole usurps the role of the other parts in an attempt to become the whole, then not only is the whole destroyed, but each part is diminished too.

After this auspicious response on Luvah's part, and particularly in view of the harmonious cooperation between the Winegrower and the Corngrower, inspired by and overseen by Albion, we would seem to be entering into the final stage of the realization of universal love and brotherhood. But again Blake takes us through the experience of contrasts — more strident than ever:

> As he* arose from the bright feast, drunk with a wine of ages.
> His crown of thorns fell from his head, he hung his living Lyre
> Behind the seat of the Eternal Man† & took his way
> Sounding the Song of Los,[158] descending to the Vineyards bright.
> His sons, arising from the feast with golden baskets, follow,
> A fiery train, as when the Sun sings in the ripe vineyards.
> Then Luvah stood before the Wine press; all his fiery sons
> Brought up the loaded Waggons with shoutings; ramping tygers play
> In the jingling traces; furious lions sound the song of joy
> To the golden wheels circling upon the pavement of heaven, & all
> The Villages of Luvah ring; the golden tiles of the villages
> Reply to violins & tabors, to the pipe, flute, lyre & cymbal.
> Then fell the Legions of Mystery in madd'ning confusion,
> Down, down thro' the immense, with outcry, fury & despair,
> Into the wine presses of Luvah; howling fell the clusters
> Of human families thro' the deep; the wine presses were fill'd;
> The blood of life flow'd plentiful. Odors of life arose
> All round the heavenly arches & the Odors rose singing this song:
> 'O terrible wine presses of Luvah! O caverns of the Grave!
> How lovely the delights of those risen again from death!
> O trembling joy!'[159]

This whole scene is imbued with the spirit and joy of resurrection when 'the Legions of Mystery' fell.

By the fall of the crown of thorns from Luvah's head Blake is saying that Christanity should now no longer be envisaged as implying the

*i.e. Luvah

i.e. Albion

worship of suffering. In his view such worship is based on an erroneous, a Urizenic view of the significance of Christ's death on the cross. Luvah, the Prince of Love, identified with Christ,[160] is transformed here from Christ as the dying, suffering God, in a physical body, to the God of Rebirth, resurrection in the spiritual body. A religion which is ruled by rationalism and blind to the spirit cannot conceive of a spiritual body and must, therefore, focus attention on physical suffering — on the crown of thorns. Such worship — whether it be in the mystery-religions of a god of vegetation, or in the mystery-religion enthroned by the Urizenic priesthood — substitutes sacrifice and corporeal war and suffering for the spiritual combats of regenerated Man. The winepress here represents both fallen corporeal warfare and redeemed 'wars' of love, the creative, spiritual strife of Eternity.

Now, with brutal abruptness, the scene of the joyous 'delights of those risen again from death', is contrasted with a situation which is more than discordant. It is terrifying. Around the winepress all is jubilation, indeed, exuberance. But the happenings within the winepress are appalling, for 'in the Winepresses is wailing, terror & despair'.[161] It is not solely 'the Legions of Mystery' who are suffering, but also 'Human Grapes' — the souls of men and women:

> But in the Wine Presses the Human Grapes sing not nor dance,
> They howl & writhe in shoals of torment, in fierce flames consuming,
> In chains of iron & in dungeons circled with ceaseless fires,
> In pits & dens & shades of death, in shapes of torment & woe;
> The Plates, the Screws & Racks & Saws & cords & fires & floods,
> The cruel joy of Luvah's daughters, lacerating with knives
> And whips their Victims, & the deadly sport of Luvah's sons.[162]

The souls still within the winepress, who have not yet become 'Odors of Life'[162a], are undergoing agonies of unparalleled inquisitorial intensity. It is true that these human souls are willing to endure torment, for they, obstinate, and

> Tho' pained to distraction, cry, 'O, let us exist! for
> This dreadful Non Existence is worse than pains of Eternal Birth:
> Eternal death who can endure? let us consume in fires,
> In waters stifling, or in air corroding, or in earth shut up.
> The Pangs of Eternal birth are better than the Pangs of Eternal death.'[163]

It is also true that the process of having the 'husks' of error separated from their human wine cannot be a pleasant one for those who are undergoing the vintage. The incrustations of thousands of years of the fallen world are not easily removed. Nevertheless, neither the latter circumstances nor the willingness — indeed, eagerness — of human souls to suffer the pains of 'Eternal Birth' rather than stagnate in a spiritless world, in 'Non Existence', would appear to justify, or explain, the sadistic glee manifested by those who 'torture' them. But, clearly, Blake would have us react differently and penetrate to the real purpose and find the regenerating function of such an orgy of violence. Perhaps we could see a partial analogue in a boil, which, over a period of time, has been causing feverish discomfort and poisoning of the body. At some stage it has to seeth, burst and exude a foul-smelling pus. In short, it has to indulge in an orgy of violence before the final health-restoring process can take place. Seen from the viewpoint of the sufferer, this health-restoring process is one of torment, but seen from that of the agents of the restorative process it is one of joy. A process of purification is torment for those being purified. Perhaps, also, we can accept that such a horrific scene of 'torture' and suffering is essential to an understanding of the interrelationship between the inflicting of suffering and the forgiveness of sins, for the very next episode in which the tormentors, Luvah and Vala, and their sons and daughters, appear, shows them repenting after they have sobered up from their bloodthirsty drunkenness — 'they reascended/ To the Eternal Man in woe'.[164] After a wintry banishment in the world of shadows they are forgiven.

Another aspect of this complex situation also needs to be considered. We have previously mentioned that, for Blake, both corporeal war and sacrificial religion (Druidism, for instance) are perversions of energy. Now, the frenzy of the cruel activity of the sons and daughters of Luvah and Vala is characteristic of such a perverted use of energy. However, Blake also expresses the conviction that 'Those who restrain desire, do so because theirs is weak enough to be restrained; and the restrainer or reason usurps its place & governs the unwilling.'[165]

Urizen, regenerated, no longer usurps Luvah's place. As we have seen, Urizen, the Graingrower, and Luvah, the Winegrower, work harmoniously together. However, the process of reintegration is not yet complete. Both Tharmas and Urthona have yet to complete their tasks in the regenerative process. Until the intuitive consciousness of wholeness and the imaginative consciousness are fully operative within man there is still 'room', as it were, for deviation from the ideal unity. The children of Luvah, representatives of various sensual delights (as yet they still have some of the nature of the unredeemed Vala), without the harmonizing influence of regenerated Tharmas and Urthona, are uncontrollable. Sensual delight, uncontrolled, is as much a usurper as fallen reason can be, for it ousts clarity of consciousness. Enhanced sensual delight, spiritualized sensual delight, is active in man when, in Blakean terms, the four Zoas, 'the Four Faces of Humanity'[166] reflect 'each in each'[167] and take joy in each other's energies and activities. They then converse 'together in Visionary forms dramatic'.[168]

We have just witnessed the torment of 'human families' in the winepresses and the cruelty of the sons and daughters of Luvah 'treading out' the 'blood of life'.[169] This 'blood of life' which remains after the 'husks' have been thrown away is what is real in the human soul, it is the truth man embodies. It remains as the essence from which the apocalyptic wine is made. The 'falsehood', that is, the parasitic Mystery, deprived of the elements of the material world which gave it form, vanishes and is annihilated.[170]

In a new transubstantiation, the blood of corporeal human sacrifice is now transmuted into the wine of eternal, spiritual life. The time has come when Albion, Eternal Man, will no longer have to lament (as he did at the beginning of Night ix).[171]

Listening to the torments of the 'Human Grapes', Albion, 'darken'd with sorrow'[172] at the gleeful sadism of the grape-treaders, calls upon both Tharmas and Urthona, 'satisfied/With Mirth & Joy',[173] to resume their unfallen state and finish the work of the great vintage by separating the wine from the lees.[174] The year, which began with Urizen sowing the 'seeds', has ended:

> ... a wintry mantle
> Cover'd the hills.[175]

And now:

> ... Urthona, limping from his fall, on Tharmas lean'ed,
> In his right hand his hammer. Tharmas held his shepherd's crook.
> ...
> Then Enion & Ahania & Vala & the wife of dark Urthona[176]
> Rose from the feast, in joy ascending to their Golden Looms.
> There the wing'd shuttle sang, the spindle & the distaff & the Reel
> Rang sweet the praise of industry. Thro' all the golden rooms
> Heaven rang with winged Exultation.[177]

As the wives (Emanations) of the Zoas work at weaving the woof of a redeemed nature, and 'All beneath'[178] the Legions of Mystery are

annihilated, Tharmas and Urthona and their sons gather the vintage
which Urizen had sown and harvested and Luvah had pressed out:

> ... they took the wine, they separated the Lees

and:

> They loaded all the waggons of heaven
> And took away the wine of ages with solemn songs & joy.[179]

Then:

> Luvah was put for dung on the ground by the sons of Tharmas and Urthona.[180]

This enigmatic image may, perhaps, be understood to mean that after
the wine of life has been separated from the sediment, the latter can still be
put to productive use to nourish a new nature. Luvah has not yet made
the reascent to the Eternal Man from the period of banishment in the
'world of shadows',[181] mentioned earlier on in this chapter. Just before
this vital step in regeneration is made, Tharmas and Urthona go down to
the winepresses and find the sons and daughters of Luvah exhausted from
their labours and, intoxicated, tormenting each other and treading on the
howling and writhing 'Human Grapes'. Luvah himself, and his
Emanation, Vala, are found sleeping the heavy, dreamless sleep of the
inebriated.[182] They symbolize, in their present state, the worshippers of
the dying god of vegetation of the mystery religions, the Bacchic cele-
brants of perverted energy — including sexual energy. A perverted
energy which turns in upon itself: the sons and daughters of Luvah
'began to torment one another'.[183] Luvah and Vala, the god and goddess
of this Bacchic orgy, are 'O'erwearied'. The divinities of the vegetative
mysteries are now coming to an end. They are dying. The 'soil' for the
regeneration of man and nature is almost ready. An essential element in
the preparation of this new, living ground is the assimilation and trans-
mutation (that is, not the rejection) of the dying-god aspect of man's
emotional life (unredeemed Luvah and Vala), and it is, therefore, 'put for
dung on the ground' to nourish the birth of nature free from the cycle of
fallen life. This having been done, the 'wine of ages', the waters of a
rejuvenated and more abundant life, are carried off in a festival of rejoicing
by the sons of Urthona and Tharmas, that is, by that which is the most
creative in man, the intuitive and creative power of imagination, and by
the instinctive, innocent sense of wholeness, that which senses and
maintains, with care and tenderness, harmonious unity in the individual
and mankind as a whole. The 'Human Wine', now liberated through

pain and suffering from mere 'natural' existence as 'grapes', stand 'wondering', and 'the heavens roll'd on with vocal harmony',[184] the music of the spheres is heard resounding.

Then:

> Los, who is Urthona, rose in all his regenerative power.[185]

Urthona and Tharmas have the final task of completing the work of bread-making begun by Urizen's sowing, reaping and threshing. The 'Mills of Urthona' and the 'Ovens of Urthona' are not so vividly described as Luvah's winepress, but the 'grains' suffer just as much as the 'grapes':

> Terrible the distress
> Of all the Nations of Earth, ground in the Mills of Urthona.[186]

The whole of Nature, in darkness, groans:

And Men are bound to sullen contemplation in the night:
Restless they turn on beds of sorrow; in their inmost brain
Feeling the crushing Wheels, they rise, they write the bitter words
Of Stern Philosophy & knead the bread of knowledge with tears & groans.[187]

Earlier in this chapter we saw that the grapes (wine) are associated with Luvah, and grain (bread) with the tiller of the soil, Urizen. Whereas, then, the suffering symbolized by the pressing of wine is of the heart, that symbolized by the making of the bread is of the head. However, there is a significant difference between the 'bread of sorrow' kneaded by the daughters of Urizen and fed to Orc in Night vii[188] and the 'bread of knowledge' being kneaded here. The 'bread of sorrow' was made from the fruit of the Tree of Mystery, the Tree of Death. The fatal fruit of that tree brings spiritual death.[189] In Night vii, Urizenic Mystery, false religion, became sorrow, producing dire suffering and further mystery. Here, in Night ix, sorrow becomes wisdom, spiritual enlightenment. The final product is the Bread of Life, the 'Bread of Ages',[190] which Urthona places:

> In golden & in silver baskets, in heavens of precious stone[191]

from which eternal humanity can be spiritually nourished.

Neither the sufferings of the families of men thrust into the wine-presses, nor their turnings 'on beds of sorrow' are the deadly sufferings of corporeal war, but the pangs which accompany the spiritual birth of true joy; a joy which echoes the music of the spheres.

This spiritual birth, the spiritual cultivation of human souls, 'seeds' and 'grapes', is made possible because, inspired by Eternal Man, Albion, the Zoas and their Emanations now cooperate in harmony with one another.

As we have already mentioned, Blake particularly emphasizes, in Night ix, the need for such harmonious cooperation between Urizen, the grower of grain, and Luvah, the grower of wine. Elsewhere Blake makes a significant remark which further illumines the necessity for such cooperation. Music, poetry and painting, he writes, are 'the three Powers in Man of conversing with Paradise, which the flood did not Sweep away.'[192] Music is the expression of pure emotion and therefore belongs to Luvah. Music is the most direct communication with Divinity, Eternity. It needs no intermediary such as words or images. Thus while music is spiritual wine, poetry and painting are prayer, the spiritual bread of life.[193]

Now a last winter falls upon what remains of the fallen world 'in the night of Time'.[194] The new age, the age of universal brotherhood, is dawning and, with it, freedom, a promise of an end to the deep sleep, the great winter of humanity and the world. This last winter is not one of death, but of repose, of an untroubled sleep from which man awakens to take his place in the Halls of Eternity:

> The Sun has left his blackness & has found a fresher morning,
> And the mild moon rejoices in the clear & cloudless night,
> And Man walks forth from midst of the fires: the evil is all consum'd.
> His eyes behold the Angelic spheres arising night & day;
> The stars consum'd like a lamp blown out, & in their stead, behold
> The Expanding Eyes of Man behold the depths of wondrous worlds![195]

All the evil in man has been destroyed and he can look at Infinity without being harmed, he can 'meet' Christ, which he was unable to do earlier.[196] As we shall soon see, he can walk 'thro' the flames' without being repelled. Man has now infinite vision. His eyes, expanding, free themselves from the restrictions of Urizenic 'caverns'. We may here draw upon Blake's remarks in his letter to Dr Trusler of 23 August 1799 to elucidate this statement:

The tree which moves some to tears of joy is in the Eyes of others only a Green thing that stands in the way. Some See Nature all Ridicule & Deformity, ... & Some Scarce see Nature at all. But to the Eyes of the Man of Imagination, Nature is Imagination itself. As a man is, So he Sees. As the Eye is formed, such are its Powers. ... To Me This World is all One continued Vision of ...Imagination.[197]

A Urizenic, contracted, limited eye, perceives only fallen reality, a caricature of the archetypal, spiritual reality. He who sees with the analytical eye only is divorced from reality. Space and time, for instance, are features of the phenomenal world, and both are but imperfect symbols of ideal attributes of the Ideal World. He who sees with the eye of Imagination, with the expanding eye, with 'Spiritual Sensation'[198] expands 'in the bosom of God',[199] becomes one with Christ, the Divine Imagination.

In this letter to Dr Trusler Blake tell us that it is the task of the creative artist to re-member from its fallen splintered state an eternal archetype of true life which most people never, or rarely, perceive. Through the intuitive power of the creative imagination the possibility is there for all men to perceive spiritual reality. In such an expanded vision man and world become one. A true unity is born. Urizen, as we have commented elsewhere, preaches a perverse distortion, a caricature of unity when he decrees that there should be:

> One command, one joy, one desire,
> One curse, one weight, one measure,
> One King, one God, one Law.[200]

This is an abstract unity, imposed upon mankind out of fear of the future and what it may bring, and out of fear of the uniqueness of every creative human being. It is an abstraction which is taken for truth by much of humanity. It is an illusory unity in which the freedom and love which prevail in universal brotherhood, in a living and creative unity, have no place. In a Urizenic world happiness cannot be universal, for in such a world the happiness of the few feeds on the unhappiness of the many. There is, in fact, no true happiness. In such a world the voice of social conscience is stilled.

It is out of the Urizenic world that Los has torn down the sun and the moon.[201] Now we see them restored in their primal, spiritual form. The spiritual sun has reassumed its rightful place, the material sun, the dark sun, is no more.[202] The very imagery Blake uses to describe the two events forms a sharp contrast:

> ... Los his vegetable hands
> Outstretch'd: his right hand, branching out in fibrous strength,
> Siez'd the Sun; His left hand, like dark roots, cover'd the Moon.[203]

Here Sun and Moon are perceived in their materiality.

But, when vision is renewed and humanized, when universal brotherhood is realized, then new-born man beholds:

> One Earth, one sea beneath; nor Erring Globes wander, but Stars
> Of fire rise up nightly from the Ocean; & one Sun
> Each morning, like a New born Man, issues with songs & joy
> Calling the Plowman to his labour & the Shepherd to his rest.[204]

The days and nights, like the seasons, of the Eternal World of Vision are instantaneously one, that is, their passage is no longer sequential as in the 'night of Time'.

Instead of the distant, cold stars of reason, the Inner Light of human imaginative perception reveals new worlds. The 'Man of Imagination', to whom 'Nature is Imagination itself', is no longer at the mercy of Urizen's laws, but perceives, 'lives', the world in its true eternal nature:

He[205] walks upon the Eternal Mountains, raising his heavenly voice, and, as in the primal condition of innocence, he is again able to converse:

> ... with the Animal forms of wisdom night & day,
> That, risen from the Sea of fire, renew'd walk o'er the Earth.[206]

Not only man, but all the creatures of the earth, and the earth itself, are regenerated when the Zoas themselves regain their prelapsarian forms.

A visionary passage now follows which describes the pastoral innocence of Tharmas, the wise and innocent sense of wholeness, and the beat of Urthona's hammer, that is, of the faculty of creative imagination in its purity:

> ... Tharmas brought his flocks upon the hills, & in the Vales
> Around the Eternal Man's bright tent, the little Children play
> Among the wooly flocks. The hammer of Urthona sounds
> In the deep caves beneath; his limbs renew'd, his Lions roar
> Around the Furnaces & in Evening sport upon the plains.[207]

The restoration of Eden nears completion. The 'Tygers' who roamed in the forests of the night have been replaced by the Lions of Urthona, royal emblems of creative power. Raising 'their faces from the Earth',[208] they converse with man. To their astonishment they find that they are not consumed, but liberated, by the fires of vision:

> How is it we have walk'd thro' fires & yet are not consum'd?
> How is it that all things are chang'd, even as in ancient times?[209]

'Things are chang'd', man — and with him all nature — has regained his primal state of innocence, but during the process of regeneration he has passed through the anguish of the fire and the torment of the world of experience, and, in so doing, his errors have been annihilated and his essential purity, reclaimed, now prevails.

In an awe-inspiring breath of peace, Blake's mighty creative effort to give birth to visions of a universe which will awaken men and women to seek true, spiritual life, is sung to its completion:

> The Sun arises from his dewy bed, & the fresh airs
> Play in his smiling beams giving the seeds of life to grow,
> And the fresh Earth beams forth ten thousand thousand springs of life.[210]

For the first time in the whole poem the mood is unqualified harmony and serenity!

In this state of regeneration, Urthona rises as a warrior whose warfare is spiritual, not corporeal. Urthona's 'Mental fight' does not obliterate, it subordinates, those Urizenic techniques of analysis which, when employed exclusively, whether by scientists or by others, lead to the destruction of Vision. When science pays heed to the visions of the creative imagination then it is free to manifest itself in its true glory as 'sweet Science':

> ... Urthona rises from the ruinous Walls
> In all his ancient strength to form the golden armour of science
> For intellectual War. The war of swords departed now,
> The dark Religions are departed & sweet Science reigns.[211]

In this last line Blake presents us with an ideal: the reign of 'sweet Science' superseding the 'bitter' science promulgated by fallen Urizen.

* * * * *

Before bringing this chapter to a conclusion, it behoves us to give some consideration to Blake's vision of 'sweet Science'. So far we have seen Blake condemning Newton, Bacon and Locke, who, he repeatedly states, were three of the major figures responsible for the materialism of modern times. However, he is clearly not condemning scientific knowledge as such. What he attacks is abstract knowledge and the one-sided rationalism upon which the science of Urizenic knowledge is based:

> They began to weave curtains of darkness,
> They erected large pillars round the Void,

> With golden hooks fasten'd in the pillars;
> With infinite labour the Eternals
> A woof wove, and called it Science.[212]

Elsewhere Blake speaks of reason and science being formed by the natural (i.e. spiritually passive) and abstract impressions of reasoning man:

The law and gospel from fire and air, and eternal reason and science
From the deep and the solid, and man lay his faded head down on the rock.[213]

The words 'solid' and 'rock' speak of the rigid nature of the Urizenic reasoner's impressions. The priests, too, form their laws and doctrines from their abstract and natural impressions, that is, impressions of the purely phenomenal world passively received.

In *The Book of Ahania* science is again knowledge based on limited, 'caverned' Urizenic sense perception. Urizen, by his science, forms the human soul in his own likeness. The analytical reasoner himself and his dead science are depicted in the lines:

> ... when Urizen shrunk away
> From Eternals, he sat on a rock
> Barren; a rock which himself
> From redounding fancies had petrified.
> Many tears fell on the rock,
> Many sparks of vegetation.
> Soon shot the painted root
> Of Mystery under his heel:
>
> It grew a thick tree: he wrote
> In silence his book of iron.[214]

The imagery is clear. It speaks of reductionist materialism. The human soul — just as the rock — is 'petrified', imprisoned in moral law, laws of oppression, and Newtonian abstract laws and principles of nature. Urizenic man writes books imprisoned in his own self-created 'cavern'.

Urizenic man's science contains the 'Seed' of fragmentation. He separates himself from others by seeking refuge in his own selfhood:

... he seeks the caves of sleep
... in his selfish cold repose
Forsaking Brotherhood & Universal Love, in selfish clay
Folding the pure wings of his mind, seeking the places dark
Abstracted from the roots of [Nature *del.*] Science; then inclos'd around
In walls of Gold we cast him like a Seed into the Earth.[215]

Science — scientific thought — separated from the realities of human relationships and creative human activity is abstract. Indeed, such abstract, 'selfish' and cold science destroys creativity. It enfolds, destroys, the creative mind in its abstract philosophy and brings about the fall of Albion, the Eternal Man. As we have already seen, before their regeneration, Urthona, Luvah and Tharmas, dominated by fallen Urizen, all lose their visionary power through the abstract science which covers them in its light-denying veil. Man then becomes, like Urizen, who before his fall 'was Faith & certainty',[216] a doubting and insecure wanderer.

The science of Urizen is bitter and negative for he journeys in hopelessness and despair:

> ... nor saw Urizen with a Globe of fire
> Lighting his dismal journey thro' the pathless world of death,
> Writing in bitter tears & groans in books of iron & brass
> The enormous wonders of the Abysses, once his brightest joy.
>
> For Urizen beheld the terrors of the Abyss wandering among
> The ruin'd spirits, once his children & the children of Luvah.[217]

The Four Zoas begins with the fall of man from universal brotherhood into division, into war, into the hands of Urizenic 'bitter' science and ends with the 'sweet Science' of unity and brotherhood.

Blake identifies 'the Antichrist ... the Tree of Death'[218] with Urizenic, bitter science. Art, on the other hand, Blake affirms, 'is the Tree of Life'.[219] By art is not meant a particular form of art, such as poetry, music or painting, but a mode of life, the life of the imagination. Such a mode of life is also 'sweet Science'. Indeed, science, in its creative sense, is usually combined by Blake with art. For instance, in his annotations to the *Discourses* of Joshua Reynolds Blake writes:

> The Arts & Sciences are the Destruction of Tyrannies or Bad Governments.

And:

> The Foundation of Empire is Art & Science. Remove them or Degrade them, & Empire is no More.[220]

By 'Empire' Blake means 'spiritual' not 'temporal' Empire.

Both art and science, Blake states, must be completely truthful:

> Art & Science cannot exist but by Naked Beauty display'd.[221]

Beauty for Blake is an order and harmony imposed on chaos, on the indefinite. 'Naked Beauty display'd' reveals what is truly human, it reveals the true lineaments of the soul. Loss of form, for Blake, is loss of beauty. It is not surprising then to hear him speak of the spectres as 'deformed' and 'repugnant to the forms of life'.[222] The Spectre, the 'Reasoning Power in Man', has to be removed so that 'Naked Beauty', the truth, may be revealed. The Spectre is:

> ... a false Body, an Incrustation over my Immortal
> Spirit, a Selfhood which must be put off & annihilated alway.
> To cleanse the Face of my Spirit by Self-examination,
> To bathe in the Waters of Life, to wash off the Not Human.[223]

To 'wash off the Not Human' is to reveal the true lineaments of the soul. To 'cleanse the Face of my Spirit by Self-examination' is to purify the soul through spiritual self-knowledge; to reveal the truth and beauty of form is to purify one's soul through selfless spiritual self-knowledge, a knowledge which has its source in the 'Living Waters flowing from the Humanity Divine'.[224]

> 'Sweet Science' and true Art:
> ... cannot exist but in minutely organized Particulars,
> And not in generalizing Demonstrations of the Rational Power.[225]

'Sweet science', spiritual science, is the wise knowledge of the Golden Age. It is the kind of knowledge Blake exhorts us to re-member, to win for ourselves again. It is knowledge of the Imagination. 'Bitter' science can be no other than the kind of knowledge which 'sees' man as an automaton, and the universe as a vast machine in which each part, each cog, plays its predestined, limited and rigid, role — fixed for all futurity. 'Imagination, Art & Science, & all Intellectual Gifts [are] all the Gifts of the Holy Ghost,'[226] writes Blake in 1810. The Last Judgement begins when mankind has completely lost sight of this truth. He describes his picture of the Last Judgement as 'a History of Art & Science, the Foundation of Society, which is Humanity itself.'[227]

In *Jerusalem*, in the address 'to the Public', Blake states: 'The Primeval state of Man was Wisdom, Art & Science.'[228] And in the address 'To the Christians' he asks:

> ... are not the Gifts of the Spirit Every-thing to Man? O ye Religious,
> discountenance every one among you who shall pretend to despise Art & Science!
> I call upon you in the Name of Jesus! What is the Life of Man but Art & Science?

... expel from among you those who pretend to despise the labours of Art & Science, which alone are the labours of the Gospel. Is not this plain & manifest to the thought? Can you think at all & not pronounce heartily That to Labour in Knowledge is to Build up Jerusalem, and to Despise Knowledge is to Despise Jerusalem & her Builders ... Let every Christian, as much as in him lies, engage himself openly & publicly before all the World in some Mental pursuit for the Building up of Jerusalem.[229]

We see, then, that Blake uses the term 'Science' — and the same may be said of the term 'knowledge' — in two different senses: the one is with reference to Newtonian science, which is solely concerned with appearances, the other, spiritual science, spiritual knowledge, concerned with essences. The 'bitter' variety of science, ignorant of any spiritual, eternal reality, confines itself to the limited realms of the corporeal world perceived by the five physical senses. Should such a science consider a world not perceptible to the physical sense (or to their mechanical extensions — telescope, microscope, etc.) it can only do so in terms of its own mode of mechanistic and rationalistic thinking.[230] As we have seen elsewhere, rationalism would have a 'Natural Cause for Any Thing',[231] whereas, for Blake, the spiritual scientist,

> ... every Natural Effect has a Spiritual Cause, and Not
> A Natural; for a Natural Cause only seems: it is a Delusion
> Of Ulro & ratio of the perishing Vegetable Memory.[232]

Every thought or action, divorced from spiritual reality, is, for Blake, inhuman. A science divorced from the divine in man is one of the 'dark Religions'. Tharmas expresses his realization of the effect of such a science (knowledge) in Night iv of *The Four Zoas* when he feels the loss of his true humanity:

> Is this to be A God? far rather would I be a Man,
> To know sweet Science, & to do with simple companions
> Sitting beneath a tent & viewing sheepfolds & soft pastures.[233]

Through 'sweet science' man can experience brotherhood and love.

Of 'bitter', inhuman, science, Blake writes, in an annotation to one of Swedenborg's works: 'Study Sciences till you are blind, Study Intellectuals till you are cold, Yet science cannot teach intellect. Much less can intellect teach Affection.'[234] However, the kind of science, 'sweet' science, which meets human needs and aspirations, which recognizes the essence, the spiritual, as being the truly human and divine in man, need not, indeed, should not, oust that faculty in him which has its task to investigate the purely physical and mechanical elements in nature and the universe. Blake himself is keenly aware of this. Exclusion of physical science from its rightful place would be a Urizenic misuse of creative energy. Blake gives clear expression to this spiritual reality when, at the end of *Jerusalem*, he includes the 'infernal' trinity, three of the great scientists and thinkers responsible for modern materialism, Bacon, Newton and Locke, in the great awakening. Regenerated, that is, risen from their satanic roles, from the spectral deformities of their true selves and functions, they appear at the side of those who were in Blake's view the greatest representatives of art — Milton, Shakespeare and Chaucer. Blake recognizes that, whatever their errors — and it is to these that Blake addresses himself throughout his life — the three men were, first and foremost, seekers of the truth.

What we have been saying here in respect of the two forms of science and scientists can also be said of art and artists. There is 'bad art' and 'good art', there are bad and good artists. Life itself is art. There are two kinds of art and two kinds of life: there is the 'good' art, good life, of the Imagination, informed by spiritual knowledge, intellectual vision, and therefore concerned with essences; and the 'bad' art, bad life, of the ratio, of the spectral selfhood, concerned only with appearances. All art — or action in life — which imitates appearances and not essences Blake calls 'Bad Art', and since, for him, 'Mental Things are alone Real',[235] it follows that 'The Last Judgement is an Overwhelming of Bad Art & Science.'[236] The Last Judgement is to be understood here as the end, not of the universe as such, but of Urizenic error, of the created illusion. It is the 'overwhelming' of 'Bad Art' and 'bitter' science by the Imagination, informed by spiritual knowledge, by Christ, the Imagination, Himself. Then His Kingdom is come on Earth — Universal Love and Brotherhood.

In Night ix of *The Four Zoas* we have seen that creative, imaginative life — as expressed through art — has set mankind on course for regeneration. But after art has fulfilled its mission it recedes into the background. After Los has initiated the process of the reawakening to the reality of Eternity[237] he is given a very minor role in the remainder of the Night. In fact, at the very end, when Urthona is 'in all ancient strength',[238] then 'the Spectre Los', 'the Spectre of Prophecy'[239] disappears.

We could understand this to mean that imaginative creativity has finally been cleansed of all traces of negating reason, of the 'poison' of spectrehood, which would, if it persisted, be destructive of inspiration. This is, no doubt, quite a true understanding of Blake's intention. But it seems more in tune with Blakean universality to suggest that he means more than this: that art is not an end, but only a means, a language of imaginative knowledge; moreover, that art itself must not set itself up on a pedestal to be worshipped. The worship of artistic creativity can itself be idolatrous. Any form of idolatory is anathema to Blake. What Blake seems to be indicating here is that we would be guilty of error if we were to fall into the trap of thinking that the ideal of human existence is synonymous with creativity for the sake of creativity.

Los, having fulfilled his role as pioneering spirit in the process of regeneration, departs, but Urthona, Los's primal self, restored to his original strength, has resumed his essential function, which is 'to form the golden armour of science/ For Intellectual war'. His task is not that of fighting the war himself, but to make the 'Sword', 'Spear', 'Bow' and 'Arrows', so that men and women may arm themselves and never cease 'From Mental Fight' till they

> ... have built Jerusalem
> In England's green and pleasant land.[240]

Blake, in short, does not place the artist above, but rather as the servant to, the rest of humanity. As if to emphasize the role of the regenerated artist as the servant rather than the lord of mankind, Blake here equates Urthona with Hephaestus, the lame smith of the Greek pantheon.[241] The stature of the artist is reduced, as it were. He is even shown as having to be supported by Tharmas.

Blake's concern is not restricted to the artist. His concern embraces the whole of humanity. He sees it as his task to help all men and women explore inwards into spiritual reality, into essences, and thus to expand into the bosom of Christ, Universal Man. His concern is with the resurrection to unity; with the reattainment of full humanity by every human being — be she a harlot or virgin, be he beggar or king; with Universal Brotherhood and Love.

THE REBIRTH OF VISION

After the well-known lyric with which Blake begins *Milton*[1] he quotes Moses' words in answer to Joshua's urging that Eldad and Medad be prevented from prophesying in the camp: 'Would to God that all the Lord's people were Prophets.'[2] In the lyric Blake expresses the hope that all men will participate with him in building the community of universal brotherhood, the City of Peace and Liberty, Jerusalem. Blake emphasizes here the message of the prose preface which precedes the lyric. There he calls upon 'Young Men of the New Age' to 'Rouze up' and 'set' their 'foreheads against the ignorant Hirelings! For we have Hirelings in the Camp, the Court & the University, who would, if they could, for ever depress Mental and prolong Corporeal War.'[3] This idea of the development of creative vision by the whole human community, for every man and woman is a potential creator, a potential artist, comes to clear expression in Blake's last great epic, *Jerusalem*.

The concluding pages of this epic poem, with which we shall primarily concern ourselves in this chapter, confirm and underline its dominant theme: the loss and rebirth of Vision. Before considering these pages in some detail, a few words are in order regarding (1) the cosmology of *Jerusalem*; (2) Blake's conception of Albion and of Albion's Emanation, Jerusalem; and (3) the structure and themes of each chapter.

In *Jerusalem* Blake's cosmology is more developed than in any of his previous works. In Eden, the spiritual world, Divine Vision enfolds everyone. There man is truly spiritually alive and creative. Around Eden is Beulah, a place of rest for weary spirits from the 'warfare' of ideas of Eden.[4] It is also a place which mortals may 'see' and 'enter' in dreams. Beyond Beulah is the vegetative world, the world of generation. This world is essential to Blake's conception of Providence, for without it the Incarnation would be impossible. Furthest of all from Eden is Ulro, or chaos, the 'place' of non-entity and formlessness.[5] But the Eternals in

Eden care for those in Ulro, and Los, Imagination, is given the task of building and rebuilding the city of Golgonooza, which, foursquare like the New Jerusalem, not only guards against chaos, but is also a 'refuge' for those souls who are striving to rise out of chaos.

Albion is the Eternal Man whom we have already met in *The Four Zoas*.[6] Jerusalem is his Emanation. Here Blake draws upon all the resources of the Old Testament love for the Holy City and fuses them with the significance of Jerusalem as the city where Christ was crucified and its final reappearance as the Bride of the Lamb in Revelation. As in *The Four Zoas*, and in *Milton*, the dominant myth in *Jerusalem* is that of the sleep of the Eternal Man and the consequent disorder of various forces within his soul — and spiritual activity. In *Jerusalem*, the Fall and Resurrection of Albion are studied in much more detail than in *The Four Zoas*, where, as we have seen, the conflicts between the Zoas form the main theme. In *Jerusalem*, Los, the major positive force, is the central figure of the poem. Admittedly, Albion himself being 'darkened', spiritually asleep, Los is, *ipso facto*, also without true vision, but, by his courageous use of creative energies, he nevertheless continues to act as the guardian of Vision throughout the dark period of its eclipse.[7]

Whereas in *The Four Zoas* Albion is described as being the father of all mankind[8] — corresponding to the Adam Kadmon of the Kabbalists, in *Jerusalem* Blake specifies that the Universal Man is to be seen in Albion, in Britain, on his island-rock, rather than as an ancestor of the Jews. In short, in *Jerusalem*, we see a personified Albion who subsumes all Britons — past, present and future — together with their island. However, Blake is not guilty of false patriotism here, for, towards the end of the first chapter of *Jerusalem*, we learn that Albion remembers the primal concord of all nations:

In the Exchanges of London every Nation walk'd,
And London walk'd in every Nation, mutual in love & harmony.
Albion cover'd the whole Earth, England encompass'd the Nations,
Mutual each within other's bosoms in Visions of Regeneration.[9]

Albion is also to be seen as an 'entity'. We could say that he is a 'person' himself, looking upon and interacting with his own elements — primarily, in *Jerusalem*, with the Britons, whom Blake calls Sons and Daughters of Albion.

Albion is clearly more than a personification. He is an eternal reality, a living spiritual being in Eden. In Blake's vision, a person, a spiritual being, in Eternity attains a wholeness completely unknown and unattainable in vegetative, earthly life. All the opposing principles and characteristics of life on earth — vitally necessary for an evolving community — are harmoniously blended together in Eternity. Ordinary men and women on earth cannot fully experience characteristics other than their own. Man cannot really know, in his ordinary everyday consciousness, what it is to be a piece of metal, a plant or a four-legged animal. In Eternity, in the spiritual world, however, Blake sees the individual spiritual being able to contain all these forms — and their experiences — within himself:

> All Human Forms identified, even Tree, Metal, Earth & Stone: all
> Human Forms identified, living, going forth & returning wearied
> Into the Planetary Lives of Years, Months, Days & Hours; reposing
> And then Awakening into his Bosom in the Life of Immortality.[10]

Every person in his earthly frame is part of the eternal Albion.

The final line of the poem, following on those just quoted, is:

And I heard the Name of their Emanation: they are named Jerusalem.[11]

In the title of the poem Blake refers to his vision of 'Jerusalem, The Emanation of the Giant Albion'.[12] At the outset, then, Blake is saying that Albion, encompassing all the nations, should look towards the coming of the New Jerusalem as described in Revelation.

As in the Bible, Blake's Jerusalem appears in many forms. For instance, as the City of Peace, Liberty and Universal Brotherhood, besieged by Babylon, the City of Lust, by natural religion or deism, by the Goddess of Nature, and by moral virtue (i.e. the state Rahab).[13] She also appears as a woman, led astray and captive by Babylon, or redeemed, and a bride of Eternity. As the Bride of the Lamb[14] she is communion with God, 'the Mystic Union of the Emanation in the Lord'.[15] Orthodoxy interprets the marriage of the Lamb and Jerusalem as the Union of Christ and His Church. Blake extends the meaning of 'Church' to signify not only the whole of mankind but the whole of nature too, united in the mystical ecstasy.[16]

In *Jerusalem* Blake unites the two notions of Albion and Jerusalem in a remarkable way. Albion is envisaged in universal greatness in the realms of ideal truth; Jerusalem is envisaged as being the goal to be realized in everyday life — at home, in England, anywhere. As in *The Four Zoas* and in *Milton*, so also in *Jerusalem* Albion is asleep, that is, he is sunk in the deadly sleep of materialism. He dreams perverted ambitions of war and conquest;[17] he is trapped by mistaken laws of righteousness,[18] and is consequently unable to wake to the vision — and freedom — of his true destiny, which is embodied in Jerusalem. He scorns her love and forgiveness as folly. Christ, through Blake, cries repeatedly to Albion:

> Awake awake O sleeper of the land of shadows, wake! expand!
> I am in you and you in me, mutual in love divine:
> Fibres of love from man to man thro' Albion's pleasant land.
> ...return Albion! return!
> Thy brethren call thee, and thy fathers and thy sons,
> Thy nurses and thy mothers, thy sisters and thy daughters
> Weep at thy soul's disease, and the Divine Vision is darken'd,
> Thy Emanation that was wont to play before thy face,
> Beaming forth with her daughters into the Divine bosom:
> Where hast thou hidden thy Emanation, lovely Jerusalem,
> From the vision and fruition of the Holy-one?
> I am not a God afar off, I am a brother and friend;
> Within your bosoms I reside, and you reside in me:
> Lo! we are One, forgiving all Evil, Not seeking recompense.
> Ye are my members, O ye sleepers of Beulah, land of shades![19]

The 'sleepers' — Albion, all of us — are called on not only to wake but to 'expand', for we cannot be saved but by 'expanded' perception.

All the themes of *Jerusalem* are heard in these lines. Here we note particularly that the 'sleeper of the land of shadows' is he who has fallen from unity into division, from Imagination into limited memories, from 'Existence' into the 'Void'. Christ, God, is not an abstract being but is a brother and a friend Who can exist among human beings on earth and manifest Himself in human relationships. In the bosoms of awakened men, in whom Christ resides, imaginative 'fibres of love' join men, in freedom, one to another, in universal brotherhood. Such love must exist, if England, if mankind, is to be liberated from the 'vegetative' fibres which form the chains of selfhood and jealousy. A nation, a society, which is free from self-righteousness and Urizenic suppression of man by man, is the Emanation of the Divine. It is to this Divine Vision that Blake urges us to hold.

In a Urizenic/Newtonian world man is spiritually asleep. He then, like

> ... the perturbed Man away turns down the valleys dark;
> Saying, we are not One: we are Many ...[20]

The denial of unity is also a denial of the reality of vision. The Divine Vision is darkened. Blake is alluding here to the cry of wisdom in Proverbs.[21] Divine Wisdom, Jerusalem, is hidden by man himself when he formulates the delusory idea that God is a Heavenly Father hidden beyond the skies. Jerusalem is the 'Emanation' of the 'Divine Vision' manifest in selfless and loving human relationships.

Albion, spiritually asleep, rejects Christ and, jealous, hides Jerusalem, his Emanation, who should be the Bride of the Lamb. But Los, the personification of the imaginative spirit, continues to struggle against the perverted visions of Albion and of Albion's children (that is, ordinary men and women). Blake identifies himself with Los, the true artist, but Los is greater than any one man. Whenever a man or woman sees visions of Eternity and gives them freely to the world of humanity — in the living and creative form of a simple or a great deed — the spirit of Los is awake and active. Los himself cannot bring about the millennium when Albion will awake, but he can keep the possibility of that day, when the New Jerusalem will be built, continually alive before us. He can work ceaselessly towards that day when Albion will be reunited with his Emanation, Jerusalem, and thus be redeemed.[22]

The structure of the poem *Jerusalem* is founded upon an antithesis between two contrary forces which metamorphoses and intensifies from chapter to chapter.

In the first chapter these contraries are between the tendency towards mental chaos and the organizing and creative element. In this chapter Blake describes the origins of Albion's spiritual sickness. It has two main themes: Albion's state, and the labours of Los, who ceaselessly struggles to contain the evils, the errors, resulting from Albion's spiritual sleep.

In the second chapter we see that this antithesis takes the form of the process by which Los seeks to create an image of salvation from the repetitive cycle of nature that Albion has fallen into. We witness the further weakening of Albion. This chapter is addressed to the Jews and the theme is the growth and triumph of moral law, resulting in the tyranny of the nation's leaders, the harsh and righteous judgements of the Church, and the abstract reasonings of Urizenic scientists and philosophers.

This process, in the third chapter, is intensified in the opposition between deism and Blake's conception of Christ. Here we witness the growth of rationalism against the confused and perverted background of war. The Spectre (reason) proclaims himself God.

From the opposition we witness in the third chapter there crystallizes, in the fourth and final chapter, a clarifying confrontation between Truth and Error, which, catalystically, causes a Last Judgement, a spiritual awakening to begin. This chapter, addressed to the Christians, contains the triumph of the Female Will (see p. 273 and note) — the epitome of all errors.[23] This triumph is no more than transitory, however, and is finally overcome by the self-sacrifice of Albion, which leads on to the final reunion of all things.

*****

The final awakening of Albion and the redemption of Jerusalem is described in the last few plates of *Jerusalem*. The poem as a whole depicts the travails of creation — including man — to find its true nature. It recounts a difficult and gradual opening and expanding of the organs of perception until finally the vision of the 'prophet' is attained by everyone. The work ends, as we have already intimated, with Blake's conception of the renewal of creation.

Mention was made earlier that Los consistently labours and is the central character of the poem. He is humanity's great hero. So long as his creative activity can transform abstractions into living realities, hope for mankind remains. His guardianship of Vision is the key to the new hope for humanity, for all creation. Without his foresight and faithful adherence to creative activity, Albion would not have heard the call to awaken. Let us therefore look at the activities and prophetic utterances of Los just prior to Albion's awakening.

There is a certain moment when Los is confirmed in his belief that in his eternal nature as Urthona he is the 'keeper of the Gates of Heaven'.[24] This moment of self-knowledge — the incidents which trigger it off need not concern us here — is a turning-point in the final section of the poem. From now on he asserts himself with such vigour that his goal, the awakening of Albion, is achieved. His love for Albion draws him down into the generative world. He now finds 'Corruptability [*sic.*]' appearing on Albion's limbs and resolves never more to leave the sleeper's side, 'but labour here incessant till thy awaking'.[25] His task is not easy. It involves control of his Spectre, who labours by day while Los keeps watch at night. Also, because he is not yet reunited with his Emanation, Enitharmon, he is accompanied by the Dogs of Leutha, that is, the physical, natural desires which threaten to break out into an independent and destructive existence.[26] Los experiences fierce intimations of triumph, his creation 'concentering in the majestic form of Erin'.[27] But his enjoyment of the fruits of his labour is short-lived, for he has not yet resolved the crisis in regard to his own Emanation, Enitharmon, who now appears before him enticing him into a fantasia of desire. Here we have a repetition of the scenes enacted in the first Night of *The Four Zoas*; the same pattern of strife between the two sexes:

> Two Wills they had, Two Intellects, & not as in times of old.[28]

At this stage Enitharmon still refuses to be reunited with him:

> I have Love's of my own; ...
> Cast thou in Jerusalem's shadows thy Love, ...
> Jerusalem divides thy care, while thou carest for Jerusalem,
> Know that I never will be thine ...[29]

Enitharmon mistrusts the love Los has for Jerusalem and is jealous of it.[30]

Los replies by praising the human relationships of Eternity, of spiritual relationships, where the brotherhood of man is achieved and made possible by the union of each man with his Emanation:

> When in Eternity Man converses with Man, they enter
> Into each other's Bosom (which are Universes of delight)
> In mutual interchange, and first their Emanations meet
> Surrounded by their Children; if they embrace & comingle,
> The Human Four-fold Forms mingle also in thunders of Intellect;
> But if the Emanations mingle not, with storms & agitations
> Of earthquakes & consuming fires they roll apart in fear;
> For Man cannot unite with Man but by their Emanations
> Which stand both Male & Female at the Gates of each Humanity.
> ...
> When souls mingle & join thro' all the fibres of Brotherhood
> Can there be any secret of joy on Earth greater than this?[31]

We need not concern ourselves further with the strife between Los and Enitharmon (soon to be overcome) other than to mention Los's prophetic vision that

> Sexes must vanish & cease
> To be when Albion arises from his dread repose, O lovely Enitharmon:
> When all their Crimes, their Punishments, their Accusations of Sin,
> All their Jealousies, Revenges, Murders, hidings of Cruelty in Deceit,
> Appear only in the Outward Spheres of Visionary Space and Time,
> In the shadows of Possibility, by Mutual Forgiveness for evermore.[32]

Their separation will also vanish and, with it, all crimes, accusations of sin, and so forth, will also disappar, to remain only as vague memories in a world permeated by 'Mutual Forgiveness', by mutual acceptance and understanding.

A witness to the strife between Los and Enitharmon is the Spectre of Urthona, who throughout has laboured with Los against his own will. He is not only a witness, but the cause of their division, the 'veil' which caused their separation,[33] in the sense that their mundane prides are keeping them apart:

> A sullen smile broke from the Spectre in mockery & scorn;
> Knowing himself the author of their divisions & shrinkings, gratified
> At their contentions, ...
> Thus joy'd the Spectre in the dusky fires of Los' Forge, eyeing
> Enitharmon who at her shining Looms sings lulling cadences
> While Los stood at his Anvil in wrath, the victim of their love
> And hate, ...[34]

This spectral, self-centred 'joy' prepares the way for a revelation of the mightiest of all Spectres, the Antichrist himself:

> Thus was the Covering Cherub reveal'd, majestic image
> Of Selfhood, Body put off, the Antichrist accursed,
> ...
> In three nights he devour'd the rejected corse of death.[35]

For the Covering Cherub, the Antichrist, to appear now is an omen of an even mightier revelation. Here Blake expresses his conception of the reign of the Antichrist that had to precede the Second Coming of Christ. The last line contains the idea that the uncovering of Antichrist suggests the revelation of Christ, Who, on the third day, leaves His 'rejected corse' to the devouring 'dragon' of death and rises to a more abundant spiritual life.

The selfhood is revealed as a figure of selfish holiness.[36] The Cherub's brain is described as enclosing 'a reflexion of Eden all perverted', the land of anti-vision, Egypt, with all its tyranny and 'brick-kilns', as opposed to Eden.[37] In its bosom are all the visionless cults of sensuality[38] and

> His Loins inclose Babylon on Euphrates beautiful
> And Rome is sweet Hesperia: there Israel scatter'd abroad
> In martyrdom & slavery I behold, ah vision of sorrow![39]

Both Rome and Babylon are symbolic here of tyrannizing moral law. Jerusalem, the guiding vision, exists only in the 'devouring Stomach'.[40]

The ruling power is seen as being that of the Double Female, 'a Dragon red & hidden Harlot', religion 'hid in war',[41] who 'become One with the Antichrist & are absorb'd in him'.[42]

This description of the nature of the selfhood is immediately followed by a scene describing the nature and effects of the Fall from Eternity — of which an essential element is the separation of the Feminine 'from the Masculine & both from Man'.[43]

In his response to the revelation of selfhood and the fall of man into division Los's next declaration touches a new height of prophetic vision. It centres upon the theme:

> No Individual ought to appropriate to Himself
> Or to his Emanation any of the Universal Characteristics
> Of David or of Eve, of the Woman or of the Lord,
> …
> Those who dare appropriate to themselves Universal attributes
> Are the Blasphemous Selfhoods, and must be broken asunder.[44]

The ultimate sin of the individual, Los is saying here, lies in appropriating to himself eternal states. States such as David or Eve have valid existence, but it is the task of the individual to pass through them, not to rest in them. To 'appropriate' one particular state is to create a selfhood. The appropriation of universality by the individual implies the denial of universal brotherhood and the unity of all in the Divine Family. Moreover, Los continues,

> When the Individual appropriates Universality
> He divides into Male & Female, & when the Male & Female
> Appropriate Individuality they become an Eternal Death.[45]

Here we recognize Los as 'the Prophet of Eternity' who reveals basic truths.[46]

Los's growing grasp of truth finds its most vivid expression in his next loud 'peals'.[47] Here much of Blake's wisdom, gained by a disciplined poetic vision and gleaned from a lifetime of honestly confronting conflicts within his own soul, is gathered together:

> It is easier to forgive an Enemy than to forgive a Friend.
> The man who permits you to injure him deserves your vengeance:
> He will also recieve it; go Spectre! obey my most secret desire
> Which thou knowest without my speaking. Go to these Fiends of
> Righteousness,

Tell them to obey their Humanities & not pretend Holiness
When they are murderers: as far as my Hammer & Anvil permit.
Go, tell them that the Worship of God is honouring his gifts
In other men; & loving the greatest men best, each according
To his Genius: which is the Holy Ghost in Man; there is no other
God than that God who is the intellectual fountain of Humanity.
He who envies or calumniates, which is murder & cruelty,
Murders the Holy-one. Go, tell them this, & overthrow their cup,
Their bread, their altar-table, their incense & their oath,
Their marriage & their baptism, their burial & consecration.
I have tried to make friends by corporeal gifts but have only
Made enemies. I never made friends but by spiritual gifts,
By severe contentions of friendship & the burning fire of thought.
He who would see the Divinity must see him in his Children,
One first, in friendship & love, then a Divine Family, & in the midst
Jesus will appear; so he who wishes to see a Vision, a perfect Whole,
Must see it in its Minute Particulars, Organized, & not as thou,
O Fiend of Righteousness, pretendest; thine is a Disorganized
And snowy cloud, brooder of tempests & destructive War.
You smile with pomp & rigor, you talk of benevolence & virtue;
I act with benevolence & Virtue & get murder'd time after time.
You accumulate Particulars & murder by analyzing, that you
May take the aggregate, & you call the aggregate Moral Law,
And you call that swell'd & bloated Form a Minute Particular;
But General Forms have their vitality in Particulars, & every
Particular is a Man, a Divine Member of the Divine Jesus.[48]

This speech summarizes Blake's apocalyptic humanism. Many of the
points raised have been discussed in earlier chapters. Here we may confine
ourselves to a few observations.

We need to note that Los's speech is directed to his Spectre, to every-
thing in man which inhibits creative activity. In the third line of the
speech we hear Los commanding his Spectre to tell the Giants (the Sons of
Albion) — who have previously set themselves up as deists — to obey
their humanities and not pretend holiness when, in fact, they are
'murderers' of divine, creative impulses in their fellow men. Los Blake
then unfolds the Gospel of Humanity, which is also the Gospel of Genius,
of the indwelling spirit and of joy in the genius in other men. Then, again
through the Spectre, Los commands the Sons of Albion to overthrow the
ritual paraphernalia of Christian worship. This, it should be emphasized,
it is not to be understood as iconoclasm or sacrilege. It is an example of

Blake's persistent opposition to the church of 'self-righteousness' which he sees as 'conglomerating against the Divine Vision'.[49] To turn one's back on the Divine Vision is to be in the state of Hell, it is the 'Negation of the Poetic Genius' which is God.[50] Communion — the experience of transubstantiation, of inner transformation — Blake sees as continually taking place through 'severe contentions of friendship & the burning fire of thought',[51] the agents of transformation being the strife of contraries. Los/Blake then emphasizes and supplements the experience of oneness with the Divine by reinterpreting the word of Christ: 'Where two or three are gathered together in my name, there am I in the midst of them', and 'Verily I say unto you, Except ye be converted, and become as little children, ye shall not enter into the kingdom of heaven.'[52] God can be seen only in his children:

> He who would see the Divinity must see him in his Children
> One first, in friendship & love; then a Divine Family, & in the midst
> Jesus will appear ...[53]

Such is Blake's vision of communion with the Divine.

Shortly after this speech Los declares his conviction that Albion has become one with him and prophetically states that all men and women shall be united in Christ:

Fear not, my Sons, this Waking Death; he is become One with me.
Behold him here! We shall not Die! we shall be united in Jesus.
Will you suffer this Satan, this body of Doubt that Seems but Is Not,
To occupy the very threshold of Eternal Life? if Bacon, Newton, Locke
Deny a Conscience in Man & the Communion of Saints & Angels,
Contemning [sic.] the Divine Vision & Fruition, Worshipping the Deus
Of the Heathen, The God of This World, & the Goddess Nature,
Mystery, Babylon the Great, The Druid Dragon & hidden Harlot,
Is it not that Signal of the Morning which was told us in the Beginning?[54]

The nadir of existence has been plumbed and now the 'ascent' can begin.

The 'waking death' is an allusion to the forthcoming awakening of Albion from his sleep of death in materialism. If materialism denies eternal spiritual life, and if natural religion leads to the worship of Mystery, then a nadir has been reached in the life and history of mankind. Such a point, Blake affirms, is the promised signal of apocalypse in the Bible.[55]

It is at this point that Los's firm adherence to his prophetic and creative role brings its reward — Albion begins to awaken:

Time was finished! The Breath Divine breathed over Albion.[56]

This sudden climax is the act of divinity forseen by Los.

'England, who is Britannia'[57] awakes from death on Albion's bosom. She is the feminine aspect of Albion, a compound of Jerusalem and Vala.[58] This is the beginning of the redemption of Albion. He, in turn, awakes his true Emanation, Jerusalem.[59]

Britannia awakes 'pale & cold',[60] and is immediately aware of previous nightmare states in which she committed acts of 'murder' in her mistaken dreams. She cries out:

O Piteous Sleep, O Piteous Dream! O God, O God awake! I have slain
In Dreams of Chastity & Moral Law: I have Murdered Albion! Ah!
In Stone-henge & on London Stone & in the Oak Groves of Malden
I have Slain him in my Sleep with the Knife of the Druid.[61] O England!
O all ye Nations of the Earth, behold ye the Jealous Wife![62]

Jerusalem and Vala are twin aspects of Albion's 'wife'. Here she has spoken in her Vala aspect, as laws of nature and of natural religion. Such laws are 'dreams', mere shadows of spiritual reality; they 'murder' the spiritual in man. In her Jerusalem aspects, Britannia may be interpreted as being the England of Blake's vision of a New Age England, of spiritual freedom and universal brotherhood.

Britannia's voice pierces Albion's 'clay, cold ear' and

... he moved upon the Rock.
The Breath Divine went forth upon the morning hills. Albion mov'd
Upon the Rock, he open'd his eyelids in pain, in pain he mov'd
His stony members, he saw England. Ah! shall the Dead live again?[63]

The Divine Breath is the breath of Eternal Life, the wind of inspiration.

As a risen body Albion takes his Bow and 'his arrows of flaming gold'[64] and induces three of his soul-components, Tharmas, Luvah and Urizen, to assume their proper order and function: Urizen to his furrow, Tharmas to his sheepfold, and Luvah to his loom. Urthona, of course, in his 'Vehicular Form'[65] of Los, has continued throughout his labours:

Therefore the Sons of Eden praise Urthona's Spectre* in songs
Because he kept the Divine Vision in time of trouble.[66]

The praise for Los is not dedicated to him alone, but to all men and women who, as 'artists', have kept their vision throughout times of

*i.e. Los separated from Enitharmon.

adversity, that is, of Urizenic suppression and exploitation of creative imagination and energy.

Now, at last, the time has come for Britannia, in anticipation of the awaking of Jerusalem, to assume her place in Albion's heart:

> As the Sun & Moon lead forward the Visions of Heaven & Earth
> England, who is Brittannia, entered Albion's bosom rejoicing.[67]

After this reunion between Britannia and himself and the re-integration of 'the Four Elements'[68] Albion can resume his total humanity. Here we may remind ourselves of the statement made earlier in this chapter. With the exception of Los, the activities of the Zoas are less prominent in *Jerusalem* than in *The Four Zoas*. In *Jerusalem* it is the rehumanization, or we could also say, the redivinization, of the universe — man, nature, the heavens — which is emphasized. A universe in which every object, freed from the Urizenic shackles which imprison it, assumes its own identity.

The essential Blakean humanism of the Apocalypse is now fully revealed:

> Then Jesus appeared standing by Albion as the Good Shepherd
> By the lost Sheep[69] that he hath found, & Albion knew that it
> Was the Lord, the Universal Humanity; & Albion saw his Form
> A Man, & they convesed as Man with Man in Ages of Eternity.
> And the Divine Appearance was the likeness & similitude of Los.[70]

Albion opens his eyes and rises when the Divine Vision comes close enough to him to be sensed as a life-giving breath — an exhalation like a gentle breeze or like the warming breath of another human being. To Albion's fully integrated and expanded senses the Divine Vision emerges in the human form of another man.

In the spiritual Eden, the 'dwelling place' of the Divine Family, of those who have achieved spiritual brotherhood, everything is 'human' and can be 'conversed' with. God Himself is no longer a transcendent abstraction. He 'stands' face to face with us and lives in every human being. There is no 'dim Chaos',[71] for Chaos is the confused mind of the man without Vision. In the spiritual world there are no dark and unknown, remote places, no areas of unconsciousness. All is translucent. 'Dim Chaos' is 'brightened beneath, above, around'.[72] God, Christ, is present for the risen, spiritual body.[73] The 'Lord, and the Universal Humanity' may take many forms. Here He takes the form of creative and imaginative man, Los, whose activities have been entirely devoted to the Divine Vision and who has walked safely in the fiery furnace of the creative imagination.

Albion now perceives that his selfhood still 'marches against' Jesus Christ:

> O Lord, what can I do? my Selfhood cruel
> Marches against thee, deceitful, ...
> I behold the Visions of my deadly Sleep of Six Thousand Years
> Dazling around thy skirts like a Serpent of precious stones & gold
> I know it is my Self, O my Divine Creator & Redeemer.[74]

Albion's 'Selfhood', 'Self', is the Covering Cherub[75]; it is that self-centredness and self-seeking which Blake sees as the root of all Christian errors. It is the final error, the last 'enemy' to be revealed and to be 'slain'.

The Covering Cherub has been waiting for his prey and has yet to be dealt with. Albion, on awakening, puts off his error, but the accumulation of that error — in the guise of the Covering Cherub — still remains. The revelation of the ultimate error, of the Covering Cherub, which Albion now experiences is a sure step towards the rejection, or, rather, overcoming, of that error.

Albion sees 'the Covering Cherub coming on in darkness',[76] and, overshadowing them, fears that it will overpower the Redeemer. But Christ tells him that, although He must die, He will not be destroyed:

> Jesus replied: 'Fear not Albion: unless I die thou canst not live;
> But if I die I shall arise again & thou with me.
> This is Friendship & Brotherhood: without it Man Is Not'.[77]

These few lines form the 'keystone' to Blake's philosophy of life, religion and sociology.

Albion has yet to take the final step into full spiritual illumination, and asks:

> Cannot Man exist without Mysterious
> Offering of Self for Another? Is this Friendship & Brotherhood?
> I see thee in the likeness & similitude of Los my Friend.[78]

The very use of the term 'mysterious' shows that, though it is fading, Albion is still under the influence of the Covering Cherub, 'the false dogmas of the Church Militant'.[79] The final resolve to take the step of 'self-annihilation' is roused in Albion by Christ Himself:

> Wouldest thou love one who never died
> For thee, or ever die for one who had not died for thee?
> And if God dieth not for Man & giveth not himself
> Eternally for Man, Man could not exist; for Man is Love
> As God is Love; every kindness to another is a little Death
> In the Divine Image, nor can Man exist but by Brotherhood.[80]

Albion's full recognition of the 'doctrine' of true friendship occurs simultaneously with a last desperate measure undertaken by the Covering Cherub, the 'cloud', for he, Albion, sees himself and Los/ Jesus being overshadowed and divided 'asunder' and he

> ... stood in terror, not for himself but for his Friend
> Divine, & Self was lost in the contemplation of faith
> And wonder at the Divine Mercy & at Los's sublime honour.[81]

Albion now realizes the extent of his error:

> Do I sleep amidst danger to Friends? O my Cities & Counties,
> Do you sleep? rouze up, rouze! Eternal Death is abroad![82]

In complete forgetfulness of his own self and fearing for the life of his friend Los/Jesus, Albion throws himself into the 'Furnaces of affliction'.[83] As he does so they become

> Fountains of Living Waters flowing from the Humanity Divine.[84]

With this transformation a new, re-formed brotherhood of man comes into being:

> All the Cities of Albion rose from their Slumbers, and All
> The Sons & Daughters of Albion on soft clouds, waking from Sleep.[85]

Men and women of all the 'Nations of the Earth' wake up from 'Newton's sleep'.

Albion, fully united with the Four Zoas, stands 'Fourfold among the Visions of God'[86] and can now call upon his Emanation, Jerusalem, to wake:

> Awake! Awake! Jerusalem! O lovely Emanation of Albion,
> Awake and overspread all Nations as in Ancient Time;
> For lo! the Night of Death is past and the Eternal Day
> Appears upon our Hills. Awake, Jerusalem, and come away![87]

The 'Bow of burning gold'[88] which Blake calls for in his prefatory stanza to *Milton* is taken when 'Albion stretch'd his hand into Infinitude',[89] and, because he is fully integrated fourfold Man, four men seize their bows:

> ... Fourfold the Vision; for bright beaming Urizen
> Lay'd his hand on the South & took a breathing Bow of carved Gold:
> Luvah his hand stretch'd to the East & bore a Silver Bow, bright shining:
> Tharmas Westward a Bow of Brass, pure flaming, richly wrought:
> Urthona Northward in thick storms a Bow of Iron, terrible thundering.[90]

Albion's act is reflected in all the four parts of his being, for all four are now united.

Albion's bow, like Blake's, is of gold, the metal signifying intellect, which, as always in Blake, means 'imaginatively used mental powers', not mere reason. And the arrows with which he slays the Covering Cherub are also of 'flaming gold':[91]

> And the Bow is a Male & Female, & the Quiver of the Arrows of Love
> Are the Children of this Bow, a Bow of Mercy & Loving-kindness laying
> Open the hidden Heart in Wars of mutual Benevolence, Wars of Love.[92]

The Bow is 'Male & Female', that is, it is whole. Let us look at this statement a little more closely.

Earlier we heard Los saying to his Emanation, Enitharmon,

> Sexes must vanish & cease
> To be when Albion arises from his dread repose, O lovely Enitharmon.[93]

That is, in Eternity, in the non-temporal and non-spatial world, the spiritual world, in purest consciousness, Divine Humanity, there is no division between 'Male & Female', or, as Jerusalem says,

> Humanity is far above
> Sexual organization ...[94]

It is relevant to note here, in passing, that Satan's, Urizen's, bow is the exact contrary to risen Albion's. It is a bow of hate, not love, of revenge, not mercy, of death, not life:

> When Satan first the black bow bent
> And the Moral Law from the Gospel rent,
> He forg'd the Law into a Sword
> And spill'd the blod of mercy's Lord.[95]

Fallen Urizen's black stone-bow is clearly that of Satan. It is made of the ribs and sinews of the 'enormous dread serpent' of nature, and the arrows are poisoned with hatred.[96] But, as we have just seen, when Urizen is redeemed then his weapon becomes 'a breathing Bow of carved Gold'.

At the drawing of the fourfold Bow of Love the Druid Spectre meets his final elimination when the 'Arrows of Intellect' and love are sent through the wide heavens. One act of love — self-annihilation — leads towards the slaying of the Spectre. Then:

> ... at the clangor of the Arrows of Intellect
> The innumerable Chariots of the Almighty appear'd in Heaven,
> And Bacon & Newton & Locke, & Milton & Shakespear & Chaucer.[97]

The Chariots here are symbols of the creative energy by which contraries are reconciled: men of reason are accompanied by the masters of poetic vision. Urizen embraces and is embraced by his brothers. They are prepared for the 'Mental Fights' of the regenerated life.

We have just seen that when Albion, the Eternal Man, reaches for his Bow, the four Zoas reach for their own bows; but there is but a single 'horned Bow Fourfold'.[98] In his description of the risen man, Blake underlines the unison of the fourfold functioning of the body and soul and the process of harmonious cooperation:

And every Man stood Fourfold; each Four Faces had. One to the West,
One towards the East, One to the South, One to the North, the Horses
                                                        Fourfold.
And the dim Chaos brighten'd beneath, above, around: Eyed as the Peacock,
According to the Human Nerves of Sensation, the Four Rivers of the Water
                                                        of Life.[99]
South stood the Nerves of the Eye; East, in Rivers of bliss, the Nerves of the
Expansive Nostrils; West flow'd the Parent Sense, the Tongue; North stood
The labyrinthine Ear:[100] Circumscribing & Circumcising the excrementitious
Husk & Covering, into Vacuum evaporating, revealing the lineaments of
                                                        Man,
Driving outward the Body of Death in an Eternal Death & Resurrection,
Awaking it to Life among the Flowers of Beulah, rejoicing in Unity
In the Four Senses, in the Outline, the Circumference & Form, for ever
In Forgiveness of Sins which is Self Annihilation; it is the Covenant of
                                                        Jehovah.[101]

The natural senses, as we generally conceive them, are here replaced by the 'body' awakened Albion, that is, by a fourfold organ of imagination. We could say that the natural organs of perception — 'eye, ear, mouth, or skin, or breathing nostrils,'[102] functioning in egotistic separation, 'shrunk up from existence',[103] are point-like contractions of the originally 'all-flxible',[104] fourfold, 'four-dimensional', risen body. Like the 'ancient Poets' Albion perceives through 'enlarged & numerous senses', for the four eternal senses are each fourfold faces — each commands North, South, East and West. In short, Albion can perceive in all directions at one and the same moment. He does not have to place himself in any one particular and isolated position to perceive an object; he is not restricted to one viewpoint or to the one-faceted directional and analytical fragmentation of natural, physical vision, but can perceive an object in the round, from all viewpoints at once. He perceives the totality, not merely the part. Risen Man, Spiritual Man, has countless organs of perception. He is, indeed, 'Eyed as the Peacock'. Together they form his creative faculty of vision. Similarly, his other senses are all-encompassing, 'Contracting or expanding ... at will'.[105]

It would be more appropriate to describe Albion's new 'body' as a risen 'activity' rather than as a risen 'body'. A body we usually think of as having a set, visually perceptible form, but the risen 'body' Blake describes exists in activity and in motion. The only visual image Blake gives of the risen 'body' is that of the fourfold chariots in motion, which is certainly beyond the powers of the natural eye to encompass.

Before trying to gain a more living picture and experience of man's risen 'body' as Blake portrays it in *Jerusalem*, it seems relevant to refresh our minds in regard to his description of the resurrection of Albion in the ninth Night of *The Four Zoas*. There the resurrection of man, of Albion, takes place through the successive regeneration of his four members, the Zoas, and their subsequent reintegration into a harmonious cooperation in creative acivity. The first Zoa to be called, by Albion, 'Regenerate Man',[106] to 'Come forth' and 'Arise to Eternal births!'[107] is the Prince of Light, Urizen. The key action of Night ix is seen in Urizen's twofold surrender: that of self-centredness and that of the quest to determine futurity with a tyrannical will and a restrictive, circumscribing reason. And the main theme of Night ix is the reintegration of consciousness into the regenerated, complete 'body' of man. A redeemed Urizen leads the process of regeneration. It is he who sows the 'Seed of Men'[108] and reaps 'the wide Universe'.[109] As the joyful labour of creating a new human condition progresses the Spectres are consumed in the fires of Urizen's expanded consciousness and re-emerge in new, purified 'bodies'. The Emanations, Enitharmon, Vala, Ahania and Enion, return to the Zoas — 'in joy ascending to their golden Looms'[110] — and the Zoas themselves all return to their proper stations. They celebrate their reunion and, embracing the 'New born Man',[111] recognize with their renovated total vision:

> That Man subsists by Brotherhood & Universal Love.
> ...
> Not for ourselves, but for the Eternal family we live.
> Man liveth not by Self alone, but in his brother's face
> Each shall behold the Eternal Father & love & joy abound.[112]

All aspects of Albion's 'body' are now 'Co-operating in the bliss of Man obeying his Will' for 'their disorganiz'd functions/Again reorganize.'[113]

In Night ix Blake is speaking to us of an expansion of consciousness beyond the confines of the selfhood and of the rationality grounded in a philosophy of the five senses. The inner development Blake urges us to go through is to take the step from reason to 'Intellect', Imagination, from Baconian atheism to a true Christian philosophy.

The Resurrection in *The Four Zoas* is founded in a harmonious reorganization of action; in a conscious re-emergence of a sensibility for the Whole which breaks through the barriers of limited self-consciousness; and, in an all-permeating realization of the power and *cornu copiae* of brotherhood. *Jerusalem* reaffirms these motifs, but the Apocalypse, as Blake now treats it, is more radical and direct in its assertions.

In *Jerusalem* the influence and the stubbornness of the selfhood are stronger than in *The Four Zoas*, and the sense of conflict and affliction is more acute because it is experienced by the central characters — Albion and his Zoas — and not attributed in a general way to society at large, to the 'Human Grapes', as it is in *The Four Zoas*. *Jerusalem* does not treat of a harvest and vintage as a necessary painful prelude to the Resurrection, but of a battle against the Covering Cherub, the embodiment of the satanic selfhood. Of vital significance also is that in *Jerusalem* Blake lays emphasis, not only on self-sacrifice, but also on forgiveness. In short, the creative energies of brotherhood are strengthened by self-sacrifice and forgiveness, on which the regeneration of man ultimately pivots.

In the following passage Blake gives us his fullest portrayal of the regenerated 'body'. The state of true humanity is revealed by the 'conversations' between men in Eternity:

And they conversed together in Visionary forms dramatic which bright
Redounded from their Tongues in thunderous majesty, in Visions
In New Expanses, creating exemplars of Memory and of Intellect,
Creating Space, Creating Time, according to the wonders Divine
Of Human Imagination throughout all the Three Regions immense
Of Childhood, Manhood & Old Age; & the all tremendous unfathomable Non Ens
Of Death was seen in regeneration terrific or complacent, varying
According to the subject of discourse; & every Word & Every Character
Was Human according to the Expansion or Contraction, the Transluence or
Opakeness of Nervous fibres: such was the variation of Time & Space
Which vary according as the Organs of Perception vary; & they walked
To & fro in Eternity as One Man, reflecting each in each & clearly seen
And seeing, according to fitness & order.[114]

Words and vision are one here — the image being evident and manifest the moment it is spoken. The creative mind, spirit, directly creating space and time, even regenerates the 'Non Ens of Death', the non-existence of death. Time and space are no longer abstractions, but immediate realities in the impulses of the risen 'body'. Los has worked ceaselessly to humanize time and space.[115] In the Edenic state, as a result of Los's continued creative activity, time and space are reintegrated in, fully returned to, man, who now creates them in the rhythmic expansions and contractions of his risen 'body'. 'True Man'[116] is not subject to temporality and spatiality as we know them in mundane life. For the imaginatively creative and inspired man, who is not imprisoned by the temporality of clock time and the visual space of the unredeemed, 'shrunken' and 'clouded over' eye,[117] time and space, as we know them with our finite senses, are rendered non-existent.[118]

In the Edenic state there is no distinction between perceiving and creating, nor between the activity of Imagination and that of the senses. The 'body' has become, is one with, the soul.[119] The senses are so enhanced that they perceive all that the creative Poetic Genius can imagine. The form of the risen 'body' is at one with changes in impulse, desire, intention and action, in that its outlines continuously change, like a flame, in harmonious empathy. The vision of such sympathetic 'vibrations' should not lead us to think that Blake is here advocating the fusion of the various faculties into one undifferentiated sense. On the contrary he is not erasing distinctions between different kinds of sensation, but puts before us the vision of each sense gaining in intensity. We may understand this in the following way: in everyday life in the world of generation each sense endeavours to 'tyrannize', dominate, the others. This is particularly so in the case of the sense of sight, Urizen's sense. The natural eye — the unredeemed eye of 'cavern'd man' (as distinct from the visionary eye) — exerts tyrannical power over the other senses.[120] The visionary eye, on the other hand, is no longer enclosed and drastically separated from the other senses, but reintegrated into Albion's fourfold 'body'. Through this process of reintegration it does not become weaker, but stronger, but now in a 'selfless' mode of operation. Through the process of regeneration, renewal, each sense gains in the same way in richness and power as it is brought into harmonious relationship with the others. Brotherhood — and therefore great spiritual strength — reigns among the senses in risen Spiritual Man. Here we may recall that any separation, be it of the senses, of the sexes, of space and time,[121] or of body and soul, is seen by Blake as a manifestation of the Fall of man, of 'His Fall into Division'.[122]

The process of reintegration, no matter how intense the process of unification may be, does not involve the loss of individuality, for the integrity would also be lost:

> Let the Human Organs be kept in their perfect Integrity,
> ...
> Every one knows we are One Family, One Man blessed for ever.[123]

Earlier in *Jerusalem* Los/Christ says to Albion, who had turned away from universal love:

> Albion! Our wars are wars of life, & wounds of love
> With intellectual spears, & long winged arrows of thought.
> Mutual in one another's love and wrath all renewing
> We live as One Man; for contracting our infinite senses
> We behold multitude, or expanding, we behold as one,
> As One Man all the Universal Family, and that One Man
> We call Jesus the Christ; and he in us, and we in him
> Live in perfect harmony in Eden, the land of life,
> Giving, recieving, and forgiving each other's trespasses.[124]

This is an important statement, for it summarizes Blake's vision of the ideal state of spiritual Eden, of the spiritual brotherhood of man, of man who has become one with Christ. But such 'identification' with Christ is always accompanied by the spiritual freedom of the individual. Individual identity, integrity, is always kept intact. Otherwise true love and mutual forgiveness, freely given and received, would be impossible. Blake constantly stresses the essentiality of individual identity. For instance, even when Albion, spiritually asleep, has uttered the words: 'Hope is banish'd from me,'[125] it is made quite clear that the merciful Christ preserves his 'Eternal Individuality'.[126] Each individual is sacred — this applies to the individual senses as much as it does to each man and woman. Of man we can say, with Blake, that to deprive him of his individuality would be to commit the only unforgiveable sin, for it would be against the Holy Ghost, Christ, the Imagination.[127]

Albion's risen and fully awakened spiritual body is engaged in an activity which is a form of speech in which all four Zoas are involved in harmonious intercourse. In this heavenly conversation — the action of all the soul and spiritual faculties in harmony — 'the Tongues ' create thunderous 'Visionary Forms'. A new, creative language is spoken. It is like the speech of the Poetic Genius; like poetry, but poetry realized, manifested. That is, the 'Tongue', the Logos, creates the universe.

As the Edenic state evolves, more and more forms of existence are reclaimed by the new 'language' and regain their divinity, their humanity, as they join in the all-embracing and continually expanding 'conversation' of the risen 'body'. Albion is now perceived as the new Jehovah, who is now no longer the God of vengeful Justice, but the God of Mercy and Forgiveness; no longer the Urizenic God of repression, but the Christ-Love imbued and renovated man, who is the creator of his own universe. The God of Mercy, Christ, speaks 'terrific from his Holy Place',[128] which is co-extensive with the risen 'body' and the newly created universe, in perceptible words of the mutual Covenant Divine.[129] This new Covenant is conveyed

On Chariots of gold & jewels, with Living Creatures, starry & flaming
With every Colour, Lion, Tyger, Horse, Elephant, Eagle, Dove, Fly, Worm
And the all wondrous Serpent clothed in gems & rich array, Humanize
In the Forgiveness of Sins according to thy Covenant, Jehovah.[130]

The new Covenant is the forgiveness through which all things can realize their divinity, their true humanity. It is a divine assent that everything has human form, that everything is holy. All animate and inanimate nature is returned to humanity, to divinity. It is, indeed, a call for lion, 'Tyger', fly and worm to assume human form. All animals 'humanize' under the influence of love and forgiveness, including the 'all wondrous Serpent'. In the final apocatastasis,[131] the plants, animals, the earth itself, and the rest of the universe, will become merged in the Union of God and man.[132] No one, Blake would have us understand in *Jerusalem*, can find heaven until all do. Spiritual brotherhood embraces all things and all men and women.

The animals enquire among themselves concerning the nightmare states which they dimly remember: states of natural religion; of the Tree of Good and Evil; of the oppression of nations; of Albion taking nations into desolation. They give voice to their awareness of the disappearance of their generative state. The world of generation is free, and, as all identities discover what it is to 'Humanize in the Forgiveness of Sins', the 'Cry from all the Earth'[133] rings out:

Where is the Tree of Good & Evil that rooted beneath the cruel heel
Of Albion's Spectre, the Patriarch Druid?[134] where are all his Human
                          Sacrifices
For Sin in War & in the Druid Temples of the Accuser of Sin, beneath
The Oak Groves of Albion that cover'd the whole Earth beneath his
                          Spectre?
Where are the Kingdoms of the World & all their glory that grew on
                          Desolation,
The Fruit of Albion's Poverty Tree, when the Triple Headed Gog-
                          Magog Giant[135]
Of Albion Taxed the Nations[136] into Desolation & then gave the
                          Spectrous Oath?
Such is the Cry from all the Earth, from the Living Creatures of the
                          Earth
And from the great City of Golgonooza in the Shadowy Generation,
And from the Thirty-two Nations[137] of the Earth among the Living
                          Creatures.[138]

And, finally, the inanimate — 'Tree, Metal, Earth & Stone' — is redeemed and returned to humanity.

In the world of Imagination, unimpeded by gross nature, when 'Man converses with Man, they enter into each others Bosom'.[139] That is, there is an immediacy and spontaneity of communication which transcends the 'clouded' and imperfect, distorted exchanges of viewpoints by people who are unable to free themselves from the limitations imposed upon them by their fallen senses.

If, as Blake contends, reality is mental, spiritual, then it must correspond to the 'form' of creative human minds. Or, as he expresses it in a letter to Thomas Butts:

> ... Each grain of Sand,
> Every Stone on the Land,
> Each rock & each hill,
> Each fountain & rill,
> Each herb & each tree,
> Mountain, hill, earth & sea,
> Cloud, Meteor & Star,
> Are Men Seen Afar.[140]

Blake makes the same point in *Jerusalem* where

> ... Cities
> Are Men, fathers of multitudes, and Rivers & Mountains
> Are also Men: every thing is Human, mighty! sublime![141]

To converse in 'Visionary forms dramatic' is to 'Enter into Noah's Rainbow or into his bosom, to 'make a Friend & Companion'[142] of the Divine Image in one's imagination, to 'humanize' all life and thus to make it divine.

Forgiveness of sins is, on the moral level, the act of entering another's bosom. This can be accomplished only through intuitive imagination. On the visionary level it is the act of 'Awaking into his Bosom in the Life of Immortality'.[143] When this happens all men are one man — as each man is all men. Then the human form is recognized as being divine — as the divine is seen in all life.[144] To awake 'into' God's bosom is to raise the temporal to the eternal and the human to the divine; it is to humanize all life:

> ... Villages, Towns, Cities, Sea-Ports, Temples, sublime Cathedrals,
> All were his Friends ...
> For all are Men in Eternity, Rivers, Mountains, Cities, Villages,
> All are Human, & when you enter into their Bosoms you bear your
> Heaven
> And Earth & all you behold; tho' it appears Without, it is Within,
> In your Imagination, ...[145]

To become One — through intuitive imagination — is another way of saying that a universe is 'within' rather than 'without', that one individual enters into the 'Bosom' of another.[146]

In such a vision everything has life and is divine, holy.

> ... even Tree, Metal, Earth & Stone: all
> Human Forms identified, living, going forth & returning wearied
> Into the Planetary lives of Years, Months, Days & Hours; reposing,
> And then Awaking into his Bosom in the Life of Immortality.[147]

In the moment of fully imaginative perception all things live as men, or as 'One Man', to whom one speaks as a friend in love and brotherhood. This is the final great vision of *Jerusalem*.

In this visionary condition all forms possess their true identity, going forth in the sublime light of fourfold Edenic vision and returning in the restful light of Beulah, of threefold vision. It is not, then, the natural cycle of the world of generation which is described here, but the eternal alternation of contrary states, of the Edenic state of conscious creative spiritual activity, and of rest from 'Mental Fight'[148] in the realm of Beulah, in which 'contrarieties are equally True'.[149] Beulah is the source of both dreams and of inspiration. It is the realm in which fresh inner strength and inspiration are gathered without which the 'Mental Fight' would be wanting in creative activity and imagination.

The brotherhood of Eden, fully conscious spiritual relationships imbued with brotherly love, cannot be described as being a restful kind of unison. On the contrary, in such relationships, if they are to be fruitful, there excels an exuberant 'warfare' of ideas and creative processes.

True spiritual life, Blake is saying in the last four lines just quoted, manifests itself in a rhythm of energy and repose — a 'cycle' parodied in the world of generation by the natural cycle of birth and death, of the natural seasons. Creative Spiritual Man periodically departs from his pure Edenic state for a restful sojourn in Beulah, but, in contrast to the natural cycle, such a sojourn in the threefold realm of Beulah is not a spiritual death, but may be likened to a refreshing and rejuvenating sleep.

The 'Human Forms identified' are the 'Human Four-fold Forms' which mingle 'in thunders of Intellect',[150] that is, human forms which speak the 'Words of the Mutual Covenant Divine',[151] which makes all things take human form, 'Humanize' — 'even Tree, Metal, Earth & Stone'.

The name of the Emanations of 'All Human Forms identified' is Jerusalem. It is these Emanations which unite man with man (see p. 344). It is through their 'mutual interchange'[152] that Jerusalem can come into being.

Jerusalem, the Emanation of Albion, is not only the community of freely creative humanity, but is also the emanative force which creates unity out of 'Mutual Forgiveness' and individual liberty. In one passage Blake shows us Jerusalem as being perceived as the translucency of the Purely Spiritual Edenic state:

In Great Eternity every particular Form gives forth or Emanates
Its own peculiar Light, & the Form is the Divine Vision*
And the Light is his Garment. This is Jerusalem in every Man,
A Tent, & Tabernacle of Mutual Forgiveness, Male & Female Clothings.
And Jerusalem is called Liberty among the Children of Albion.[153]

Here Blake makes an all-important statement. He identifies Jerusalem with liberty, mutual forgiveness, the Divine Vision and form. 'Visionary forms dramatic' are forms which are 'particular' and which are 'peculiar' so far as the 'Light' they shed is concerned. When all the 'Particular' and 'Peculiar' characteristics of man find free expression then the human harvest described in *Jerusalem* becomes divine. The Human Form Divine holds converse with every particular form he has 'identified'.

The human harvest at the end of *Jerusalem* is a visionary act describing the creative processes which build

... Jerusalem
In England's green & pleasant Land.[154]

Jerusalem is the perfect 'Counterpart' for Everyman. 'Jerusalem' is both the first and the last word of Blake's great poem, which suggests that he is concerned — first and last — with spiritual freedom. It is the ideal for society as a whole and for every individual, for on spiritual freedom, liberty, is founded the brotherhood of man. In the final spiritual union of all human forms the name of their Emanations is Jerusalem:

And I heard the Name of their Emanations: they are named Jerusalem.[155]

The final pages of *Jerusalem* confirm the poem's thematic coherence: the account of man in his primal spiritual, Edenic state; man restored to that state through conscious and creative endeavour inspired by the Divine Vision; Los guarding the Divine Vision throughout the trials of the period of its eclipse. These are the basic elements of a single theme: the loss and renewal of vision and, therewith, of universal brotherhood.

Here we should note a very significant point. Creative Man, Los, even

*i.e. Christ.

when he stands on 'Albion's Rock'[156] or sits 'on the Stone of London',[157] retains the inner urge to bring about the transformation of death into new life, to work towards renewal, regeneration. It is, indeed, a decisive Blakean theme that everything in man's, Albion's, prelapsarian spiritual existence survives the Fall in what we could call a 'diluted' or 'diminished' form and that, as a consequence, the Apocalypse is a development of potentialities which are always with us and in us — now and in the future.

The visionary conversion of which Blake writes in *Jerusalem* is, like the Word, the Logos, in the Gospel of John, a creative force. New life is created. It is analogous to the creation of a work of art, of any creative act. We may say that a work of art is the manifestation of the invisible conversation, of the interplay, intercourse, of creative forces within the imagination of Visionary Man. The more this manifestation expresses this inner, spiritual conversation, the more it communicates, 'speaks', the more it is 'humanized'. We may conceive of the act of original creation by the Word as being an act analogous to that of the imaginative, creative artist. Indeed, as Blake himself says, Christ was, is, an artist.[158] It was through Christ, the Word, *the* Imagination, that the world was created.

THE POWER
OF THE WORD

In *Milton* Blake writes:

And in the Nerves of the Ear ...
On Albion's Rock Los stands creating the glorious Sun each morning,
And when unwearied in the evening, he creates the Moon,
Death to delude, who all in terror at their splendor leaves
His prey, while Los appoints & Rintrah & Palamabron guide
The Souls clear from the Rock of Death, that Death himself may wake
in his appointed season when the ends of heaven meet.[1]

The point to note here is that it is 'in the Nerves of the Ear' that Los, whose sense-organ is the ear, creates the possibilities of transforming 'Death' so that it may 'wake' in its 'appointed season'.

Elsewhere Blake writes: 'Poetry, Painting & Music [are] the three Powers in Man of conversing with Paradise, which the flood did not sweep away.'[2] In *Milton* we are told that

... in Eternity the Four Arts, Poetry, Painting, Music
And Architecture, which is Science, are the Four Faces of
Man.[3]

And in *Europe* Blake asserts that ears can hear the 'music of the spheres'.[4]

It is Los who maintains the potential ability of man to hear the Music of the Spheres and to converse with Paradise. It is not incidental that Blake speaks of 'conversing with Paradise', with the spiritual world in which man is conceived, through art — even in reference to the visual arts of painting and architecture. For, relatively free from the Urizenic conditions of a self-orientated viewpoint and limited horizon, the sense of hearing is suggestive of the liberty of the creative imagination.

Now, a frequent Blake image for the lack of immediacy between man and the objects of his perception is the muting of nature's voices:

A Rock, a Cloud, a Mountain,
Were now not Vocal as in Climes of happy Eternity.[5]

These two lines occur in a description of Urizen's exploration of his dens and it relevant here to quote a longer passage in which they occur:

Then he beheld the forms of tygers & of Lions, dishumaniz'd men.
Many in serpents & in worms, ...
His voice to them was but an inarticulate thunder, for their Ears
Were heavy & dull, & their eyes & nostrils closed up.
Oft he stood by a howling victim Questioning in words
Soothing or Furious; no one answer'd; every one wrap'd up
In his own sorrow howl'd regardless of his words, nor voice
Of sweet repose could he obtain, tho' oft assay'd with tears.
He knew that they were his Children ruin'd in his ruin'd world.

Oft he would stand & question a fierce scorpion glowing with gold;
In vain; the terror heard not. Then a lion he would sieze
By the fierce mane, staying his howling course; in vain the voice
Of Urizen, in vain the Eloquent tongue. A Rock, a Cloud, a Mountain,
Were now not Vocal as in Climes of happy Eternity
Where the lamb replies to the infant voice, & the lion to the man of years
Giving them sweet instructions; where the Cloud, the River & the Field
Talk with the husbandmen & shepherd.[6]

Here, in the 'dishumaniz'd' Urizenic world, no 'conversation' with the Divine is possible as there used to be 'in climes of happy Eternity' and as there is between men in their regenerated 'bodies'.

In a world which is governed by the tyrannical and 'shrunken' eye, 'Cavern'd Man', who does not accept the reality of the spirit in himself or in his fellow men — or in the universe itself — cannot hear the voice of the Divine. Now, it is true that the natural, physical ear is as enclosed and externalized as the natural, physical eye, and its whorled form images the whirlpool of fallen perception.[7] Nevertheless, it remains a link with the spiritual world from which we have fallen and Blake describes its winding spiral as ascending rather than descending. In *The Four Zoas* we see

... the Ears
As a golden ascent winding round to the heavens of heavens.[8]

In his water-colour drawing 'The Ladder of Angels' or 'Jacob's Dream' (c. 1803–1805) Blake shows Jacob contemplating the angels of God ascending and descending a spiral 'ladder'. They are bearing scrolls, food and drink, and even the compasses which Blake usually associates with the unimaginative limit-setting propensity of Urizenic reason. A similar ascending spiral is spoken of in a poem Blake dedicated to Mrs Anna Flaxman:

> You stand in the village & look up to heaven;
> The precious stones glitter on flights seventy seven;
> And My Brother is there & My Friend & Thine
> Descend & Ascend with the Bread & the Wine.
>
> The Bread of sweet Thought & the Wine of Delight
> Feeds the Village of Felpham by day & by night.[9]

Poetry and painting are the bread of life,[10] music is the wine.[11] For Blake, as we have seen already, 'Poetry, Painting & Music [are] the three Powers in Man of conversing with Paradise.'

Blake describes inspiration as an act of 'hearing' a voice. The source of inspiration is mediated through the 'inner' sense of 'hearing'. This source is spiritual. It is not of our sense-perceptible world, as the materialist would claim.

The notion of mediation is fundamental to Blake's conception of artistic creation. He states on more than one occasion that he 'receives' his poetry through immediate spiritual dictation. In letters to Thomas Butts he writes:

I may praise it, since I dare not pretend to be any other than the Secretary; the Authors are in Eternity.[12]

Now I may say to you, what perhaps I should not dare to say to any one else: That I can alone carry on my visionary studies in London unannoy'd, & that I may converse with my friends in Eternity.[13]

And in a letter to William Hayley, written a few months before he wrote the poem he dedicated to Mrs Flaxman, he expresses the conviction

... that our deceased friends are more really with us than when they were apparent to our mortal part. Thirteen years ago I lost a brother & with his spirit I converse daily & hourly in the Spirit ... I hear his advice & even now write from his Dictate.[14]

Elsewhere Blake writes:

> ... when I came
> Into my parlour and sat down and took my pen to write,
> My fairy sat upon the table and dictated EUROPE.[15]

At the beginning of *Jerusalem*, in the address 'To the Public', we read:

Reader! *lover* of books! *lover* of heaven,
And of that God from whom *all books are given*,
Who in mysterious Sinai's awful cave
To Man the wondrous art of writing gave:[16]
Again he speaks in thunder and in fire!
Thunder of Thought, & flames of fierce desire:
Even from the depths of Hell his voice I hear
Within the unfathom'd caverns of my Ear.
Therefore I print; nor vain my types shall be:
Heaven, Earth & Hell henceforth shall live in harmony.[17]

In a letter to Dr Trusler Blake calls Milton himself to witness as a supporter of his notion of mediation:

... tho' I call them* Mine, I know that they are not Mine, being of the same opinion with Milton when he says That the Muse visits his Slumbers & awakes & governs his Song when Morn purples the East.[18]

A similar vision of the moment of inspiration is depicted in Blake's sixth illustration to Milton's *L'Allegro*. In the first part of his description of this illustration Blake writes: 'The youthful Poet, sleeping on a bank by the Haunted Stream by Sun Set, sees in his dream the more bright Sun of Imagination.'[19] In the illustration itself Milton is shown reclining with his eyes closed. He appears to be greeting the gift of inspiration with his upraised left hand and, with his right, to be transferring that inspiration to an opened book lying beside him. The fact that his eyes are closed gives us the clue that his inspiration is not derived from the external, sense-perceptible world — and that he is writing from inwardly audible dictation.

It is in such moments as these, 'that Satan cannot find',[20] that creative and imaginative man is awakened to new vision. Such spiritual awakenings are not to be equated with a simple 'opening' of the physical eyes, for they are due to 'inner' eyes which have been 'opened' as the consequence of 'hearing' an 'inner' voice, as the result of inspiration flowing from the spiritual world which is at one with the spirit 'within' man.

Here we need to pause a while to consider the implications of this statement.

Blake, as we have seen on several occasions, does not accept the existence of a deity who is solely transcendent, remote and mysterious. For Blake, He Whom 'we call Jesus the Christ' is 'in us, and we in him'.[21]

*i.e. Blake's 'Designs'.

With Christ, Blakean Man says, 'I and my Father are one' (John 10:30), 'the Father [is] in me, and I in him' (John 10:38). God is both 'above' and 'below', 'without' and 'within'.

Now, belief in the competely transcendent deity — a conception which, in the main, has been that of the Christian churches — implies that all knowledge of an exalted kind comes from an unknowable 'above', that it is 'breathed in', in-spired, from an external source. It involves, as it did, for instance, for the mystic, St Mechthild of Hackeborn (1240–1298), a complete elimination of inner activity as a preparation to passive reception of the Divine as something 'flowing in' from 'without'.

Blake's conception is clearly quite different. The imagination, active and creative intellect within man, is a gift of the Holy Ghost and is part of the Divine Logos; the spirit of man is at one with the spirit of the whole, and, therefore, it does not behove man to harbour the thought and feeling that he is, ultimately, at the mercy of an external domination which leaves him no direct access to the 'fountain of Life' (Rev. 21:6). To such passivity — and apathy — imaginative man responds vehemently by reminding us that we are denying the Divine 'within' if we stand 'here trembling around/ Calling on God for Help, and not ourselves, in whom God dwells'.

A most exquisite moment of inspiration is described by Blake in *Milton*. There the lark, a spiritual messenger — Los's messenger — appears as inspiration in the dawn:[22]

> His little throat labours with inspiration; every feather
> On throat & breast & wings vibrates with the effluence Divine.
> All Nature listens silent to him, & the awful Sun
> Stands still upon the Mountain looking on this little Bird
> With eyes of soft humility & wonder, love & awe.[23]

In his description of 'The Lark', the second of his illustrations to Milton's poem *L'Allegro*, Blake writes 'The Lark is an Angel on the Wing. Dull Night starts from his Watch Tower on a Cloud. The Dawn with her Dappled Horses arises above the Earth. The Earth beneath awakes at the Lark's Voice.'[24] In the picture the lark is conceived as a naked boy with magnificent golden wings, indicating his spirituality, and with a human body, thus asserting his relationship and relevance to man. Of this picture, Pamela Dunbar writes:

The Lark is a felicitous symbol for poetic inspiration, for it suggests the lofty and inspired flights of the Romantic poet as well as the beauty and apparent spontaneity of his utterances. The Lark of *L'Allegro II* is associated as well with the preternatural reconciliation of oppositions — humanity and divinity, motion and fixity, minuteness and sublime proportions, fleeting appearance and duration. His size on the plate indicates his true grandeur but it also reveals the discrepancy between the way in which he appears to mortal eyes and his 'visionary' dimensions. Both his size and his 'divine humanity' affirm that he has been perceived and depicted by an artist ... who is possessed of that Divine Vision which he himself embodies.[25]

The moment 'that Satan cannot find', the moment which heralds a new day, a new beginning, is analogous to that in which the creative artist is inspired.

Such a moment when

> ... ears have heard
> The Holy Word
> That walk'd among the ancient trees,[26]

such a moment sows a spiritual seed and helps create the gigantic apocalyptic moment in which the regeneration of the whole of humanity and the universe itself will take place. Such a moment of inspiration, of 'inner' hearing of the 'inner' spiritual voice, gives birth in Creative Man to the vision:

> In futurity
> I prophetic see
> That the earth from sleep
> (Grave the sentence deep)
>
> Shall arise and seek
> For her maker meek;[27]

Cleansing the organs of perception — all sense organs are organs of perception, not only the physical eyes — implies not only harmonious working together of all the senses in brotherhood, but, above all, the overcoming of the tyranny of the 'dark' and 'clouded' Urizenic eyes. Perception is 'cleansed' through the transformation of Urizenic 'seeing', which is spiritually blind, into an 'inner', spiritual seeing-hearing, or hearing-seeing, faculty. The apocalyptic moment, which occurs time and again in Blake, when a 'voice' cuts into 'Single vision & Newton's sleep',[28] suggests that the 'Ear' is the most potent means of breaking through the limitations of spiritual sleep. Here we may recall that Albion's 'clay cold ear'[29] is pierced by Britannia's voice preparatory to the

'Breath Divine' touching him and giving him new life. Another good example of this breakthrough is given us right at the beginning of *Jerusalem*. Here Blake begins a communication of his vision in the first person, invoking the aid of the Divine Spirit:

> Of the Sleep of Ulro! and of the passage through
> Eternal Death! and of the awaking to Eternal Life.

> This theme calls me in sleep night after night, & ev'ry morn
> Awakes me at sun-rise; then I see the Saviour before me
> Spreading his beams of love & dictating the words of this mild song.

> Awake! awake O sleeper of the land of shadows, wake! expand![30]

The faculty of 'inner' hearing-seeing is not exclusive to those with the poetic gift. As we have noted elsewhere, Blake asks all of us to help build Jerusalem 'In England's green & pleasant Land'. This faculty is present within us, within anyone, at any time. But we need to become aware of it. The visionary Los does not 'see' what others cannot 'see' — the Divine Vision, Jerusalem, the Covering Cherub, and so on — but, as prophet and creative artist, he is able to articulate moments of inspirational vision, to give them 'form', 'identity', 'outline', without which they would evaporate into nothingness. In Blake the sound that awakes 'to Eternal Life' is usually that of speech.

All speech involves, to a greater or lesser degree, the task of formulating, giving form to, an idea, an inner vision. But Blake goes a step further. For him the Word has greater power than this: he believes that it has a creative and sustaining force, that it creates and sustains our world and, in addition, has the power to change both man and the world. We see an example of the power of the Word when Albion, after having cursed Jerusalem, humanity, and himself, and, as a consequence, has fallen into the world of death, the 'Abyss of sorrow & torture',[31] cries out:

> What have I said? what have I done? O all-powerful Human Words!
> You recoil back upon me in the blood of the Lamb slain in his Children.[32]

Blake frequently figures the power of the spoken word as a creative wind, or breath of prophecy. Sometime the 'wind' is destructive, sometimes mild and regenerative. For instance, when, at the end of *The Four Zoas*, Luvah speaks to Vala 'with voice mild', she experiences him first as a 'vocal wind' and, rising 'from the dews of death', asks:

> Whose voice is this, in the voice of the nourishing air,
> In the spirit of the morning awaking the soul from its grassy bed?[33]

In *Jerusalem*, Los's 'words' create phenomena. To speak them is to call them into 'being'. When Jerusalem is finally 'released' she is 'perceived', heard, in the 'Cry from all the Earth'. Los is now not the only one who can articulate her; all 'the Living Creatures of the Earth'[34] can do so. The time which the ancients called the Golden Age[35] is restored in Jerusalem, because man is once again creator, not merely a creature. When he speaks, the creator, the 'Universal Father' speaks 'in him'[36] and the Dark Night of Death is past.[37]

In Jerusalem the Covenant between Christ, the Creator, the Word, and man is a continuing dialogue.[38] Human life itself may be called a 'dialogue'; if life is lived creatively and imaginatively it is a constant 'giving' and 'receiving', a constant 'speaking' and 'listening', 'hearing'. The original act of creation was speech, the Word.[39] Each moment in life is a creation of the Word. Every event in life, be it large or small, comes about through 'Dialogue', through 'response' to a challenge, through an answer to a question, audibly or inaudibly uttered, through a 'conversation' with one's destiny. He who can no longer respond, who can no longer 'converse', is spiritually 'asleep', he is devoid of imagination and a victim of 'Single vision & Newton's sleep'.[40] The whole evolution of mankind and the universe is a continuing dialogue between the Divine and its manifestations, between Christ and man. A true dialogue is one in which both participants are spiritually free and creative, in which each is able to speak his own independent, free 'word'. Once man has grasped the bow of 'burning gold' with 'Arrows of desire' he can converse with Christ, with God, and rejoice in the 'Fourfold Annihilation'[41] of the dark and cold night of death, of space and time, which has hitherto ruled his life and world.

Urizenic Man is incapable of Intellect[42] and cannot drink from 'the intellectual fountain of Humanity'.[43] Unless man 'puts on Intellect' and 'puts off' Urizen he cannot receive 'the Gifts of the Holy ghost',[44] the Gifts of the Spirit'.[45] It is he who receives these gifts, who enters into images in his imagination, who, says Blake, becomes one with creative Los, the likeness and similitude of Christ.[46] One of the greatest, if not the greatest, gift man can receive is the ability to create through the power of the Word. 'It is man's fault if God is not able to do him good, for he gives to the just & to the unjust, but the unjust reject his gift.'[47]

EPILOGUE

William Blake is one of the great poets of the modern city. It is true that in his earliest works, *Poetical Sketches*, he reflects the anti-urbanism which characterizes his near-contemporaries. He even explicitly dismisses the city as a source of inspiration, in favour of the country:

Clamour brawls along the streets, and destruction hovers in the city's smoak [*sic.*]; but on these plains, and in these silent woods, true joys descend.[1]

Indeed, several utterances from this early period in his life emphasize Blake's antipathy towards the city and love of the countryside. He depicts cities as symbols of corruption and stupidity.[2] Yet even in his earliest works Blake does not reject the city out of hand, but attacks it as a place where the selfhood flourishes.

However, we find the maturing Blake assuming an attitude towards the city which becomes increasingly positive. Here we need to note that

it is not fair to say that his attitude towards nature *per se* became entirely negative, but he rejected ideas of human community based on 'natural' premises as utterly as he scorned similarly grounded theories of perception and systems of theology. Stages along the way of this development are marked by the forms of cities which become increasingly marvellous affirmations of the power and transcendent value of Imagination.[3]

It would take us well beyond the bounds of these few concluding pages to go into any detail as to how Blake's conception of the city gradually evolves.[4] What we can say here is that he asserts that the city is a place of infinite richness and creative possibilities, and that it devolves upon each one of us as individuals whether a Babylon or a Jerusalem comes into being; whether we choose to exert our creative imagination or allow ourselves to be dictated to by inhuman abstractions.

In *The Four Zoas, Milton* and *Jerusalem*, we find that a large part of

Los's, Imagination's, endeavour is to create a form, or 'vehicle', for the life of imagination upon the opaque and contracted limits of fallen human nature, that is, to build a Golgonooza.[5]

The vital difference between the two cities built by Urizen (rationalism) and Los (creative imagination) is the subtle error — not, of course, seen as such from a strictly rational (Urizenic) viewpoint — of accepting man's perceptual limitations as being fixed for all time (see Prologue). Another way of expressing the difference between Babylon and Jerusalem would be to say that Urizen's city manifests a destructive, Los's city a constructive, creative mode of consciousness.

In a Urizenic city, that is, in a city in which rationalism prevails over all other human faculties — individual actions, emotions and creative impulses — Blake makes the significant point that, although the 'Chimney Sweeper',[6] the office and factory worker, are undeniably victims, repression is nevertheless not simply the consequence of restrictions imposed by an uncaring authority, but is just as much, if not more, the outcome of a passive acceptance. In other words, we ourselves shackle our spirits into obeying such restrictions, or 'bans', as Blake calls them in the poem 'London'.[7] Consciously or unconsciously we acquiesce to being 'tyrannized' by Urizen.

It is the task of the 'artist's' vision to awaken the 'vision' in his fellow men so that the city they build allows, indeed, encourages and nurtures, individual freedom and creativity. It is not the fault of the city as such, but faults which men and women bring upon themselves, which bring about the state of 'mind forg'd manacles'.[8] This is not to suggest that reason should not play a role in man's life. Blake never advocates such an absurdity, for without the guidance of reason chaos ensues. When emotion rules supreme, 'Triumphant in the bloody sky',[9] then humanity is also lost and the reaction is inevitable: 'One Law for the Lion & the Ox'.[10] As Margoliouth expresses it: 'Rationalism and planning are evils used to fight the evils of chaotic emotion'[11] — both exaggerations (aberrations) are inhuman.

Life in the modern Urizenic city of today is depicted in these few lines in *The Four Zoas*:

> ... many stood silent & busied in their families.
> And many said, 'We see no Vision in the darksom air.
> Measure the course of that sulphur orb that lights the darksom day;
> Set stations on this breeding Earth & let us buy & sell'.[12]

These are, in a nutshell, the conditions of life without Imagination: Nature 'de-natured', reduced to scientific measurement; marriage and sexual relationships debased to mere breeding contracts; and, most important from the Urizenic point of view, commerce carries on as usual.

Reason (Urizen) constructs a reinforced concrete and rigidly geometric city which is the fitting form of such a life devoid of Imagination:

In right lined paths outmeasur'd by proportions of [weight &
measure *del.*] number, weight
And measure, mathematic motion wondrous along the deep,
In fiery pyramid, or Cube, or unornamented pillar square
...
... Such the period of many worlds.
Others triangular, right angled course maintain. Others obtuse
Acute [& Oblong *del.*], Scalene, in simple paths, but others move
In intricate ways, biquadrate, Trapeziums, Rhombs, Rhomboids,
Paralellograms triple & quadruple, polygonic
In their amazing hard subdued course in the vast deep.[13]

Such a city is a far cry from the ideal of imaginative man. Nevertheless, as we have seen, Urizen's rational skills are necessary to man's full redemption. They are only destructive when set to work in isolation. We have to give Urizen (Reason) credit for the clear-cut beauty of his construction, despite its mechanical rationalism.

The ultimate contrast to Urizen's 'dry-cleaned' and sterile city is the humanized city described in *Jerusalem*:

What are those golden builders doing?
... near mournful
Ever weeping Paddington? ...
... Lo!
The stones are pity, and the bricks, well wrought affections
Enamel'd with love & kindness & the beams & rafters are forgiveness:
The mortar & cement of the work, tears of honesty: the nails
And the screws & iron braces are well wrought blandishments
And well contrived words, firm fixing, never forgotten,
Always comforting the remembrance: the floors, humility:
The cielings, devotion: the hearths, thanksgiving.[14]

Los, Imagination, the architect of this city, knows the intimate relationship between man and city. Whereas Urizen's city is a mere utilitarian construction, a substance without soul and spirit, Los's city is a spirit- and soul-imbued living organism. Imagination gives form to a city which breathes and pulsates with creative life. Rationalism, unless it works in creative harmony with Imagination, remains cold and abstract and constructs a form which reduces man to the existence of a heartless robot.

In *Milton* Blake says that 'every Space that a Man views ... is his Universe'.[15] That is, in the act of perceiving, consciousness creates its own universe. Our creations — cities, poems, paintings and so forth — are all expressions of our inner life. In terms of the creation of Urizenic cities we can say that they are 'dead', for reason can only comprehend death, only has consciousness of death.

Now, a city makes considerable impact upon its surroundings. Indeed, we could say that a nation's capital city focuses the whole country. The form of life in the capital city is the form of a nation's consciousness. The vital question is: Is it Imagination or Reason which is the forming agent? If the former, then spiritual 'death' is the keynote; if the latter, then creative life is the 'expanding centre' of the city.[16] The relation between city and country in a Urizenic society is one in which the former exploits, dominates and represses the latter. From the iron-girdered concrete and glass towerblocks of commerce and industry orders are issued which devastate the life of both man and nature. Nature, indeed, is destroyed and man's life is debased. But where the Imagination is dominant — by its very nature, it is never repressive — it, or its city, does not tyrannize or exploit either man or nature's 'green and pleasant land'.[17] On the contrary, in a creative and living city, in which love and brotherhood reign, there:

> Our souls exult & London's towers,
> Recieve the Lamb of God to dwell
> In England's green & pleasant bowers.[18]

Imagination gives a living form to nature; gives it new life; rescues it from the sentence of death and dissolution which emanates from Urizen's, rationalism's, cold and heartless abstractions.

Imagination always seeks to enliven, enspirit.

William Blake is a modern man. Far from destroying the city, the factory, commerce and industry, he would transform them — through the creative imagination — from oppressive tyrants, depriving the individual of free expression and initiative, to creative havens in which man can find inspiration and new life. In his eye of Imagination Blake has a vision of

England — of every nation — being renewed through her cities. He has a vision of the cities of the world uniting the whole of humanity in universal brotherhood.

In the letter to Dr Trusler, from which we have quoted on several occasions already, Blake writes:

I feel that a Man may be happy in This World. And I know that This World Is a World of imagination & Vision ... to the Eyes of the Man of Imagination, Nature is Imagination itself. As a man is, So he Sees ... You certainly Mistake, when you say that the Visions of Fancy are not to be found in This World. To Me This World is all One Continued Vision of Fancy or Imagination ...[19]

Blake sees the Imagination as engaged in a conversation with everything the senses perceive — a creative spiritual conversation with a living nature.

The Age of Universal Brotherhood will be ushered in when we expand our organs of perception to embrace the spiritual order which endows the universe and man with creative life. Then 'A Rock, a Cloud, a Mountain', Man and Nature, will again be

Vocal as in Climes of happy Eternity.[20]

APPENDIX 1:
BLAKE'S THEOLOGY

Damrosch makes the following points which can help us come closer to an understanding of Blake's theology:

He sought to renew Christianity, not replace it ... The Puritans fought the good fight against that triple enemy: the world, the flesh and the devil; Blake redefined them drastically, but they remained his enemies too — the fallen world of Newton and Locke, the flesh of Generation's endless cycle, the Satan who is god of this world ...

Blake's religion was never that of the orthodox, and to the end of his life he continued to assert the humanity of Jesus the only God. 'GOD IS JESUS', he proclaimed in the *Laocoon* aphorisms, and set up a kind of equation between the Imagination, 'God himself' or 'the Divine Body', and Jesus of whom we are all 'Members'.[1] 'GOD IS JESUS' not because God is confined to the *merely* human, but because he does not exist in the superhuman or inhuman fictions of conventional religion. If Blake had wanted to say only that the human imagination is our sole experience of the divine, it would not have cost him so many years of brooding and such tortuous formulations to say so. As Frye reminds us, 'Though God is the perfection of man, man is not wholly God; otherwise there would be no point in bringing in the idea of God at all.'[2] Among Blakeans, however, it is customary to deny the existence of a transcendent realm and to assert that God or Jesus is wholly human. Against the prevailing tendency to demythologize all references to transcendence and the divine, I shall argue that Blake found that he needed them and had to conceive of a Divine-Humanity that was divine as well as human. Other writers, and perhaps our age in general, have found that they can do without the transcendent ... But I shall try to show that we cannot describe his poetry fairly or do justice to its peculiar emphasis if we suppose that he simply grounds in man all the values that used to be grounded in God.

Blake's thought is so consistently religious that even the early polemical aphorisms about the divinity of man are not so thoroughly humanist as they may seem. In *The Marriage of Heaven and Hell* Blake offers what looks like an Enlightenment theory of the origin of religion. Ezekiel says that all gods will be proved to originate in the Hebrew faith, and Blake ironically adds, 'All nations believe the jews' code and worship the jews' god, and what greater subjection can be?.'[3] The nations have taken literally Jehovah and his moral code, evolving from these a grotesque natural religion in which 'the Father is Destiny, the Son a Ratio of the five senses, & the Holy-Ghost Vacuum'.[4] But an imaginative interpretation of Ezekiel's speech can easily be assimilated to Blake's analysis in the preceding plate: religion began by a poetic *animation* of the natural world, and went wrong only when it deified the gods as external beings. 'Thus men forgot that All deities reside in the Human breast.'[5] To say that there is no God outside the human breast — no vengeful Nobodaddy[6] on high — is not to say that there is no God. 'Reside in' suggests real existence, not subjective projection. And the same is true of the much-quoted statement, 'The worship of God is Honouring his gifts in other men each according to his genius, and loving the greatest men best. Those who envy or calumniate great men hate God, for there is no other God.'[7] This implies that God does exist and does bestow his gifts even though the gifts have no existence apart from human beings.

... 'All deities reside in the human breast' is a formulation intended to emphasize the divine element in man rather than to demote God to a metaphor of individual human imaginations; it is in God that the individual is freed from isolation and solipsism. Blake's position may be paradoxical, but it responds to the same problem that all the deepest thinkers of his time had to face, confronted as they were with the demolition job of the Enlightenment that Blake surveys in 'Mock on'.[8] As Hegel put it, in terms that are exactly congruent with Blake's, 'God is God only in so far as he knows himself; his self-knowledge of himself is moreover his self-consciousness in man, it is man's knowledge *of* God that goes on to become self-knowledge of man *in* God.'[9] Both Hegel and Blake would regard a reductive humanism as disastrous. If all reality is mental, then God, who is the supreme reality, must be supremely mental. Berkeley denied that anything would exist if no one were thinking it, and postulated a God who always thinks everything. Blake simply makes the relationship reciprocal: God thinks us and we think him. For we can only think at all, according to Blake, if we participate in the divine imagination; and if we do that, then the divine imagination dwells in the human breast — not in the brain, which is wrongly localized by Urizen as 'the uppermost innermost recesses/ Of my Eternal Mind'.[10] It would make no sense to postulate a God who could exist outside our thoughts, for 'Where is the Existence Out of Mind or Thought?'.[11]

Blake needs this conception of the divine because, unlike ordinary humanists, he is unwilling to give up its saving role.

Then Los grew furious, raging: 'Why stand we here trembling around Calling on God for help, and not ourselves, in whom God dwells, Stretching a hand to save the falling Man?'...[12]

God dwells in us, but he must *stretch out his hand*, and a few pages later we hear that while Los stood before his furnaces 'the Divine hand was upon him, strengthening him mightily'.[13] Los's speech is not a cocky assertion of his own divinity; everywhere in Blake's myth the divine is invoked because it is the only agent that can reverse the Fall.[14]

APPENDIX 2:
OPACITY AND
TRANSLUCENCE

When man falls from his state of spiritual perfection then, in Blake's myth, a space must be created to set a limit to his fall: 'The Divine Hand found the Two Limits, first of Opacity, then of Contraction.'[1] These two limits are personified as Satan and Adam,[2] and represent (1) the lower boundaries of man's fall into spiritual darkness beyond which the barriers to his perception cannot be intensified, and (2) the shrinking of his soul into an egotistic self-enclosed organism. 'But', says Blake/ Los, 'there is no limit of Expansion; there is no Limit of Translucence.'[3] The limits to contraction and opacity are set by the Mercy of the Divine Saviour;[4] they prevent a further Fall into Non-Entity. Of Satan Blake states that he is 'Opake against the Divine Vision'.[5]

Two of Blake's best-known designs, 'Albion Arose',[6] and the frontispiece to *Europe, a Prophecy*,[7] exemplify the contrast between Expansion/Translucence and Contraction/Opacity. The figure captioned 'Albion rose from where he laboured at the Mill with Slaves ...' expands in a great burst of radiance; he is depicted as the light-source of all the colours of the rainbow. Just below Albion's knee his radiance seems to dispel the very darkness of materiality around his feet. The ground beneath his feet, corresponding to the spiritual darkness from which he has arisen, is presented as a conglomeration of opaque pigments, similar to those Blake uses to depict the rock on which Newton is sitting at the bottom of the ocean (note the polypus beside him on the sea-floor).[8]

The contrasts between 'Albion Arose' and the frontispiece to *Europe* are revealing. Urizen, 'The Ancient of Days' (Jehovah), is shown with his body bent and contracted, enclosed in a circle. His one outward gesture is a thrust downward with his left arm (materialism) into the darkness to inscribe another limiting circle on the abyss.[9] Unlike Albion, who is shown as the dynamic radiating centre, Urizen is subjected to the elements — as is revealed by the wind blowing his hair and beard, and the clouds closing in on him and obscuring his radiance. Urizen is the creator of that restricting circle through which Albion is bursting.

Urizen appears here as the presiding genius of the fallen world, but Blake subtly undermines the traditional benevolence of the act of creation by an ironic use of pictorial language. Urizen's head is shown lower than his shoulders, a posture associated in Blake's art with despair; he is confined within the circumference of a rather solid looking and sombre sun; and he holds a pair of dividers, a symbol of mathematical science (in his left hand), in order to circumscribe the universe. The white-bearded figure is unmistakably God the Father in the tradition of the universally familiar image of, say, Michelangelo's 'God creating Adam' in the Sistine Chapel. But the way in which Blake reinterprets the act of creation (see chapter 'The Myth of Creation') reverses our customary expectations and understanding of the Father principle.

The fourth and final chapter of *Jerusalem* is introduced by a redemptive image, for the end of the age of Deism (third chapter) initiates the phase leading to the Last Judgement. Albion, arms raised in exultation (as in 'Albion Arose'), is shown gazing upwards to the Christ crucified on the Tree of Knowledge of Good and Evil. The new dawn for all the kingdoms of nature is suggested by the spiritual sun rising in the west.[10] In this glorious image (plate 76) Blake brings together Albion's awakening from spiritual sleep with Christ's cosmic deed of sacrifice.

In the final stage of the engraving of 'Albion Arose', dating from after 1800, Blake added the inscription: 'Albion rose from where he laboured at the Mill with Slaves: Giving himself for the nations he danc'd the dance of Eternal Death.' The exultant image of Albion is, therefore, a 'dance of Eternal Death' for it implies the annihilation of selfhood. It is a radiant image of spiritual regeneration.

The concepts of expansion and translucence, contraction and opacity, are not to be thought of in simple terms of 'good' and 'evil'. Blake always has a 'contrary vision' in mind, in which any given symbolic organization could assume the opposite meaning. For instance, the act of creation is certainly a demonic act in Blake's myth in that it encloses man in the 'Mundane Shell', but it is also, from another point of view, an act of mercy because it prevents man from falling endlessly into the 'Indefininite'. Similarly, there is a sense in which contraction is good, as in the state of innocence when the mother creates a womblike space to protect the growing child. Opacity also has its beneficial aspect, as can be seen in both text and illustration of 'The Little Black Boy', where it serves as a temporary protection against the radiant light and heat, the translucence, of God:

> ... thus I say to little English boy
> When I from black and he from white cloud free,
> And round the tent of God like lambs we joy,
>
> I'll shade him from the heat, till he can bear
> To lean in joy upon our father's knee.[11]

The protective functions of opacity and contraction as portrayed in *The Songs of Innocence* assume quite a different guide in *The Songs of Experience*. For instance, the tranquil, angel-guarded darkness described in the poem 'Night',[12] gives way to the threatening opacity of the 'forests of the night' in 'The Tyger'.[13]

Expansion and translucence are not unequivocally good. In fact, Blake often presents the figures of warfare and bloody revolution as bright, radiating youths. The figure of Orc, the personification of corporeal rebellion against the restrictive and repressive order of Urizen, is often depicted as a bright, youthful nude in an expansive pose. A fine example of this can be seen in Plate 10 of *America, a Prophecy* (1793),[14] which shows Orc surrounded by flames, his arms extended in a parody of the exultant expansion and translucence of 'Albion Arose'. The real, 'good' solution is, Blake makes clear, not Orc, corporeal revolt, but Christ, spiritual revolution.

APPENDIX 3:
THE IMPORTANCE OF
GIVING FORM

In general terms we could compare the giving of 'form' with the act of exploring 'the interiors of the mind'.[1] To explore one's own mind, or, rather, one's own soul — thoughts, feelings, motivations, and so on — to look at oneself in a new light in an endeavour to give form to what has hitherto been largely haphazard and out of control, misguided and erroneous, to give form to what had hitherto been chaotic, formless — such an exploration can lead to an expurgation of 'dense falsities'.[2] The very act of 'exploring', of entering into, error — be it incarnating into a physical body, or examining a falsehood — contains within it the possibility of its clarification and exposure. To clarify error, to confront it and consciously formulate it, give it form, is the first step towards its exposure and, ultimately, its annihilation. The purpose of 'giving form' is to bring that which is in error, misguided, 'fallen', in oneself into the light of awareness. To become aware of one's failings is the first painful step which has to be taken in the process of regeneration. This process is affected by exposure to the fires of purgation, or, in Blakean terms, to the fires of 'affliction'.

It is the task of Los, of creative imagination, to give form to a world which would otherwise fall into chaos, into formlessness, were Satan/Urizen to hold complete dominion over it. To give form to error is an essential poetic function, or, we could say, a function which only Christ/Los can perform — Los being understood here as Christ's spiritual representative. It is either Christ or Los who sets the two limits (Opacity and Contraction) to prevent man from falling completely into 'the State of Death & not a Human Existence'.[3]

To the condition of formlessness, of the indefinite, Blake gives the name Udan-Adan.[4] Los, the creator of form, therefore builds Golgonooza, the City of Art, in its close vicinity.[5] In Udan-Adan:

... Souls incessant wail, being piteous Passions &
Desires
With neither lineament nor form, ...[6]

We have seen that, in *The Book of Urizen*, the events of the Creation and the Fall of Man are instigated by Urizen's banishment from Eternity. He brings banishment by the other Eternals upon himself by first separating himself from them and then seeking to dominate them by his laws. Through his 'assum'd power'[7] Urizen devizes religion. He falls into Chaos. The creation of man in a physical form — and of the phenomenal world — is performed by Los in order to give Urizen coherent form and to confine his domain to the created universe. After the separation of Urizen from Eternity, the first stage in the Fall is, in Blake's mythology, the formation of the world, the second is the fall of Los into division, in which the sexes are created. In *The Book of Urizen* we see Los denying his redemptive role. He suppresses his fiery child, Orc, and thus enables Urizen to ensnare man in his net of religion.

The separation of reason from the other faculties of man's soul is the immediate cause of the Fall from unity, true brotherhood. As an autonomous facet of the human soul, reason seeks to suppress man's power of imagination. Los, the artist, exists in the world of generation as the voice of Imagination, of Christ, but he, too, has to struggle with reason, not only within himself, but also as a force which dominates the fallen world in which he has existence.

The creation of the form of Urizen is a primal task and purpose of Los. If Urizen were to remain 'disorganized', without form, then man would be unable to discern his true nature. By 'organizing', giving form to, Urizen, Los gives man a tangible and recognizable image of him.

Blake, in his image of the creation of Urizen, reveals the true nature of the dominant deity of the world of men. A number of illustrations emphasize Blake's intention. For instance, the title-page of *The Book of Urizen* shows Urizen in his most organized form. He is depicted as a symmetrical, squatting figure. Behind him are the Tablets of the Law (the Ten Commandments, the repressive code of Jehovah). With both eyes closed — and with both hands — he appears to be writing in his 'Book/ Of eternal brass'.[8]

Urizen's squatting position implies spiritual despair, his sightless eyes, indicate spiritual blindness — he is ensnared, imprisoned, by his own dark creation.[9]

We saw in the chapter, 'The Creation Myth', that after the degeneration of man under Urizen's laws:

> ... Fuzon call'd all together
> The remaining children of Urizen,
> And they left the pendulous earth.
> They call'd it Egypt, & left it.[10]

— Egypt here being symbolic of slavery, subjection to the repressive and restrictive power of Urizen.

We can see in these last few lines from *The Book of Urizen* a stage in the process in which man has to involve himself if he is to free himself from the dominance of abstract reason; a process which was initiated by Los in that he gave reason a 'human' form, thus making it possible for man to perceive its errors and, eventually, to allocate it to its rightful place in the human soul.

Textual Note

All textual references, unless otherwise indicated, are to *Blake: Complete Writings with Variant Readings*, edited by Sir Geoffrey Keynes, Oxford University Press, 1966, etc. Quotations are given by the page number in Keynes (K), followed by the abbreviation of the work, then plate, and finally line number(s). Thus the lines in *Jerusalem*,

> I gave thee liberty and life, O lovely Jerusalem,
> And thou hast bound me down upon the Stems of Vegetation,

will be located as K692 J60:10-11. However, in the cases of *The Four Zoas* and *Tiriel*, which have no plate numbers, references are given by section and line, thus the lines in *The Four Zoas*,

> How is it we have walk'd thro' fires & yet are not consum'd?
> How is it that all things are chang'd, even as in ancient times?

are located as K379 FZix:844-5. In quotations from Blake's prose (and from poems whose titles are not given in the Table of Contents of *Blake: Complete Writings*) the Keynes pagination is given.

Abbreviations

AllR	*All Religions are One*
Am	*America, a Prophecy*
BA	*The Book of Ahania*
BL	*The Book of Los*
BU	*The (First) Book of Urizen*
Cor	*Corinthians*
CR	H. Crabb Robinson, in Arthur Symons, *William Blake* (1907)
Damon	S. Foster Damon, *A Blake Dictionary* (1979)
DesC	*A Descriptive Catalogue*
EG	*The Everlasting Gospel*

Erdman	David V. Erdman, *The Illuminated Blake* (1975)
Eur	*Europe, a Prophecy*
FR	*The French Revolution*
Frye	Northrop Frye, *Fearful Symmetry* (1969)
FZ	*The Four Zoas*
GoP	*The Gates of Paradise*
IslM	*An Island in the Moon*
J	*Jerusalem*
K	Sir Geoffrey Keynes, ed., *Blake: Complete Writings with Variant Readings* (1966, etc.)
Laoc	Laocoon plate
M	*Milton, a poem*
Matt	Matthew
MHH	*The Marriage of Heaven and Hell*
NNR	*There is no Natural Religion*
'On Bacon'	Annotations to Bacon's *Essays*
'On Berkeley'	Annotations to Berkeley's *Siris*
'On Dante'	Notes on the illustrations to Dante
'On Lavater'	Annotations to Lavater's *Aphorisms on Man*
'On Reynolds'	Annotations to Sir Joshua Reynold's *Discourses*
'On Swed DL'	Annotations to Swedenborg's *Wisdom of Angels Concerning Divine Love and Divine Wisdom*
'On Swed DP'	Annotations to Swedenborg's *The Wisdom of Angels Concerning Divine Providence*
'On Watson'	Annotations to Watson's *Apology for the Bible*
PubA	Public Address
Rev	Revelation
SoE	*Songs of Experience*
SoI	*Songs of Innocence*
SoL	*The Song of Los*
Stevenson	W.H. Stevenson, ed., text by David V. Erdman, *Blake: The Complete Works* (1972)
Thel	*The Book of Thel*
Tir	*Tiriel*
VDA	*Visions of the Daughters of Albion*
VLJ	*A Vision of the Last Judgement*

NOTES

Prologue

1. William Blake was born on 28 November 1757, in London and died on 12 August 1827, in London. Henry Crabb Robinson reports Blake to have said: 'I should be sorry if I had any earthly fame for whatever natural glory a man has is so much detracted from his spiritual glory. I wish to do nothing for profit. I wish to live for art. I want nothing. I am quite happy.' (*Blake, Coleridge, Wordsworth, Lamb, etc.* Selection from the Remains of Henry Crabb Robinson, edited by Edith J. Morley (1922), p. 5).
2. Extract from the University of Toronto Quarterly, XXVII (Oct. 1957), pp. 10–21.
3. K794 Letter to Dr Trusler, 23 Aug. 1799.
4. K793.
5. K794.
6. K445 'On Reynolds'.
7. K407 'On Bacon'.
8. K476-7 'On Reynolds'.
9. Cf. K793 Letter to Dr Trusler, 23 Aug. 1799.
10. K216 SoE 'London'.
11. K481 M1:8
12. K216 SoE 'The Little Vagabond':1-2. In the first typographical edition of the *Songs of Innocence and Experience*, published in 1839, this poem was considered too subversive of authority and was omitted.
13. K752 EGd:75-6.
14. 'If Blake refuses to acknowledge the existence of original sin, his belief in the loss of original vision provides him with a no less exacting yardstick for the judgement of human conduct'. John Beer, *Blake's Humanism* (1968), p. 12.

15. Beer, op. cit., pp. 14–15.
16. *Kritik der reinen Vernunft*, first published in 1781.
17. *Novum Organum* I, 41–4.
18. K98 AllR.
19. K716 J77.
20. K750 EGc:41–2.
21. K506 M22:40–1.
22. John Howard, *Blake's Milton. A Study in Selfhood* (1976), p. 138.
23. K473 'On Reynolds'.
24. K96 NNR. 2nd Series.
25. Cf. K629 J10:20–1.
26. K679 J49:21–2.
27. Rev.1:8; 21:6; 22:13.
28. K775 'On Berkeley'.
29. K513 M26:44–6.
30. Agnes Arber, *The Manifold and the One* (1967), p. 85.
31. K110 Tir 8:24.
32. K659 J33:5–7.
33. K639 J17:29.
34. Kathleen Raine, 'Blake's "Eye of the Imagination"'. In *Harvest*, Vol. xxx (1982), p. 40.
35. K98 AllR.
36. Plato named *Nous* (intellect) as the 'true man'. Kathleen Raine writes: 'How close Blake's conception of the Imagination is to Plato's "intellect" may be seen from his description of the "Treasures of Heaven" as "Realities of Intellect", "the Eternal Births of Intellect from the Divine Humanity". Blake's world of the Imagination is, like Plato's Intellect, a world filled with forms.' *The Inner Journey of the Poet* (1982), p. 188.
37. K776 Laoc.
38. K614 VLJ.
39. K605–6 VLJ.
40. K533 M41:15.
41. K756 EG:h.
42. Kathleen Raine, *The Inner Journey of the Poet* (1982), p. 181.
43. K605 VLJ.
44. 'Blake's "Eye of the Imagination".' In *Harvest*, Vol. xxx (1982), p. 41.
45. K709 J71:17–19.

46. K534 M41:37.
47. K702 J66:9.Cf.ibid.6–7.
48. K976 J63:18.
49. K330 FZvii:408–9.
50. K117 SoI 'The Divine Image'.
51. K110 Tir 8:24.
52. Cf. K418 'Mock on, Mock on'.
53. K716–17 J77.

1 Blake's Christianity of the Future

1. K782 'On Wordsworth's "Poems"'.
2. I.Cor. 2:14–15.
3. K623 J5:17–20.
4. K346 FZviii:217.
5. K470 J42:17.
6. K719 J78:20.
7. K621 J3.
8. Cf. K513 M26:44–6; K403 'On Bacon'.
9. K498 M17:9.
10. K671 J42: 57, 62.
11. K210 SoE 'Introduction':4–7.
12. In his *Annotations to Lavater* Blake writes: 'It is the God in all that is our companion & friend, for our God himself says: "you are my brother, my sister & my mother", & St John: "Whoso dwelleth in love dwelleth in God & God in him", & such a one cannot judge of any but in love.' He then goes on to say that God, Christ, is 'in the lowest effects as well as in the highest causes; for he is become a worm that he may nourish the weak. For let it be remember'd that creation is God descending according to the weakness of man, for our Lord is the word of God & every thing on earth is the word of God & in its essence is God.' (K87).
13. K612 VLJ.
14. K87 'On Lavater'.
15. K512 M26:31–2.
16. Cf. K670 J42:29–35.
17. K741 J94:1–4.
18. K742 J94:18, J95:2–5.
19. K743 J96:14–16.
20. Ibid. 20–1.

21. Ibid. 23–8.
22. K744 J96:33–4.
23. Plate XVIII.
24. K709 J70:19.
25. K776 Laoc.
26. K775 'On Berkeley'.
27. K98 AllR.
28. K579 DesC.
29. K605–6 VLJ.
30. W. T. Stace, *Mysticism and Philosophy* (Philadelphia, 1960), p. 61.
31. K804–5 Letter to Butts, 2 Oct. 1800.
32. K793 Letter to Dr Trusler, 23 Aug. 1799.
33. Ibid.
34. K817 Letter to Thomas Butts, 22 Nov. 1802.
35. K617 VLJ.
36. K747 J99:1.
37. K160 MHH27; K289 FZii:366.
38. K87 'On Lavater'.
39. The doctrine of the apocatastasis was accepted by many, including Erigena, until Rome pronounced against it. But it was revived during the Reformation. Milton (*Christian Doctrine*), Thomas Vaughan, Ruysbroeck, Tauler, and many others accepted it — and so did William Blake.
40. K483 M4:11.
41. K532 M40:13.
42. Cf. K153 MHH11.
43. K513 M26:44–5.
44. K483 M4:12.
45. K646 J23:29–30.
46. K293:FZiii:64.
47. K521 M32:17–21.
48. K154 MHH14. A large part of *The Four Zoas* speaks of the exploration of 'the Caverns of the Grave' (Cf. also K558), and the 'dens' of spiritual darkness, i.e. our present physical world.
49. K679–80 J49:32–9.
50. Cf. K484 M5:19–24.
51. K659 J3:5–7.
52. K818 Letter to Thomas Butts, 22 Nov. 1802.
53. CR 255.

54. Cf. K222 BU3:6.

55. On one occasion Blake writes of his own seduction by abstractions: 'my Abstract folly hurries me often away while I am at work, carrying me over Mountains & Valleys, which are not Real, in a Land of Abstraction where Spectres of the Dead wander.' K809 Letter to Thomas Butts, 11 Sept. 1801.

56. K733 J88:3–4.

57. K805 Letter to Thomas Butts, 2 Oct. 1800.

58. Henry Murray (ed.), *Myth and Mythmaking* (1968), p. 314.

59. K659 J32:6. Cf. K661 J34:57.

60. K717 J77.

61. Ibid.

62. Cf. K97–8.

63. K317 FZvi:208–16; cf. K315 FZvi:133–8.

64. K665 J38:48–9.

65. K315 FZvi:149–50.

66. K222 BU1:4.

67. K815 Letter to Thomas Butts, 22 Nov. 1802. Cf. K387 'On Watson'.

68. K743 J96:14–28.

69. K776 Laoc.

70. K651 J27:57–64, 71. Cf. K663–4 J36:54–5.

71. K224 BU4:40.

72. K158 MHH24. Cf. K109 Tir 8:10–11.

73. K159 MHH27. *Milton*, plate 16 (illustration) leaves us in no doubt that 'the Great Selfhood/Satan, Worship'd as God by the Mighty Ones of the Earth' (K659 J32:17–18) is the God of the Ten Commandments. Here we are shown the poet — 'the inspired man' — pulling down the God of the Decalogue, 'the Selfhood of Deceit and False Forgiveness'. One of Blake's *Job* engravings (plate 11) shows Satan disguised as God but recognizable by his cloven foot.

74. K662 J35:11–16.

75. K154 MHH14.

76. K626 J7:70.

77. K771 GoP 'Epilogue'. Cf. 2 Cor. 4:4.

78. K393 'On Watson'.

79. K626 J7:65, 67.

80. K314 FZvi:116. Cf. K344 FZviii:116–22.

81. K680 J49:45–6.

82. K481 M1:13–16.
83. Numbers 11:29.
84. K158 MHH23.
85. Cf. K316 FZvi:167–75; K235 BU23:23–7.
86. Cf. K754 EGe:9–22.
87. K776 Laoc.
88. Ibid.
89. K679 J49:24–30.
90. K90 'On Swed. DL'.
91. K714 J73:43.
92. K713 J73:31.
93. K774 'On Berkeley'.
94. K775 ibid.
95. K718 J77:24–8.
96. K616 VLJ.
97. K738 J91:5–7.
98. Cf. John 14:16–21; also Blake's *Job* engraving, plate 17.
99. Cf. K158 MHH23.
100. K690 M58:44.
101. K685 J54:16–25.
102. K671 J43:2.
103. K282 FZii:105.
104. K753 EGd:99–100.
105. K433 'Auguries of Innocence' 107–10.
106. K397 'On Bacon'.
107. K386 'On Watson'.
108. K152 MHH10.
109. Cf. K718 J77:18–20.
110. Cf. K397, K407 'On Bacon'.
111. K758 EG, Supp. 1:1–4.
112. K758 EG, Supp. 2:19–20.
113. K608.
114. K759 EG, Supp. 2:30–37.
115. K775 Laoc.
116. K777 Laoc.
117. K752–3 EGd:73–7.
118. K217 'The Human Abstract':7–8, 11–12. Consistent with his attitude to humility as demanded by natural religion and his statement that 'God wants not Man to Humble himself', Blake very

rarely speaks of, or depicts, Man as kneeling before God. In fact, it would appear that there are only two instances of such a posture: in *The Ghost of Abel* Adam and Eve kneel before Jehovah; and in his description of a sketch of *A Vision of the Last Judgement* they kneel in humiliation before the Throne of Christ (K780 and K443, respectively).

119. K83 'On Lavater'.
120. K612 VLJ.
121. Blake 'illustrates' this experience in one of his *Job* engravings (plate 17). At the foot of this plate, books and written scrolls, symbolizing the Book of Life, are opened. All twelve passages engraved are, with some characteristic Blakean alterations, from the Gospel of the Creative Word, John's Gospel. Ten of these passages are from Chapter xiv, which contains the key passage (not quoted by Blake, but clearly implied): 'I am the way, the truth, and the life.' All the passages Blake refers to speak of the unity and identity of the Father and the Son, and several state that both Father and Son are *in* Man. That Heaven is 'within' Man is expressed particularly clearly in John xiv: 20 — '... ye shall know that I am in my Father & you are in me & I in you.'
122. K612–13 VLJ.
123. K741 J98:7.
124. K631 J12:13.
125. K347 FZviii:228–9.
126. Rev 22:2. Cf. K731 J86:18.
127. K630 J10:47–9.
128. K681–83: J52.
129. K777: Laoc.
130. K652 J28:15–16.
131. K673 J43:60.
132. K653 J28:19.
133. K174 'The Human Image'. Cf. K217 SoE 'The Human Abstract'.
134. Cf. K294 FZiii:95 & K655 J29:74.
135. K613 VLJ.
136. Cf. Blake's *Job* engraving, plate 16.
137. K202–203 Am. plate 16.
138. Cf. K328 FZvii: 339–423.
139. Cf. K98 AllR.: 'Principle 3'.
140. K651 J27: 79–80.

141. K733 J88:14–15.
142. Matt. 25:1–13. Illustrated by Blake, from 1805 onwards, in several versions.
143. K623 J5:20.
144. Cf. K701 J65: 75, 79.
145. The 'mark' or 'sign' of the Beast is rendered 'character bestiae' in the Latin Bible.
146. K718 J77:24–5.
147. K613 VLJ.
148. Ibid.
149. Cf. Rev. 13; 17; also K734 J89:10; K735 J89:62; K777 Laoc.; K758 EG Supp. 1:11–14.
150. K345 FZviii:157–9.
151. K670 J42:35.
152. K352 FZviii:420–8.
153. Cf. K272 FZi:290; K279 FZi:558; K280 FZii:2; K622 J4:22.
154. Cf. K613 VLJ.
155. K530 M38:37–42.
156. CR 270.
157. K622 J4:1–2.
158. K797, 6 May 1880.
159. K776 Laoc.
160. K707 J69:25. Cf.K679 J49:13.
161. K717 J77.
162. Ibid.
163. Cf. K771 GoP 'Epilogue':1–2.
164. K605 VLJ.
165. K240 Eur 5:6.
166. K779 'The Ghost of Abel'.
167. In the lower border of his first illustration of the Book of Job Blake engraves the words of St Paul: 'The Letter Killeth. The Spirit giveth Life.' (2 Cor. 3:6).
168. K736 J90:34–5.
169. K356 FZix:2–4. On the plate 'To Tirzah' (K220 SoE) Blake quotes the last clause of St Paul's declaration: 'It is sown a natural body; it is raised a spiritual body.' (1 Cor. 15:44).
170. K793 23 Aug. 1799.
171. K79 NNR 2nd Series.
172. K709 J71:17–19.

173. K775 'On Berkeley'.
174. K672 J43:12–14.
175. K684 J53:11.
176. K517 M29:32–3.
177. K433 'Auguries of Innocence':126.
178. Ibid. 125.
179. K818 Letter to Thomas Butts, 22 Nov. 1802.
180. Moments of revelation are, of course, presented to the most rationalistic of men in times of stress, acute worry, bereavement, or, for instance, a sudden realization 'out of the blue' that 'all is not gold that glitters', that life hitherto has been confined to chasing an elusive and deceptive will-o'-the-wisp.
181. K640 J18:30.
182. An instance of Vala's power to induce false concepts in the mind of man is found in *The Four Zoas*, K292–3 FZiii:44–103 — repeated, almost verbatim, in *Jerusalem*, K654–5 J29:33–82.
183. K612 VLJ.
184. K517 M29:32.
185. K606 VLJ.
186. K304 FZiv:265.
187. K241 Eur 10:10–11.
188. K605 VLJ.
189. Ibid.
190. K647 J24:17–24.
191. K481 M1.
192. K679 J49:21–2.
193. K675 J45:8–16.
194. Ibid. 17.
195. K776 Laoc.
196. K649 J27.
197. K622 J4:1–2.

2 Creative Imagination, Perception and Particulars

1. K707 J69:25.
2. K617 VLJ. Frye comments on this passage: 'The unit of this mental existence Blake calls indifferently a "form" or an "image" ... these two words mean the same to him. He makes no consistent use of the term "idea". Forms or images, then, exist only in perception.' Northrop, Frye, *Fearful Symmetry* (1969), p. 15. '"Mental" and "intellectual" ... are synonyms of "imaginative"

everywhere in Blake's work.' (op. cit. p. 19).

3. *Leviathan*, 1651, pp. 3,5.
4. K605 VLJ.
5. *Rasselas*, Chap. xliv, 'The Dangerous Prevelance of Imagination'. Engell rightly points out: 'Blake is not a stray outsider on the idea of the imagination. He is, in some respects, very much the insider, attempting to restore what he considers to be an age-old conception of prophecy and imaginative art.' J. Engell. *The Creative Imagination* (1981), p. 248.
6. K604 VLJ.
7. In philosophical terms we would speak of Plato's Idea.
8. K605 VLJ. Cf. also K517 M29:22; K709 J71:19 and K717 J77.
9. Urizen in Blake's myth of the creation. See Chapter 6.
10. K522 M32:36-8.
11. K776 Laoc.
12. K522 M32:32.
13. K576 DesC.
14. K709 J70:19-20.
15. K775 'On Berkeley'.
16. K776 Laoc.
17. Cf. Damon, pp. 186d-187a-d.
18. K604 VLJ.
19. K752 EG d:45.
20. K784 'On Wordsworth': *The Excursion*.
21. K518 M29:65.
22. K793 Letter to Dr Trusler, 23 Aug. 1799.
23. A panentheist recognizes God as an inviolable unity (as a separate Being), yet sees Him also as a presence dwelling in each of his creations.
24. 'Fallen' for Blake means being separated from God/Christ; it is not 'sinful' in the usual personal and guilt-ridden sense. The latter is, for Blake, a Urizenic 'invention'.
25. K742 J95:20.
26. K605 VLJ.
27. Cf. Genesis 1.
28. K777 Laoc.
29. K617 VLJ.
30. K746 J98:31-2.
31. K794. The term 'entertaining' is used here in the sense of afford-

ing mental sustenance.

32. K774.
33. K474 'On Reynolds'.
34. K476 ibid.
35. Cf. Damrosch, Leopold, Jr., *Symbol and Truth in Blake's Myth* (1980), p. 16.
36. K153 MHH 11.
37. K459 'On Reynolds'.
38. K611 VLJ.
39. K451 'On Reynolds'.
40. K459 ibid. Blake's attack on generalization was also aimed at Edmund Burke (1729–1797), who had argued that a degree of obscurity, that is, lack of particularity, was necessary to the Sublime: 'Burke's Treatise on the Sublime & Beautiful is founded on the Opinions of Newton & Locke; on this Treatise Reynolds has grounded many of his assertions in all his Discourses. I read Burke's Treatise when very Young; at the same time I read Locke on Human Understanding & Bacon's Advancement of Learning; on Every one of these Books I wrote my Opinions, & on looking them over find that my notes on Reynolds in this book are exactly similar. I felt the Same Contempt & Abhorrence then that I do now. They mock Inspiration & Vision.' (K476–477 'On Reynolds').

A similar statement regarding Reynold's attitudes towards inspiration was made by Blake in the margin of the fifth page of the first *Discourse*: 'Reynold's Opinion was that Genius may be Taught & that all Pretence to Inspiration is a Lie & a Deceit, to say the least of it.' (K452 'On Reynolds'). And when Reynolds writes: 'My notion of nature comprehends not only the forms which nature produces, but also the nature and internal fabrick and organisation ... of the human mind and imagination,' Blake annotates: 'Here is a Plain Confession that he Thinks Mind & Imagination not to be above the Mortal & Perishing Nature. Such is the End of Epicurean or Newtonian Philosophy; it is Atheism.' (K475 'On Reynolds').

It is obvious that Newton, Locke and Bacon, Burke and Reynolds, and all of their persuasions, are, in Blake's view, ruined by Satanic/Urizenic fallen reason and can know nothing of the Golden Age which Art and Poetry, inspired by Imagination, strive to restore.

41. K457 ibid.
42. K453 ibid.
43. K473 ibid.
44. K738 J91:21–2, 30. 'Sacrifice the Parts, What Becomes of the Whole?' (K462 'On Reynolds').
45. K466 'On Reynolds'.
46. K672 J43:19–20.
47. K738 J91:30–1.
48. The work Blake is referring to is his painting of Chaucer's *Canterbury Pilgims*.
49. K576–7 DesC.
50. K457 'On Reynolds'.
51. K565 DesC. Cf. K571 DesC.
52. K576 DesC.
53. K473 'On Reynolds'.
54. K458 ibid.
55. Ibid.
56. K459 ibid.
57. Elsewhere Blake writes: 'I know that where there are no lineaments there can be no character.' (K575 DesC).
58. K611 VLJ.
59. K585 DesC. In *The Four Zoas* we find Los beginning his process of recovery, regeneration, by drawing 'a line upon the walls of shining heaven' (K332 FZvii:467).
60. K595 PubA.
61. K585 DesC.
62. K573 ibid. Artists of whom Blake speaks with approbation include Raphael, Michelangelo, Albrecht Dürer and Julio Romano. He vehemently disapproves of, among others, Titian, Rubens, Rembrandt and Correggio. Blake's criticism is particularly evident in his annotations to Reynold's *Discourses*; in the 'Public Address' (*c.* 1808); and in *A Descriptive Catalogue* (1809).
63. 'True Science is eternal and essential, but it turns bad when it cuts loose from Humanity and runs wild, abstracting, generalizing, and domineering.' Damon, p.359 b-c.
64. K687 J55:60–4.
65. K672 J43:22–3.
66. K687 J55:51–3.
67. K737 J91:31.

68. K708, J69:42.
69. K579 DesC.
70. K673 J43:51–62.
71. K656–7 J31:7, 17–20.
72. See note 59.
73. K557 DesC.
74. Entuthon Benython — or, simply, Entuthon — is described as 'a world of deep darkness, where all things in horrors are rooted' (K296 FZiii:181).
75. K624 J5:56–58.
76. With few exceptions, words which imply lack of form have derogatory connotations in Blake, e.g. formless, general form (as distinct from particular form), indefinite, spectrous, un- or disorganized, un-shaped, soft, and so on.
77. K258 BL4:30.
78. K226 BU6:7–8.
79. Ibid. 8–9.
80. K234 BU23:2–4.
81. K258 BL4:55–. See note 85. Regarding the significance of the 'Polypus' as a symbol, see p. 73.
82. K723 J80:51–4. The symbolic significance of Rahab is complex. In the Old Testament she was the harlot of Jericho. Blake applies the name Rahab to the Whore of Babylon — 'Mystery, Babylon the Great, the mother of harlots and abominations of the Earth' (Rev 17:5; K349 FZviii:333). She symbolizes the false Church of this world, the opponent of Jerusalem and the crucifier of Christ (Cf. K351 FZviii:406). Rahab is natural religion and, as such, is the seductive harlot. She insinuates herself into the Reasoning Spectre which 'stands between the Vegetative Man & his Immortal Imagination' (K663 J63:23), and thus is the source of the materialistic system of society. The Reasoning Spectre (spoken of in *Jerusalem* as 'Hand & Hyle', 'evil' son of fallen Albion) is responsible for the Satanic Mill of the Industrial Revolution (J19:19; 43:50; 60:43). Insinuating herself into the Reasoning Spectre, Rahab 'sat, deep within him hid ... brooding Abstract Philosophy to destroy Imagination, the Divine Humanity' (K709 J70:18–20), 'to destroy the Divine Saviour, the Friend of Sinners' (K641 J18:37).

It is a characteristic feature of Rahab to remain secret, refusing to take on a definite form. But finally she is exposed as being completely in error. In *The Four Zoas* this happens at the trial and crucifixion of Christ (Night viii); in *Milton* in a Last Judgement, when natural religion is denounced (plate 40); and in *Jerusalem* at the revelation of the Covering Cherub, the ultimate meaning of which is the Selfhood, within which are both Rahab and Satan (plate 89). Being thus exposed, assuming, in other words, a definite form, she can be cast out (cf. Appendix 3). In the Last Judgement, Mystery is burned up (Rev xvii; K359 FZix:67; K609 VLJ), but it is only her errors which are destroyed: 'Sin, even Rahab, is redeemed' (K361 FZix:159).

83. K220 SoE 'To Tirzah'.
84. K346 FZviii: 201, 220.
85. K704 J67:34. A 'Polypus' — in common with the 'indefinite hovering Cloud' — is amorphous and formless. Both are characterized by a lack of an enduring and definite 'outline'. In Blake both are common symbols for materiality and the material, natural world. See p.73.
86. K304 FZiv:266-8.
87. K707 J69:2-3.
88. K703 J3:53-6.
89. K708 J69:42-3.
90. K684 J54:1-2. See p. 261.
91. K685 J53:6-8.
92. Named thus for the first time in *The Four Zoas* (K304, FZiv:265). Regarding 'sea' as a symbol of materiality, see pp. 163-5.
93. K280 FZii:19-21.
94. K360 FZix:129.
95. K360-1 FZix: 146-7.
96. K361 FZix:150.
97. In *Jerusalem*, Rahab is described as sitting deep within rational man 'Brooding Abstract Philosophy to destroy Imagination, the Divine-Humanity' (K709 J70:19-20). Cf. note 82.
98. K776 Laoc.
99. From *A Midsummer Night's Dream*, V. i. 14-17, 'And, as Imagination bodies forth/The forms of things unknown, the poet's pen/Turns them to shapes, and gives to airy nothing/A local habitation and a name.' Blake alters the emphasis and meaning significantly. To him Theseus's 'airy nothing' is the invisible

imaginative reality.

100. K514–15 M28:1–5.
101. K482 M3:7–9.
102. K623 J5:19–20.
103. K878 Letter to George Cumberland, 12 Apr. 1827.
104. K516 M28:62–M29:3.
105. K516 M28:48.
106. K516 M29:4–13.
107. We could pursue this thought further and say that the Divine Imagination, Christ, awakens the spirit of imagination in the creative artist, Los, who, in turn, must awaken the same spirit in his fellow men.
108. K516–17 M29:15–24.
109. Og and Anak are enemies of Jerusalem. They symbolize the two-fold attempt by moral and natural law to prevent the human soul from opening the heart to the world of imagination.
110. K520–21 M31: 28–62.
111. K526 M35:54 and 63.
112. K527 M36:12.
113. K618 'Descriptions of the Illustrations to Milton's "L'Allegro" and "Il Penseroso"'.
114. K527 M36:10.
115. Cf. K525–7 M36.
116. As it was also for Paracelsus and Jakob Boehme, who both wrote books with the title *Aurora*.
117. Satan and his 'Watch Friends', Og and Anak, would deter man from listening to any inspiration and from using his power of creative imagination.
118. K526 M35:42–5.
119. See, for instance, Mircea Eliade, *Patterns in Comparative Religion* and *The Myth of the Eternal Return*.
120. K509 M24:50.
121. K500 M19:21.
122. We are reminded here of Portia's words: 'How far that little candle throws his beams!/So shines a good deed in a naughty world.' *The Merchant of Venice*, V. i. 90–1.
123. K633 J34–6. The line following on the three quoted runs: 'And the abstract Voids between the Stars are the Satanic Wheels ...' Commenting on these four lines, Beer writes: 'The symbolism of

this becomes clear as soon as we grasp the antithesis involved. The Vegetative Universe exists between the two limits of Eternity. Eternity can be traced either at the heart of a flower or in the realm of light beyond the regions of the stars. Calculators and reasoners may go on measuring to the utmost limits of human perception at either direction, but Eternity will lie always beyond them: they are worshipping the mechanism of the flower instead of its heart, the abstract voids between the stars instead of the light of the stars themselves. Their diagrams to analyse the courses of the planets become Satanic wheels which bind humanity.' Beer, J., *Blake's Visionary Universe* (1969), pp. 243–4.

124. K689 J57:17–18.
125. K709 J71:7.
126. K708 J69:41–2.
127. K622 J4:7 and 18–20. Cf. K709 J71:17. The spirit of Inspiration, Christ, distinguishes Himself from the remote God of Judgement.
128. In Blake's description of Urizen in *The Book of Urizen* we have a telling picture of the processes of 'contracting' and 'shrinking'. See Chapter 6.
129. K670 J42:32–3.
130. K623 J5:20.
131. K314 FZvi:94.
132. K224 BU4:16–17.
133. K640 J18:2–4.
134. K153 MHH 11.
135. K709 J71:6–7.
136. K471 'On Reynolds'.
137. K513 M26:41.
138. K267 FZi:100.
139. K361 FZix:147.
140. K431.
141. 'This is but a part we see, and not a whole ... His knowledge is measur'd to his state and place/His time a moment, and a point in space.' Alexander Pope, *Essay on Man*, Epistle I.
142. K709 J71:6.
143. K154 MHH 15. The Cave is one of Blake's major symbols of the fallen world and fallen mind. See Chapter 5.
144. Jakob Boehme expresses the same vision in very simple terms: 'When I take up a stone or clod of earth and look upon it, then I see

that which is above and that which is below, yes, I see the whole world therein.' *Mysterium Magnum*, London (1965), p. 4.

145. K418.

146. K659 J33:8.

147. K878 Letter to George Cumberland, 12 Apr. 1827. The Democritian theory was further developed by Epicurean philosophers and others, among whom Blake singles out Franics Bacon, who, he states, 'is only Epicurus over again', and whose 'philosophy has ruined England' (K456 'On Reynolds'). Newton's corpuscular theory is of the same school of thought.

148. K659 J33:3.

149. 'Though traditional religions and Churches seem dead, their errors are perpetuated. Voltaire's worldly scepticism and Rousseau's Natural Religion still encourage self-righteousness, deny the value of enthusiasm and self-sacrifice, support the State, are legalistic, are able to pervert true vision, condemn true liberty, and allow divine matters to remain in the hands of Mystery, when they should be the province of all men's capacity for spiritual vision.' A. Ostriker (ed.), *William Blake. The Complete Poems* (1981), footnote: *Milton* 22:41, p. 976.

150. See D. Ault, *Visionary Physics: Blake's Response to Newton* (1974), pp. 54–6 and 146.

151. K90.

152. K97 NNR 2nd Series.

153. K44–63 Islam (c. 1784–5).

154. Egypt symbolizes tyranny and slavery because of the bondage of Israel.

155. K656–7 J31:2–4; 7; 17–20.

156. K672 J38:20.

157. K738 J91:30–1.

158. As Plato did.

159. K672 J43:19–23.

160. K621 J3.

3 'Cavern'd Man' and the Sanctity of True Individuality

1. K237 Eur 1–6.

2. K98 AllR.

3. Cf. Proverbs 9:17; also K194 VDA7:3–11.

4. K517 M29:32–3.

5. K793 Letter to Dr Trusler, 23 August 1799.
6. K481 M1:13.
7. Cf. K502 M20:41–2; K507 M23:22; K526 M35:39; K529 M37: 53–9.
8. K636 J15:14–20.
9. K171:1–8.
10. K154 MHH14.
11. In VDA, Oothoon is the central figure and represents thwarted love. She is the Emanation of Theotormon.
12. K191 VDA2:30–6. In the *Book of Urizen* Blake develops this image fully as part of the narrative of the Fall.
13. K189 VDA1:3.
14. K191 VDA:2–6.
15. K508 M24:12.
16. K192 VDA4:22.
17. K516–7 M29:17–22.
18. K154 MHH14.
19. K149 MHH4.
20. Cf. K689 J57:17–18.
21. The idea that the body is not a separate thing from the soul is obviously not unique to Blake. It dates back to Xenophanes of Colophon fl. *c.* 500 B.C.
22. K98. The body is the effective 'circumference' of imagination at any moment. In order that the 'Poetic Genius', the Imagination, in every man and woman may be actualized, the 'cavern' of naturalistic perception must be broken through — in much the same way, Blake contends in the poem 'To Tirzah' (K220), in which Christ 'rejects' the mother of his mortal part.
23. K90.
24. K878. 12 April 1827.
25. K604 VLJ.
26. K154 MHH14. Cf. K679 J49:21–2.
27. That is, 'Druidism', deism, the religion of Natural Man.
28. K672 J43:11–14.
29. K716–17 J77.
30. K774 'On Berkeley'.
31. K397 'On Bacon'.
32. K731 K86:18.
33. K154 MHH 14.

34. Cf. K223 BU3:37-8; K288 FZii:295-98; K308 FZv:118-126. This is what Blake means when he says that 'the whole creation will ... appear finite and holy ... by an improvement of sensual enjoyment'. (K154 MHH14).
35. K149 MHH4.
36. K76 'On Lavater'.
37. K777 Laoc.
38. 1 Cor. 3:1-3.
39. K149 MHH4.
40. Cf. CR 291.
41. K617 VLJ.
42. K774 'On Berkeley'.
43. Cf. K516 M28:62-M29:3.
44. Cf. K526 M35:42-7.
45. K818. Letter to Thomas Butts, 22 November 1802.
46. K81 'On Lavater'. 'The abstract universe which man's mind creates by 'deducting' the qualities from things is the hell that Blake will call "Ulro" — 'Abstract Philosophy Warring ... against Imagination'. Morton D. Paley, *Energy and the Imagination* (1970), p. 99.
47. K607 VLJ.
48. K777 Laoc.
49. K88 'On Lavater'.
50. Ibid.
51. K97 NNR 2nd Series.
52. Alfred North Whitehead, *Science and the Modern World*, Lowell lectures, (1925), p. 250.
53. K98 AllR.
54. Ibid.
55. Ibid.
56. K431 'Auguries of Innocence'.
57. K158 MHH24.
58. *Tiriel* is an analysis of the decay and failure of materialism.
59. K109 Tir7:21.
60. K109 Tir8:10-11.
61. K110 Tir8:31.
62. Ibid. 35-41.
63. Ibid. 42-3.
64. K360-3 FZix:123-93.

65. K689 J57:17–18.
66. K708 J69:40.
67. K530 M39:2.
68. K341 FZviii:20–3.
69. K342 FZviii:33.
70. K351 FZviii:379–83. Cf. K521–2 M32:8–35.
71. In Night ix of *The Four Zoas* the whole process takes place after 'death'; in *Milton*, the woes and sufferings involved have not merely reference to contemporary 'corporeal' wars, but can be seen in a larger context as depicting the decline of mankind in its old form — 'Ah weak & wide astray' (K484 M5:19) — and the preparation for the New Age of 'Mental Fight'. Cf. also Rev 19:14–20.
72. K483 M4:8.
73. K521–2 M32:14–29.
74. K681–3 J52.
75. K682 J52.
76. K684–5 J54:1–8.
77. K686 J55:8–10.
78. K686–7 J55: 36, 46.
79. K687 J55:49–50; 52–3.
80. K689 J57:11.
81. K699 J64:24.
82. K595 PubA.
83. K304 FZiv:268.
84. 'Obedience to the Will of the Monopolist is call'd Virtue' (K595). Blake had booksellers and picture-dealers in mind when he wrote these words, but in a period of rapid capitalist expansion of power concentrated in the hands of a privileged few and of the concomitant mushrooming of industralist power, centred in 'dark Satanic Mills', such an observation is axiomatic. In Blake's writings we can see the earlier imagery of tyranny gradually changing from 'crowns' and 'sceptres' to 'machines'. In the last two decades of his life, 'Money' is opposed to 'Art', 'Commerce' and 'Empire' to 'Poetry' and 'Painting', 'Cogs' and 'Wheels' to 'Wings'.
85. K717 J77.
86. K379 FZix:855.
87. K459 'On Reynolds'.

88. K561.
89. K716 J77.

4 Universal Brotherhood and Our Social Conscience

1. Geoffrey Keynes, *William Blake, Poet, Printer, Prophet* (1964), p. 26.
2. W. R. Harris, *Romanticism and the Social Order, 1780–1830* (1969) pp. 36–7.
3. K481 M1:8.
4. K216 SoE.
5. K646 J24: 42–3.
6. K11 'Gwin, King of Norway' 5–8.
7. K216 SoE.
8. K212 SoE.
9. See Elizabeth Burton, *The Georgians at Home* (1897), p. 33.
10. K18 'King Edward the Third' 25–34.
11. K290 FZii:404–7. See also 408–13 and 417–18.
12. See K65–88, 'On Lavater'.
13. See K383–96, 'On Watson'.
14. K65.
15. K88.
16. K122 SoI 'On Another's Sorrow' 1–4.
17. K151 MHH 7.
18. K210.
19. K115.
20. K214.
21. Cf. K155 MHH 16.
22. K115 SoI 'The Lamb' 8.
23. K112 SoI 'The Little Girl Lost' 1–8.
24. K115 SoI 'The Lamb' 12–18.
25. K111 SoI 'Introduction' 19–20.
26. K148 MHH 2.
27. K488 M8:34.
28. Cf. K272 FZi:297; K348 FZviii:274; K494 M13:27.
29. K211–12 SoE 'Holy Thursday'.
30. My italics.
31. K217 SoE.
32. In the illustration to 'The Human Abstract' Urizen, the creator, is himself shown entangled in the nets of Religion, in his own creation.

33. K117 SoI 'The Chimney Sweeper' 1–3.
34. K117–18 ibid.10–14 and 17–20.
35. Cf. K345 FZviii:176–81.
36. K126 SoI 'The Voice of the Ancient Bard'.
37. K629 J10:20–1.
38. K211 SoE 'Earth's Answer' 11–12.
39. K617 VLJ.
40. K211 SoE 'Earth's Answer' 6–10.
41. Ibid. 21–4.
42. Ibid. 25.
43. Ibid.15.
44. K211 SoE 'The Clod & the Pebble' 1–6. Cf. K129 Thel. 4:10.
45. Cf. K216 SoE 'London'.
46. K211 SoE 'The Clod & the Pebble' 7–12.
47. K151 MHH 7.
48. K117 SoI.
49. K217 SoE.
50. K117 SoI 17–20.
51. K83 'On Lavater'.
52. K775 'On Berkeley'.
53. See Arthur Symons, *William Blake*, 1907.
54. Blake did distinguish, however, between the Eternal, spiritual body, and the Mortal, the natural body. In the latter body Christ could err.
55. K98 NNR (2nd Series).
56. K774 'On Berkeley'.
57. K775 ibid.
58. Ibid. Re Blake's attitude to Plato, Aristotle, and Neoplatonism see Harper, Paley and Raine.
59. See also Psalm 82:6.
60. K155 MHH 16.
61. K158 MHH 22. Cf. K738 J91:5–13.
62. K483 4:8.
63. K738 J91:10.
64. K158 MHH 24.
65. K649 J54:5.
66. K215 SoE 'The Garden of Love'.
67. K216 SoE 'London' 8.
68. i.e. Christ, God. Cf. K521 M32:14. See also J28:26; 61:43 and

M15:2.
69. K149 MHH 4.
70. Blake discusses this theme with particular cogency in *Visions of the Daughters of Albion*.
71. K163.
72. Cf. K139–40 FR 126–7; K167 'Infant Sorrow' 36–9; K149 MHH 17–18.
73. K241 Eur 10:10–22.
74. K97 NNR (1st Series).
75. K635–6 J15:8–20.
76. Blake often illustrates falling man as being entwined with serpents.
77. K124 SoI 'The School Boy' 16–30.
78. K218–19 SoE.
79. K213 SoE 'The Fly'.
80. K767.
81. K771.
82. K767.
83. K760.
84. K617 VLJ.
85. K154 MHH 14.
86. K753 EGd:103–6.
87. K98 AllR.
88. K672 J43:12–14.
89. K604 VLJ.
90. K673 J43:74.
91. K776 Laoc.
92. K98.
93. K777 Laoc.
94. K579 DesC.
95. K717 J77.
96. K716–7 J77.
97. K413 'On Dante'.
98. K660 J33:52.
99. K689 J57:10–11.
100. K600 PubA.
101. K620 J1.
102. K709 J70:19–20.
103. K155 MHH 16.
104. K366 FZix:366–9.

105. Damon makes the point that the adjectives 'human' and 'divine' in Blake are virtually interchangeable. Damon, p. 191.
106. K748 EGa:1–2.
107. K757 EGi:45–8.
108. K738 J91:5–7.
109. K771 GoP 'Epilogue'.
110. Ibid.
111. K489–90 M9:21–31.
112. K491 M10:21.
113. K493 M13:5.
114. K510 M25:12–14.
115. K579 DesC.
116. K682 J52.
117. Ibid.
118. K222 BU4:24–40.
119. Cf. FZi:290, 558; ii:2; J4:22,
120. K670 J42:29–37.
121. K615 VLJ.
122. K513 M26:44–5.
123. K403 'On Bacon'.
124. K573 DesC. See also K480 M. 'Preface'.
125. K615 VLJ.
126. See K604–17 VLJ.
127. K210 SoE 'Introduction'.
128. K496 M14:30.
129. K495–96 M14:28–9.
130. K631 J12:13.
131. K500 M19:6–14.
132. Plate 15 of Copy A in the British Museum.
133. K497.
134. K773 'On Berkeley'.
135. K681–2 J52.
136. K631 J11:24–5. Vala is here the goddess of Nature.
137. K616 VLJ.
138. K659 J33:17–18.
139. Ibid. 6.
140. K110 Tir8:24.
141. K90 'On Swed DL'.
142. K384 'On Watson'.

143. K260 BoL 5:52–7.
144. K266 FZ 1:75.
145. K97 NRR.
146. K266 FZi:87.
147. K272 FZi:288–303.
148. Ibid. 304.
149. K481 M1:13.
150. K775 'On Berkeley'.
151. K793. Written on 23 August 1793.
152. K281 FZii:38.
153. K581 DesC.
154. K521 M32:6.
155. Blake distinguishes between 'Contraries' and 'Negations'. Negations affirm one quality and simultaneously deny the other. *Good* and *evil, beautiful* and *ugly*, are Negations. Contraries, on the other hand, are contrasting but complementary qualities. For example, *elegant* and *grotesque* are contraries. Satan is not a Contrary but a Negation, who merely denies.
156. K533 M40:30–7; 41:1–6, 12–15.
157. K645 J23:4.
158. K793 Letter to Dr Trusler, 23 August 1799.
159. K222 BU3:6–7.
160. K224 BU4:38–40.
161. The title is not Blake's, but is derived from the opening sentence: 'In the Moon is a certain Island ...' (K44).
162. K48 Is1M.
163. K48 Ibid.
164. K62 Ibid.
165. K46 Ibid.
166. Dr Robert South (1634–1716) and Dr William Sherlock (1641–1707) were both writers of religious tracts. Blake contrasts them here with the philanthropist, Thomas Sutton (1532–1611), founder of Charterhouse, a charitable boys' school and hospital for the aged. Sherlock was the author of *A Practical Discourse concerning Death* (1689).
167. K57 IsIM.
168. K59 Ibid.
169. K110 Tir8:25–33. Tiriel, the king, who revolted, set himself up as a tyrant, became a hypocrite, and ruined his children by his curse, is

a foreshadowing of Urizen.
170. See K767 GoP, illustration 11.
171. K480 M1.
172. K481 Ibid.
173. *Paradise Regained*, Book iv: 143–5.
174. K155 MHH 16.
175. K685 J54:29.
176. K483 M3:38.
177. K484–5 M5:19–6:37. See also K679–80 J49:32–41.
178. K289 FZii:366.
179. See K351 FZviii:406.
180. K595 PubA.
181. K816. Letter to Thomas Butts, 22 November 1802.
182. K595 PubA.
183. K483 M4:6–7.
184. K485 M5:22.
185. K741 J93:22.
186. K620 J1.
187. K604 VLJ.
188. K153 MHH11.
189. K150 MHH6.
190. John Beer: *Blake's Visionary Universe* (1969), p. 314.
191. K684 J53:11.
192. K171 'To Nobodaddy', 1–8.
193. K521 M32:6.
194. K679 J49:24.
195. Ibid. 30.
196. K680 J49:67.
197. K529–30 M38:39–49.
198. Cf. K220 'To Tirzah'.
199. K622 J4:1–5.
200. K743 J96:8–28.
201. See note 155.
202. K639 J17:33–8.
203. K533 M40:34.
204. Ibid. 40:35–6.
205. Cf. K738 J91:12–15.
206. K776 Laoc.

5   Blake's Symbolism

1. Much can be, and has been, said by a number of scholars about the sources of Blake's symbols (see, for instance, Damon, Harper, Raine). Our concern, however, is not with his sources but rather with what he does with them.
2. I am indebted to Stanley Gardner here. See his book on Blake in the Literature in Perspective Series, London, 1968.
3. K628 J10:21.
4. The reader is referred again to the works of Damon, Harper and Raine.
5. K623 J5:13.
6. Cf. K639 J17:34–5.
7. K533 M40:34–6.
8. K295 FZiii:142–4.
9. K144 FR:218–19.
10. K155 MHH17.
11. K190 VDA2:9.
12. K634 J13:38–40.
13. K625 J7:22. Cf. FZviib:298; M26:26; FZviii:224–9; J13:25; FZviii:227; M21:2.
14. K673 J43:59–60.
15. K656 J31:2–6.
16. K698 J63:44–J64:1.
17. K660 J34:11.
18. K662 J36:5.
19. Damon 6b.
20. K661 J34:55–6.
21. K226 BU6:7.
22. K354 FZviii:507, 513–20.
23. K251 BA3:45–6.
24. K701–2 J66:2–9. Stevenson comments: 'This does not mean "this building symbolizes Natural Religion alone", but rather that such an evil creation is derived from an attitude of mind which might create many such temples in religion, politics, or private life. Natural Religion is not an elegant creation of sophisticated minds, but a creation such as this, a refuge of despair.' (p. 767n).
25. K304 FZiv.265–6.
26. K674 J44:11–12 and 15–16.

27. K729 J84:7.
28. K702 J66:14.
29. K741 J94:3–11 and 14–17.
30. K245 SoL 3:15.
31. K339 FZviib:235–8.
32. K622 J4:9–10.
33. K508 M24:5.
34. K525 M35:2.
35. K773 'On Berkeley'; K745 J98:12–18. Cf. Genesis 2:10–14. From the 'River of Life' flow four branches — the Four Zoas:

> The Four Living Creatures, Chariots of Humanity Divine Incomprehensible,
> In beautiful Paradise expand. They are the Four Rivers of Paradise
> And the Four Faces of Humanity, fronting the Cardinal Points
> Of Heaven, going forward, forward irresistible from Eternity to Eternity
> (K745 J98:24–7).

The four Divine Senses are debased by Urizen (including his own) in his creation:

> ... his Brain in a rock & his Heart
> In a fleshy slough formed four rivers
> Obscuring the immense Orb ... (K260 BL5:52–4).

The 'immense Orb' is the Spiritual Sun which fallen Urizen can neither conceive nor perceive, for in a Urizenic world the senses are limited. (Cf. K294 FZiii:86–9; K655 J29:67–70). Through the one-sided influence of Urizen the River of Life becomes the River of Death.

36. K636 J15:14–20.
37. Stevenson, p. 655n.
38. K672 J43:11.
39. K649 J27.
40. For an interesting discussion of the effect of Druidism on Blake's thinking, see Peter F. Fisher, 'Blake and the Druids', JEGP LVIII (1959) pp. 589–612.
41. K708 J70:15–16.
42. K674 J44:32. Cf. K701 J65:75 and 79.
43. K674 J44:37.
44. K746 J98:48–50.
45. Verulam, of course, never has had a cathedral, nor did St Albans

until 1877 (fifty years after Blake's death). Blake, however, makes Verulam one of his four major Cathedral Cities, which he placed in the South under Urizen (cf. J46:24 an J74:3). He chooses the name doubtless because Francis Bacon, who 'put an End to Faith' (K398 'On Bacon'), was created Baron Verulam and Viscount St Albans.

46. In *The Marriage of Heaven and Hell*, the Angel is, satirically, an orthodox, 'good' person, the contrary of the Devils, who are the unorthodox Geniuses, the 'evil' revolutionaries against established Urizenic order. In the passage quoted from *Europe, a Prophecy* 'Man' has become such an 'Angel' as we find in *The Marriage*.

47. K241 Eur10:16–23.

48. Cf. K527 M37:11; K673 J43:65.

49. K241 Eur10:10–15.

50. K238 Eur2:4–6.

51. K252 BA3:69–70.

52. K252 BA4:2–4.

53. K215 SoE.

54. K530 M39:2.

55. The foot is traditionally the most materialistic part of the human body.

56. K321 FZvii:31–3.

57. Ibid. 36–7.

58. K333 FZviib:1.

59. Ibid. 21–9.

60. Blake is also alluding to Ezekiel 7:22.

61. K226 BU4:40.

62. K7.

63. K116 SoI:11–13.

64. K1–2.

65. K36.

66. K115–16 SoI.

67. K125 SoI.

68. K317 FZvi:208.

69. Ibid. 213–15.

70. K125 SoI:17–20.

71. K119 SoI:9–12;

72. K199 Am9:4–8.

73. K106 Tir4:90.

74. K156 MHH17–18.

75. K287 FZii:266–86.
76. K474 'On Reynolds'.
77. K673–4 J43:80–J44:13.
78. We should note, however, that Blake makes the significant point that Man cannot be 'saved' without an act of will on his own behalf.
79 K635 J15:5.
80. Ibid. 6–13.
81. K3.
82. K610 VLJ.
83. K609 VLJ.
84. K204 Amb:5–7.
85. K310–11 FZv:218–24.
86. K316 FZvi:196–7.
87. K317 FZvi:235–6.
88. Ibid. 237.
89. K632 J12:51.
90. K717 J77:1–6.
91. Cf. Genesis 3:24.
92. K717–18 J77:1–23.
93. K718 J77:36–9.
94. K632 J12:51.
95. K346 FZviii:218.
96. K490 M9:41.
97. K210 SoE 'Introduction' 16–20.
98. Total Chaos, or non-existence, could here be understood to mean a life on earth completely devoid of any spirituality.
99. Cf. K304 FZiv:271–4.
100. K509 M24:51. Here Bowlahoola is a workshop of Los in Golgonooza where unborn souls receive bodies.
101. The 'Polypus' is symbolic of materiality. A society which is ruled, held prisoner by, the tentacles of the Polypus is the antithesis of the Brotherhood of Man.
102. K509 M24:37–8.
103. K636 J15:14–20.
104. K634 J13:57–8.
105. K606 VLJ.
106. K505 M22:29–34.
107. K771 GoP 'Epilogue':2.

108. K331 FZvii:439–41.
109. K342 FZviii:37–9.
110. Cf. K341 FZviii:28.
111. Cf. K341–2 FZviii:24–39.
112. K346 FZviii:202–15.
113. K328 FZviii:323.
114. K626 J7:65.
115. K512 M26:31–6.
116. K517 M29:22. Cf. K709 J71:19; K717 J77.
117. K509 M24:34–6.
118. K346 FZviii:218–27.
119. K347 FZviii:230–3.
120. Ibid. 236–7.
121. K362 FZix:190–3. Cf. Blake's engraving, colour printed, 'Albion arose'.
122. K294 FZiii:106–7;
123. K346 FZviii:200–22. Cf. K517–18 M29:51–65.
124. K486 M6:28–9.
125. K345 FZviii:176.
126. K235 BU25:22.
127. K512 M26:2–7 and 10–12. Cf. Exodus 28:33; Numbers 15:38. Also Matt 9:20 and 14:36.
128. K495 M14:13.
129. K150 MHH5.
130. K530 M38:34.
131. K529 M38:8.
132. K533 M40:35–6.
133. Ololon appears only in *Milton*. Milton had never 'discovered', i.e. he had never understood, the female sex.
134. K533 M41:36.
135. K535 Written on the back of M43.
136. K499 M18:20, and 35. Cf. K512 M26:16–17.
137. K351 VZviii:397.
138. K533 M41:12.
139. Ibid. 21–8.
140. Cf. K499 M18:4–38; Ezekiel 28:16; K734 J89:9–13.
141. K645 J22:34–5.
142a. K728 J83:71–3.
142b. Cf. K668 J41:7–9.

143. K684 J54:1–5.
144. K660 J34:3–6.
145. Cf. K418 'Mock on' 9–10.
146. K693 J60:39–44.
147. K483 M4: 9–12 and 17.
148. K480 M1:1.
149. K483 M3:41–3. Cf. K490 M10:1.
150. K491 M11:6–14.
151. Cf. K483 M4:17.
152. K510 M25:10–12.
153. K485 M6:12–13.
154. K374 FZix:653.
155. Ibid. 656.
156. K510 M25:29. Cf. K508 M23:61–M24:16.
157. K346 FZviii:201.
158. K713 J73:38.
159. K662 J36:7.
160. K361 FZix:176–7. Cf. K651 J27:77–80.
161. K535 M43:1.
162. K742 J95:16.
163. K488 M8:20.
164. K485 M6:12–13.
165. Ibid. 18. Cf. K511 M25:55; K712 J72:35–6; K720 J79:22; K744 J97:1–2.
166. K374–5 FZix:657–9, 662. Here we may note that 'nation' is cognate with *natus* (birth) and with 'nature'. The annihilation of 'Mystery' is the annihilation of all that springs from Urizen's evil-doing, as well as that of the delusive harlot Rahab.
167. K535 M43:1.
168. K745 J98:18–19.
169. K775 'On Berkeley'.
170. K530 M38:46–7.
171. K533 M40:35–6.
172. Cf. K738 J91:27–31 and K483 M4:8.
173. K738 J91:19–22.
174. K686 J55:8–10.
175. K491 M11:10.
176. Cf. K490 M9:25–6;
177. K330 FZvii:402. To use the faculty of spiritual perception is to

have, to use, 'a concentering vision'. Here 'concentering vision' synthesizes a multiplicity of entities into a One, which Blake sees as a Man. It is characteristic of Blake that he sees Reality in vision not as a boundless Ocean of Being, but 'human-formed'. 'Jesus, as also Abraham & David, consider'd God as a Man in the Spiritual or imaginative Vision' (K774 'On Berkeley'). In Blake's writings, the epithet 'Human' comes to be equivalent to 'spiritual' or 'real'.

178. K672 J43:35–6.
179. K413 'On Boyd'.
180. K684 J54:1–3.
181. K661 J34:57.
182. K374 FZix:629–31.
183. K235 BU25:9–22. Cf. K318 FZvi:243–4.
184. K236 BU25:29–32.
185. Cf. K227 BU8:7. See Chapter 6 regarding Los's role here.
186. The poem, 'The Golden Net' (K424) is a vision of the 'net' or 'veil' of Nature.
187. Cf. K656 J30:40; K686 J55:16; K701 J65:61–2.
188. K193 VDA5:17–20.
189. K246 SoL4:1–4.
190. K696 J62:13.
191. K702 J66:8–10. The 'Building' is the Druid Temple at Stonehenge.
192. On one occasion Vala is described as being the mother of Urizen (K326 FZviii:244).
193. Cf. K686 J55:11; K701 J65:61; K736 J90:4–5.
194. K691 J59:2–7.
195. K643 J21:15; K646 J23:22, 31.
196. K677 J47:12.
197. K688 J56:40; K692 J59:55.
198. K656 J30:40; K686 J55:16; K701:61; K355 FZviii:556.
199. Cf. K643 J20:30; K671 J42:81; K721 J80:1.
200. K671 J42:81. Cf. K691 J59:2–3.
201. K677 J47:12.
202. K330 FZvii:402. See note 177.
203. Ibid. 409.
204. K646 J23:22.
205. K691 J59:2–9. Cf. K770 GoP 'Of the Gates' 17–18.
206. K281 FZii:38.

207. K286 FZii:245–6 and 248.
208. K498 M17:21–2. A 'Concave Earth' is a universe like the inside of an egg.
209. K513 M26:44.
210. K744 J96:35.
211. K624 J5:39.
212. K727–28 J83:33–9. A 'Fluctuating Globe' has an 'indefinite' form.
213. K740 J92:24–7.
214. K634 J13:52–4.
215. K614 VLJ.
216. K87 'On Lavater'.
217. K691 J59:7–9.
218. K523 M35. The Zoas are represented as four intersecting circles surrounded by the flames of the fallen world. In the centre is the Mundane Egg, within whose blue 'shell' man lives, with its two 'Limits', Satan and Adam. Adam/Man is entirely in the circle of Urthona. This is appropriate for he is capable of being regenerated through the indwelling Christ of Imagination. Satan, on the other hand, straddles the other three Zoas, i.e. the ruined world created by the Fall. The line designated as 'Milton's Track' passes through the intersecting circles of Urizen and Luvah and joins Adam in Urthona. Milton, here a figural representation of Christ, passes through the spheres of repressive law (fallen Urizen) and the will-to-power (fallen Luvah) to become incarnate in regenerate man. Cf. Morton D. Paley, *Energy and the Imagination* (1970), pp. 240–1.
219. K223 BU3:24–6.
220. Cf. K659 J33:1–24 and K685 J54:6–24.
221. Cf. K502 M20:42.
222. Cf. K709 J71:17–19.
223. K236 BU27:39.
224. We could say that the symbol of the Mundane Shell originated in Blake's intuitive response to the deistic perception of the starry heavens as a prison, an obstacle which encloses the beholder. When it is intellectualized as an infinite space in which the stars shine onwards into infinity, then, for Blake, it becomes a vision of despair. In the Urizen Newtonian mind the stars are the visible machinery of the astronomical universe and may be seen as symbolic of deterministic Fate, in which there is no room for

individual creative energy, for free will. For the man of vision the stars are not perceived as mere dead matter, subject to the inescapable laws of cause and effect of the physical world, but as living, spiritual aids — as 'human' aids — helping man to see through the obstructing and constricting 'Shell' to a living spiritual realm beyond. Cf. Leopold Damrosch Jr., *Symbol and Truth in Blake's Myth* (1980), p. 88.

225. K776 Laoc.
226. K623 J5:20.
227. K481 M1:13.
228. K617 VLJ.
229. K653 J29:1–5.
230. K622 J4:3–5.
231. K674 J44:30.
232. K505 M22:5–12.
233. K818:55–8.
234. CR291.
235. Ibid.
236. K92 'On Swed. DL'.
237. K283 FZii:127–32.
238. Cf. K204 Am:b:7; K503 M21:20ff.
239. K528 M37:46–53.
240. One of Blake's illustrations of the *Book of Job* (plate xiv) shows Urizen depicted as Apollo driving his chariot of light.
241. 'Emanation' is a term used to describe post-Newtonian theories of light.
242. Cf. John Beer, *Blake's Visionary Universe* (1969), pp. 39–40.
243. K97 NNR 1st series.
243a. K688 J56:18.
244. Cf. Isaiah 14:12–15.
245. K851–2. Letter to William Hayley, 23 Oct. 1804. The Truchsessian Gallery was a collection of pictures brought to England by Joseph, Count Truchess, and exhibited in August 1803.
246. K852.
247. K92 'On Swed. DL'.
248. K98 AllR.
249. K421 'To Morning'.
250. Whereas the physical sun rises in the east, the Spiritual Sun rises in

the west.

251. K618 'On the Illustrations to Milton'.
252. K94 'On Swed. DL'.
253. K272 FZi:302–3.
254. K760 GoP, Frontispiece.
255. Cf. K310–11 FZv:189–241.
256. K301 FZiv:141.
257. K338 FZviib:201. Cf. K271 FZi:264; K292 FZiii:30–2; K300 FZiv: 111–13; K310 FZvi:206–9; K359 FZix:91–4.
258. K277 FZi:480.
259. K294 FZiii:106.
260. K278 FZi:504–5.
261. K503 M21:20.
262. K345 FZviii:176.
263. K344 FZviii:145.
264. Ibid. FZviii:131–45.
265. K345 FZviii:180–1.
266. K362 FZix:188 and 190–3.
267. K271 FZi:264.
268. K292 FZiii:44–5.
269. Ibid. 46.
270. K293 FZiii:58.
271. K294 FZiii:81–2. There is obvious allusion here to Job 2:7. In *Jerusalem*, in a like situation, Albion cries out:

> The disease of Shame covers me from head to feet. I have no hope.
> Every boil upon my body is a separate & deadly Sin.
> Doubt first assail'd me, then Shame took possession of me.

(K643 J21:3–5)
272. K490 M9:26.
273. K682 J52.
274. 'In the human mind Satan is the death-impulse or Selfhood which reduces men to becoming either death-dealing tyrants or torpid and inert victims of them'. Northrop Frye, *Fearful Symmetry* (1969), pp. 134–5.
275. K654–5 J29:60–1.
276. K351 FZviii:382–3.
277. K742 J95:20.

278. K98 AllR.
279. K293 FZiii:74–6.
280. K351 FZviii:382–3.
281. Cf. Numbers 21:8–9 and John 3:14.
282. K337 FZviib:166–7.
283. K349 FZviii:325–6.
284. K359 FZix:69.
285. K330 FZvii:414–16.
286. K287 FZii:264.
287. K744 J96:35.
288. K743 J96:22.
289. Ibid. 13. Cf. K362–3 FZix:219–24; K670 J42:32–4; and Blake's illustration to *Paradise Lost* 'The Creation of Eve'.
290. K664 J37:11.
291. Ibid. J38:7.
292. Ibid. 10–13.
293. K699 J64:20–24.
294. Cf. K700 J65:33–6.
295. K641 J18:37.
296. Cf. K719 J78:12–14.
297. K623 J5:29.
298. K640 J18:11.
299. Cf. K735 J89:17–23.
300. K485 M6:8–13. Here Rintrah, Palamabron, Theotorn and Bromion are Los's four faithful sons.
301. On three occasions Blake associates Tyburn with Golgotha. i.e. K632 J12:26–8; K665 J38:54–9; K698 J63:33. Cf. also: K281 FZii:39–40; K531 M39:32–8; K652 J28:4; K653 J29:3; K696 J62:34.
302. K282 FZii:72–7. Cf. K625–6 J7:30–5.
303. Cf. K283 FZii:117–18.
304. Cf. K702 J66:15.
305. Cf. K271 FZi:271–4; K272 FZi:284–9.
306. K852 Letter to William Hayley, 23 Oct. 1804.
307. K280 FZii:22.
308. K282 FZii:80.
309. Ibid.
310. Ibid. FZii:99–100.
311. K316 FZvi:167, 173.

312. K314 FZvi:85. Cf. K224 BU4:32–3 and 44. See also Chapter 6.
313. K728 J83:53.
314. K627 J8:26.
315. K630 J10:63.
316. K746 J98:55.
317. K329 FZvii:380.
318. Cf. K632–3 J12:45–J13:29.
319. K743 J96:28.
320. Cf. K363 FZix:225–9; K364–6 FZix:291–353; K372 FZix: 579–86; K374 FZix:650–3; also K743–4 J96.
321. K728–9 J83:76–8.
322. Blake combines the classical Golden Age with the Judaeo-Christian symbolism of the recovery of Eden in the New Jerusalem, the golden City with 'golden pillars high' and 'golden arches' built by 'golden Builders' (K650 J27:10–11 and 25).
323. K745 J98:18–19.
324. K744 J97:7–8, 11.
325. K743 J96:28.
326. Ibid. 21.
327. K744 J96:35, 37.
328. Cf. K721 J79:53–5.
329. K743 J96:26–7.
330. K611 VLJ.
331. K320 FZvii:10.
332. K241 Eur10:18.
333. K605 VLJ.

6   The Creation Myth

1. Erdman makes the very valid point that Blake never really ceased to comment — for the most part critically — on social and political matters but, fearing the consequences of too overt utterances, 'clothed' his opinion and meaning in a complex symbolic and mythological 'garment'. 'It has been possible', Erdman writes, 'to trace through nearly all of his work a more or less clearly discernible thread of historical reference.' David V. Erdman, *Prophet against Empire* (1977), xiv–xv.
2. In his quest, Blake consulted many of the works of the esoteric tradition — hermetic, gnostic, Neoplatonic and alchemical. The

interested reader, wishing to know more of Blake's affinities with this 'occluded' knowledge, is referred to the work of such scholars as Kathleen Raine, George Mills Harper, Morton D. Paley, and Leopold Damrosch (see Bibliography).

The present author cannot refrain from referring the reader to a remarkable — and exceptional — statement made by another Blake scholar, Harold Bloom. He vehemently denies that Blake had any association with arcane traditions. But he goes further than this, and one cannot help wondering whether his senatorial condemnation of those who do see such associations is not an obvious example of academic 'Urizenism'. Bloom's statement runs as follows: 'A lunatic fringe of enthusiastic occult Blakeans is likely to abide as the left wing of Blake studies until the veritable apocalypse, and all one can do is to counsel students and readers to ignore them'(!) These lines are quoted from his otherwise most illuminative book, *Blake's Apocalypse* (1963), p. 249.

3. H. Jonas, *The Gnostic Religion* (1963), p. 111.
4. K222 BU2:1–4.
5. K222 BU3:1–7.
6. K223 BU3:21.
7. K98.
8. Especially in contrast with eternal life as Blake describes it in the quatrain:

> Earth was not: nor globes of attraction;
> The will of the Immortal expanded
> Or contracted his all flexible senses;
> Death was not, but eternal life sprung. (K223 BU3:36–9)

9. K224 BU4:10.
10. Ibid. 34–40.
11. Ibid. 24–33.
12. K252 BA3:55–8, 63–4.
13. K158 MHH24.
14. K224 BU4:10–11.
15. Ibid. 7–8.
16. K530 M39:1–2.
17. Cf. ibid. 2.
18. K224 BU4:12–13.
19. Ibid. 14.

20. K621 J3. Blake's italics.
21. K225 BU4:45.
22. Ibid. 48.
23. All Eternity suffers a 'fall' when a single 'part' falls. All powers are weakened.
24. K225 BU5:3-11.
25. Cf. K743-7. J96-9.
26. K225 BU5:2.
27. Ibid 17-18. Flames which emit no light, i.e. are black, are traditionally associated with conventional Hell. They torment (give heat) but give no insight (light). See also Blake's Job Engraving, Plate 11, and Am 4-11.
28. K223 BU3:21.
29. K225 BU5:19-27.
30. K225 BU5:28-9. The 'womb' is here an image of restriction.
31. K226 BU6:9.
32. K226 BU5:38-40.
33. K226 BU6:11-12.
34. K226 BU7:5.
35. K226 BU5:39-40.
36. K226 BU6:9.
37. Ibid. 5-6. The Illustration shows the Eternals falling, wreathed around by snaky selfhoods.
38. Cf. K530 M38:37ff.; K494 M13:40.
39. K226 BU7:8-9.
40. Ibid. 1-3. Plate 7 shows Los howling in agony, 'his physiognomy distorted like a Fuselian damned soul'. D. Bindman, *Blake as an Artist* (1977), p. 92.
41. K227 BU8:4.
42. K226 BU7:4.
43. Ibid. 5-7.
44. Blake stresses the need for meaningful, 'organized' form. He who is 'unorganized' is unable to act, create or associate with creative purpose. Los, the creative artist, limits the disaster by creating an organic form for Urizen; admittedly a fallen, restricted form, but better than no form at all, better than non-existence. See also Appendix 3.
45. K631 J12:13.
46. K226 BU7:9.

47. K227 BU8:12.
48. K227 BU10:15–16.
49. K226 BU7:8.
50. K227 BU8:9–11. The illustration shows Urizen's skeleton in an embryo-like posture.
51. K227 BU10:10.
52. Ibid. 12.
53. Ibid. 17–18.
54. At this stage of creation space has not yet come into being. Los is in being before his Emanation, Enitharmon, who is the mythical representative of Space. However, it is Los who creates the sun 'to measure Time and Space to mortal Men every morning' (K517 M29:24).
55. K229 BU13:13–14.
56. The west is assigned to Tharmas, who symbolizes the five senses, i.e. West is the 'body', it is that 'portion of Soul discern'd by the five senses' (K149 MHH4). Water, which symbolizes 'Matter', is the Western element.
57. K227–8 BU10:19–27. Lines BU10:19 to BU13:27, metrically adapted, recur in FZiv:208–46. The description of the 'Eternal Mind' as being as 'white as the snow' is an illusion to the *tabula rasa* of Lockian psychology, a 'blank slate', empty of innate, intrinsic ideas, only capable of passively receiving — and combining — external impressions. Clearly, Urizen's mind should not be 'blank', but it is rapidly becoming so.
58. K228 BU10:31–4.
59. Ibid. 35–41.
60. K223 BU3:36–9. These lines combine two related notions: Blake's dislike of any form of confinement and restriction; and Newton's system, which asserted that the universe was governed by such control — the law of gravity being paramount. Blake asserts that in Eternity there are no 'globes' (such as planets, stars, etc.) subject to such a law. Eternity — the reality — is non-Newtonian. Expansion and contraction are effected by spiritual, divine Will, not by the law of gravity.
61. K228 BU1:1–7. The 'Round Globe' is the heart; the 'ten thousand branches' are the blood vessels.
62. Ibid. 11–14. The 'branches' issuing from the brain constitute the whole system of nerves.

63. K229 BU11:21–4. A 'close volution' is the spiral of the inner ear.
64. K229 BU11:27–BU13:3.
65. K229 BU13:4–9. The 'craving Hungry Cavern' is the digestive system.
66. Ibid 18–19.
67. Cf. Plato in *Timaeus*.
68. See earlier discussion on 'roots' in Chapter 5.
69. K230 BU13:52. Cf. K488 M8:19–20. This division becomes the Globe of Blood, which develops into Los's Emanation, Enitharmon, the first separate female. Cf. also K483 M3:30; K732 J86:50–4.
70. K228 BU11:2–4.
71. Ibid. 15–16.
72. K229 BU13:1.
73. Ibid. 13–16.
74. Blake's poetic imagery is given added weight and poignancy by his illuminations.
75. K229 BU13:27.
76. Ibid. 21.
77. K230 BU13:28–34.
78. Ibid. 37–40. Cf. K483 M3:28.
79. K227 BU8:10–11.
80. K230 BU13:41–7.
81. Lines BU13:37–47 could also be interpreted as representing the mental fate of creative man who fails to respond to his inspiration.
82. K629 J10:21.
83. K229 BU13:27.
84. K224 BU4:11.
85. K117 SoI.
86. K217 SoE 'the Human Abstract'. Printed in 1794, the same year as *The Book of Urizen*.
87. K235 BU25:3.
88. K227 BU8:10–11.
89. K230 BU13:48–53.
90. Bindman makes the point that 'pity is associated with the failure of inspiration'. By feeling pity for Urizen, Los attributes to him a humanity which he does not possess; thus Urizen becomes an idol. Los consolidates his own fall when 'he loses his will to depict the true face of Urizen, as the material world comes into existence'. D.

Bindman, *Blake as an Artist* (1977), p. 92.

91. K230 BU15:1-2.
92. K231 BU18:1-16.
93. K231 BU19:5.
94. Ibid. 8-9.
95. A comparison here between John Milton's *Paradise Lost* and Blake's *Book of Urizen* is illuminative. In the former all created nature was perfect until Satan fell. On account of his fall — and his subsequent deeds — all natural creation eventually became debased and perverted. In Blake's work, however, the natural creation does not even begin until *after* Lucifer/Satan, or Satan/Urizen, has fallen. Moreover, creation acquires final human lineaments — separate male and female forms — only after the divine faculty of creative imagination has also fallen.
96. Urthona is the spiritual existence of Los. Conversely, Los is described as being 'the vehicular Form of strong Urthona' (K684 J53:1) until, ultimately, Los is reabsorbed into Urthona. Urthona is the cosmic blacksmith, constantly occupied in creating forms (Cf. K278 FZi:519; K742 J95:17-18). He is the 'keeper of the gates of heaven' (K298 FZiv: 42; K727 J82:81). Los, towards the end of *Jerusalem* is praised by the Sons of Eden for keeping the 'Divine Vision in time of trouble' (K742 J95:19-20).
97. 'Los is by mortals nam'd Time, Enitharmon is nam'd Space' (K509 M24:68).
98. K473 'On Reynolds'.
99. In the World of Generation, Space and Time are twin manifestations of what, in Eternity, is one, a 'Oneness'. Enitharmon, who is Pity (BU19:1), creates Spaces (K271 FZi:241) which are protective (cf. for instance, K707 J69:19-24). Whereas Time is Mercy (K510 M24:72), Space is Protection, born of pity.
100. K231 BU19:10-13.
101. K232 BU19:14-16.
102. Ibid. 40.
103. Ibid. 41-3.
104. K233 BU20:2.
105. Cf. K517 M29:22; K709 J71:19 and K716-17 J77.
106. K233 BU20:8-25.
107. Jealousy can only arise after the soul has been 'divided' into more than two 'entities'. A fully integrated soul could not harbour such

an aberration.

108. K233 BU20:26–9.

109. Ibid. 30–2.

110. Urizen, exploring his 'dens' with a dim lamp (see remarks regarding Enlightenment in Chapter 5), is illustrated at the foot of plate 23.

111. K233–4. BU20:33–41.

112. K217 SoE.

113. K234 BU20:42–4.

114. Los is both the Spirit of Time and the Eternal Prophet. In Eternity there is no need for prophecy because there is no time. We need to be aware of the nature of prophecy as Blake understands it. His prophets are not to be understood as being foretellers of future events, but as revealers of eternal truths. For Blake, the Prophets of the Old Testament, for example, were 'poets'. When Bacon sneered at pagan religion because the 'chief doctors and fathers of their church were the poets', Blake underlines the word 'poets' and adds 'prophets' (K399 'On Bacon').

115. In Eternity, where Man is androgynous, the Emanation is an integral 'part' of any Spiritual Being. In 'Whole' Man the Emanation is experienced as Inspiration which nourishes and 'houses', gives Space to, the Creative Imagination. In the Fall the Emanation becomes a separate being. In order to gain re-entry to Universal Brotherhood the split in the personality, the division of the Emanation from the Individual, must be healed. The Emanation is necessary for the union with God as well as Man: 'Man is adjoin'd to Man by his Emanation portion, who is Jerusalem in every Individual Man' (K675 J44:38. Cf. K733 J88:3–11).

116. K234 BU20:45.

117. K234 BU23:2–4. This episode is given again, in expanded form, in FZvi.

118. K617 VLJ.

119. K234 BU23:8–18. Cf. K663 J36:31–7 where the four elements are associated with the Four Zoas.

120. K617 VLJ. Fuzon, 'first begotten, last born' (K234 BU23:18) appears again in *The Book of Ahania* (1795) where he is crucified by Urizen on the topmost stem of the Tree of Mystery (K251–22 BA3:52–BA4:8). But Fuzon does not reappear in later works.

Damon writes: 'Blake suppressed the book [i.e. *The Book of Ahania*] probably because of his dissatisfaction with his symbols. Passion (Fuzon) could not possibly be the child of Reason (Urizen); he is merely the element of Fire. Also, it was Jesus, not Fuzon, who was crucified on the Tree of Mystery. Therefore, Blake never published his book, and dropped Fuzon entirely from his mythology.' (Damon, 51d). In *The Four Zoas* Urizen's antagonist is Luvah, the Prince of Love, who is closely associated with Christ.

121. Urizen's laws are inevitably followed by his curse. Cf. Galatians 3:10–11.

122. K235 BU23:22–6.

123. K235 BU23:27–BU25:2.

124. K235 BU25:3–4.

125. Ibid. 5–22. Cf. Rev. 17:5; K349 FZviii:330; K356 FZviii:603; K506 M22:48; K529 M38:23. Orthodox religion is, for Blake, not the 'Religion of Jesus', for 'Jesus supposes every Thing to be evident to the child & to the Poor & Unlearned. Such is the Gospel' (K774 'On Berkeley'). There is no 'Mystery' in the 'Religion of Jesus'.

126. K235 BU25:5–22. It is, of course, not to the inspiration of religion that Blake objects, but to the ecclesiastical control of men's beliefs and lives. He objects to the 'Net' which catches the free-flying spirit, and to the 'Web' which ensnares the spirit and devours it.

127. Cf. K682 J52. Also: John 12:31; 14:30; 16:11; 2 Cor. 4:4; K771 GoP, 'Epilogue'; K749 EGb:31, 44; K758 EG suppl.2:13. Blake labels all religion and philosophy which dispenses with spiritual inspiration 'Deist'.

128. K349 FZviii:326. Cf. K252 BA4:5–8.

129. Here we are reminded again of Blake's assertion that 'every Natural Effect has a Spiritual Cause' (K513 M26:44).

130. The association of the invisible infection, pestilence, bred in the dark with the spiritual effects of 'false' religion, is the basis of the poem 'The Sick Rose' (K213 SoE). Blake associated all repressive law and authority — indeed, all repressive and restrictive acts — with the imagery of blight and sickness. One of the 'Proverbs of Hell' in *The Marriage of Heaven and Hell* illustrates this point clearly: 'As the catterpillar [*sic.*] chooses the fairest leaves to lay her eggs on, so the priest lays his curse on the fairest joys.' (K152 MHH9).

131. K235–6 BU25:23–30.
132. K236 BU25:31–6.
133. Ibid. 39–42.
134. The cities become 'heart-formed Africa', the cradle of civilization. Cf. K245 SoL3:3.
135. K236 BU25:43–BU28:3.
136. K236 BU28:4–7.
137. K237 BU28:23.
138. K236 BU28:8–10. Egypt symbolizes slavery because of the bondage of Israel.
139. Ibid. 17–18.
140. K252 BA4:8.
141. K237 BU28:19–22.
142. K236 BU28:16.
143. Mencius (?371–?289 BC). Quoted by Agnes Arber in *The Manifold and the One* (1957) p. 36.
144. Cf. John 14:20.
145. K776 Laoc.
146. Arber writes: 'The conception of the microcosm and the macrocosm is particularly congenial to Chinese thinkers, in its correlation with their innate feeling of man's unity with nature. In the second century before Christ, Tung Chung-shu said that man is a shadow in brief of the universe, while the universe may be described as man on a vast scale; and, in the twelfth century, Lu Chiu-yuan declared "The universe is my mind; my mind is the universe." The same idea finds expression in our modern world, when Pierre, in *War and Peace*, glancing up from his prison encampment into the night sky, says to himself, "And all that is me, all that is within me, and it is all I." ' (op.cit., p. 37).
147. See earlier remark regarding Blake's triple doctrine.
148. K473 'On Reynolds'.
149. Cf. the point made earlier in the chapter regarding the necessity of reason and imagination working together in harmony.
150. K746 J98:28, 39.

    7 *The Four Zoas: The Triumph of Imaginative Life*

1. K273 FZi:336.
2. K605 VLJ 69–70.
3. K273 FZi:337–41.

4. Frye, p. 270.
5. Ibid.
6. K264 FZi:21–3.
7. K363 FZix:225–31.
8. *The FOUR ZOAS, the Torments of Love & Jealousy in the Death and Judgement of Albion, the Ancient Man*, was the final title of Blake's longest poem, originally named *Vala, or the Death and Judgement of the Ancient Man. A Dream of Nine Nights.*
9. Frye, p. 127.
10. K790 Letter to Cumberland, 6 Dec. 1795.
11. K640 J18:29–30.
12. Their two names, as first suggested by Erdman, are derived from ENITHARMON. D. Erdman, *Prophet against Empire* (1954), p. 275, n. 27.
13. K635 J14:13–14.
14. K264 FZi:9–13.
15. Ibid.24.
16. Ibid.21.
17. K328 FZviii:347–8 and K659 J33:1–2.
18. K621 J3.
19. K743 J96:20–8.
20. Cf. K605 VLJ 69–70.
21. K266 FZi:87.
22. K224 BU4:44.
23. Cf. K431 'Auguries of Innocence' 1–4.
24. K267 FZi:99–100.
25. K510 M24:72.
26. Cf. K280–7 FZii:22–267.
27. K281 FZii:38.
28. K286 FZii:245–6.
29. All the ante-Nicene Fathers taught that Christ, the Logos, created Man and the Universe. Thus, according to Theophilus of Antioch, it was not the Father, 'but his word, through whom he made all things' (*To Autolycus*, II, xxii). Blake adapted this belief when he wrote of 'The Holy Word that walk'd among the ancient trees, calling the lapsed Soul' (K210 SoE, 'Introduction' 4–5). See Damon 450c–d.
30. K87 'On Lavater' 630.
31. i.e. the veil. The 'veil', which enclosed the material world, was

first made by Vala for her own purposes of control. Here it is used by Los to keep the evil influences out of the World of Generation as much as possible.

32. K691 J59:2–9.
33. In Urizen's hands Brass is symbolic of tyranny. In its positive aspect it is the metal of social organization, of the Brotherhood of Man. Therefore when man rises, regenerated, 'his feet become like brass' (K199 Am8:16).
34. For Blake, anything opposed to the Everlasting Gospel, is Anti-Christian.
35. Keynes suggests that 'temper' is probably an abbreviation of 'temperance'. See K323 and K902.
36. K323 FZii:110–29.
37. See Schorer, pp. 277–8.
38. K323–4 FZii:135–49.
39. K271 FZi:264.
40. K324 FZvii:152–6.
41. Ibid. 158.
42. Ibid. 161.
43. K752 EG d:34. See also: K149 MHH 2:17–18 and K158 MHH 23.
44. Ibid. 59.
45. K751 EG d:29–30.
46. Ibid. 2.
47. K752 EG d:66.
48. K323–4 FZvii:137–65.
49. K338 FZvii:214. See also FZviii:382–3 and 509; also FZix:69 and K110 Tir8:35–9.
50. K351 FZvii:382–3.
51. Cf. K198–199 Am8:1–14.
52. K359 FZix:69–70.
53. K280 FZi:5.
54. Ibid. 2.
55. K647 J24:23–4.
56. K324 FZvii:164–5.
57. K342 FZviii:61–4. See also K335 FZviib:113–22.
58. Cf. K252 BA4:5–8.
59. K349 FZviii:325–26.
60. Cf. K348 FZviii:268–74.
61. Cf. K665 J38:54. See also D. Erdman, p. 305.

62. K749 EG b:53–4.
63. K484 M5:3. The term 'Christ' has been used consistently by the present author. It should be noted, however, that Blake himself nearly always uses the name 'Jesus'.
64. K301–5 FZiv:161–295.
65. K321 FZvii:33.
66. K324 FZvii:170–1.
67. K323 FZvii:113.
68. Ibid. 114–16.
69. Cf. K34–5 FZviii:184–208.
70. Cf. Schorer p. 279; also Wilkie and Johnson (1978), pp. 89–90.
71. Bloom pp. 252–3.
72. Cf. K300 FZiv:92–106 and K327 FZvii:278–95.
73. Here we need to recollect that, in reality, Los, Enitharmon, and the Spectre, are all aspects of the primal Urthona. But as long as they 'think' of themselves, 'see' themselves, as separate beings they appear as disparate and independent 'persons'.
74. *America, The Book of Urizen, Europe, The Song of Los, The Book of Ahania. The Book of Los.*
75. K325 FZvii:218.
76. K279 FZi:565–6.
77. K309 FZv:177–8. Cf. K803 Letter to Thomas Butts, 23 Sept. 1800.
78. K271–2 FZi:260–80.
79. K271 FZi:249.
80. K272 FZi:309. See also K273 FZi:337.
81. K274 FZi:355.
82. K272 FZi:281.
83. Ibid. 308.
84. K328 FZvii:315. See also K326–7 FZvii:231–310.
85. K349 FZviii:330.
86. K327 FZviii:295.
87. K328 FZviii:317.
88. Ibid. 327–31.
89. Frye, p. 298.
90. K526 M35:42. It is like a moment of inspiration when the 'Poet's Work is done ... within a moment, a Pulsation of the Artery' (K516 M29:1–3).

91. Note the symbolic use of language to denote the ensnarement of the material world.
92. K328 FZvii:332–41.
93. K327 FZvii:305–6.
94. Ibid. 296–7.
95. K684 J53:1. 'Vehicular form' means 'that Los is the eternal Urthona as he acts in the fallen world. This [is] an important element in *The Four Zoas*, but is scarcely relevant in *Jerusalem*'. Stevenson, p. 735, footnote 53.1.
96. K328 FZvii:342–8.
97. Cf. K326–7 FZvii:267–310.
98. K329 FZvii:353–60.
99. Ibid. 361–9.
100. Ibid. 373–83.
101. Cf. K733 J88:3–11.
102. i.e. Christ's self-sacrifice on the Cross.
103. K329–30 FZvii:387–94.
104. K330 FZvii:396–7.
105. Ibid. 398.
106. Ibid. 399–400.
107. K323 FZvii:114, 116.
108. K328 FZvii:333–4.
109. K329 FZvii:385.
110. K330 FZvii:397.
111. K273 FZi:341.
112. Cf. K270 FZi:237–8.
113. Cf. K285 FZii:211–12.
114. K307 FZv:73–8.
115. See *Book of Urizen* and Chapter 6.
116. Cf. K278–9 FZi:510–34.
117. K330 FZvii:403–10.
118. K327 FZvii:310.
119. Ibid.
120. K346 FZvii:208.
121. K809 Letter to Butts, 11 Sept. 1801.
122. K327 FZvii:304–5.
123. K329 FZvii:384–5.
124. K330 FZvii:411–23.
125. K330–1 FZvii:425–30.

126. K331 FZvii:440–1.
127. Ibid. 438.
128. Ibid. 443–4.
129. Ibid. 444–5.
130. Ibid. 446–55.
131. Ibid. 456–8.
132. 'The activity of the artist is now to preserve the Divine Vision by creating the order of art rather than to demonstrate the causes and consequences of war to an unheeding society.' Paley (1970), pp. 159–60.
133. K332 FZvii:467–9.
134. K512 M26:26 and 28. In *Milton* we see Antamon, a son of Los and Enitharmon, an agent of spiritual regeneration, also drawing an 'indelible line' to the same purpose. (See K515 M28:16.)
135. Cf. K576 DesC.iv and K585 DesC.xv.
136. Cf. K659 J33:2; K740 J92:22.
137. Cf. K331 FZvii:443–4, 455.
138. Cf. K743 J96:16 and K694–5 J61:17–26.
139. K761 GoP 'Prologue'.
140. Cf. K743 J96:22.
141. Cf. K771 GoP 'Epilogue'; also K758–9 EG Suppl.2:13 and 34; K746 J98:49.
142. K332 FZvii:482–5. Cf. K307–9 FZv:70–154 and K232–3 BU19:45–20:25.
143. Cf. K514–15 M28:1–20.
144. K331 FZvii:461–2.
145. K332 FZvii:476–81.
146. Cf. K510 M24:75.
147. K245 SoL3:11.
148. K246 SoL3:18–19.
149. With the exception of the Satan-Palamabron myth in Milton, see K484–92, plates 5–11.
150. Cf. K350 FZviii:357–67 and K234 BU20:45.
151. Damon makes the point that Los and Enitharmon may be said to have had only one child, Orc, 'for every real poet is in some measure a revolutionist'. Damon p. 253.
152. Cf. K366 FZix:358–62.
153. K332 FZvii:486–7. Cf. K264–6 FZi:24–93.
154. Reunion finally takes place in Night ix:590–620.

155. K745 J98:17.
156. K264 FZi:24.
157. K332 FZvii:492.
158. Cf. K343 FZviii:86–99. Also K333–4 FZviib:1–38.
159. K332 FZvii:496–9.
160. K777 Laoc.

8 *The Four Zoas: The Culmination of Errors*

1. The Limits of Contraction and Opacity (or Adam & Satan) were fixed by Christ as an act of Mercy. Bounds were put to Error. In *Jerusalem* Los is once named the fixer of the two Limits. See K713 J73:24–8.
2. Cf. 2 Kings 4:35 and K341 FZviii:16–19.
3. K340 FZviib:295.
4. K332 FZvii:496–7.
5. K341 FZviii:20–1.
6. 'The "Female will"', as Blake calls it, has no necessary connection with human women, who are part of humanity, except when a woman wants to make a career of being a "harlot coy", or acting as nature does. The female will is rather the elusive, retreating, mysterious remoteness of the external world.' Northrop Frye, 'Blake's Introduction to Experience', *Blake. Twentieth Century Views* (1966), p. 29.
7. K341 FZviii:22.
8. K342 FZviii:32–44.
9. K341 FZviii:23.
10. Luvah is the Zoa of Love. Cf. FZi:325; ii:104; iv:142; v:42; ix:700. However, Luvah includes all emotions. Not only love but also its contrary, hate. Cf. FZv:42.
11. K342 FZviii:61–4.
12. K343 FZviii:96. The collusion between Urizen and Orc is foreshadowed in the negotiations between Urizen and Luvah towards the end of Night i.
13. K343 FZviii:97–100.
14. Ibid. 86.
15. Ibid. 102–6.
16. K343–4 FZviii:108–15.
17. Cf. FZix:32; 80–90; 114; 188–9, etc.
18. K345 FZviii:153.

19. K670 J42:35.
20. K346-7 FZviii:194-9 and 236-45. Cf. Rev. 22:20.
21. K347 FZviii:247-58.
22. Cf. Rev 2:9; John 11:47.
23. K348 FZviii: 277-82.
24. K349 FZviii:330.
25. K348 FZviii:263.
26. Ibid.
27. Cf. ibid. 265.
28. Ibid. 267.
29. K345-6 FZviii:182-93.
30. Enemies of the Israelites, i.e. of God's Chosen People.
31. i.e. the state of Error. Ulro, Void, Chaos, Udan-Adan and Enthuthon Benython are equivalent symbols.
32. K346-7 FZviii:217-29.
33. Cf. K625 J7:22.
34. Cf. K307 FZv:76.
35. K512 M26:26-7.
36. K530 M39:11-12.
37. K347 FZviii:230-1.
38. Cf. ibid. 232-7.
39. K342 FZviii:61-2.
40. Cf. FZi:271-8; 284-9; 408-9.
41. Cf. K660 J33:48-J34:1.
42. K348 FZviii:265-7.
43. Cf. for instance K286 FZii:231-5.
44. K348 FZviii:276.
45. K349 FZviii:325-7.
46. K350 FZviii:341-6.
47. Ibid. 347.
48. Ibid. 351-5.
49. K351 FZviii:379-81.
50. K348 FZviii:286.
51. K743 J96:21.
52. K351 FZviii:410-14.
53. K352 FZviii:415.
54. Cf. ibid. 422-37.
55. Ibid. 424-5.
56. Ibid. 429.

57. Ibid. 437.
58. K353 FZviii:458–9.
59. K346 FZviii:195–9.
60. K352 FZviii:428–31.
61. K353 FZviii:463–6.
62. K352 FZviii:416, 420.
63. K277–9 FZi:480–549.
64. K264 FZi:22.
65. K376 FZix:709.
66. K571 DesC.iii. Cf. also K366 FZix:363–74.
67. Cf. Kathleen Raine, *The Human Face of God. William Blake and the Book of Job* (1982), pp. 247–9.
68. K353 FZviii:467–8.
69. Ibid. 477–80.
70. Ibid. 463.
71. K353–6 FZviii:492–584.
72. K291 FZvii:421–4.
73. K353 FZviii:491.
74. Ibid. 489.
75. K354 FZviii:505–32.
76. K346 FZviii:196. Cf. also K353 FZviii:484.
77. K290 FZii:386.
78. Ibid. 391–418.
79. Cf. Matt. 25:6.
80. K354–5. FZviii:534, 536–47, 555–7.
81. K669 J41 illustration.
82. K284 FZii:181.
83. Cf. K285 FZii:186–96.
84. K355 FZviii:548–54.
85. Cf. K355 FZviii:553 and Rev 21:4. As Wilkie and Johnson point out, there are clear parallels here between Blake and 1 Cor 15:13–20. Paul's contrasts between natural and spiritual, corruptible and incorruptible, sowing and raising, form the very substance of the dialogue between Ahania and Enion. The naturalistic vision of those who doubt and are without hope — whom Paul is addressing — is precisely Ahania's position. Enion's reply to Ahania parallels Paul's contradiction of Error. Wilkie and Johnson (1978), p. 200.
86. K355–6 FZviii:555–63, 581–3.

87. Cf. K220, illustration to the poem 'To Tirzah'; also 1 Cor 15:44.
88. K297 FZiii:204.
89. K297 FZiv:9.
90. K743 J96:27–8.
91. K355 FZviii:574–5.
92. K351 FZviii:397–8.
93. Cf. Kathleen Raine, *Blake and Tradition* (1968), Vol.I, pp. 352–3.
94. K356 FZviii:580–3.
95. K330 FZvii:402.
96. K356 FZviii:597–600.
97. K349 FZviii:340.
98. K356 FZviii:593–5.
99. K356–7 FZviii:604–13. Cf. Joshua 2:6 and 11; also 1 Kings 10:5.
100. Cf. K351 FZviii:406.
101. K350–1. FZviii:351–409.
102. K357 FZviii:614–20.
103. Cf. K681–3 J52.
104. K604 VLJ.
105. K745 J98:18–21.

9 The Four Zoas: The Last Judgement

1. Harold Bloom, *Blake's Apocalypse* (1963), p. 266.
2. Frye, p. 305.
3. K357 FZix:1–3.
4. Ibid. 4–5.
5. Ibid. 12–13. Cf. K365 FZix:331 and K373 FZix:615.
6. Ibid. 5–9.
7. Cf. Matt 24:29–31.
8. Cf. Rev 6:14–15.
9. K357 FZix:10–23.
10. K154 MHH14.
11. To 'consume' ('consummation') in Blake is equivalent to the annihilation of Error. Spiritual fire consumes nothing but Errors. Cf. K154 MHH 14 and K617 VLJ; also Rev 20:14.
12. K154 MHH 14.
13. Ibid. We may remind ourselves here that, for Blake, a last Judgement occurs 'Whenever any Individual Rejects Error & Embraces Truth' (K613 VLJ). The Last Judgement is also symbolic of 'an Overwhemlming of Bad Art & Science' (K617 VLJ).

14. Cf. K353 FZviii:477.
15. i.e. K357 FZix:18–23.
16. K363 FZix: 241–77.
17. 'The spectre of a female emanation or counterpart is unusual, but Blake has grown used to Enitharmon as a personality in herself ...' Stevenson, p. 431 9:24.
18. K358 FZix:24.
19. Ibid. 26–31.
20. Ibid. 32. See note 11.
21. Ibid. 34.
22. K579 DesC.
23. K358 FZix:33.
24. Ibid. 43–5.
25. Ibid. 52–8.
26. K359 FZix:67–70.
27. Ibid. 79.
28. K357 FZix:9.
29. K358 FZix:46–8.
30. K651 J27:77–80. The adjective 'soft' and the noun 'softness' are used in a derogatory sense by Blake on more than one occasion. Cf. K457 'On Reynolds'. 'Soft Family Love' is 'one of the most formidable bulwarks of social conservatism' (Frye p. 73). Individualism in its selfish sense is fostered by it.
31. K359 FZix:76.
32. Ibid. 82-7. 'liking' = 'licking'.
33. K358 FZix:45.
34. K359 FZix:91.
35. Ibid. 93–4. See also K271 FZi:264.
36. K359–60 FZix:98–101, K107–14.
37. K360 FZix: 115–20.
38. John 11:43.
39. Cf. K252 BAiv:11–26.
40. K360 FZix: 124–32.
41. K252 BAiv:11.
42. K360 FZix:133–5.
43. K282 FZii:105.
44. K116 SoE 'The Ecchoing Green' 11–12.
45. K360 FZix:138.
46. Ibid. 137–9.

47. Ibid. 140–3.
48. K360–1 FZix:146–50.
49. In Night ii, Albion blames both Luvah and Urizen but nevertheless considers Urizen to be a competent deputy (Cf. K280 FZii:1–8). Here in Night ix, Albion will chastise Luvah (Cf. K366 FZix:363–74), but he clearly holds Urizen responsible for the Fall of Man, for Reason should have greater powers of discrimination than Passion.
50. K361 FZix:151–7.
51. It is by a 'line of scarlet thread in the window' that the harlot Rahab was to be recognized and so spared the destruction meted out to Jericho. Cf. Joshua 2:18.
52. K361 FZix:158–61.
53. i.e. the open drains down the middle of the streets.
54. K361 FZix:162–78.
55. K362 FZix:183.
56. Ibid. 184–7.
57. Ibid. 191–3. Here we are reminded of the jubiliant young man in Blake's print generally known as 'Glad Day', or 'Albion Arose'.
58. Cf. K292 FZiii:27–104.
59. Cf. Blake's letter to George Cumberland, 6 Dec. 1795 (K790).
60. K362 FZix:222.
61. K362–3 FZix:206–24.
62. K355 FZviii:543.
63. Ibid. 548.
64. In *The Book of Ahania*, Ahania's last words (K255 BA5:39–47) are very similar to those of Earth in the poem 'Earth's Answer' (K211 SoE 11–15). Urizen himself recalls his work as farmer when he casts out Ahania. He speaks of her 'clods' and of his 'plow', and in *The Book of Ahania* she reminds him that he is both husband and farmer (K255 BA5:29–34). Cf. Kathleen Raine, *Blake and Tradition*, Vol.1, pp. 154 and 159.
65. K230 BUxiii:39–40.
66. K250 BAii:34.
67. K295 FZiii:113.
68. K149 MHH 4.
69. K362 FZix:198–9.
70. There are obvious parallels between the role of Ahania and that of Persephone.

71. K82.
72. K366 FZix:363.
73. The word 'Lock' is not merely a reference to the kind of lock used on waterways which, in Blake's lifetime, had been greatly extended, but also to Locke's philosophy of the five senses.
74. K363 FZix:225–9.
75. This is not the first time that Urizen has recognized his fallen state. In Night v he chants his woes in a song which includes recollections of his former self. See K310 FZv:198–201.
76. Beer (1969) p. 147.
77. When all things 'revers'd flew from their centers' then the Urizenic law of gravity ceases. Re 'rattling bones' cf. Ezekiel 37:7.
78. K363 FZix:230–4.
79. Ibid. 246–9.
80. Blake uses the title 'Son of Man' only in one other place (K293 FZiii:68), but there it is used of Luvah, not directly of Christ.
81. K364 FZix:280–1.
82. Ibid. 289.
83. FZix:354–7.
84. K264 FZi:9.
85. K366 FZix:354.
86. K364–5 FZix:291–2, 304–5, 308–11.
87. K365 FZix:316.
88. K366 FZix:342.
89. Cf. K366 FZix:344–7.
90. K366 FZix:353.
91. Ibid. 358–9, 361. Smoke is the product of Orc's burnt-out fires.
92. Ibid. 363–74.
93. K367 FZIx:375–6.
94. Cf. K370 FZix:486ff.
95. K367 FZix: 381–2. Cf. K372 FZix:559.
96. Cf. K366 FZix:371.
97. K369 FZix:484.
98. K371 FZix:538–42.
99. K366 FZix:365.
100. K367 FZix:380.
101. Ibid. 386.
102. K368–9 FZix:434–46, 455–7.
103. K367 FZix:408–9.

104. K368 FZix:410–17.
105. Cf. Thel, K127–30.
106. K368 FZix:418–21.
107. Ibid. 423–5.
108. Ibid. 433.
109. The ram symbolizes the Land of 'organised innocence'. See the illustration to page 7 of *America, a Prophecy*, Erdman, p. 145.
110. Cf. K287 FZii:263–5 and K349 FZviii:323–4, for instance.
111. K370 FZix:481–94.
112. Cf. Enion's Song, K354–6 FZviii:534–83.
113. K301 FZiv:146–7.
114. Tharmas is described as the 'Parent pow'r, dark'ning in the West' (K264 FZi:24). The 'West' is the realm of man's body in Blake.
115. In the poem, 'The Little Black Boy' (K125 SoI), the little black boy says:

> And we are put on earth a little space,
> That we may learn to bear the beams of love;
> And these black bodies and this sunburnt face
> Is but a cloud, and like a shadowy grove.

> For when our souls have learn'd the heat to bear,
> The cloud will vanish; we shall hear his voice,
> Saying: 'Come out from the grove, my love & care,
> And round my golden tent like lambs rejoice'.

Here the 'cloud' is our body, which conceals Eternity from us. Most frequently the 'cloud' is associated with anything which obscures the spirit, e.g. 'clouds of reason' (K126 SoI, 'The Voice of the Ancient Bard', 4); 'clouds of learning' (K683 J52:7); 'clouds of War' (K420:17).
116. K266 FZi:71–6.
117. K370 FZix:490–4.
118. Ibid. 495.
119. Cf. K369 FZix:458–63.
120. K370 FZix:509–11.
121. Cf. also *The Book of Urizen* and *Tiriel*.
122. K370 FZix:513.
123. K282 FZii:105.
124. K371–2 FZix:547–54. 'He', of the first line, is Tharmas.
125. K432:56–62.

126. K371 FZix:538-43.
127. K369 FZix:460.
128. We have seen in relation to Enion and Tharmas that dreams are not mere pleasant pastimes, but have definite functions. Changes in the soul can result. So, too, Urizen and his sons, 'the sleepers entertain'd upon the Couches of Beulah' (K372 FZix:558), are changed by such a pastoral interlude. They are now ready to begin bringing in the ripened grain.
129. K372 FZix:585-9.
130. Cf. 1 Kings 19:11-12 and Ezekiel 37:1-10.
131. K372-3 FZix:590-9.
132. K372 FZix:556.
133. Cf. K269 FZi:179-82.
134. K373 FZix:614.
135. Ibid. 613.
136. Ibid. 604-16. In Night iv, Los began to rebuild Urizen's world which had been hurled into ruins in Night iii, but he was trapped by the chaos and 'became what he beheld'. Cf. K301-2 FZiv:161-207.
137. K374 FZix:627-31.
138. Ibid. 663-42.
139. Both the threshing process and the winnowing fan, or whirlwind, used by Tharmas are prophesied by Isaiah (41:15-16.) and John the Baptist (Luke 3:17).
140. K374 FZix:650-6. The perspective here is that of Eternity — the harvest and vintage of nations is the Last Judgement. If we are limited to a fallen and temporal perspective and do not recognize the reality of spiritual processes of purification and redemption, then we would probably interpret this scene as being no more than a powerful poetic description of tremendous conflicts (wars, perhaps) and disasters of nature on a devastating scale.
141. Parenthetically we may note here that often in Blake's work — and this is particularly relevant for the last section of Night ix of *The Four Zoas* — we need to read the actions and the events put before us as simultaneous projections of visions of fallen and regenerated man, not as a mere temporal sequence of happenings — be they cosmological, personal (psychological) or historical.
142. K379 FZix:854.
143. K709 J70:19-20.

144. K369 FZix:460.
145. K210.
146. K372 FZix:559–K373 FZix:824.
147. K157 MHH Pl.20.
148. The annihilation of Mystery is the annihilation of all that which springs from fallen Urizen's 'evil doing', as well as of delusive Rahab. Cf. K349–50 FZviii:325–57; K356–7 FZix:597–617; K321 FZvii:28–35. Also Rev 17:5 and 18.
140. K374–5 FZix:657–69.
150. Cf. Am K198 plate 6. Blake is, of course, using the term 'slaves' in a comprehensive sense, i.e. everyone oppressed by Urizenic might. But it is not irrelevant to note that the slave trade was not abolished in British territories and ships until 1807 — some three years after Blake had finished working on *The Four Zoas*.
151. K375 FZix:670–81.
152. K375 FZix:683.
153. Ibid. 686.
154. Ibid. 687–91.
155. K367 FZix:375–6.
156. Cf. K366 FZix:363–5.
157. K376 FZix:709.
158. The 'Song of Los' may be recalling *Asia* (plates 6 and 7 in *The Song of Los*) (K247–8), for its subject is the imminent overthrow by Orc of the power of Priest and King, who serve fallen Urizen. The last three lines of *Asia* describe the revival of the dead for Judgement in terms suggesting a Bacchanalian Feast. Luvah's transformation is also accompanied by Dionysiac overtones.
159. K376 FZix:710–30. In the first line 'he' refers to Luvah. The 'Eternal man' is Albion.
160. Cf. K337 FZviib:166.
161. K376 FZix:732.
162. K377 FZix:748–54.
162a. The nose is the sense-organ of Luvah, the Prince of Love. We may understand the expression 'Odors of life' as suggesting that such souls have not yet assumed the ethereal form of Love.
163. K376–7 FZix:738–42.
164. K378 FZix:796–7.
165. K149 MHH5.
166. K745 J98:26.

167. K746 J98:39.
168. Ibid. 28.
169. K376 FZix:726.
170. Cf. ibid. 732–7.
171. Cf. K360 FZix:121–22.
172. K377 FZix:772.
173. Ibid. 774–5.
174. K378 FZix:790.
175. K377 FZix:772–3.
176. Urthona has, in fact, no Emanation. Enitharmon is really the emanation of Los, who is the manifestation in time and space of Urthona.
177. K377–8 FZix:775–82.
178. K378 FZix:782.
179. Ibid. 790, 793–4.
180. Ibid. 791.
181. Ibid. 798.
182. Ibid. 785–8.
183. Ibid. 787.
184. Cf. ibid. 779–800.
185. Ibid. 801.
186. Ibid. 807–8.
187. K379 FZix:817–20.
188. Cf. K322 FZvii:92–107.
189. Cf. K343 FZviii:84.
190. K379 FZix:822.
191. Ibid. 823.
192 K609 VLJ.
193. In his illustrations of the *Book of Job* — plates 18 and 20 — Blake makes the association of poetry and painting with bread, and music with wine, very clear.
194. K379 FZix:824.
195. Ibid. 825–30.
196. Cf. K364 FZix:285–90.
197. K793.
198. K794. Letter to Dr Trusler, 23 Aug. 1799.
199. K623 J5:20.
200. K224 BU4:38–40.
201. Cf. K357 FZix:8–9.

202. Cf. K617 VLJ.
203. K357 FZix:6–8.
204. K379 FZix:831–4.
205. i.e. the one Sun who is 'like a new born man'.
206. K379 FZix:836–7. In a note written on the original pages of *The Four Zoas* Blake says:
    Unorganiz'd Innocence: An Impossibility
    Innocence dwells with Wisdom, but never with Ignorance.
    (K380)
207. K379 FZix:838–42.
208. Ibid. 843.
209. Ibid. 844–5.
210. Ibid. 846–8.
211. Ibid. 852–5.
212. K231 BU 19:5–9.
213. K138 FR:95–6.
214. K252 BA3:55–62.
215. K374 FZix:627–32.
216. K282 FZii:105.
217. K314 FZvi:83–8.
218. K777 Laoc.
219. Ibid.
220. K445.
221. K663 J36:49.
222. K347 FZviii:254.
223. K533 M40:35–M41:1.
224. K744 J96:37. Cf. John 4:10–15; Rev 21:6.
225. K687 J55:62–3.
226. K604 VLJ.
227. K613 VLJ.
228. K621 J3.
229. K717 J77. Here, as in the other passages just quoted, 'Science' should be understood to be 'Sweet Science'.
230. 'Blake saw in Druidism the prototype of all systematic theology which attempted to explain the paradoxes of spiritual life in the rational terms of fallen man and his world of nature.' Peter F. Fisher, 'Blake and the Druids', *The Journal of English and Germanic Philology*, LVIII (1959), 589–612.
231. K403 'On Bacon'.

232. K513 M26:44–6. Cf. also K621 J3.
233. K301 FZiv:146–8.
234. K93 'On Swed. DL'.
235. K617 VLJ.
236. Ibid.
237. K357 FZix:6–9.
238. K379 FZix:853.
239. Ibid. 850–1.
240. K481 M:15–16.
241. Cf. K377 FZix:775.

10   The Rebirth of Vision

1. Beginning with the words: 'And did those feet in ancient time/Walk upon England's mountains green?' K480 M1.
2. Numbers 11:29.
3. K480 M1 'Preface'.
4. Cf. K677–8 J48:13–20.
5. Cf. K632 J12:45ff.
6. In terms of the Hebrew cabbalistic tradition he would be named Adam Kadmon.
7. Los's concern is the salvation of Albion who has turned his back on the Divine Vision. Cf. K622 J4:13, 22.
8. K281 FZii:43.
9. K647–8. J24:42–5. We should note, that, for Blake, 'Exchanges' are not mere centres for the making of money, but are places designed for brotherly and international commerce. Cf. also K652 J27:85–8.
10. K747 J99:1–4.
11. Ibid. 5.
12. K620.
13. Cf. J18:29; J42:63; J52; J75:19; J93:25. In *Jerusalem*, Babylon is spoken of as the city of Vala, of natural religion, or deism, the Goddess of Nature. Generally speaking, Jerusalem is a symbol for eternity, Vala a symbol for nature, and Rahab a symbol for the reasoning power in man which 'invents' a nature devoid of spirit.
14. Rev 21.
15. K684 J53:24.
16. Blake adhered to the doctrine of apocatastasis.
17. Cf. K623 J5:1–15, for instance.

18. Cf. K622 J4:31–2.
19. K622 J4:6–21. Cf. also John 14:20.
20. K622 J4:22–3. The 'perturbed man' is Albion.
21. Proverbs 8:22–30.
22. Cf. K684 J53:15–24.
23. In Blake's view, the over-idealization of woman is one of the major errors of historical Christianity. In *Jerusalem* we hear the voices of the 'Living Creatures', the four Zoas, saying:

    Establishment of Truth depends on destruction of Falsehood continually,
    On Circumcision, not on Virginity, O Reasoners of Albion

    (K687 J55:65–6)
    Circumcision, a Blakean symbol for sacrifice of the selfhood, must take the place of unnatural repression.

    Los, Imagination, frequently deplores the dominance of the female will, that is, of the Moral Law, which, like freedom and inspiration on the higher plane — and nature on the lower — is represented as feminine.
24. K727 J82:81.
25. K727 J83:1–3.
26. K729 J83:82.
27. K731 J86:45. 'Erin' is a symbol of Blake's philosophy of love.
28. K732 J86:61.
29. K732–3 J86:18–22.
30. Enitharmon is jealous because Los is labouring to release Jerusalem. She wrongly assumes that his intentions are dishonest.
31. K733 J88:3–15.
32. K739 J92:13–18.
33. Cf. J10:32ff; J30:14; J95:19.
34. K733–4 J88:34–6 and 44–7.
35. K734 J89:9–13.
36. Containing the hypocrisy of Pharisees, Sadducees and other religious sects. Cf. K734 J89:5–8.
37. Cf. K734–5 J89:14–19.
38. Cf. K735 J89:24–37.
39. K735 J89:38–40.
40. Ibid. 43.
41. Ibid. 53.
42. K736 J89:62.

43. K736 J90:1. Thomas R. Frosch commenting on this and similar passages in Blake writes: 'The tearing apart of man into two sexes is the fundamental duality of his life in nature, and Blake sees in it the separation between art and life, desire and act, imagination and love, perceiver and object-world, and all the other fallen schisms.'

    With reference to J90:1–2, 52–4 Frosch continues: 'Note that Blake distinguishes male and female, on the one hand, from man, or humanity, on the other: all sexual being is inevitably fragmented.' *The Awakening of Albion*, 1974, p. 164.

44. K736 J90:28–33.

45. K737 J90:52–4.

46. In *Jerusalem* Los is equated with the ideal prophet, Elijah. K674 J44:30–1.

47. K737 J90:67.

48. K737–8 J91:2–31. Cf. K158 MHH22 and K717 J77.

49. K634 J13:52.

50. K90 'On Swedenborg DL'. Cf. also K616 VLJ.

51. K738 J91:18.

52. Matt 18:20 and 18:3.

53. K738 J91:19–21.

54. K741 J93:18–26.

55. Cf. Matt 24:3–15.

56. K742 J94:18.

57. Ibid. 20.

58. In J36:28 she is 'divided into Jerusalem and Vala'. Now, conversely, the two Emanations of Albion meet and are united in Britannia.

59. Cf. K744 J97:1–5.

60. K742 J94:21.

61. 'London Stone' is consistently regarded by Blake as symbolically equivalent to the Temples of Stonehenge and other Druid monuments. For Blake Druidism is synonymous with the error of natural religion (cf. K701–2 J66:1–9). The Stone is usually associated with expressions of repressive morality — with Stonehenge, for example, as a place of human sacrifice. One slab at Stonehenge is known as 'the slaughter stone'. It is at Stonehenge that the Daughters of Albion torture their victims (K702 J66:20) and that Britannia, 'In Dreams of Chastity & Moral law', murdered Albion 'with the Knife of the Druid' (K742 J94:23, 25).

62. K742 J94:22–6.
63. K742 J95:1–4.
64. Ibid. 13.
65. K684 J53:1.
66. K742 J95:19–20. 'Urthona's Spectre' is Los separated from Enitharmon.
67. K743 J96:1–2
68. K742 J95:10.
69. Cf. John 10:11 and Matt 18:12–14.
70. K743 J96:3–7.
71. K745 J98:14.
72. Ibid. cf. K709 J71:6.
73. Ezekiel 39:29.
74. K743 J96:8–13.
75. The term comes from Ezekiel 28:16.
76. K743 J96:17.
77. Ibid. 14–16.
78. Ibid. 20–2.
79. Damon, p. 94a.
80. K743 J96:23–8.
81. Ibid. 30–2. Los's honour is 'sublime' because Christ chooses his, Los's form, in which to meet the Covering Cherub.
82. K744 J96:33–4.
83. Ibid.35.
84. Ibid.37. Here we have several biblical ideas mingled together. The 'Furnaces of Affliction' are like that of the Book of Daniel in which the three loyal Jews, Shadrach, Meshach and Abed-nego, in the presence of 'the form of the fourth', Christ, remained unharmed (Daniel 3:19–28). They also resemble Hell — 'the lake of fire and brimstone' — into which the Devil is cast (Rev 20:10); but Hell itself turns into the 'living water' offered to mankind by Christ (John 4:10), which, in turn, resembles the 'fountain of the water of Life' given to man by Christ in the New Jerusalem (Rev 21:6).
85. K744 J96:38–9.
86. Ibid. 43.
87. K744 J97:1–4.
88. K481 M1:9.
89. K744 J97:6.
90. Ibid. 7–11.

91. K742 J95:13.
92. K744 J97:12–14.
93. K739 J92:13–14.
94. K721 J79:73–4. Blake's most pervasive metaphor for the 'fall into Division' is the separation of the sexes. In particular, the apparent division of the world into space and time is described as a sexual antimony. Originally, Blake says, 'Time & Space are Real Beings, a Male & a Female. Time is a Man, Space is a Woman' (K614 VLJ), or, Los and Enitharmon, respectively. In Blake's myth, the sexes do not exist as part of the ultimate reality, but are the product of pride and egotism: 'When the Individual appropriates Universality/ He divides into Male & Female' (K737 J90:52–3). The danger is, according to Blake, that this sexual polarity will be mistaken for the final nature and reality of things: 'When the Male & Female / Appropriate Individuality they become an Eternal Death' (K737 J90:53–4).
95. K683 J52:17–20.
96. K250–1 BA3.
97. K745 J98:7–9. It may surprise us to see Bacon, Locke and Newton keeping company with Milton, Shakespeare and Chaucer in Eden. We might be tempted to think that Blake is exercising some form of moral generosity. This, however, would be to miss the point altogether. The Urizenic Trio enter Eden quite simply because, in Blake's Spiritual World, all men are freed from their relative states. Once such men as Bacon, Locke and Newton are no longer dominated by the Spectres who influenced and directed them in their works on earth their Energy is no less spiritual and creative than that of Milton, Shakespeare and Chaucer. We must also remember that at the end of *Jerusalem* Blake does not cease from 'Mental Fight'. In short, Forgiveness is not to be mistaken for Urizenic acceptance or intellectual apathy. Forgiveness is a characteristic of spiritual 'warfare' because it is cleansed of the selfhood and is founded in the honesty and true love of Brotherhood. Blakean forgiveness and brotherhood do not dilute spiritual 'fury'. True forgiveness is the perception of divine humanity in one's fellow men. It is true understanding.
98. K744 J98:3.
99. The 'Four Faces' belong to the four Zoas (living creatures) of the Book of Ezekiel and Rev 4; the horses to the four horsemen of Rev

6. The four living creatures of Rev 4:6 are 'full of eyes before and behind'. The four rivers of Paradise (Genesis 2:1–14) are identified with the River of Life of Rev 22.

100. Cf. K228–9 BU11; also K632 J12:54–60.

101. K745 J98:12–23.

102. K191 VDA3:8–9.

103. K236 BU25:39. Cf. K500 M19:21; K691 J59:17.

104. K223 BU3:38; K288 FZii:296.

105. K288 FZii:296. Elsewhere in *Jerusalem* Blake says that his vision enables him to 'see the Past, Present & Future existing all at once' (K635 J15:8. Cf. also K210 SoE 'Introducton':1–2). Visionary Man sees time, history as a unity. Time as we know it in ordinary life ceases. Similarly, space is also 'finished', for the visionary sees in all directions at once. The end of time is prophesied in Rev 10:6. then the 'sea' (i.e. of time and space) shall give up its dead (Rev 20:13). Cf. K742 J94:18.

106. K372 FZix:587.

107. K360 FZix:129–30.

108. K365 FZix:316.

109. K372 FZix:584.

110. K378 FZix:779.

111. K374 FZix:643.

112. Ibid. 638–42.

113. K366 FZix:373, 371.

114. K746 J98:28–40.

115. In the World of Generation, time and space assume spectral, dehumanized form. Spectral time is counted in the mere additive amassing of seconds; spectral space in the additive accumulation of units of measurements. If Los were unable to maintain man's ability to converse with the Divine, then, in such a spectral, mechanistic time-space continuum, spectral forces would completely eliminate those of creative imagination.

116. K98 AllR.

117. K236 BU25:31.

118. Cf. K742 J94:18.

119. Cf. K154 MHH14.

120. In *Milton* Blake associates the eye with spiritual death:
But in the Optic Vegetative Nerves, Sleep was transformed
To Death in old time by Satan the father of Sin & Death.

(K517 M29:32–33)

121. Just as sexual polarity can be mistaken for the final nature of things, so also time and space, if they 'Appropriate Individuality they become Eternal Death'. In other words, if space becomes an end in itself — an 'individual', as it were — it becomes a prison-house, the 'Mundane Shell' of matter which is mistakenly supposed to assume reality independent of consciousness. In like manner, time becomes an abstract, non-human phenomenon, the 'dull round' (NNR 1st Series) of a fatal, mechanistic determinism.

122. K264 FZi:21. See note 94.

123. K686–7 J55:36, 46.

124. K664–5 J38:14–22.

125. K677 J47:18.

126. Ibid. J48:3.

127. K738 J91:10–13. Cf. Matt 12:31.

128. K746 J98:41.

129. Christ was 'sent' to replace the Old by his New Covenant. Against the Law, with its long lists of sins and punishments, He taught 'Judge not' and the Forgiveness of Sins. The clearest example of this teaching is the case of the woman taken in adultery — whom the Law would have stoned to death, but He forgave her. Cf. K754 EG:e:9–42; also 'On Dante' K785.

130. K746 J98:42–5.

131. Not only are 'tall men to be saved' (1 Timothy 2:4), but nature too.

132. Cf. K747 J99:1–4.

133. K746 J98:54.

134. Cf. K217 SoE 'The Human Abstract'.

135. Cf. Ezekiel 38–9.

136. As Caesar did at the time of Christ's birth. Cf. K699 J64:34.

137. Cf. K712 J72:32–44. 'The thirty-two Nations are a prophetic view of a brotherhood of the great nations which shall protect liberty ("dwell in Jerusalem's gates")'. Damon p. 294d.

138. K746 J98:47–56.

139. K733 J88:3–4.

140. K804–5. Letter to Thomas Butts, 2 Oct. 1800.

141. K665 J38:46–8. In the spiritual world, in fourfold vision, everything is 'human', divine, and can be 'conversed' with. Christ/God is no longer a transcendent abstraction, but 'stands' face to face with us and lives in each one of us. There is no 'dim chaos' (K745

J98:14), for chaos only exists in the confused mind of the man who is without vision. As Blake says elsewhere in *Jerusalem*: 'everything in Eternity is translucent' (K709 J71:6). 'Dim Chaos' is 'brightened beneath, above, around' (K745 J98:14) and there are no 'dark' areas of consciousness.

142. K611 VLJ. The rainbow, God's Covenant with man, symbolizes here the spiritual body. It is the promise of immortality.
143. K747 J99:4.
144. Cf. MHH27 'Every thing that lives is Holy'.
145. K709 J71:13-19.
146. This is another way of expressing the idea that subject and object interpenetrate one another.
147. K747 J99:1-4.
148. Supporters of natural religion and 'corporeal' war are powerless against spiritual warfare, 'Mental Fight':

For a Tear is an Intellectual thing,
And a Sigh is the Sword of an Angel King,
And the bitter groan of a Martyr's woe
Is an Arrow from the Almightie's Bow. (K683 J52:25-8)

True Christianity, the Religion of Christ, 'Forgiveness of Sin, can never be the cause of a War nor of a single Martyrdom' (K683 J52).
149. K518 M30:1; K677 J48:14.
150. K733 J88:7.
151. K746 J98:41.
152. K733 J88:5.
153. K684 J54:1-5.
154. K481 M1:15-16.
155. K747 J99:5.
156. K517 M29:41.
157. K658 J32:3-4.
158. K777 Laoc.

11   The Power of the Word

1. K517 M29:40-6.
2. K609 VLJ.
3. K514 M27:55-6.
4. K237 Eur 3:2.
5. K315 FZvi:134-5.

6. K314–15 FZvi:116–17, 124–38.
7. K130 Thel6:17; Cf. K728 J83:36–7.
8. K318 FZvi:250.
9. K800 Enclosed in a letter from Mrs Blake to Mrs Flaxman, 14 Sept. 1800. 'My Brother' refers to Robert who had died thirteen years before.
10. Illustration to *The Book of Job*, plate xviii, margin.
11. Ibid., plate xx, margin.
12. K825 Letter to Thomas Butts, 6 July 1803.
13. K822 Letter to Thomas Butts, 25 Apr. 1803.
14. K797 Letter to William Hayley, 6 May 1800.
15. K238 Eur3:22–4.
16. Blake's reading of Exodus 24:4,7,12–15.
17. K621 J3:1–10.
18. K792 Letter to Dr Trusler, 16 Aug. 1799. Blake is referring to some of his designs.
19. K618 'On the Illustrations to Milton'.
20. K526 M35:42.
21. K665 J38:20. Cf. John 15:4.
22. K672 J43:12–13. Kathleen Raine sees the Lark of *Milton* as an image of that 'minute center in which eternity expands'. *Blake and Tradition* (1968), Vol.II, p. 162.
23. K520 M31:34–8. 'The importance of the Lark in *Milton* is clear: he is the new idea which inspires the entire poem.' Damon, p.234d. Cf. K526 M35:67, K527 M36:12.
24. K618 'On the Illustrations to Milton'.
25. Pamela Dunbar, *William Blake's Illustrations to the Poetry of Milton* (1980), p. 127.
26. K210 SoE 'Introduction' 3–5.
27. K112 SoI 'The Little Girl Lost' 1–6.
28. K818.
29. K742 J95:1.
30. K622 J4:1–6.
31. K646 J23:39.
32. K646 J24:1–2.
33. K367 FZix:393–4.
34. K746 J98:54.
35. Cf. Isaiah 35.
36. K744 J97:5–6.

37. The Dark Night of Death began when man's emanations refused form in each other's bosom, causing man, causing everything, to 'roll apart in fear' and the Gates of Jerusalem to be walled up. Cf. K733 J88:3–15.

38. In *Jerusalem* the symbolism of the 'Covenant' is paramount, that of the 'Harvest' subordinate — in *The Four Zoas* it is predominant (much abbreviated in *Milton*).

39. 'All things were made by him' (John 1:3), by Christ, the Word (Logos).

40. K818.

41. K745 J98:7.

42. K580 DesC.

43. K738 J91:11.

44. K604 VLJ.

45. K613 VLJ.

46. K743 J96:7.

47. K392 'Annotations to Watson'.

Epilogue

1. K37 'Contemplation'.

2. Cf. K40–3 'Then She bore pale Desire'. Written when Blake was still in his teens.

3. Kenneth R. Johnston, 'Blake's Cities: Romantic Forms of Urban Renewal', in David V. Erdman and John E. Grant (eds.), *Blake's Visionary Forms Dramatic* (1970), p. 415.

4. The interested reader is referred to Johnston's essay mentioned in the previous note.

5. Golgonooza is more than a city. For a fuller discussion of its symbolic richness and possibilities see, for instance, John Middleton Murray, *William Blake* (1933), 196–210, and Harold Bloom, *Blake's Apocalypse* (1963), 377–82.

6. Cf. K212 SoE.

7. K216 SoE 'London'.

8. Ibid.

9. K275 FZi:409.

10. K158 MHH24.

11. H. M. Margoliouth, *William Blake* (1951), p. 111.

12. K283 FZii:126–9.

13. K287 FZii:273–86.

14. K632 J12:25–37.
15. K516 M29:5–7.
16. Cf. K689 J57:17–18.
17. K481 M1:16.
18. K718 J77:10–12.
19. K793 Letter to Dr Trusler, 23 Aug. 1799.
20. K315 FZvi:134–5.

Appendix 1   Blake's Theology

1. K776 Laoc.
2. Frye, p. 31.
3. K154 MHH 13.
4. K150 MHH 6.
5. K153 MHH11.
6. Nobodaddy ('nobody's daddy') is Blake's name for the false God of this World. Cf. K171.
7. K158 MHH 22–3.
8. K418.
9. *Encyclopedia*, Third Part (*Die Philosophie des Geistes*), *par.564*, quoted by Charles Taylor, *Hegel* (1975), p.481.
10. K490 M9:27–8.
11. K617 VLJ.
12. K672 J38:12–14.
13. K671 J42:56.
14. Leopold Damrosch, Jr., *Symbol and Truth in Blake's Myth* (1980), 244–8.

Appendix 2   Opacity and Translucence

1. K494 M13:20.
2. Ibid.
3. K670 J42:35.
4. Cf. K517 M29:35–49; K670 J42:29–33.
5. K490 M9:31.
6. Engraving colour printed. San Marino, California, Huntington Library.
7. Relief etching colour printed. London, British Museum.
8. Colour print finished in watercolour. London, Tate Gallery.
9. Blake's conception has two literary sources: one from *Proverbs*, viii,27; the other from *Paradise Lost*, vii:225.

10. Erdman, p. 355.
11. K125 SoI 'The Little Black Boy', 22-6.
12. K118-19 SoI.
13. K214 SoE.
14. Erdman, p. 148.

Appendix 3   The Importance of Giving Form

1. Emanuel Swedenborg, *The Apocalypse Explained*, n. 536.
2. Ibid., n. 533.
3. K680 J49:67. Cf. K304 FZiv:269-74; K713 J73:24-8.
4. K625 J7:22.
5. K307 FZv:76.
6. K512 M26:26-7.
7. K222 BU2:1.
8. K224 BU4:32-3.
9. Erdman, *The Illuminated Blake*, p. 183. Cf. also p. 89.
10. K237 BU28.

SELECT BIBLIOGRAPHY

Adams, Hazard: *Blake and Yeats. The Contrary Vision* (1968).
Arber, Agnes: *The Manifold and the One* (1957).
Ault, Donald: *Visionary Physics. Blake's Response to Newton* (1974).
Beer, John: *Blake's Humanism* (1968).
_____,*Blake's Visionary Universe* (1969).
Bindman, D.: *Blake as an Artist* (1977).
Bloom, Harold: *Blake's Apocalypse* (1963).
Curran, Stuart: 'The Structure of *Jerusalem*'. In *Blake's Sublime Allegory*. Eds. Curran, Stuart and Joseph Anthony Wittreich, Jr. (1973), pp. 329-46.
Damon, S. Foster: *A Blake Dictionary* (1979).
Damrosch, Jr., Leopold: *Symbol and Truth in Blake's Myth* (1980).
Davis, Michael: *William Blake. A New Kind of Man* (1977).
Digby, G. Wingfield: *Symbol and Image in William Blake* (1957).
Dunbar, Pamela: *William Blake's Illustrations to the Poetry of Milton* (1980).
Eaves, Morris: *William Blake's Theory of Art* (1982).
Engell, James: *The Creative Imagination: enlightenment to romanticism* (1981).

Erdman, David V.: *The Illuminated Blake* (1975).

_____,*Blake. Prophet against Empire* (1977).

_____,Ed., commentary by Harold Bloom: *The Complete Poetry & Prose of William Blake* (1982).

Fairchild, B. H.: *Such Holy Song* (1980).

Ferber, M.: *The Social Vision of William Blake* (1985).

Fisher, Peter F.: 'Blake and the Druids'. In *Blake. A Collection of Critical Essays*. Ed. Northrop Frye (1966), pp. 156-78.

Frosch, Thomas R.: *The Awakening of Albion* (1974).

Frye, Northrop: 'Blake's Introduction to Experience'. In *Blake. A Collection of Critical Essays*. Ed. Northrop Frye (1966), pp. 23-31.

_____,*Fearful Symmetry. A Study of William Blake* (1969).

Gardner, Stanley: *Blake* (1968).

Gilchrist, Alexander: *The Life of William Blake*. Ed. Ruthven Todd (1942).

Grimes, Ronald L.: 'Time and Space in Blake's Major Prophecies'. In *Blake's Sublime Allegory*. Eds. Stuart Curran and Joseph Anthony Wittreich, Jr. (1973), pp. 59-81.

Hagstrum, Jean H.: *William Blake. Poet and Painter* (1964).

_____,'William Blake rejects the Enlightenment'. In *Blake. A Collection of Critical Essays*. Ed. Northrop Frye (1966), pp. 142-55.

_____,'Christ's Body'. In *Essays in Honour of Sir Geoffrey Keynes*. Eds. Paley, Morton D. and Michael Phillips (1973) pp. 129-56.

Harper, George Mills: *The Neoplatonism of William Blake* (1961).

Hilton, N.: *Literal Imagination: Blake's Vision of Words* (1984).

Hirst, D.: *Hidden Riches. Traditional Symbolism from the Renaissance to Blake* (1964).

Howard, John: *Blake's Milton. A Study in the Selfhood* (1976).

Howard, J.: *Infernal Poetics: Poetic Structures in Blake: Lambeth Prophecies* (1985).

Johnston, Kenneth R.: 'Blake's Cities: Romantic Forms of Urban Renewal'. In *Blake's Visionary Forms Dramatic*. Eds. David V. Erdman and John E. Grant (1970), pp. 413-42.

Keynes, Sir Geoffrey: *William Blake. Poet, Printer, Prophet* (1964).

_____,Ed., *Blake. Complete Writings with variant readings* (1979).

_____,Ed., *The Letters of William Blake with related documents* (1980).

Klonsky, M.: *William Blake. The Seer and his Visions* (1977).

Larrissy, E.: *William Blake* (1985).

Lesnick, Henry: 'Narrative Structure and the Antithetical Vision of

Jerusalem'. In *Blake's Visionary Forms Dramatic*. Eds. David V. Erdman and John E. Grant (1970), pp. 391-412.

Lindsay, Jack: *William Blake* (1978).

Mitchell, W. J. T.: *Blake's Composite Art* (1978).

Nurmi, Martin K.: *William Blake* (1975).

Paley, Morton D.: *Energy and the Imagination* (1970).

_____, 'The Figure of the Garment in *The Four Zoas, Milton,* and *Jerusalem'*. In *Blake's Sublime Allegory*. Eds. Curran, Stuart and Joseph Anthony Wittreich, Jr. (1973), pp. 59-81.

William Blake (1978).

Raine, Kathleen: *Blake and Tradition* (1968), 2 vols.

_____, *Blake and the New Age* (1979).

_____, *The Human Face of God. William Blake and the Book of Job* (1982).

_____, *The Inner Journey of the Poet* (1982).

_____, 'Blake's "Eye of the Imagination"'. In *Harvest.* Journal for Jungian Studies (1984), vol. xxx, pp. 37-47.

Raine, Kathleen and G. Mills Harber, Eds.: *Thomas Taylor the Platonist* (1969).

Robinson, H. Crabb: *Blake, Coleridge, Wordsworth, Lamb, etc.* Ed. E. Morley (1922).

Rose, Edward J.: ' "Forms Eternal Exist For-ever": The Covenant of the Harvest in Blake's Prophetic Poems'. In *Blake's Visionary Forms Dramatic*. Eds. David V. Erdman and John E. Grant (1970), pp. 443-62.

Sabri-Tabrizi, G. R.: *The 'Heaven' and 'Hell' of William Blake* (1973).

Schorer, Mark: *William Blake. The Politics of Vision* (1959).

Sloss, D. J. and J. P. R. Wallis, eds.: *The Prophetic Writings of William Blake* (1926), 2 vols.

Stevenson, W. H., ed., text by David V. Erdman. *Blake. The Complete Poems* (1972).

Stock, R. D.: *The Holy and the Daemonic from Sir Thomas Brown to William Blake* (1982).

Sutherland, John: 'Blake and Urizen'. In *Blake's Visionary Forms Dramatic* Eds. David V. Erdman and John E. Grant (1970), pp. 244-62.

Tannenbaum, Leslie: *Biblical Tradition in Blake's Early Prophecies* (1982).

Warner, J.: *Blake and the Language of Art* (1985).

Watson, J. R.: *English Poetry of the Romantic Period* (1985).

Wicksteed, Joseph: *William Blake's Jerusalem*. Foreword by Sir Geoffrey Keynes (1954).

Wilkie, Brian and Mary Lynn Johnson: '*The Four Zoas:* Inscape and Analogy'. In *Blake's Sublime Allegory.* Eds. Curran, Stuart and Joseph Anthony Wittreich, Jr. (1973), pp. 203-32.

_____,*Blake's Four Zoas. The Design of a Dream* (1978).

Wilson, Mona: *The Life of William Blake.* Ed. Sir Geoffrey Keynes (1971).

Wright, A.: *Blake's Job. A Commentary.* (1972).

Wright, Thomas: *The Life of William Blake* (1972).

INDEX OF NAMES

SUBJECT INDEX